AIEL Series in Labour Economics

AIEL Series in Labour Economics

For further volumes:
http://www.springer.com/1863-916X

Sergio Destefanis • Marco Musella
Editors

Paid and Unpaid Labour in the Social Economy

An International Perspective

Physica-Verlag
A Springer Company

Editors
Professor Sergio Destefanis
Università degli Studi di Salerno
Dipartimento di Scienze
Economiche e Statistiche
Via Ponte Don Melillo
84084 Fisciano (SA)
Italy
destefanis@unisa.it

Professor Marco Musella
Università degli Studi
di Napoli Federico II
Facoltà di Scienze Politiche
Via Rodinò 22
88138 Napoli
Italy
marmusel@unina.it

The publication of this book has been made possible thanks to the financial support of the Ministero dell'Università e della Ricerca and of the Dipartimento di Scienze Economiche e Statistiche, Università degli Studi di Salerno.

ISBN: 978-3-7908-2136-9 e-ISBN: 978-3-7908-2137-6
DOI: 10.1007/978-3-7908-2137-6

Library of Congress Control Number: 2008943922

AIEL Series in Labour Economics ISSN: 1863-916X

Cover design: SPi Publishing Services

Printed on acid-free paper

9 8 7 6 5 4 3 2 1

springer.com

Contents

Contributors

Ben-Ner, Avner
Carlson School of Management, University of Minnesota,
Minneapolis, Minnesota 55455, USA

Borzaga, Carlo
Department of Economics, University of Trento and European Research Institute on Cooperative and Social Enterprises, Via Inama 5, 38100 Trento, Italy

Degli Antoni, Giacomo
Centro interuniversitario EconomEtica, University of Milano-Bicocca, Edificio U9, Viale dell'Innovazione 10, 20126 Milano, Italy

Destefanis, Sergio
Department of Economics and Statistics and CELPE, University of Salerno, Via Ponte Don Melillo, 84084 Fisciano (SA), Italy

Fiorillo, Damiano
Department of Economics, University of Napoli Parthenope, Via Medina, 40, 80133 Napoli, Italy

Flint Paulson, Darla
Carlson School of Management, University of Minnesota, Minneapolis, Minnesota 55455, USA

Galera, Giulia
European Research Institute on Cooperative and Social Enterprises, University of Trento, Via Inama 5, 38100 Trento, Italy

Livraghi, Renata
Department of Education and Territorial Sciences, University of Parma, Borgo Carissimi 10, 43100 Parma, Italy

Maietta, Ornella Wanda
Department of Agricultural Economics and Policy, University of Napoli Federico II, and Centro per la Formazione in Economia e Politica dello Sviluppo Rurale, Via Università 96, 80055 Portici (NA), Italy

Michelutti, Miriam
Department of Economics, University of Udine, Via Tomadini, 30/a, 33100 Udine, Italy

Mosca, Michele
Department of Economic Theory and Applications, University of Napoli Federico II, Via Rodinò 22, 80138 Napoli, Italy

Musella, Marco
Department of Economic Theory and Applications, University of Napoli Federico II, Via Rodinò 22, 80138 Napoli, Italy

Pappadà, Gabriella
Faculty of Management and Organization Sciences, University of Viterbo La Tuscia, Via S. Maria In Gradi 4, 01100 Viterbo, Italy

Pastore, Francesco
IZA, Bonn and Faculty of Law, University of Napoli II, Palazzo Melzi, Piazza Matteotti, 81055 Santa Maria Capua Vetere (CE), Italy

Ren, Ting
Carlson School of Management, University of Minnesota, Minneapolis, Minnesota 55455, USA

Sanson, João R.
Department of Economics, Federal University of Santa Catarina, 88049-970 Florianopolis (SC), Brazil

Schenkel, Marina
Department of Economics, University of Udine, Via Tomadini, 30/a, 33100 Udine, Italy

Tortia, Ermanno C.
Department of Economics, University of Trento and European Research Institute on Cooperative and Social Enterprises, Via Inama 5, 38100 Trento, Italy

Troisi, Roberta
Department of Economics and Statistics, University of Salerno, Via Ponte Don Melillo, 84084 Fisciano (SA), Italy

Young, Dennis R
Nonprofit Studies Program, Andrew Young School of Policy Studies, Georgia State University, Atlanta, Georgia 30303, USA

List of Abbreviations

Adj. R^2	Adjusted R^2, coefficient of determination corrected for degrees of freedom
AIEL	Associazione Italiana Economisti del Lavoro, the Italian Association of Labour Economics
CECOP	Confédération Européenne des Coopératives de Production, the European Confederation of worker cooperatives, social cooperatives and social and participative enterprises
CE	Certainty equivalent
CEE	Central and Eastern Europe
CNA	Certified nursing assistants
CIS	Commonwealth of Independent States
Coeff.	Coefficient
DEA	Data envelopment analysis
ECHP	European Community Household Panel
EFTA	European Fair Trade Association
EMES (referring to EMES European Research Network)	Emergence de l'Entreprise Sociale
EV	Expected value
FIVOL–FEO	(referring to FIVOL-FEO dataset) FIVOL: Fondazione Italiana per il Volontariato, the Italian Foundation for Voluntary Service; FEO: Fondazione Europa Occupazione: Impresa e Solidarietà, the Foundation Europe, Employment, Enterprise and Solidarity
FP	For-profit organizations, firms
FT	Fair Trade
G	Public, or local government, organizations
ISFOL	Istituto per lo sviluppo della formazione professionale dei lavoratori, the Institute for the Development of the Vocational Training of Workers

ISTAT	Istituto nazionale di Statistica, the Italian National Institute of Statistics
IV	Instrumental variable
LPN	Licensed practical nurses
LLR	Log Likelihood Ratio
Max	Maximum
MDH	Minnesota State Department of Health
MDHS	Minnesota State Department of Human Services
Min	Minimum
MNHES	Minnesota Nursing Homes Employer Survey
N	Number of observations
NH	Nursing home
NP	Nonprofit organizations
NP1	Social cooperatives and religious nonprofit organizations
NP2	Non-religious nonprofit organizations
OLS	Ordinary least squares
OSCAR	Online Survey, Certification and Reporting data of nursing facilities
OU	Operating unit
Pseudo-R^2	McFadden's measure of fit for the binary regression
RN	Registered nurses
R^2	Coefficient of determination
SHIW	Survey of household income and wealth, Bank of Italy
St. Dev.	Standard deviation
UNDP	United Nations Development Programme

Introduction and Overview

Sergio Destefanis and Marco Musella

This book provides an up-to-date analytical and empirical treatment of some important interactions between paid and unpaid labour and the social economy.[1] The emphasis on the preferences of paid and unpaid labour and on their role in the efficient provision of social services makes a vital contribution to clarifying the definition of social economy, a concept which has attracted considerable interest in the recent literature on the welfare system. Particular attention is paid to the differences among different countries' experiences.

The analysis of paid and unpaid labour in the social economy could appear at first sight a marginal theme within labour economics. For various reasons, however, this would be a very misleading impression.

1. The third sector encompasses a host of organizations, different from for-profit and public bodies, and which has been growing in weight and importance in the last ten to fifteen years both in terms of size (and, thus, its presence in society) and economic importance. The contribution of this sector to GDP has increased significantly in percentage terms (to name just two examples, in Italy it has reached 3.1% in 2001, while it was already 7.3% in 1999 in the US). The impact of nonprofit organizations in the labour market is important too. In Italy, employment in cooperatives, associations, voluntary organizations and other nonprofit bodies (not counting conscientious objectors and volunteers) has reached 2.6% of total employment in 2001. In the UK and the US, broadly comparable aggregates had reached percentage values of about 6.2 and 7.8

[1] We shall use the expressions nonprofit, third sector, and social economy interchangeably. Even though there are some differences among them, they broadly stand for the same area of economic activity and the same set of issues for economic analysis. However, we believe that social economy, by explicitly referring to the social mission bestowed to organizations engaged in the provision of social utility services, best conveys the broadness of the topic.

S. Destefanis (✉)
Department of Economics and Statistics and CELPE, University of Salerno,
Via Ponte Don Melillo, 84084 Fisciano (SA), Italy

S. Destefanis and M. Musella (eds.), *Paid and Unpaid Labour in the Social Economy*,
AIEL Series in Labour Economics, DOI: 10.1007/978-3-7908-2137-6_1,

(share over non-agricultural employment).[2] Also in other countries, including CEE and the CIS, there is a significant growth in the economic and labour-market impact of nonprofit organizations. There is, therefore, a quantitatively based case for trying to understand better the evolution of labour relationships in this sector, among the few to have recorded in recent years a positive balance between jobs created and jobs lost.[3]

2. It is in nonprofit organizations that we more frequently find paid and unpaid labour coexisting side by side. It follows that the analysis of this somewhat peculiar sector is crucial in obtaining more precise information about this phenomenon, increasingly important throughout the economy. The coexistence of various forms of labour differing in terms of the type of the contractual agreements struck between employers and employees, the variety of legal forms taken by those agreements, the existence and role of monetary and non-monetary remuneration, are all elements that can arguably be best appraised in the social economy.
3. A third element making the "paid and unpaid labour in the social economy" theme interesting relates to the nature of nonprofit organizations as a very large set of case studies for the analysis of post-Fordist industrial relations. Because of the largely intangible nature of output they produce and of their unique ownership structure, cooperatives, foundations, voluntary organizations, etc., provide a particularly clear model of the growing importance of intangible aspects for industrial relations.

The above considerations inspired the idea of devoting a session of the twenty-first annual conference of AIEL, the Italian Association of Labour Economists (University of Udine 2006), to the topic of paid and unpaid labour, with particular reference to social utility services. These papers constituted an up-to-date and stimulating body of findings, and we feel that there are ample grounds for bringing them together in a single volume.

The papers presented at the Conference bring to the fore the following analytical issues which, to a varying extent, are also taken up by way of empirical analysis: preferences of paid and unpaid labour and human resource management in the third sector, the incentive and remuneration system, ownership structure and risk, choice-theoretical analysis of unpaid labour and household production.

The first set of papers (Borzaga, Young, Musella and Troisi, Sanson) focuses on the conceptual and theoretical treatment of these issues. The remaining papers are essentially of an empirical nature. The target of the empirical studies is first and foremost the Italian social economy. This is understandable for contingent reasons,

[2] As all these data are basically taken from national censuses, comparable data for more recent years are not readily available. However, also the latest period has been characterized by a strong presence of the nonprofit sector in advanced economies. See for instance the data available from the Center for Civil Society Studies, Johns Hopkins University.

[3] Note that the above quoted statistics are likely to underestimate the weight of the social economy, because they are based on a fairly restrictive notion of nonprofit sector, stressing the role of the profit non-distribution constraint. Broadly speaking, these figures leave out most cooperatives, whose social mission is very close to that of the pure nonprofit organizations.

but can also be justified on deeper grounds. Among other things, the growth in economic size of the Italian third sector in recent years has been truly impressive.[4] Moreover, Italian third-sector legislation is examined with particular interest not only in many countries of Continental Europe, including CEE and CIS countries, but also, outside Europe, in Japan and Korea as well as in some Latin American nations. At any rate, empirical analyses also deal with other countries. Descriptive evidence of the nonprofit sector, particularly of paid and unpaid labour within this sector, is provided for countries (CEE, CIS, Malta, Spain) where there is relatively little information on these matters. State-of-the-art quantitative techniques are also applied to a dataset for the US never previously utilized.

The following brief presentation of the contents of the papers roughly arranges them under three headings according to the above discussion. However, as will become clear, there are close links among the papers.

1 Analytical Issues

Carlo Borzaga begins by observing that empirical and experimental analyses, and especially research on under-remunerated workers in nonprofit organizations with an explicit social mission, show that volunteers are also driven by self-regarding preferences, while remunerated workers may have preferences that are different from the maximization of immediate or deferred monetary income. Borzaga proceeds by showing that it is possible to take account of this pluralism of motivations and agents by modifying the utility function so that it includes all the different types of motivation. The resulting allocation of workers and volunteers among sectors and enterprises can therefore be considered efficient also in the presence of individuals who are not paid or who are systematically paid less than others.

The purpose of the paper by Dennis Young is to identify the kinds of decisions where nonprofit organizations need to manage their risks in a strategic fashion, to review what we know about how they approach these decisions, and to offer a conceptual framework that nonprofits can use to develop a more sophisticated and effective approach to their risk management decisions in the future. He argues that, for various reasons, nonprofits have not taken a sufficiently robust view of risk management, and presents a simple framework for nonprofits to address their risk-related decisions in a strategic fashion.

Marco Musella and Roberta Troisi analyze social cooperatives as a typical delivery service firm focusing on employee incentive systems characterized by ‘role tension’ linked to the dual position of being employee and owner at the same time. They then develop an incentive system which is designed and measured on effort rather than on output. In social cooperatives, workers’ satisfaction depends not just on remuneration, but also on intrinsic incentives and consumption of relational goods

[4] In Italy, according to various surveys by ISTAT (the Italian National Statistical Institute), between 1991 and 2001 nonprofit organizations more than doubled, nonprofit employees increased by 75%, and voluntary workers increased tenfold to over three million.

on the job. Because social cooperatives are better able to structure a richer incentive set, these organizations are more efficient in the provision of social utility services even though they pay lower wages than public organizations and for-profit firms.

The main objective of João Sanson is to formulate a model of household production in which labour is one of the productive activities whose output may be sold in the market. A Beckerian model with a joint-production technology, where at least one of the outputs is labour, is presented. Sanson shows that different estimates of the opportunity cost of time naturally appear within this model and, as the consumer - producer cannot alter the time endowment, the definition of net result of the worker is related to economic rent. As a result, the household production model, including labour supply, might be more easily integrated into general equilibrium theory.

2 Empirical Studies: Evidence from an Italian Microeconometric Survey

The papers collected under this heading all refer to empirical studies based on a microeconometric dataset for social utility services in Italy, the FIVOL–FEO survey (see, for more details, Borzaga 2000; Depedri 2003). This survey includes information on 228 Italian public, private for-profit and private nonprofit organizations providing social utility services (care and guardianship, nursing and rehabilitation, educational, cultural, recreational, school and school-to-work guidance, job-search assistance, others). For organizational reasons, data could be gathered only in ten North-Centre provinces and in five Southern provinces. It is, however, believed that the dataset offers a sufficiently accurate image of the population of organizations as far as territorial distribution, type of service provided and institutional category are concerned.

Miriam Michelutti and Marina Schenkel attempt to understand the factors determining the satisfaction that volunteers derive from their own activity, and then to compare them with those determining the satisfaction of paid workers. The novelty of their approach is that they use the same measure of rewards and reported satisfaction for volunteers and paid workers within the same dataset. They find that, while the determinants of satisfaction are not exactly the same for volunteers and paid workers, both of them attach special consideration to the users' well-being.

Ermanno Tortia concentrates on the comparative analysis of the determinants of worker satisfaction, measured by job-satisfaction and loyalty to the organization. Special attention is given here to the role of workers' fairness perceptions. A clear difference emerges between the public and the private sector in general, with the former at a disadvantage. Furthermore, while for-profit firms and nonprofits show similar levels of job-satisfaction, religious nonprofits best guarantee distributive fairness and social cooperatives score highest when procedural fairness is considered. Given the more significant role of procedural fairness in influencing job-satisfaction, social cooperatives turn out as an innovative and successful organizational form, at least as far as labour relations are concerned, the difficulties in retaining their more educated and skilled workforce notwithstanding. Essentially, the democratic scheme of governance in cooperatives in general, and in social cooperatives more specifically, guarantees more autonomy to workers and provides them with the opportunity to have their say even with regard to managerial decisions.

In their assessment of the relative impact of different recruitment channels, and of informal networks in particular, Michele Mosca and Francesco Pastore analyze the returns to education on wage structures across organizations in the social service sector. While the impact of recruitment methods on wages has been addressed in several previous contributions, none of them focuses on social services. Comparison of outcomes across organization types within the same sector is in itself another novelty, as compared to previous studies that generally focus on differences across sectors or, more recently, across countries. Mosca and Pastore find that nonprofit organizations prefer informal recruitment methods to better select the most motivated workers, namely those workers who share the nonprofit mission.

The paper by Sergio Destefanis and Ornella Wanda Maietta analyzes the relatively novel concept of a downward-sloping demand for voluntary labour. Indeed, both their descriptive and econometric evidence shows that the prices of volunteer labour (as proxied by its shadow price) is negatively related to the number of volunteer hours. Further, the demand for volunteer labour is higher in areas relatively well endowed with social capital (Putnam 1993), where there is also evidence that organizations refrain from substituting volunteers for paid workers when the latter become more expensive. This finding is related to evidence from papers that shall be presented below (Degli Antoni, Fiorillo) and has some relevance for the debate on economic and social convergence across European regions.

3 Empirical Studies: Comparative Evidence from Italy and Other Countries

The papers under this heading refer to empirical studies, both for Italy and other countries, based on various datasets. The Italian studies emphasize issues of a regional nature that to some extent have already come up in the paper by Destefanis and Maietta.

Damiano Fiorillo examines the evidence in favour of different motivations for voluntary labour in volunteer service associations, using an Italian micro dataset constructed by ISTAT, which allows use of a measure of household income. It turns out that the donation of unpaid activity to a volunteer service association is determined both by the consumption and the investment motivation, confirming the evidence of studies for the US, Canada and the UK. Interestingly, however, regional patterns of volunteer labour reflect the pattern of participation described in the social capital literature (Putnam 1993). People who live in regions relatively well-endowed with social capital do significantly more volunteer labour.

On a similar tack, Giacomo Degli Antoni studies the level of trustworthiness across Italian regions in relation to three variables: membership in cultural and recreational associations; membership in ecological, civil rights and peace associations; voluntary participation in (voluntary service) solidarity associations. The main result is that voluntary participation has a positive and significant effect on the regional level of trustworthiness. Consequently, and providing a new perspective to the results in Destefanis and Maietta, and in Fiorillo, it is unpaid labour of solidarity associations that crucially contributes to the creation of propitious conditions for the diffusion of trustworthy behaviour throughout the community.

In their paper, Avner Ben-Ner, Ting Ren, and Darla Flint Paulson investigate ownership-related wage differentials using a sample of US nursing homes, distinguishing between nonprofit, for-profit and local government organizations. They focus on within-organization across-occupation wage dispersion, controlling for important factors that may affect this variable. Their results do not support widespread opinions about wage dispersion across the three ownership types. Neither the intrinsic motivation perspective's prediction of less inequality among employees in nonprofit and government sectors, nor the agency theory prediction that higher level employees will use their influence to increase their own well-being without increasing the well-being of others, is supported. Adopting a combination of both the intrinsic motivation and agency approaches may thus be essential to understand wage determination. Moreover, the relative strength of each of these approaches is likely to be industry-specific.

Renata Livraghi and Gabriella Pappadà present the outcomes of fieldwork carried out in Italy, Spain, Malta and France with the aim of providing evidence about the main features characterizing fair trade organizations and the volunteers involved in them. The case studies have been selected taking into consideration both the areas where Fair Trade has deeper roots (as in some French, Italian and Spanish regions) and the areas where the sector is younger (like Malta and the south of Italy). It turns out that Fair Trade mainly attracts women and young people and that there are some skills that emerge across all volunteers, such as relational team-working skills.

Following a brief introduction on the relevance of institutional pluralism for economies characterized by poorly developed markets and welfare systems under construction, Giulia Galera analyzes social enterprises in CEE and CIS countries. Starting from a definition of social enterprise grounded in the European tradition, and therefore considered more appropriate for these countries, she focuses on both the history of social entrepreneurial organizations and current social enterprise development paths in the region, with special regard to the role played by the social enterprise in fostering socio-economic development. This is due to its ability to supply general goods and services for the community, generate new employment, contribute to a more balanced use and allocation of resources, and enhance the social capital that is accumulated at the local level.

4 Main Results

In systematizing some general issues relating to the new role adopted by the social economy in the labour market, we believe that this book can contribute both to a more precise understanding of quantitative and qualitative aspects of paid and unpaid labour in the social economy, and of the social economy itself. Topics of particular interest, that are dealt with in several essays, include: preferences and satisfaction of paid and unpaid labour; ownership structure and risk; ownership structure, remuneration and incentives for paid labour; characteristics of volunteer labour and its relationship with social capital endowment across Italian regions; comparative analysis of labour in the nonprofit sector across Europe.

The role of preferences of paid and unpaid workers in shaping the social economy and in making it an efficient tool for the provision of social utility services is taken up from a conceptual point of view by Borzaga, and by Musella and Troisi, who point out the relevance of some institutional aspects of Italian social cooperatives in solving the role tensions arising from the dual position of being employee and owner at the same time. Empirical content to these propositions is given by the analyses in Michelutti and Schenkel, and in Tortia, who apply state-of-the-art quantitative techniques to the FIVOL-FEO dataset. On the other hand, Young suggests ways in which nonprofits could improve their efficiency, by approaching their risk-related decisions in a strategic fashion that properly reflects the mission and circumstances of the organizations.

In using not-readily-available datasets for the US and for Italy respectively, Ben-Ner, Ren, and Paulson, and Mosca and Pastore also provide novel evidence on the relationships between ownership structure, remuneration and efficiency of different incentive schemes for paid labour. The finding by Mosca and Pastore that nonprofit organizations prefer informal recruitment methods to better select the workers who share the nonprofit mission of the organization has a clear correspondence with the above quoted results on the preferences of paid and unpaid workers. When motivation is an important quality in candidates, informal recruitment methods may be better suited. On the other hand, Ben-Ner, Ren, and Paulson do not find support for some widespread opinions on wage dispersion across ownership types, and conclude that both intrinsic motivation and agency approaches may be essential to understand wage determination. It is easy to concur with these considerations, Yet, it is worthwhile adding that both Ben-Ner et al. and Mosca and Pastore, in very different labour markets, do *not* find that nonprofit organizations employ lower productivity workers and pay them consistently less than other ownership types within the same industry, as is sometimes surmised. Furthermore, both studies (as well as Tortia) find that wage determination in nonprofits is consistent with various strategies of workforce selection and motivation. The results by Ben-Ner et al. on the use of merit-related pay incentives also chime in with the analytical conclusions of Musella and Troisi.

The measurement of productivity of voluntary labour and its relevant role in the social economy are analyzed by Destefanis and Maietta, who find some new kind of evidence in favour of the existence of a downward-sloping curve for unpaid labour. Their evidence, according to which the productivity of voluntary labour is higher in areas well endowed with social capital has interesting relationships with the findings in Fiorillo, to the effect that people who live in regions relatively well endowed with social capital are more likely to provide volunteer labour. It would appear that nonprofits in social capital-rich regions can draw more motivated and skilful volunteers from a larger pool of potential applicants. The findings in Degli Antoni, however, also imply that unpaid labour of volunteer service associations contributes to the diffusion of trustworthy behaviour throughout the community. As a whole, the results from these papers have some relevance, not only for understanding the development path of the social economy, but also for the debate about economic and social convergence across European regions.

The wider relevance of the above results is well illustrated by the more descriptive evidence of the nonprofit sector, particularly of paid and unpaid labour within this sector, provided by Livraghi and Pappadà, and Galera, for countries (Malta, Spain, CEE, CIS) where there is relatively little information on these matters.

Another point that is highlighted from many of the book's contributions (mainly Borzaga, Musella and Troisi, Tortia, Livraghi and Pappadà, Galera) is that cooperatives, and especially social cooperatives, may exemplify a distinctly successful institutional form within the social economy. Introduced in Italy in 1991 (Law 381/1991), social cooperatives are a still young and growing organizational form and represent an interesting case of institutional hybridization. They are firms but retain many of the features of nonprofit organizations, such as non-distributable and mission-devoted assets with an explicit social aim.

The legislation both in Italy and other countries is in fact now moving along similar lines, recognizing that socially-minded entrepreneurs are a fundamental element in the production of social services. Dees (2001) maintains that an increasing number of nonprofits are beginning to appreciate the increased revenue, focus and effectiveness that can come from adopting a for-profit business approach.[5] Increasingly, they are reinventing themselves as social entrepreneurs, combining the passion of a social mission with business-like discipline, innovation, and determination. Social entrepreneurs play the role of change agents in the social sector, by:

- Adopting a mission to create and sustain social (not just private) value
- Recognizing and pursuing new opportunities to serve that mission
- Engaging in a process of continuous innovation, adaptation, and learning
- Acting boldly without being limited by resources currently in hand
- Exhibiting heightened accountability to their constituencies.

Also according to Yunus (2008) social enterprises employ workers in order to produce goods or services to be sold at a price consistent with their basic aims. Paramount among their aims (and among their evaluation criteria) is to bring about a positive change in the social conditions of the people with which they get in touch. However, this does not mean that social enterprises are charities. They are full-fledged enterprises that must cover all their costs while pursuing their aims.

Keeping in mind the above considerations, social cooperatives represent a new and interesting system of industrial relations, not losing focus on monetary incentives, but also very receptive about democratic management, inclusiveness, and fair procedures. Social cooperatives are able to respect workers' rights and can thus employ highly motivated paid and unpaid labour.[6]

---

[5] This point is well illustrated by the analyses of Musella and Troisi, Galera, and also Young (from a slightly different perspective).

[6] The case in point is here the paper by Tortia. Yet Michelutti and Schenkel, Mosca and Pastore, Destefanis and Maietta, Livraghi and Pappadà also bring about indirect pieces of evidence on this issue.

The book as such is not devoted to policy analysis. However it is easy to derive important policy implications from its analyses. As shown in the essay by Galera, social enterprises are extremely sensitive to changes in public policy, especially regarding their eligibility for public subsidies. Legal systems can also play either an enabling or a restrictive role in their development. Hence, policies can foster a more efficient distribution of economic activity across sectors by exploiting the strengths of the social economy. Some of the latter, linked to the strategic role of paid and unpaid labour, have been highlighted throughout the book. Given the importance that the social utility services have acquired (and will acquire), research on these matters has high policy relevance, both in predicting the possible evolution of welfare systems and in improving their efficiency.

It is perhaps not inappropriate to close this introduction by noting that the development itself of the social economy has policy consequences of its own. Voluntary labour, being one of the pillars of social capital accumulation, may be a crucial contextual variable in determining the success or failure of various kinds of economic policies. In the field of development policies, this is well highlighted by the results obtained in Burnside and Dollar (2004) who find that the impact of foreign aid on growth in poorer countries crucially depends on the quality of national institutions. Even closer to our institutional set-up, (Ederveen et al. 2006) find that European Structural Funds are effective in speeding up the process of regional convergence only when the quality of institutions is good. Among the indicators of good-quality institutions they include proxies of trust and membership to solidarity associations. All these results support the existence of a significant direct relationship between the effectiveness of growth policies in a given area and its endowment in an array of factors linked to the notion of social capital, whose accumulation can be favoured by the development of the social economy.

Acknowledgments We gratefully acknowledge financial support from the Italian Ministry of Education, University and Research (PRIN 2005) and from the DISES, University of Salerno. We also wish to thank Francesco Amati, Sharon Gleave, Alexander Kirichenko and Roger Meservey for editorial assistance.

References

Borzaga C (2000) Capitale umano e qualità del lavoro nei servizi sociali. Fondazione Italiana del Volontariato, Roma

Burnside C, Dollar D (2004) Aid, policies, and growth: Revisiting the evidence. World Bank Policy Research Working Paper 3251

Dees JG (2001) The meaning of social entrepreneurship. Duke University. http://www.fuqua.duke.edu/centers/case/documents/Dees_SEdef.pdf

Depedri S (2003) La ricerca: metodologia campione e principali risultati. In: Borzaga C, Musella M (eds.) Produttività ed efficienza nelle organizzazioni nonprofit. Edizioni31, Trento

Ederveen S, Groot HLF, Nahuis R (2006) Fertile soil for structural funds? A panel data analysis of the conditional effectiveness of European cohesion policy. Kyklos 59:17–42

Putnam R (with Leonardi R, Nanetti R) (1993) Making democracy work. Princeton University Press, Princeton

Yunus M (2008) Creating a world without poverty: Social business and the future of capitalism. PublicAffairs, New York

Chapter 1
A Comprehensive Interpretation of Voluntary and Under-Remunerated Work

Carlo Borzaga

Abstract The aim of the essay is to contribute to development of an unitary interpretation of the supply of labour in nonprofit organizations. The paper shows that agents supply their labour on the basis of a mix of motivations, whose composition is influenced by numerous personal, cultural, and vocational factors. Empirical and experimental analyses, and especially research on under-remunerated workers in nonprofit organizations with an explicit social mission, show that volunteers are also driven by self-regarding preferences, while remunerated workers may have preferences that are different from the maximization of immediate or deferred monetary income. It is possible to take account of this pluralism of motivations and agents by modifying the utility function so that it includes all the different types of motivation. The resulting allocation of workers and volunteers among sectors and enterprises can therefore be considered efficient also in the presence of individuals who are not paid or who are systematically paid less than others.

1.1 Introduction

In recent years, the interest of social scientists in the evolution of nonprofit and collective-interest organizations delivering social services has grown significantly. Among the aspects of greatest interest are free or voluntary work, and work paid at rates lower than market ones.[1]

[1] The distinction between the two types of work is not always clear in the literature. Whilst normally considered to be volunteers are persons who work for an organization, or directly for the beneficiary of a service, on a gratuitous basis or with the sole reimbursement of expenses, some international organizations (e.g. ILO and UN) still use the concept of 'remunerated volunteers', meaning by this term persons who perform paid work for a nonprofit organization from which they receive remuneration below the market rate. Aside from the difficulty of quantifying 'market remuneration', in the most recent literature these workers are generally considered to be remunerated, and are treated as such.

C. Borzaga
Department of Economics, University of Trento and European Institute for Cooperative and Social Enterprise, Via Inama 5, 38100 Trento, Italy

S. Destefanis and M. Musella (eds.), *Paid and Unpaid Labour in the Social Economy*, AIEL Series in Labour Economics, DOI: 10.1007/978-3-7908-2137-6_2,

In regard to voluntary work, attempts have been made to estimate its magnitude, evolution, intensity, and sectors of employment. Different interpretations have been put forward on the basis of theoretical models and empirical surveys. Analyses of paid work have instead sought to identify the determinants of the capacity of nonprofit organizations to attract workers and to obtain from them high levels of commitment, loyalty and satisfaction – not inferior to those of public organizations and for-profit enterprises – even though they generally offer lower pay rates.

Although various studies have shown that the two forms of work in the social services sector have many features in common – also because changes from voluntary to remunerated work are frequent, and many paid workers have had experience of voluntary work – they have always been studied separately. That is to say, both theoretical and empirical analyses have always concerned themselves with either voluntary or paid work, but never the two of them jointly. Moreover, only rarely have these studies connected these types of work with the characteristics of the sectors in which they are most widespread, and of the organizations in which they are generally performed. They have not connected analysis of these forms of work with the fact that both voluntary and under-remunerated work are especially present in nonprofit organizations[2] engaged in advocacy activities or in the production of social and collective-interest services: that is, activities always characterized by multiple forms of work – not only voluntary or paid at various rates, but also the gratuitous work of family members, friends and neighbours, and of irregular or non-standard workers. Indeed, one may argue that the sector of personal care services comprises all the possible forms of work, from that performed gratuitously by necessity or choice to the well-paid work of professionals employed by public agencies.

As long as voluntary work and nonprofit organizations were quantitatively limited phenomena and were regarded as about to be cut back, the results obtained by these studies could be considered satisfactory. However, the recent growth in the number and size of nonprofit organizations engaged in the production of social services and, internally to them, in the number of voluntary and paid workers, as well as the expected accentuation of these tendencies due to increased demand for social and collective-interest services and the difficulty of expanding their public supply, warrant closer examination. Required in particular is analysis of the dynamics of the labour supply in the social services sector which can yield a unitary interpretation of the presence a multiplicity of types of work. Such interpretation should, on the one hand, aid understanding of why particular organizations and activities comprise forms of work that differ in important respects – pay, working time, and other characteristics – from standard ones; and on the other, predict their evolution.

The aim of this paper is to contribute to development of this unitary interpretation. Sections 1.2. and 1.3 conduct brief analysis of the recent evolution of the nonprofit sector and of the theoretical and empirical literature on voluntary and paid work, paying particular attention to studies on the wage levels and satisfaction of these workers. Section 1.4 examines work motivations in general, highlighting their

[2] Voluntary workers are also often present in public organizations delivering social services, above all when they have a community connotation (see Borzaga 2000).

complexity and proposing their possible classification. Section 1.5 summarizes the distinctive features of social and collective-interest services, with particular regard to those features which distinguish these goods from traditional ones, both public and private, and which justify the presence of nonprofit delivery units. This analysis will show that there is neither a single nor a predominant determinant of either voluntary or remunerated work. Agents supply their labour on the basis of a mix of motivations which varies from individual to individual, and whose composition is influenced by numerous personal, cultural, and vocational factors. The possibility to obtain remuneration from work – and above all the maximum possible remuneration – is only one reason for working, and it is not necessarily the most important one. As argued in Sect. 1.6, by using this approach it is possible to account for both the existence of voluntary or under-remunerated work, and for the predominant or exclusive presence of these forms of work in some sectors and in nonprofit organizations. It will thus be possible to furnish a unitary interpretation of the results of empirical research on these various forms of work and their recent growth.

It becomes useful to make an attempt to draw on analyses of voluntary and under-remunerated work in order to explain the determinants of the labour supply. Especially in light of the increasing diffusion of activities which share many of the features typical of the social services sector. This diffusion may profoundly influence the future of industrial relations and the perceptions of work among an increasing number of people; and it will raise a major challenge to the way in which economists have to date treated the labour supply.

1.2 The Evolution of the Nonprofit Sector and of Voluntary Work

In recent decades, an increasing body of research, both comparative and on single countries, has reported the generalized consolidation of the nonprofit sector. This concerns both countries like the United States, where the nonprofit sector was already substantial, and those where it had been previously cut back, mainly owing to the growth of public intervention. This consolidation has assumed two different forms: quantitative and qualitative.

In quantitative terms, consolidation of the nonprofit sector is evidenced by the growth in the number of organizations, in the numbers of their volunteers and paid workers, in the number of users served, and in the progressive expansion of the sectors in which nonprofit organizations operate. This clearly emerges from the wide-ranging research conducted by Johns Hopkins University (Salamon and Anheier 1998; Salamon et al. 1999), which has analyzed the evolution of the nonprofit sector in several countries, showing a general increase in the number of organizations, workers, and in contribution to gross domestic product. Evidence of the wide extent of voluntary work comes from the United States, where in 2006 about 61.2 million people, 26.7% of the population, volunteered through or for an organization at least once (data from the US Department of Labour). The growth of voluntarism and the nonprofit sector has been particularly marked in the European countries, where over 32% of the adult population is now engaged in voluntary work. In Great Britain, for instance, nonprofit organizations increased in number from 98,000 in 1991 to 169,000 in 2004, involving around 50% of the adult population in voluntary work. Also in Italy, according to various surveys by the National Institute of Statistics, between 1991 and 2001 nonprofit organizations grew from 106,000 to over 253,000, voluntary workers increased tenfold in number from 317,300 to over 3 million, and nonprofit employees increased by 75%, to account in 2001 for 2.6% of the labour force. In regard to the number of users served and contribution to the production of welfare services, suffice it to point out that Italian social cooperatives, non-existent until the 1980s, served 3.3 million users and employed 244,000 workers and 30,000 volunteers in 2005 (Istat 2007).

In qualitative terms, the most significant change has perhaps been the evolution into productive and entrepreneurial forms of a large part of the nonprofit sector, above all the organizations that have arisen in the past 30 years. Organizations engaged mainly in advocacy actions, which previously constituted the nonprofit sector, have been progressively flanked and partially replaced by new organizations engaged in the direct provision of social and collective-interest services: so-called 'social enterprises'. This evolution has also given rise to major changes in the institutional features and the ownership and governance forms of these organizations. The nonprofit distribution constraint typical of the large donative foundations has lost importance, whereas of growing significance are the social goal pursued, the nature of the goods produced, the types of stakeholders owning the organization, and the form of governance. Alongside the traditional non-proprietary organizations (Hansmann 1996), there have spread enterprises only partly constrained in their distribution of profits and characterized instead by the allocation of property rights to users, volunteers, and workers, or simultaneously to more than one of these categories, which has helped re-launch the cooperative form in new activities and produce a new proprietary structure also known as 'multi-stakeholder' (Borzaga and Mittone 1997). These changes have been recently institutionalized through legal recognition of the new, entrepreneurial types of organization. First in Italy (Law 381/1991), and then in other countries, various types of social cooperative have been recognized and regulated. In 2004 the United Kingdom created the 'Community interest company', and enacted 2 years later in Italy was a law instituting the 'social enterprise' (Law 155/2006).

It is widely believed that two factors have been mainly responsible for the changes just described: the greater responsibilization and increased dynamism of civil society in face of the difficulties encountered by welfare systems in coping with growing needs, and the increasingly widespread tendency of public administrations to outsource the production of social services to private actors. The former factor explains the increase in the number of volunteers and nonprofit organizations. The latter, besides reinforcing this trend, has contributed to the increase in employment, revenues, and the number of users of the nonprofit sector. However, because this growth has come about in the presence of stringent budget constraints, also due to contracting-out practices intended to curb public spending, the pay rates of workers in nonprofit organizations are generally below the market averages, or at least below the wage paid by public units producing similar services.

This evolution of the nonprofit sector has been analyzed from different perspectives and evaluated in different ways. Firstly, attempts have been made to determine whether the growth of the nonprofit sector can be explained by the possession of competitive advantages deriving from the characteristics of these organizations. These advantages were initially identified in the ability of the nonprofit distribution constraint to foster fiduciary relationships in transactions characterized by significant problems of information asymmetry (Hansmann 1996), and to attract donors and users interested in the greater production of particular services (Weisbrod 1988; Ben-Ner and Van Hoomissen 1991). These early interpretations were subsequently integrated, deepened, and subjected to empirical verification by a large number of studies, which cannot be described in detail here but have generated an autonomous strand of analysis within the economic and social sciences (see the surveys in Anheier and Ben-Ner 1997; Borzaga and Defourny 2001).

Analyzed accordingly have been the consequences of these developments for national welfare systems. Two very different positions have been taken up: that of those who believe that this evolution may help increase both the quantity and the quality and the diversification of the supply, with evident advantages for the users of services; and the position of those who instead fear that it may justify progressive abandonment of the principle of universality of services and the consequent cutting back of public intervention.

A specific group of research studies deal with the consequences of this evolution for the quality and characteristics of work in the new services supply units. In this case, too, diverse positions have been taken up by authors. Some have emphasized the advantages in terms of a net increase in employment, often for the weakest components of the labour market. Others have seen the growth of the new organizations as a way to curb the cost of labour and to reorganize rights previously guaranteed to workers in the public social services. And they sometimes also interpret voluntary work as a form of exploitation.

Consequently, very different evaluations are made of the new role assumed by nonprofit organizations, and they require time and a great deal of research. A contribution in this regard comes from analysis of how voluntary and remunerated employment relationships are structured in nonprofit organizations, and particularly in the social enterprises, verifying whether there are matches between the characteristics of these organizations and those of the workers in them.

1.3 Work in Nonprofit Organizations: Interpretations and Empirical Verification

As said in the introduction, theoretical interpretations and empirical research on the volunteers and workers of nonprofit organizations have to date been conducted separately for the two types of workers, and generally without reference to the specific features of the organizations in which they work. Analyses of voluntary work have sought mainly to explain its existence and growth, while studies on paid work have sought not only to interpret the reasons for the increase in under-remunerated jobs within nonprofit organizations, but also for the levels, often high, of loyalty and satisfaction shown by these workers. Although they have been conducted separately, these strands of research have often assumed very similar hypotheses and used very similar explanations. It is therefore useful to summarize the contributions furnished by this literature, grouping them according to their arguments, regardless of whether the object of analysis is voluntary or under-remunerated work.[3]

A first strand of studies has sought to interpret voluntary and under-remunerated work in nonprofit organizations without abandoning the standard economic model of rational choice and self-interested behaviour, doing no more than add a new factor to the classic individual utility function. The distinctive feature of studies belonging to this strand is the nature of this additional factor: third-party advantage for a first group, and the agent's direct advantage for a second. For contributions classifiable in the first group, a volunteer is someone who incorporates into his/her utility function the well-being of one or more individuals different from him/her (Schwartz 1970; Becker 1976), or the benefit deriving from the psychological pleasure (the 'warm glow') felt upon satisfying a preference to behave altruistically (Andreoni 1989, 1990). Coherent with this conception of altruism are also the interpretations of voluntary work as resulting from genetically determined or pre-constituted preferences (Hirschleifer 1977; Frank 1987, 1988) or as a way to build a reputation and to induce recipients to reciprocate, according to a far-sighted strategy of self-interest (Axelrod 1984). Even if incorporation of preferences for others' well-being into the utility function has been used mainly to interpret voluntary work, it has also been applied to under-remunerated work in nonprofit organizations, interpreting the differences in pay as 'labour donations' (Preston 1989). Analyses that have instead viewed voluntary or under-remunerated work as directly able to increase utility mainly rely on models of investment in human capital, according to which the individual decides to undertake these kinds of work in order to increase his/her future employment opportunities and future earnings (Menchik and Weisbrod 1987; Musella and Nappo 2008; for an empirical verification Day and Devlin 1998), or to acquire information about job vacancies or to demonstrate work abilities (Prouteau and Wolff 2004; Ziemek 2006). What attracts both volunteers and workers to nonprofit organizations are therefore also opportunities for on-the-job training (Borzaga and Tortia 2006) and for professional development. On this interpretation it is therefore possible to argue that the increase in voluntary and under-remunerated work does not necessarily imply an increase in the number of altruists, but it may be due to rational behaviour by non-altruists who decide to signal themselves as more productive, or more inclined to cooperate (Katz and Rosenberg 2005).

[3]Deliberately excluded from this survey are interpretations according to which these two forms of work are due to a lack of occupational alternatives, because they derive more from casual observation that from research conducted with scientific methods, and are therefore of little interest for the purposes of this study.

Added to these benefits are non-economic ones, such as the esteem and social prestige associated with these activities (Cialdini et al. 1981, Godderis 1988), and the opportunity to enjoy new and more intense relationships (Gui and Sugden 2005; Borzaga and Depedri 2005; Musella and Nappo 2008). In regard to situations of under-remunerated work, also pointed out are the advantages that may derive from the lesser pressure applied by the organization on the workers (Mirvis and Hackett 1983), and from better working conditions, especially in terms of stability, flexibility and autonomy (Borzaga and Tortia 2006).

A second interpretative strand consists of studies which abandon the standard economic approach to the supply of labour and emphasize the importance of motivations. They therefore interpret voluntary and under-remunerated work in nonprofit organizations as resulting from the presence of motivations different from self-interest. Some authors have distinguished the motivations underlying the supply of labour into extrinsic and intrinsic, where the former refer mainly to the material benefits deriving from the work, and the latter to the self-fulfilment that it makes possible (Frey 1997). Other authors have used the concept of social preferences: these, internalized by the individual, favour the adaptation of his/her behaviour to the cultural and moral conditions of the social context. On these bases, different theoretical models have been developed, and much empirical and experimental research has been conducted. A first group of studies has stressed the ideological motivations underlying both voluntary action and under-remunerated work in nonprofit organizations (Weisbrod 1983; Rose-Ackerman 1996). They thus reprise, albeit in a different analytical context, the explanatory importance of unconditioned altruistic attitudes.

A second group of studies have shown that one of the main explanations for the choice to undertake voluntary work is explicitly requested by relatives, friends, and colleagues (Freeman 1997), which signals the presence of motivations definable as 'conformist' (Grimalda and Sacconi 2003). Other authors have instead dwelt on the ethical dimension of human action, arguing that where the production of public goods is involved, as in the case of most nonprofit organizations, choices are also guided by moral obligations or norms that originate directly from the conscience of individuals (Sen 1977, 1998). Yet others have confirmed the importance of the reciprocity principle, which, by requiring people to reciprocate benefits received, acts as a stimulus for voluntary work or the performance of particular activities with below-average remuneration (Sudgen 1982, 1984; Sacco and Zamagni 2002). When the object of the analysis has been under-remunerated work, attention has centred on other motivations, such as the preference for the greater retributive and procedural fairness guaranteed by nonprofit organizations (Levine 1991; Leete 2000; Tortia 2007 and Chap. 6 in this book) and for greater opportunities to participate in decision-making processes (Michie and Sheehan 1999; Borzaga and Tortia 2006; Tortia 2007 and Chap. 6 in this book). Finally, recognition of the importance of non self-interested motivations has made it possible to show that low wages can be used as an efficient mechanism for the selection of intrinsically motivated workers: that is, ones more concerned with the social and relational, rather than economic, characteristics of the work (Handy and Katz 1998).

The numerous empirical studies conducted in recent years on both the volunteers and workers of nonprofit organizations have often confirmed the validity of the one or the other of the above interpretations. But none of them has provided a definitive and convincing explanation of the two phenomena and their dynamics. When the data have made it possible to determine the presence of several motivations, and therefore to test different interpretations simultaneously, several of them are found to explain the phenomenon. Almost always of importance in both voluntary and under-remunerated work are altruistic motivations or social norms; but these are generally flanked by preferences for other aspects of the work: conditions, the degree of autonomy, involvement in decision-making processes, the perception of fairness, and the opportunity to increase human capital (Borzaga 2000; Borzaga and Tortia 2006; Tortia 2007 and Chap. 6 in this book). Moreover, when it is possible to use several explanatory variables, none of them proves to be exclusive or even predominant. In other words, the decision to donate part of one's labour seems always to depend on a mix of motivations which varies according to the characteristics of the individual, the social value of the activity performed, the features of the organization, and the context in which it operates. It can therefore be argued that the intensity and direction of altruistic or ideological motivations, or the perception of a possible moral obligation, determine the willingness – which differs from individual to individual – to work for organizations able to satisfy such motivations. However, whether this willingness turns into actual and continuous commitment depends on another set of conditions which respond to the needs of the potential worker and which the organization must be able to satisfy.

To continue the analysis, it is therefore first necessary to classify both voluntary and remunerated workers' motivations more precisely, and then concentrate on the characteristics of the activities in which voluntary or under-remunerated work is undertaken, that is, the specific features of the sector of social services.

1.4 The Motives Underlying Work Choices

Analyses of voluntary and remunerated work in nonprofit organizations constitute only part of the broader strand of studies recently conducted on work motivations, and on the complexity of the determinants of the labour supply. These studies raise serious doubts concerning the explanatory capacity of the labour supply models proposed by the standard economic approach. These doubts have assumed increasing importance with the spread of new forms of work and the increase in the number of people employed in the production of goods and services of collective interest. In light of these studies, it is therefore useful to try to draw up a classification of work motivations that can be applied to any context.

In its endeavour to reduce the variables explaining human behaviour to the essential minimum, economic analysis has put forward a view of individuals, and of the organizations that they create, where the only goal pursued is personal advantage, defined very restrictively as the maximization of monetary variables (profit for the enterprise, profit for the investor, immediate or deferred earnings for the worker). This interpretation of human action does not consider motivations different from self-interest; or it does not give them an importance such that they influence individual behaviour in any significant way. It is hypothesized, that is to say, that such different motivations are unable, either singly or jointly, to explain the behaviours of individuals, or at any rate gainsay the importance that they give to monetary income.

However, these assumptions, and the conception of work that derives from them, are increasingly regarded as reductive. Indeed, recent empirical and experimental evidence not only disputes the existence of a significant relationship between pay and work utility or satisfaction, but has amply demonstrated the importance of non-selfish motivations (Fehr et al. 1998; Fehr and Falk 1999; Fehr and Götte 2005), denying the existence of a direct relationship between wealth and happiness (Blanchflower and Oswald 2005).

These findings have prompted a search for new paradigms with which to interpret the supply of labour, and which comprise motivations different from the mere pursuit of self-interest. Without entering into details on the (by now) large and growing literature on this topic, it is still possible to summarize the main results and to propose a classification of the main work motivations for analytical purposes.

The first studies that sought to gain better understanding of the structure of work motivations (deCharms 1968; Deci 1975) distinguished them between extrinsic and intrinsic: where, as said, the former relate to the material consequences of work and the economic benefits that derive from it, whilst the latter refer to the desire to work solely for the interest and the personal satisfaction to be gained therefrom.[4] In regard to these two components, much emphasis has been placed on the crowding-out effect (Frey 1997): that is, the possibility that an excess in the provision of extrinsic incentives (for instance, a higher wage) reduces intrinsic motivation (for instance, in personal interest and the voluntary nature of the action), leaving work commitment unchanged or even diminished. This distinction suggests that the wage enters the individual's choice function no longer solely as a positive determinant, but also with a negative influence intermediated by possible distortionary effects on the other motivations.

However, simple analysis of extrinsic and intrinsic motivations does not seem able to account for the numerous aspects of behaviour by workers; above all because both categories comprise very different motivations. A further step towards more complete understanding of the phenomenon can be made by considering two further elements: social preferences and organizational processes. These two concepts have been used by Ben Ner and Putterman (1998), according to whom the action of individuals is simultaneously influenced by self-interested (or 'self-regarding' preferences), altruistic (so-called 'other-regarding') and procedural ('process-regarding') components. By cross-referencing these motivations with the previous ones it is possible to draw up a new classification.

[4] For more detailed analysis of motivations see the self-determination theory of Gagné and Deci (2005).

Self-regarding preferences include both extrinsic and intrinsic motivations. They comprise all those preferences that are satisfied firstly in monetary form (the wage) or by other economic incentives (for instance, opportunities for professional growth and career advancement) and, secondly, through the satisfaction of non-material needs of a personal and psychological nature. Belonging in particular to this latter category is the opportunity to express one's creativeness, to establish new relationships, and to enjoy satisfactory work relationships with colleagues, superiors and customers, and which can be considered 'on-the-job consumption' of relational goods (Gui and Sugden 2005; Borzaga and Depedri 2005).

Altruistic (other-regarding) preferences have only to do with intrinsic motivations, and they are closely connected with social preferences. They induce the worker to evaluate whether and to what extent others can benefit from his/her work or from the good or service produced by the organization where s/he is employed. The more these motivations are developed, the more the worker will decide whether, how, for what organization, and with what commitment s/he will work, also on the basis of the advantage that the beneficiaries derive from it. Among these preferences are both pure altruism and behaviours dictated by conformism, or by compliance with the reciprocity principle, when this gives rise to disinterested behaviour in response to the behaviour of colleagues or to decisions by the organization deemed correct. Also connected with the reciprocity principle are the preferences for fairness, whereby the worker is more satisfied if s/he regards the wages paid to all the workers as right, and if s/he regards the division among stakeholders of organization's economic results as equitable.

Finally, process-regarding preferences are those that refer to organizational processes, to the ways in which career paths are created and information is transmitted, as well as the way in which the work is organized (also in terms of flexibility and autonomy). In other words, these preferences relate to the way in which the work is performed, and to the processes by which the worker is integrated into the productive activity. Perhaps the most frequently cited of these motivations is 'participation', meaning involvement in decision-making processes in regard to both strategic decisions and the practical organization of work. Added to these are preferences for transparency, and the completeness of informational processes within the enterprise concerning the various aspects of the work, as well as the rules applied in establishing pay levels and career paths. In the literature, all these aspects have been synthesized into the concept of 'procedural fairness' (Solari 2003).

This classification satisfactorily encompasses the complexity of work motivations. But it requires at least two further components. First to be considered are the possible control methods used by enterprises and their effects on workers' motivations, effort and satisfaction. And secondly the possibility that the importance given by each worker to the various groups of motivations may evolve over time under the influence of various factors.

Control over a worker can be exercised (Minkler 2004) both by the employer, in the traditional form of threatened punishments of differing degrees of severity, and by colleagues in the form of peer pressure. In the former case, control is used to avoid opportunistic behaviours, but it cannot be taken for granted that control will induce greater effort by the worker. In fact, if control is interpreted as a lack of trust, or is considered detrimental to autonomy, the positive effect may be attenuated by the negative influence exerted on other- and process-regarding preferences. In the latter case, control is informal in nature and is the consequence of compliance, voluntary or otherwise, with social norms and values shared by the other workers. It generally takes the form of mutual pressure among colleagues, but it may also be exercised by other interest stakeholders, especially when these come into direct contact with the worker.

Stating that attention should also be paid to the possible evolution of motivations means that they are not given parameters. Rather, they change over time for different reasons: for instance, the worker's learning, needs, and expectations; the policies adopted, deliberately or otherwise, by the organization; and the behaviour of the others belonging to the work group or those people with whom the worker interacts. When it is the organization that determines the evolution of its workers' preferences, these come to assume a partially endogenous character (Bowles 1998, 2004). This means that not only are the workers differently motivated, but they are also differently disposed to modify their preferences, to learn from the work environment and, ultimately, to motivate themselves.

Whilst the standard theories on the labour supply assume, with few exceptions, that workers have identical and only self-regarding preferences, this survey supports instead the idea that work motivations are manifold, and that each of them may assume different weights according to the characteristics of workers themselves, but also those of the sectors and the organizations towards which they direct their labour supply. The differences between the interpretative capacity of the standard approach and the approach emphasizing the plurality of motivations are unremarkable as long as the labour supply consists of homogeneous subjects (adult male heads of household), and as long as workplaces have similar characteristics (as in the manufacturing firm organized according to the Taylorist model). But they increase with growth in the complexity of the labour supply and demand: in the presence of workers with different cultures, interests and needs, jobs able to satisfy not solely the extrinsic preferences of those workers, and organizations whose exclusive purpose is not the interest of their owners. It is therefore possible to hypothesize that there exist different models of labour supply, both remunerated and voluntary, based on mixes of different motivations, and of which the neo-classical model is only one of those possible. The efficiency of these models also depends on the characteristics of the sector and the organizations in which they are applied. Whence derives the interest of examining the characteristics of the sector of social and collective-interest services (Fig. 1.1).

1.5 The Distinctive Features of Social and Collective-Interest Services

Economic analysis has to date only marginally concerned itself with social and collective-interest services, notwithstanding their increasing economic and occupational importance. Consequently, statistical classifications are not sufficiently developed to allow their precise description. Indeed, every author attributes a different meaning

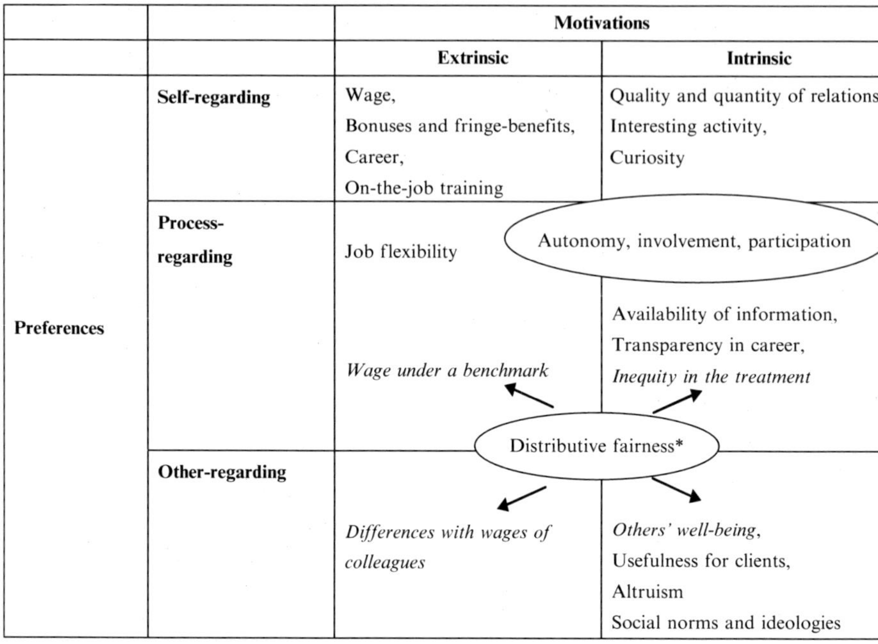

Fig. 1.1 A schematization of workers' motivations (* Motivations influenced by distributive fairness in italics)

to the term. Adopted in what follows is a broad definition of these services which extends beyond traditional care work to encompass health, educational, cultural, recreational services, and in general all those services to which citizens are entitled. This aggregate almost coincides with that of the so-called communal services which employ percentages ranging, according to the country, between 25 and 35% of the overall labour force.

However, compared with other sectors, that of social and collective-interest services has important features which also influence the relationships between workers and organizations engaged in the delivery of services. In general, it can be argued that, with few exceptions, the social and collective-interest services sector is the one in which the traditional market mechanisms work less well, for various reasons which can be summarized into two main ones: (1) the marked information asymmetry in the relationships among the various agents; (2) the nature as merit (or public) goods of the services produced, owing to their high social importance.

Social and collective interest services are generally characterized by 'multidimensionality', in the sense that they comprise several dimensions both quantitative and, especially, qualitative. Consequently, their value does not depend solely on the number of users served (and therefore solely on the quantity produced). Quality, in turn, can be understood both as the efficiency of service furnished (in terms of results) and as the possibility to obtain also relational and affective benefit from the service. However, multidimensionality in itself does not cause market failures:

in theory, in fact, it is possible to stipulate a complete contract for every dimension of the service, so that organizations consequently compete with each other according to neo-classic logic. The problem arises when, owing to incompleteness or information asymmetry, it is not possible to stipulate complete contracts for one or more of these dimensions and to verify compliance with them. In these cases, production by for-profit enterprises is inefficient, above all when the services are characterized by situations of 'third-party payee': that is, when the cost of the service is borne by an actor different from the user (the public administration, the donors, indirect users of the service). Information asymmetry may therefore create difficulties both for clients in monitoring the quality of the service and its correspondence with the price agreed, and for the entrepreneur in controlling the performance of workers (Bacchiega and Borzaga 2001). In particular, if the workers are driven solely by self-regarding motives, when the principal is unable to monitor their actions there may ensue a general tendency to reduce work commitment. Consequently, also the standard mechanisms of economic incentive are inefficient, because it is not possible to stipulate complete or productivity-linked contracts and determine when punishment should be inflicted, and because control on the performance of workers has very high costs. In this situation of asymmetry and contractual incompleteness, the costs of the relationship between enterprise and consumers or donors, and between enterprise and workers, can only be reduced by using different incentives, or by trying to limit the counterparty's opportunism by 'convincing' it to show greater commitment, with the same (or similar) economic incentives offered and the same control exercised (Borzaga and Musella 2003).

These problems are greater for services with high relational content, where the quality of the service – understood as users' satisfaction – depends to a great extent on the quality of the relationship established by the deliverer of the service, whether worker or enterprise. This means that in this sector the value of the service is influenced essentially by the effort of the workers and by the motivations and the relational skills of the workers or volunteers. However, on one hand, due to its intrinsic nature, relationships and quality of the individual performance of workers cannot be controlled and cannot be increased with material incentives. No contractual clauses are able to define minimum standards for relationships and affects, since incompatible with intrinsic motivations and social preferences. And also monitoring become difficult to carry out. On the other hand, relationships may be costly (in terms of commitment and time), so that some individuals (typically those maximizing their economic utility alone) are little inclined to invest in them, while the organization is unable to adopt any economic incentive to stimulate greater worker commitment to relations.

In regard to the second specific feature of the sector – the social importance of the goods produced – many social and collective-interest services are considered 'meritorious' by the community, or they also produce significant positive externalities. In the former case, it is generally agreed that all citizens should be eligible for services, regardless of their income and their ability to purchase them at market prices. In the latter case, a situation is created where the organization producing the service is unable to internalize all the value produced, and therefore finds itself with margins and profits systematically lower than those obtainable from other activities. Hence, frequently not only the organizations producing these services assume a well-defined social mission, but the latter is shared by the workers, who are asked to relinquish that part of the economic value of which the consumers or the community are the beneficiaries.

These observations on the specificities of the social services sector explain in the first place the existence, alongside public organizations, of private ones which expressly forgo profit maximization in order to strengthen their fiduciary relationships with consumers (Hansmann 1996) and produce goods and services with little profitability. But they also explain the presence of workers – voluntary and remunerated – who have utility functions in which, for some reason, the non extrinsic self-regarding preferences have important weight. The satisfaction of these workers and their intention to stay with the organization therefore depend on the ability of the latter to adopt coherent incentive policies and to sustain the relative costs. However, such costs are not the same for all organizations – for-profit, public and nonprofit – since they possess different capacities to provide incentives to workers, different abilities to transmit organizational goals, to organize work, and to exploit the skills of individuals, as well as different costs of control (which may be borne only not by the organization, but also by work colleagues in the case, for example, of peer pressure). It means that each organizational form has a specific comparative advantage in supplying and enforcing different types of incentives and in answering to different types of workers' motivations.

Consequently, organizational efficiency in human resources management will differ according to the proprietary and organizational form adopted. Not surprisingly, therefore, the sector of social and collective-interest services comprises different organizational, managerial, and industrial relations models, and differently remunerated workers.

1.6 A Possible Encounter Between Multiple Motivations and the Sector's Characteristics

It is now possible to propose a model able to describe, within a single interpretative framework, the labour supply of both volunteers and paid workers, and the willingness of the latter to accept pay rates below the market average, or below those which they could earn in other occupations. On the basis of the foregoing analysis, it is possible to state that employment relationships, both remunerated and gratuitous, are characterized by numerous exchanges between the organization and workers. On the one hand, they influence the production functions of organizations and the utility functions of workers. On the other, they are influenced by the characteristics of the parties, and particularly by the nonprofit or for-profit nature of the organization. There are three essential features that define the boundaries within which the employment relationship is constructed: the motivations of the workers; the characteristics of the sector; the specific features of the organization.

In regard to the first of these features, the previous sections have shown that workers (remunerated and voluntary) can draw utility from a plurality of factors, and that their behaviour is dictated simultaneously by selfish, altruistic and procedural motivations and preferences. This means that, for every individual, the participation constraint in the work and the level of effort selected are functions of both the mix of motivations and the mix of incentives offered. These will differ between remunerated workers and volunteers. Moreover, remunerated workers may also positively evaluate elements different from the wage, and volunteers may also work for motivations other than altruistic ones. To grasp all these components, it is therefore necessary to rewrite the utility function of individuals, re-aggregating the various factors of which it is composed into self-, other- and process-regarding. Whilst the last two factors should be understood as described in Sect. 1.4, the first (self-regarding) can be usefully divided into extrinsic and intrinsic. The extrinsic factors include the wage and all the forms of deferred economic incentive (e.g. career opportunities, training on the job, etc.). The intrinsic factors instead reflect non-monetizable aspects (e.g. relationships, involvement, autonomy, personal development, etc.). All these factors enter the individual's utility function as arguments and parameters: the former represent the quantity received of each incentive (or factor), while the latter capture the different weight assigned by workers to each incentive received on the job. Therefore, the parameters of the utility function represent the workers' motivations or their preferences.

The utility function of each subject becomes:

$$U_j = f(c\,(e), e, i, o, p_p, m_e, m_i, m_o)$$

with $0 < m_e < 1$ and $0 < m_i < 1$, where: $c(e)$ = cost of effort;[5] e = self-regarding incentives of extrinsic type offered by the organization; i = self-regarding incentives of intrinsic type obtained from the work; o = advantages accruing to other subjects (other-regarding); p_p = perception of procedural fairness[6] as a synthesis of the procedural

[5] In order to simplify study of the utility function and restrict the analysis to motivations and incentives, it is assumed here that the cost of effort enters the utility function in a fixed amount and that it reduces the utility in the same way and to the same amount for each worker. It will be aim of future analysis, on the one hand, to verify the sign of the correlation between effort and job satisfaction and, on the other, the determinants of the cost of effort. In regard to the former aspect, it will be assumed that effort is a source not only of costs but also of satisfaction (entering also with a positive sign into the utility function). In regard to the latter consideration, it will be assumed that social preferences and intrinsic motivations may decrease the perception of the cost of effort.

[6] Procedural fairness is included in the function as the value received by the workers. It could be broken down, like the other components, into p = the procedural fairness effectively provided in the organization, and m_p = importance attributed to fairness by the worker. However, the two factors are often evaluated jointly because it is difficult, especially from an empirical point of view, to split the fairness component between its objective value and the weight assigned to it by the worker. One may therefore assume that the worker expresses with p_p a subjective evaluation of the process-regarding aspects.

components; m_e = extrinsic self-regarding motivations; m_i = intrinsic self-regarding motivations; m_o = altruism, or importance given to others' well-being.

In a simple configuration, the utility function can be written as a non-linear function of the self-regarding elements, at which workers add the utility coming from their other- and process-regarding preferences, as formalized in many models on social preferences (see for example, Fehr and Schmidt 2001).[7] In regard to self-regarding elements, a different weight is assigned to intrinsic and extrinsic incentives, but there is no perfect substitutability among them, that is they have a different marginal rate of substitution.

The utility function can thus be rewritten as:

$$U_j = (e^{m_e} \; i^{m_i}) + m_o o + p_p - c(e)$$

Hence, given constant the value of $c(e)$, the individual's utility increases: (1) with an increase in extrinsic incentives, and all the more so when these are important for the worker; (2) with an increase in intrinsic incentives and in the weight assigned to them by the individual; (3) the more that the worker is altruistic and the activity performed has consequences on the well-being of third parties (users or colleagues); (4) the greater the worker's perception of procedural fairness.[8]

Volunteers and remunerated workers have the same utility functions. However, both the incentives offered by the organization and motivations differ between them. In regard to the incentives, the main differences concern the extrinsic aspects of the work. Offered to remunerated workers are a wage, a career and training; while volunteers are provided incentives as human capital accumulation, job opportunities in the organization, and knowledge or reputation spendable in the labour market. In regard to the motivations, assuming $m_e + m_i = 1$, such that the first element of the utility function has the properties of a Cobb-Douglas, and assuming that altruism is an independent component endogenous to the individual, it is possible to state that if $j = r, v$, with r = remunerated workers and v = volunteers, will be $m_e^r > m_e^v$; $m_i^r < m_i^v$ and $m_o^r < m_o^v$,

[7]Although the theoretical explanation assumes that workers must be offered a mix of incentives, it mainly refers to a mix of intrinsic and extrinsic incentives. Instead, by assuming that other- and process-regarding preferences enter the utility function in an additional way, the model stresses that the greater the importance of social preferences and the provision of fairness and altruistic behaviours on the job (i.e. the higher $m_o o$ and p_p), the greater the workers' final utility. But the utility is not equal to zero when the treatment is unfair or the job does not influence the well-being of others, when self-regarding aspects are sufficiently high. It should be instead assumed that inequality and organizational egoism decrease the utility of workers (i.e. $m_o o + p_p$ becomes negative) and the final utility decreases, also with the risk of diminishing the worker's reserve utility.

[8]In a different assumption of the model (for a detailed study of the utility function, see Depedri 2007) and as also found by empirical analyses on social cooperatives and nonprofit organizations (see Borzaga and Depedri 2005), the utility function also includes minimal requested levels of intrinsic and extrinsic incentives. In a similar way, there exists a minimum threshold for one or more of these elements below which workers will decide not to work for the organization, or below which their utility level is unsatisfying.

where intrinsic motivations and altruism are stronger among volunteers,[9] whilst remunerated workers are more motivated than volunteers by the extrinsic components of the work. However, this does not mean that all remunerated workers assign greater weight to extrinsic aspects than to intrinsic ones; hence for some of them job satisfaction, may be influenced more by intrinsic incentives than by the wage.

This formulation of the utility function shows that, firstly, when workers are interested in intrinsic aspects of the job it is not sufficient to offer solely economic incentives. Secondly, the more the organization supplies a mix of incentives that privileges aspects of the job in line with its workers' motivations, the more the latter will be satisfied with their job. Specifically, for nonprofit organizations the supply of mixes in which intrinsic aspects and relationships are crucial elements will satisfy more intrinsically motivated workers. In other words, it is necessary to create a mix of incentives able to satisfy all the components of the utility function, and in a manner coherent with the mix of motivations of workers and volunteers.

Furthermore, the described utility function is not static, since it should be further extended that its parameters are endogenous, that is, they evolve over time as consequence of learning on the job and adaptation. Both the motivations and the social preferences of individuals may be influenced by the work environment and by the social norms present in the work group. Therefore, the organization can influence the compliance (or conformism) of the workers and the volunteers with the behaviour desired. It is therefore likely that the characteristics of the work and of the organization impact differently both on the mix of incentives offered and on the capacity to attract differently motivated individuals and to influence their preferences.

The analysis of the distinctive features of the sector has shown that, given the difficulties of monitoring and providing economic incentives to increase workers' effort, and given the importance of the relational contents of the work, employment relationships are strongly influenced by intrinsic, other- and process-regarding factors. Firstly, relations form an important component of activities in the sector: they are not only generated but also consumed by workers and volunteers (as relational goods), and they therefore enter their utility functions as intrinsic factors. Likewise, the multidimensionality of activities favours autonomy on the job and offers opportunities for personal as well as professional growth (both of which enter the utility function as intrinsic incentives). Moreover, the work has major consequences on social well-being (i.e. of the users) which the workers can directly ascertain. This factor, too, enters the utility function of the workers, especially if they have strong other-regarding preferences. All this evidence explains how, by offering diverse intrinsic incentives, organizations operating in the sector of social and collective-interest services can attract, satisfy, and motivate individuals most concerned with these aspects. Moreover, the presence of these incentives explains both why people

[9]This is often due to the fact that volunteers already have external work incomes and are therefore little motivated by the extrinsic component.

attend to volunteer in this sector and why average wages in the sector are often lower than in other sectors – the abilities, role and schooling of the workers remaining equal – but without this reducing the level of worker satisfaction.

Equally important are the characteristics of the various types of organization operating in the sector. These in fact may have: (1) features more or less consistent with the characteristic of the sector; (2) different constraints and costs in offering incentives; and (3) different costs in the monitoring of work. In the social services sector, nonprofit organizations are better able than others to include the well-being of external stakeholders in their missions. This is made possible by the non-distribution constraint (compared to for-profit organizations) and by the absence of self-regarding bureaucrats (compared to public agencies). In nonprofit organizations, moreover, the involvement of workers is easier because it can be achieved through their direct participation in ownership of the enterprise and not merely through consultation and involvement in work groups. This also favours the development of positive relationships, above all if the organization is of small size. The figure of the manager is perceived in nonprofit organizations as a means to transmit information, whilst in public agencies and for-profit organization managers mainly perform the role of controllers, with the consequence that they negatively influence procedural fairness and autonomy. All these considerations suggest that, in nonprofit organizations, the provision of intrinsic incentives is, other conditions remaining equal, greater and less costly. Firstly, there are no serious limitations on the promotion of these incentives and, secondly, they are easier to implement, being often foreseen in the organizational structure (as in the case of membership), and entail low control and transaction costs (i.e. decision costs). Conversely, for-profit and public organizations (especially of large size) can offer greater extrinsic incentives at lower costs, because they are less burdensome on the organization's economic resources. In public agencies and for-profit firms, moreover, job security tends to be greater.

If motivations, the features of the sector, and the differences among organizations are considered jointly, it is possible to explain why different organizations offer different mixes of incentives, endowing themselves with varying combinations of volunteers and motivated workers. Nonprofit organizations, for their part, are characterized by wages lower than those paid by the other organizations, or nil in the case of volunteers, but they use different combinations of intrinsic incentives to attract and gain the loyalty of workers and volunteers. This entails: (1) the greater satisfaction of workers (remunerated and otherwise) in nonprofit organizations, regardless of pay levels, when they give importance to intrinsic aspects – other- and process-regarding – of the work; or (2) a tendency for workers with similar motivations to join the same type of organization. Moreover, a good level of satisfaction among workers (remunerated and voluntary) improves the organizational climate and internal relationships; it fosters loyalty (reducing the likelihood of exits); it increases commitment and cooperativeness (especially if the workers place importance on social preferences and reciprocity); and it favours the positive evolution of preferences and motivations. In regard to this last point, the worker's adaptation to the context is facilitated by a work environment and membership of a work group where values, moral norms, intrinsic motivations and altruistic goals are shared. Over time, the workers may internalize the organization's mission and the social nature of the work.[10] Moreover, the intrinsic aspects of the work and the organizational environment become known and the employment relationship becomes stabler, also in the long period. This increases the satisfaction and loyalty of workers and improves individual and organizational performance.

To conclude: the encounter between organizations engaged in activities with high social importance and intrinsically-motivated workers reduces opportunism, monitoring difficulties and the costs of incentives, and consequently improves performance. There may thus arise a stable equilibrium between labour supply and demand, even if it is not based solely or principally on the wage. However, this equilibrium depends on specific features of the organization, among which is also a legal form that prevents owners and managers from exploiting the low wages paid to the workers.

1.7 Concluding Remarks

Remunerated and voluntary work have been generally interpreted with models which assume that their preferences are different, or even incompatible. Subsequently, empirical and experimental analyses, and especially research on under-remunerated workers in nonprofit organizations with an explicit social mission, have shown that (1) also volunteers are driven by self-regarding preferences, and (2) remunerated workers have preferences different from the maximization of immediate or deferred monetary income. The identification and classification of these preferences have enabled more focused empirical and experimental analysis which confirms the interpretative capacity of models which assume that agents are driven by a plurality of motivations to which they attribute different weights. As this paper has sought to show, it is possible to take account of this pluralism of motivations and agents by modifying the utility function so that it includes all the different types of motivation. It is thus possible to explain, using the same utility function, both voluntary and remunerated work, and to account for the existence in the same sector of different pay levels. It is sufficient to modify the parameters associated with each variable. In light of this new assumption, the satisfaction of the remunerated worker or volunteer depends on the characteristics of both the sector and the organization in which he/she is employed. The resulting distribution of workers and volunteers among sectors and enterprises can therefore be considered efficient also in the presence of individuals who are not paid or are systematically paid less than others.

---

[10] In other words, over time the constant stimulus to relationality, involvement and the development of autonomy and personal as well as professional growth increases intrinsic incentivation. Proximity with other motivated workers, volunteers and stakeholders, but also and especially users, internalizes the mission in preferences. The presence of social norms and coherent behaviours enhance the altruistic component. Knowledge of the work environment transmits information about procedures. And consistent organizational policies may increase the perception of fairness.

Given the importance that the sector of social and collective-interest services has acquired (and will acquire), research on these matters is particularly important, both to predict the possible evolution of welfare systems and to manage the organizations that produce these services.

Acknowledgments The ideas set out in the article result from joint reflection with various colleagues within the Department and elsewhere, and in particular with Sara Depedri, Luigi Bonatti, Ermanno Tortia, Luigi Mittone, Maurizio Pugno, Marco Musella and Maurizio Carpita. I am particularly grateful to Sara Depedri, who helped greatly to improve the article in all its parts. However, responsibility for errors or omissions remains mine alone.

References

Andreoni J (1989) Giving with impure altruism: Application to charity and Ricardian equivalence. Journal of Political Economy 97:1447–1458

Andreoni J (1990) Impure altruism and donations to public goods: A theory of warm-glow giving. Economic Journal 100:464–477

Anheier HK, Ben-Ner A (1997) Shifting boundaries. Long term changes in the size of for-profit nonprofit cooperative and government sectors. Annals of Public and Cooperative Economics 68:335–353

Axelrod R (1984) The evolution of cooperation. Basic Books, New York

Bacchiega A, Borzaga C (2001) Social enterprises as incentive structures: an economic analysis. In: Borzaga C, Defourny J (eds) The emergence of social enterprises. Routledge, London

Becker GS (1976) Altruism, egoism and genetic fitness: Economics and sociobiology. Journal of Economic Literature 14:817–826

Ben Ner A, Putterman L (1998) Economics values and organizations. Cambridge University Press, Cambridge UK

Ben-Ner A, Van Hoomissen T (1991) Nonprofit organizations in the mixed economy: A demand and supply analysis. Annals of Public and Cooperatives Economics 62:519–550

Blanchflower DG, Oswald AJ (2005) Happiness and the Human Development Index: the paradox of Australia. Australian Economic Review 38:207–318

Borzaga C (ed) (2000) Capitale umano e qualità del lavoro nel settore dei servizi sociali. Fondazione Italiana del Volontariato, Rome

Borzaga C, Defourny J (eds) (2001) The Emergence of social enterprises. Routledge, London

Borzaga C, Depedri S (2005) Interpersonal relations and job satisfaction: Some empirical results in social and community care services. In: Gui B, Sugden R (eds) Economics and Social Interaction: Accounting for Interpersonal Relations. Cambridge University Press, Cambridge UK

Borzaga C, Mittone L (1997) The multi-stakeholders versus the nonprofit organizations. University of Trento Department of Economics Discussion Paper 7

Borzaga C, Musella M (eds) (2003) Produttività ed efficienza nelle organizzazioni nonprofit. Edizioni31, Trento

Borzaga C, Tortia E (2006) Worker motivations, job satisfaction and loyalty in public and nonprofit social services. Nonprofit and Voluntary Sector Quarterly 35:225–248

Bowles S (1998) Endogenous preferences: the cultural consequences of markets and other economic institutions. Journal of Economic Literature 36:74–111

Bowles S (2004) Microeconomics: behaviour institutions and evolution. Russell Sage Foundation, Princeton

Cialdini R, Baumann DJ, Kenrick DT (1981) Altruism as hedonism: helping and self-gratification as equivalent responses. Journal of Personality and Social Psychology 40:1039–1046

Day KM, Devlin RA (1998) The payoff to work without pay: Volunteer work as an investment in human capital. Canadian Journal of Economics 31:1179–1193
deCharms R (1968) Personal causation. Academic Press, New York
Deci E (1975) Intrinsic motivation. Plenum Press, New York
Depedri S (2007) Speaking on the job: Incentives, preferences and complementarities in working relationships. PhD Thesis, University of Siena
Fehr E, Falk A (1999) Wage rigidity in a competitive incomplete contract market. Journal of Political Economy 107:106–134
Fehr E, Schmidt K (2001) Theories of fairness and reciprocity. Evidence and economic applications. CEPR Discussion Paper 2703
Fehr E, Götte L (2005) Do workers work more if wages are high? Evidence from a randomized field experiment. Journal of Monetary Economics 52:779–804
Fehr E, Kirchsteiger G, Riedl A (1998) Gift exchange and reciprocity in competitive experimental markets. European Economic Review 42:1–34
Frank RH (1987) If Homo Economicus could choose his own utility function would he want one with a conscience? American Economic Review 77:593–604
Frank RH (1988) Passion within reason. Norton, New York
Frey BS (1997) Not just for the money: an economic theory of personal motivation. Edward Elgar, Cheltenham
Freeman RB (1997) Working for nothing: the supply of volunteer labor. Journal of Labor Economics 15:S140–S166
Gagné M, Deci EL (2005) Self-determination theory and work motivation. Journal of Organizational Behavior 26:331–362
Godderis JH (1988) Compensating differentials and self-selection: an application to lawyers. Journal of Political Economy 96:411–428
Grimalda G, Sacconi L (2003) La costruzione dell'impresa nonprofit: ideali conformismo e reciprocità. In: Borzaga C, Musella M (eds) Produttività ed efficienza nelle organizzazioni nonprofit. Edizioni31, Trento
Gui B, Sugden R (eds) (2005) Economics and social interaction. Accounting for interpersonal relations. Cambridge University Press, Cambridge UK
Handy F, Katz E (1998) The wage differential between nonprofit institutions and corporations: getting more by paying less? Journal of Comparative Economics 12:246–261
Hansmann H (1996) The ownership of enterprise. The Belknap Press of Harvard University Press, Cambridge MA
Hirschleifer J (1977) Economics from a Biological Viewpoint. Journal of Law and Economics 20:1–52
Istat (2007). Le cooperative sociali in Italia Anno 2005. Statistiche in Breve. Istat, Rome
Katz E, Rosenberg J (2005) An economic interpretation of institutional volunteering. European Journal of Political Economy 21:429–443
Leete L (2000) Wage equity and employment motivations in nonprofit and forprofit organizations. Journal of Economic Behaviour and Organization 43:423–446
Levine DI (1991) Cohesiveness, productivity and wage dispersion. Journal of Economic Behaviour and Organization 15:237–255
Menchik PL, Weisbrod BA (1987) Volunteer labor supply. Journal of Public Economics 32:159–183
Michie J, Sheehan M (1999) No innovation without representation? An analysis of participation, representation, R&D and innovation. Economic Analysis 2:85–97
Minkler L (2004) Shirking and motivations in firms: survey evidence in working attitudes. International Journal of Industrial Organization 22:863–884
Mirvis PH, Hackett EJ (1983) Work and workforce characteristics in the nonprofit sector. Monthly Labour Review 106:3–12
Musella M, Nappo N (2008) Volunteering and reciprocity: a normative approach. Rivista Internazionale di Scienze Economiche e Sociali 96:77–98
Preston AE (1989) The nonprofit worker in a for-profit world. Journal of Labour Economics 7:438–445

Prouteau L, Wolff FC (2004) Relational goods and associational participation. Annals of Public and Cooperative Economics 75:431–463
Rose-Ackerman S (1996) Altruism, non profit and economic theory. Journal of Economic Literature 34:701–728
Sacco PL Zamagni S (eds) (2002) Complessità relazionale e comportamento economico. il Mulino, Bologna
Salamon LM, Anheier HK (1998) The emerging sector revisited. A summary. Center for Civil Society Studies, Johns Hopkins University, Baltimore
Salamon LM, Anheier HK, List R, Toepler S, Sokolowski SW (1999) Global civil society: dimensions of the nonprofit sector. Center for Civil Society Studies, Johns Hopkins University, Baltimore
Schwartz SRA (1970) Personal philantropic contributions. Journal of Political Economy 78:1264–1291
Sen A (1977) Rational fools: a critique of the behavioral foundation of economic theory. Journal of Philosophy and Public Affairs 6:317–344
Sen A (1998) Intervento alla Camera dei Deputati del 14 maggio 1998. Atti Parlamentari XIII Legislatura, Parlamento della Repubblica Italiana, Rome
Solari L (2003) La relazione tra lavoratore e organizzazione nelle organizzazioni nonprofit: contratto psicologico ed equità. In: Borzaga C, Musella M (eds) Produttività ed efficienza nelle organizzazioni nonprofit. Edizioni31, Trento
Sudgen R (1982) On the economics of philanthropy. Economic Journal 92:341–350
Sudgen R (1984) Reciprocity: The supply of public goods through voluntary contributions. Economic Journal 94:772–787
Tortia E (2007) Worker well-being and perceived fairness: survey-based findings from Italy. Journal of Socio-Economics 37:2080–2094
Weisbrod BA (1983) Nonprofit and proprietary sector behavior: wage differentials among lawyers. Journal of Labor Economics 1:246–263
Weisbrod BA (1988) The nonprofit economy. Harvard University Press, Cambridge MA
Ziemek S (2006) Economic analysis of volunteers' motivations. A cross-country study. Journal of Socio-Economics 35:532–555

Chapter 2
How Nonprofit Organizations Manage Risk

Dennis R. Young

Abstract The purpose of this essay is to identify the kinds of decisions where nonprofit organizations need to manage their risks in a strategic fashion, to review what is known about how they approach these decisions, and to offer a conceptual framework that nonprofits can use to develop a more sophisticated and effective approach to their risk-management decisions. For various reasons, nonprofits have not taken a sufficiently robust view of risk management, A simple framework is presented to address the risk-related decisions of nonprofits in a strategic fashion, with a view to inspire fuller attention to risk management in the nonprofit academic literature and in professional forums.

2.1 Introduction

Effective management of risk is fundamental to the proper functioning of any organization. Organizations that operate in a changing or otherwise uncertain environment in which the outcomes of their decisions, or their failure to make decisions, cannot be perfectly predicted, face risk. For nonprofit organizations, risk is encountered in many different ways. Financial, personnel, program and capital expenditure decisions all entail risk because they involve interactions with changing, complex, volatile or intrinsically stochastic economic, political and social environments. Hence their outcomes cannot be precisely determined in advance.

Risk management is important to nonprofit organizations for two closely connected reasons: First, nonprofits may wish to protect themselves as well as they can against disastrous outcomes that could threaten their survival and their capacities to address their missions. Second, as nonprofits consider alternative ways to address their missions they may often find that those options which promise greatest impact also entail greater risk. Hence, nonprofits must find combinations of risk and "return" with which they are most comfortable.

D.R. Young
Nonprofit Studies Program, Andrew Young School of Policy Studies,
Georgia State University, Atlanta, Georgia 30303, USA

S. Destefanis and M. Musella (eds.), *Paid and Unpaid Labour in the Social Economy*,
AIEL Series in Labour Economics, DOI: 10.1007/978-3-7908-2137-6_3,

The literature on nonprofit risk management falls mostly in the first category. In particular, nonprofits do pay substantial attention to how they can insure themselves against lawsuits against directors and officers, against potential liabilities from operating risky programs such as children's summer camps, or ordinary hazards such as crime, fire and flood. Less attention, however, has been paid to the second category of risk management – the strategic weighing of risks and benefits that allows organizations to have the greatest impact on their missions. Relatively recently, nonprofits have adopted principles of strategic finance, which allow them to follow a "prudent man" approach to investing financial resources in appropriately diversified portfolios that embody sensible levels of risk in order to achieve strong financial returns (Fremont-Smith 2004). While such financial decision-making is a bit more complicated for nonprofits than it is for private firms or individual investors – since nonfinancial impacts of financial decisions often matter to nonprofits – it is also clear why nonprofits have been able to approach risk strategically in the financial area. In particular, the primary metric for success in this area – financial return in dollar terms – is usually clear. In other areas of nonprofit decision making, the "return" may be less clear or tangible – measured in terms of social or mission impact, for example. Hence, the notion of thinking in terms of risk vs. return is not as natural. Nonetheless, a strategic approach to risk management is just as important – otherwise, nonprofits may find themselves making unduly conservative decisions that fail to achieve as much impact as they might, or in some cases taking unreasonable amounts of risk for a low return.

The purpose of this paper is to identify the kinds of decisions where nonprofits need to manage their risks in a strategic fashion, to review what we know about how they approach these decisions, and to offer a conceptual framework that nonprofits can use to develop a more sophisticated and effective approach to their risk management decisions in the future. The hope is that this will inspire fuller attention to risk management in the nonprofit management literature and in professional forums devoted to nonprofit management and leadership.

2.2 Special Issues of Risk for Nonprofits

There are a number of reasons why the issues of risk management are particularly complex for nonprofit organizations. It is important to highlight these issues before trying to assess current practices and research on this subject. One set of issues has to do with measurability. Others have to do with who bears the risk and how much risk it is appropriate to bear.

Measurement. As suggested above, nonprofits operate in areas where the results are not necessarily measurable in dollar terms, or even quantitatively. Nonprofit organizations address the health, education and well-being of people, look to improve the quality of the environment, produce and preserve great art, or seek social justice and change. While it is increasingly important, if only to satisfy the ever more demanding accountability requirements of funders and government overseers, for nonprofits to develop quantitative measures of their mission-related impacts, nonprofits often have their hands full trying to do so. Strategic risk management demands even more of them – not only measuring mission-related impact but also considering how that impact might vary under various contingencies. As we indicate below, measures of impact or "return" need not be terribly sophisticated in order for nonprofits to be able to consider risk in strategic terms, but a capacity for nonprofit executives to rate the value of alternative outcomes at least in relative terms is required. Moreover, nonprofit executives must be able to assess the likelihoods that different outcomes will occur – a crystal ball exercise with which nonprofit executives unschooled in contingency planning may not be comfortable.

How much risk and who should determine it? Nonprofit decisions are made by paid executives or by volunteer trustees, but the impacts of those decisions are felt by the clientele or societal groups served by nonprofits and by the volunteers and benefactors who supply the resources. In essence, nonprofit executives and trustees are agents for others, and in the largest sense, agents for a society that has commissioned nonprofits to carry out their socially worthy missions. All this complicates the accounting for risk in strategic nonprofit decision making. In a business setting, shareholders ultimately hold executives responsible for managing their assets to achieve maximum financial returns within the bounds of specified tolerance of risk. In a nonprofit, executive staff and the trustees to whom they report, are left to interpret – from the viewpoint of society or their particular constituencies – what is appropriate in terms of the risks they should assume and the levels of social return they should seek. While boards of trustees can, should and do, deliberate on these matters, and often consult with their constituents, no stock market exists for such issues to be sorted out. Within broad bounds, nonprofit trustees have discretion, and indeed many executives whose boards do not exert tight oversight, also have wide discretion. It is often only when results turn disastrous that public scrutiny comes into play.

The ambiguity of who bears the risk, and what levels of risk taking are appropriate, impacts directly on nonprofit decision making. What standard should an executive or a trustee use in determining if a particular alternative is too risky or too conservative? There are three possible levels on which this question can be approached. The first is the personal level. Some decision makers are more inclined to take risks than others. Is it therefore appropriate for a more dynamic executive to take greater risks on behalf of the organization? In one sense the answer is yes: a nonprofit board that hires an executive director implicitly takes attitude towards risk taking into account in making the hiring decision. Engaging an "entrepreneurial" chief executive can be a signal that the board, interpreting what is best for the organization, endorses a new level of risk taking in order to achieve greater impact. More generally, however, individual risk preference is not the appropriate standard for a nonprofit organization. Individuals, either executive directors or trustees, do not own the nonprofit organization nor are they engaged by shareholders who do so. Rather, they are entrusted with the organization's resources in order to achieve public purposes. Thus they are obligated to interpret what is best from the organization's or society's point of view.

However, the appropriate risk preference standard for the organization as a whole is not obvious either, for several reasons. First, resource providers may exert special influence. For example, even though major donors provide "gifts" they may expect those resources to be utilized with a particular level of prudence, such as they would apply to themselves. Government or other contractors will often impose their own standards or required practices as well, as a quid pro quo for their support. And professional codes of practice will also guide the decisions of particular nonprofit officials, such as chief financial officers and investment counselors. While each of these sources influences the risk-related behavior of nonprofit organizations, none represent the nonprofit organization as a whole or define its appropriate risk preference profile.

A nonprofit's risk preference may also be influenced by its age and life cycle stage as well as its size and asset base. A small, fledgling nonprofit may have little to risk and little choice but to take risks in order to get itself established. A more mature organization with substantial resources has more to protect and hence may approach risk in a more conservative fashion, even though it may be in a stronger position to gamble if it has accumulated reserves. Similarly, an organization that is part of a supportive network may feel more secure in taking risks than one on its own without such a safety net (Derryck and Abzug 2002).

Clearly a nonprofit's risk preference should be influenced by its mission. For example, if the organization operates in a dangerous setting, such as a war zone, it probably needs to recognize that high risk tolerance is necessary for effectiveness. Or, if it is established with the intention to achieve a certain goal, say eradication of a disease within a limited period of time as specified by a founding donor, then it may have to take more chances. By contrast a nonprofit, such as a school or a museum or community foundation, intended to provide benefits to a community into the indefinite future, must be sufficiently conservative to ensure its continued viability. Thus, it is up to the nonprofits' trustees to interpret the implications of mission for risk-related behavior and decision making.

From the viewpoint of society as a whole, one could argue that nonprofits collectively should be risk neutral – neither too conservative in their deployment of resources nor too risk-taking. The logic here is that some nonprofits may fail and others may succeed as they pursue their individual missions and approaches, but a stable society can accommodate both as long as the end result is the best possible return. Such logic, though not appropriate for individual nonprofits, allows policy makers to view the country as a large insurance pool for nonprofits experimenting with different approaches. Moreover, it raises consciousness about the societal risk tolerance for nonprofits: some should be allowed to experiment and take chances in responsible fashion while others are appropriately conservative. They cannot all be held to the same standards of risk taking.

Nonprofits can run into trouble when their individual decision-makers assume an inappropriate level of risk preference. They cannot simply impose their personal preferences approaches to risk taking onto their organizational decision-making responsibilities. Nor can they blithely assume that their organizations have an obligation to minimize risk in order to assure their survival for society's welfare.

There is no getting away from the requirement that nonprofit executives and trustees need to develop an organizational attitude towards risk taking that reflects the particular societal missions with which they are entrusted.

In actual practice, at least two broad factors influence nonprofits' attitudes towards risk. The first is a conservative tendency stemming in part from the fact that people are reluctant to take chances with resources that are entrusted to them, but which do not belong to them (Scanlan and Dillon-Merrill 2006). The second is an entrepreneurial tradition based on the understanding that nonprofits are often in the business of achieving social change, led by people inclined to take substantial risks in order to achieve the organization's goals (Young 1986). Either of these influences, if left unchecked, can lead to inappropriate approaches to risk management in the context of nonprofit strategic decision making.

2.3 Views from the Literature

It is difficult to pin down the literature on nonprofits' management of risk since risk is necessarily connected to virtually all facets of nonprofit organizational decision making. This section takes a broad view, inquiring into literature on various areas of nonprofit decision making as well as writings explicitly focused on nonprofit risk management. Even with this broad sweep, however, an interesting dichotomy emerges: most contributions focus on how nonprofits can minimize the risks that they face, rather than on the strategic trade-offs they may have to make between achieving impact or return and tolerating risk.

A good place to start is the literature on nonprofit governance, since it is at the board level that responsibility resides for decisions involving the prudent deployment of resources to achieve the organization's purposes. A recent review of research on nonprofit governance (Ostrower and Stone 2006), for example, identifies two normative models of corporate governance in the health care field – the corporate model and the philanthropic or stewardship model, the former being more sympathetic to strategic risk taking and the latter more inclined towards "asset preservation." Several other articles suggest the pervasiveness of the "asset preservation" view, with its concomitant emphasis on reducing risk rather than trading it against potential gains. For example, Gibelman and Gelman (1999) highlight the idea of "safeguarding" as a guiding principle for management of risk by nonprofit boards. Middleton (1988) describes "planning" as a way for nonprofit boards to reduce their uncertainty about actions to be taken in the future. Brown and Iverson (2004) describe four different strategic orientations of nonprofit boards, two of which ("defenders" and "reactors") are distinctly conservative in their approaches to products and services. Finally, Henson and Larson (1990) promote a comprehensive risk management approach that entails risk avoidance, risk transfer, better understanding of necessary risks, and risk reduction.

Some scholars attribute risk aversion to the economic incentives intrinsic to the nonprofit structure. For example, Wedig (1994) argues that nonprofit hospitals are risk averse in connection with cash flows and fund balances because they are constrained from paying cash dividends. Similarly, Preyra and Pink (2001) demonstrate that CEOs of for-profit hospitals are greater risk takers than their counterparts in nonprofit hospitals, receiving substantially greater compensation but with much wider variances, because the compensation structures of the two types of hospitals differ in accommodating such differentials.

Other scholars identify specific risk management strategies designed to reduce a nonprofit's exposure to risk. For example Bennett et al. (2006) argue that nonprofit commercial ventures can serve as a hedge against the uncertainty of donations. Along similar lines, Chang and Tuckman (1990) cite the accumulation of financial surpluses as a hedge against financial risk and uncertainty for nonprofit organizations. Bielefeld (1992) also argues that nonprofits tend to pursue a number of uncertainty reducing strategies such as finding new revenue sources, retrenching operations or finding ways to gain legitimacy in the eyes of funders. Similarly, Gronbjerg (1990) argues that nonprofits tend to seek less volatile funding sources, e.g., from government, despite the often substantial costs associated with complying with those sources.

In the area of institutional grant making, examples of both strategic and preservation philosophies are found. Higuera (1992) reports that most surveyed corporate giving managers are willing to assume risks by funding unproven and innovative programs, while Olenick (1988) reports that grantors tend to avoid risk by funding well-managed and reliable nonprofits even where other riskier nonprofits might ultimately yield a greater impact. Interestingly, Olenick also finds that some nonprofits make the opposite mistake, leaping into risky commercial ventures when safer and more effective options are available.

Of course there is nothing inherently unwise about seeking ways to reduce risk, especially in instances where that can be done without loss in performance, impact or contribution to mission. In fact, some classic risk management strategies such as insurance-type arrangements for risk sharing, and diversification of assets, income sources or programmatic alternatives for risk reduction, make eminent sense and are not sufficiently exploited by nonprofit organizations. However, the tenor of much of the literature suggests that mission impact or other measures of performance often get lost in the discussion about managing risk. Indeed, a key review article Tremper (1994) and a recent comprehensive text on managing risk in nonprofit organizations Herman et al. (2004) are generally focused on identifying the spectrum of possible risks a nonprofit may face (all the things that could go wrong with property, programs, people and finances, etc.) and how to minimize or protect against potential losses. To a certain extent, these references consider the probabilities and consequences of such losses, but they do not focus on decisions that may require accepting certain levels of risk in order to achieve desired goals or gains. This preventative approach to risk management is useful because many risk reduction policies may be effective and cheap, and do not preclude strategic management of risk. However, reliance on risk reduction alone may have the consequence of incurring large opportunity costs – missed chances for substantial gain caused by a failure to recognize and assume prudent risks.

2.4 Causes of Inefficient Nonprofit Decision Making Under Risk

In order to consider how nonprofits should manage risk, and how efficient they are in making decisions in the face of risk, one needs a normative framework that describes desired or "optimal" behavior. A classic model from decision theory contains the basics for identifying how rational decisions under risk should be made and what errors may preclude reaching the best decisions under risk. Figure 2.1 illustrates a simple two option choice where the consequence of one option (for example maintaining the status quo) is certain and known while the consequence of the second choice is uncertain, but could potentially lead to either a better or worse outcome than the first choice (see Behn and Vaupel 1982 for a more extensive analysis of this model).

Figure 2.1 captures most of the considerations of more complex decisions under uncertainty. The action alternative involves risk represented by probabilities p and (1 – p) that a better (A) or worse (B) outcome will result than if we followed a riskless middle path with outcome C. Clearly this is the interesting case. If A and B were both better than C, the action alternative would always be preferred; similarly if both A and B were worse than C, the no change alternative should clearly be chosen. In order to make this choice, the decision maker needs a number of important pieces of information. What are the magnitudes of the possible outcomes (gains or losses) A, B and C? What is the probability p that A will occur if the action option is chosen or 1 – p that B will occur instead? And what is the decision maker's tolerance of risk?

Characterizing risk preference in the context of this diagram requires a little more subtlety. Analysts use the concept of "expected value" to characterize the apparent worth of the action alternative. In this case, "expected value" EV can be calculated from the formula pA + (1 – p)B. For example if p is 0.5, A is 100 and B is zero, then EV is equal to 50. This is the value one can expect to receive on average from the action choice if one were to make this choice over and over

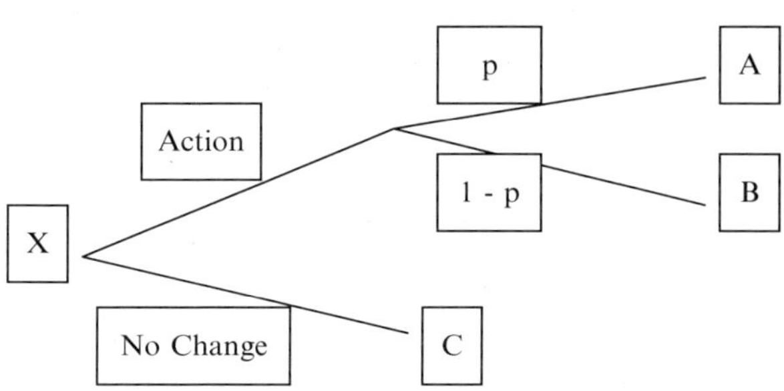

Fig. 2.1 A simple decision tree: action with uncertain outcome vs. known status quo

again (the problem, however, is that this is a single decision at one point in time). So, a decision maker who was "indifferent to risk" would choose the action alternative if the certain choice yielded a value of C less than 50. Otherwise, she would choose the certain (no change) alternative. But if the decision maker were "risk averse," she would choose the certain alternative even if C were somewhat less than 50. The more the EV would have to be in order for the decision maker to take the action choice, the more risk averse he or she is. For example, if the decision maker required EV to be 90 (a 90% chance of outcome A) before she would prefer that alternative to a certain outcome of 50, she would indeed be very conservative. In contrast, a decision maker that required EV to be only 40 for the action alternative when the certain outcome was 50 would be considered a risk-preferring gambler.

We can look at this in a slightly different way in order to get an index of a decision maker's risk preference. Let's ask the decision-maker the following question: what value of C would make you indifferent between taking the action alternative and taking the certain path? Let's call the answer to this question the "certainty equivalent," CE. If CE is less than EV then the decision maker is risk averse. If CE is equal to EV then the decision maker is risk neutral. And if the answer is CE > EV then the decision maker is risk-preferring.

With this model as background, we can now identify the various different ways in which decisions under risk can be poorly made. In particular:

- The decision maker may have a poor estimate of the consequences of different choices (A, B and C)
- The decision maker may have a poor estimate of the probabilities of good and bad outcomes (p, 1 – p) for the action choice
- The decision maker may have an inappropriate risk preference profile; e.g., relative to the mission and situational characteristics of the organization, she may be too risk averse or too risk preferring
- The decision-maker uses poor logic, failing to compare EV with her CE in order to make the best choice

In addition to these basic sources of error, there are two others implied by this model as well:

- The decision-maker fails to take advantage of sufficiently low cost information that would either give her a better estimate of p or might even yield advanced knowledge of the action outcome and whether A or B is the result
- The decision maker fails to take advantage of risk sharing arrangements such as insurance or risk pooling which might reduce the cost of a poor outcome (B)
- The decision-maker fails to exploit possible diversification or other design strategies that could increase the attractiveness of the action alternative by reducing the probability of a poor outcome

The power of this general model lies in its applicability to a wide spectrum of nonprofit strategic decisions. Some of these applications are considered in the next section.

2.5 Nonprofit Strategic Decisions Under Risk

Consider four different kinds of strategic decisions a nonprofit organization (board of trustees) may face:

1. *A New Venture*: From time to time nonprofit organizations consider doing something new – opening a new branch office, adding a new service, undertaking a commercial venture, and so on. The (more predictable) alternative is to keep going with the existing array of services and facilities.
2. *Expanding or Reducing Capacity*: Changes in demands and costs over time, or technical obsolescence may require a nonprofit to consider expanding, contracting or renovating a facility or other aspects of its infrastructure, such as its equipment, staffing or location. The (more predictable) alternative is to maintain the current capacity.
3. *Engaging New Leadership*: Boards and executives are often faced with decisions to renew the contracts of incumbents or to seek alternative candidates for executive or managerial positions. The (more predictable) alternative is to continue with the incumbent.
4. *Entering a Collaboration*: Nonprofits face multiple decisions to join associations or engage with other organizations in collaborative efforts, partnerships, or even mergers. The (more predictable) alternative is to continue going it alone.

In each of these cases, the status quo is more predictable or certain in its outcome (C) because it is a direct extrapolation of the current experience. The action decision, however, could improve matters (A) or make them worse (B). Hence, each of these kinds of decisions fits the framework of Fig. 2.1. So too, nonprofit decision making in each of these cases can be faulty in its approach to risk in the various ways considered above.

Table 2.1 elaborates on various ways in which these different types of decisions can go wrong in each of these situations. Read differently, the table points out the alternative ways in which decision making under risk can be improved for nonprofit organizations. The logic for each type of decision is very similar. One big difference in applying the decision tree logic in practice, however, is that some types of decisions are easier to quantify than others. For example, choosing a new leader is inherently more subjective than making a financial investment or undertaking a new programmatic venture. However, both cases can be accommodated. We illustrate this for two cases, as follows:

Case 1:
A profit-making venture or fund raising initiative. In this instance it is clear that the outcomes A, B and C may be quantified in dollar terms, while the probabilities must be assessed subjectively using the best available information and judgment. Suppose the status quo option was to continue the nonprofit's traditional fund raising program, yielding say \$500,000 just like last year. Suppose the new program could potentially net \$1 million (A) if successful, but might lose \$0.5 million (B) if it failed. Further suppose that a fund raising consultant firm estimated an 80% chance

Table 2.1 What can go wrong with nonprofit decisions under risk

	New venture	Change capacity	New leadership	Collaboration
Consequences	Net benefits of venture success or costs of failure are poorly assessed	Costs and/or benefits of the expansion or contraction are misestimated	Failure to anticipate what could go wrong, or what special benefits might result, with new leadership or with continuing the incumbent	Failure to anticipate what could go wrong once a collaboration is engaged or what unanticipated benefits might result from collaboration
Probabilities	Chances of success poorly estimated	Probabilities of expanded or reduced demand for service are poorly estimated	Poor assessment of the likelihood of finding a superior candidate	Chances of a successful collaboration poorly estimated
Risk preferences	Venture rejected when EV is much greater than C; or chosen when EV is much less than C	Action rejected when EV is much greater than C; or chosen when EV is much less than C	Search for new leadership rejected when EV is much greater than C; or chosen when EV is much less than C	Collaboration rejected when EV is much greater than C; or chosen when EV is much less than C
Logic	Decision is made without comparing status quo with CE of undertaking the venture	Decision is made without comparing status quo with CE of undertaking the change	Decision is made without comparing status quo with CE of undertaking a search for new leadership	Decision is made without comparing status quo with CE of entering the collaboration
Risk reduction	Failure to follow good financial or other practices that reduce probability of failure; failure to diversify venture initiatives	Failure to utilize the most effective practices, materials or technologies	Failure to follow proven policies and strategies for assessing candidates, including examining a sufficient number of candidates	Failure to provide an adequate period for mutual negotiation and consultation before a decision is reached. Failure to diversify the number of partners
Risk sharing	Failure to enter an agreement with partners or insurers that would reduce potential losses without sacrificing too much potential gain	Failure to investigate possibilities for sharing new capacity with another organization	Failure to participate in mutually-beneficial information sharing arrangements with other units or organizations in the market for leaders	Failure to negotiate a fair division of costs in the case of dissolution of the collaboration or benefits in the case of success
Information	Failure to invest in due diligence or research that could cheaply reveal a much more precise estimate of failure or success	Failure to invest in market research that could cheaply reveal a much more precise estimate of need for future capacity	Failure to invest in market research or internal programs that could cheaply reveal a much more precise estimate of available talent	Failure to invest in cost-effective research on similar collaborations elsewhere which could reveal a more precise estimate of the likelihood of success

of success and 20% chance of failure for the new program. Then the expected value is $700,000 compared to $500,000 dollars under the status quo. Thus, the trustees' CE for the action alternative would have to be less than $500,000 for them to reject the new initiative in favor of the status quo.

Clearly, the trustees can potentially make a number of mistakes in this decision. The information they have from the consulting firm could be wrong – either the probabilities or the potential gains or losses from the new venture. Or, they could be too risk averse or too risk prone. The latter is a subjective judgment they must make by discussing the mission and context of the organization and the importance of taking chances to increase their impact versus preserving the organization's capital. Certainly they could fail to follow an appropriate logic, for example determining that the action alternative had a CE more than $500,000 but then deciding against it.

As Table 2.1 suggests, other shortcomings might have to do with failure to put the decision on a firmer footing by improving its overall risk-related and pay-off parameters. Are there ways to improve the design of the initiative, for example by diversifying the donor base, in order to improve the probability of success or reduce the chance of a large loss? Are there are other nonprofit organizations that could be engaged as partners to share the risk?

One can also ask – is there additional cost-effective information that can be secured to improve the choice? For example, could an independent consulting firm carry out some market research to determine with more confidence whether success or failure will occur? Indeed, the trustees can calculate an upper limit to what such information might be worth. A perfect source of information would tell them with certainty whether the venture will or will not succeed. The chances that such a source would signal success would, as far as the trustees can determine a priori, is 80%. The option of obtaining such "perfect information" changes the "lottery" they face because if they learned that the venture was sure to fail they would take the certain alternative. Thus they would face the following new set of possibilities: an 80% chance of learning that the action alternative will succeed and hence receiving $1 million by taking the action alternative, and a 20% chance of learning that the action alternative will fail, hence going with the status quo for $500,000. Calculating the expected value of this situation yields $900,000. So indeed the trustees could be prudent in spending up to $200,000 (the difference in EV with and without perfect information) for additional market research information, depending of course on the anticipated quality of that research. In any case, the trustees would be making a mistake to spend more than that on new information (since any such information is likely to be less than perfect), but they might also err by failing to spend enough to improve their information.

Case 2

Selecting a new leader. In this instance, the foregoing logic can be applied in essentially the same way but quantification is more difficult. Suppose the choice is between undertaking a search for a new executive director and renewing the contract of the current director. If the action alternative is taken, the current director will certainly leave and a new one will be selected. A search firm has suggested that the probability of finding a more effective leader is 70% and the chance of hiring someone that turns out poorly is 30%. The trustees have a firm idea of what they can expect in the way of performance if they retain the incumbent. They might even give him a rating of say 7 on a 10 point scale. After considering the information they have about the quality of potential candidates in the market, from the search firm and colleagues in the field, they determine that a more effective leader would probably rate a 9 while a poorly chosen candidate would likely be a 5. Hence, the expected value yielded by search would be 7.8, not much above the incumbent's 7. They might be sufficiently risk averse, therefore, to reject the search and retain the incumbent. Note that, the quantitative (utility) index helps with this decision, but it is not necessary. All that is required is for the trustees to mentally consider the gamble they are facing with the search and compare in their minds the expected outcome to the incumbent in hand, given what they know about the estimated probabilities and the quality of potential candidates.

The sources of errant decision making here are the same as well. The probabilities could be badly estimated. The quality of potential candidates and their potential performance levels could also be poorly specified. Or the trustees could be inordinately conservative in rejecting an alternative that seems likely to yield a better result. Here too, risk reduction strategies might not have been sufficiently pursued, such as efforts to widen the pool of potential candidates by extending the fields or locations for search. Risk sharing strategies might also be possible, such as insurance against the loss of a new hire for just cause. Finally, information seeking through engagement of private investigators who, for a price, could uncover heretofore unknown risks associated with likely candidates, might also be possible. Trustees could determine for themselves what such information might be worth and use it to investigate likely candidates before they decide to formally undertake the search, thus reducing the risk associated with the action alternative.

2.6 Concluding Remarks

We argue here that, for various reasons, nonprofits have not taken a sufficiently robust view of risk management. While they seem to engage in a variety of sensible practices designed to reduce or minimize risk, they less commonly approach consequential decisions that involve risk in a strategic fashion. We have presented a simple framework for nonprofits to approach their risk-related decisions in strategic fashion, taking into account the probabilities of success and failure, an appropriate attitude towards risk that properly reflects the mission and circumstances of the organization, and engagement in efforts to share risks and obtain critical information to improve the likelihood of successful choices.

The paper suggests risk management as a frontier for research on effective decision making in nonprofit organizations. Areas where research can contribute include a more complete classification of nonprofit strategic decisions involving risk, methodologies to assess the nature (probabilities) and consequences of those risks, norms of risk aversion for different risk-related contexts in which nonprofits find themselves, and developing methodologies such as utility indices in nonprofit situations where the consequences of decisions and the probabilities of alternative contingencies are difficult to quantify. It would also be useful to study empirically what factors, such as organizational size, economic capacity, field of service, type of mission, organizational age or stage of development, connectedness to other organizations or networks, organizational philosophies and leadership personalities, influence nonprofits' risk-related behavior. Finally, it would be helpful to examine the legal, ethical, institutional and economic underpinnings for risk taking in a nonprofit context, what normative principles can be recommended to leaders in this decision-making milieu, and what kinds of institutional structures may bias decision-making to be inordinately conservative or risky.

The uncertainties and instabilities associated with nonprofit decision-making are not likely to diminish in the near future. All indicators point to continued change and limited options for preserving the status quo. An expanded capacity for strategic risk management will serve nonprofits well in this environment.

Acknowledgments The author would like to thank Lewis Faulk and Ron Chapman for their help in searching the literature for this paper, and Janet Johnson, David Sjoquist and Lewis Faulk for their helpful comments on the initial draft.

References

Behn RD, Vaupel JW (1982) Quick analysis for busy decision makers. Basic Books, New York.

Bennett J, Iossa E, Legrenzi G (2006) Commercial activity as insurance behavior of non-profit firms. Keele Economics Research Paper 2006/14

Bielefeld W (1992) Funding uncertainty and nonprofit strategies in the 1980s. Nonprofit Management and Leadership 2:381–401

Brown WA, Iverson JO (2004) Exploring strategy and board structure in nonprofit organizations. Nonprofit and Voluntary Sector Quarterly 33:377–400

Chang C, Tuckman HP (1990) Why do nonprofit managers accumulate surpluses and how much do they accumulate? Nonprofit Management and Leadership 1:117–135

Derryck D, Abzug R (2002) Lessons from crisis: New York City nonprofits post-September 11. Nonprofit Quarterly 9:6–10

Fremont-Smith M (2004) Investment and expenditure strategies. In: Young DR (ed) Effective economic decision making by nonprofit organizations. Foundation Center, New York

Gibelman M, Gelman SR (1999) Safeguarding the nonprofit agency: the role of the board of directors in risk management. Residential Treatment for Children and Youth 16:19–37

Gronbjerg KA (1990) Managing nonprofit funding relations: case studies of six human services organizations. In: The nonprofit sector in the United States and abroad: cross-cultural perspectives. Independent Sector, Washington DC

Henson S, Larson B (1990) Risky business: how to manage risk in your organization. Nonprofit World 8:27–29

Herman ML, Head GL, Jackson PM, Fogarty TE (2004) Managing risk in nonprofit organizations. Wiley, Hoboken NJ

Higuera JJ (1992) Risky business: how much grant-related controversy can your company tolerate? Foundation News 33:52–53

Middeton M (1988) Planning as strategy: the case of nonprofit organizations. Yale University Press, New Haven

Olenick AJ (1988) Straight talk about a nagging problem: how to improve nonprofit management. Nonprofit World 6:31–33

Ostrower F, Stone M (2006) Governance: research trends gaps and future prospects. In: Powell WW, Steinberg R (eds) The nonprofit sector: a research handbook. 2nd edn, Yale University Press, New Haven

Preyra C, Pink G (2001) Balancing incentives in the compensation contracts of nonprofit hospital CEOs. Journal of Health Economics 20:509–525

Scanlan EA, Dillon-Merrill R (2006) Risky business: understanding and managing risk in the nonprofit sector. In: Young DR (ed) Wise decision-making in uncertain times. Foundation Center and National Center on Nonprofit Enterprise, New York

Tremper C (1994) Risk management. In: Herman RD and Associates (eds). The Jossey-Bass handbook of nonprofit leadership and management. Jossey-Bass Publishers, San Francisco

Wedig GJ (1994) Risk leverage donations and dividends-in-kind: A theory of nonprofit financial behavior. International Review of Economics and Statistics 3:257–278

Young DR (1986) Casebook of management for nonprofit organizations. Haworth Press, New York

Chapter 3
Property Rights and Incentives in Social Cooperatives

Marco Musella and Roberta Troisi

Abstract This paper analyzes Italian social cooperatives as a typical delivery service firm, focusing on employee incentive systems characterized by "role tension" linked to the dual position of being employee and owner at the same time. The answers to three questions: "Why to incentivize", "What to incentivize" "How to incentivize" are searched, building on both the lack of employee's controllability in the sector and the reconstruction of property rights consistent with the characteristics of social cooperatives and the profit non-distribution constraint. The conclusion is that, because they are able to structure a richer incentive set, social cooperatives are more efficient in the provision of social utility services even though they pay lower wages than public organizations and for-profit firms.

> The pareconist internationalist says that we ought to receive for our labors remuneration in tune with how hard we have worked, how long we have worked, and how great a sacrifice we have made in our work. We shouldn't get more because we use more productive tools, have more skills, or have greater inborn talent, much less should we get more because we have more power or own more property. We should get more only by virtue of how much effort we have expended or how much sacrifice we have endured in our useful work. This is morally appropriate, and it also provides proper incentives by rewarding only what we can affect and not what is beyond our control.
>
> Michael Albert (http://www.zmag.org/zparecon/qatrade.htm)

3.1 Introduction

Under the heading of "social cooperatives", Italian law encompasses distinct types of cooperative firms and nonprofit organizations. Type A social cooperatives incorporate providers and beneficiaries of a social service as members, whereas type B social cooperatives bring together permanent workers and previously unemployed people who wish to integrate into the labour market.

M. Musella (✉) and R. Troisi
Department of Economic Theory and Applications, University of Napoli Federico II, Via Rodinò 22, 80138 Napoli, Italy

S. Destefanis and M. Musella (eds.), *Paid and Unpaid Labour in the Social Economy*, AIEL Series in Labour Economics, DOI: 10.1007/978-3-7908-2137-6_4,

Scholars in the field have reached broad agreement on two characteristics of social cooperatives which are essential for the objective of this study: (1) social cooperatives are predominantly delivery service firms[1]; (2) the social and collective services they deliver are among those services which are generally less standardized and thus more uncontrollable (Bacchiega and Borzaga 2003).

This chapter analyzes social cooperatives as a typical delivery service firm focusing on employee incentive systems, characterized by "role tension" (Rugiadini 1979) linked to the dual position of being employee and owner at the same time. Role tension is a common quality of labour-managed cooperatives in general but, in our view, the status of employee-owner in a nonprofit organization should influence the content of the property rights and, consequently, the incentives system in a social cooperative more than in a common labour-managed cooperative.

"Why incentivize?", "What to incentivize?" and "How to incentivize?" in a social cooperative are the questions we have attempted to answer. Our answer to the first question (why incentivize?) stems from an investigation into the lack of employee's controllability in a delivery service firm, and has led to an enquiry into how an incentive system may provide an alternative to a control system. The logical route to answering the second question (what to incentivize?) lies in the reconstruction of the property rights which might be more consistent with the characteristics of social cooperatives and the profit non-distribution constraint. In this way it has been possible to demonstrate how effective it could be for social cooperatives to adopt incentive models focused on the effort rather than the outcome of the performance. Finally, the answer to the third question (how to incentivize?) is linked to the following hypothesis: employee-owners' motivation is not entirely dependent on remuneration but it is also conditioned by "intrinsic incentives" as well as the production/consumption of relational goods that go together with the work activity.

Our analysis is organized as follows. Section 3.2 focuses on the reasons, according to some scholars, that show the extent to which it is essential for social cooperatives to apply incentives as an alternative to control. In our assertion that control is hard to exercise, we are saying that a part of the traditional theoretical meaning of property rights, i.e. the right to control the firm and to appropriate residual earnings (Hansmann 1996) does not make sense for the social cooperative. As such, we consider a number of topics with a view to shaping property rights in a way that is more consistent with the nature of social cooperatives. In particular, we consider it correct to appropriate *ristorni* (loosely translatable as rebates, this concept will be dealt at length in Sect. 3.2), which approximates the right to appropriate earnings in for-profit organizations.

In Sect. 3.3, the process of reconstructing the second part of the property right, defined as the right to survive, explains how it is possible to substitute control with

[1] It is well known that scholars have identified an important aspect often associated with the production and delivery of services (e.g. Normann 2000): i.e., intangibility (Kotler 1983). While manufacturing firms produce tangible products, most services cannot be seen or touched. This gives rise to information asymmetry, where both managers and customers may have difficulty controlling and evaluating the quality of service output.

incentives in social cooperatives. What follows is the idea of an incentive system which is designed and measured on the effort put in rather than the output achieved. Finally, Sects. 3.4 and 3.5 endeavour to provide some ideas on how to incentivize.

We draw on one issue emphasized in Borzaga and Musella (2003), i.e. the discovery of a highly developed incentive system for labour in use in nonprofit organizations. While economic theory of the labour market explains the supply of labour and the quantity of a worker's effort in relation to remuneration, the theory of organization pays considerable attention to the idea that the workers' duties are difficult to plan and their effort is often not verifiable (Eisenhardt 1985; Thompson 1967; Ouchi 1979). This justifies the "withdrawal of the prize" and, as will be seen later, the equivalence between a control system and a set of incentives.

The answer to the question "How to incentivize?" is theoretically based on the hypothesis that workers' satisfaction depends not just on remuneration, but also on the intrinsic incentives and consumption of relational goods on the job. Because nonprofit organizations are better able to structure a richer incentive set where room for intrinsic incentives and pro/consumption of relational goods is greater, these organizations are more efficient in some productivity sectors even though they pay lower wages than public organizations and for-profit firms. Analysis of the broader incentive set is developed in line with the literature on property rights, and the concept of the right to survive plays a pivotal role in our reconstruction of the idea that if people work "not just for money" it is not efficient to reward them just with money (Frey 1997).

Section 3.6 provides some concluding remarks.

3.2 Property Rights and Control in Social Cooperatives: Why Incentivize?

A reading of the literature on incentives in cooperatives, and in social cooperatives in particular, (Ben-Ner 1986; Borzaga 2003; Hart and Moore 1990; Ortmann 1996; Salamon and Aneheier 1997) can help to focus attention on two points of interest: (1) (social) cooperatives are predominantly delivery service firms where human resources are a strategic resource but, at the same time, are difficult to keep under control since the delivery service activity itself is difficult to control; (2) the social and collective services they deliver are among those services which by nature are generally less standardized and thus more uncontrollable.

It is well known that these circumstances give rise to problems linked to asymmetric information, chief among them being worker information advantage over owner information (more specifically, in social cooperatives the owner-employee as a worker has important information which owner-employees as owners do not have) as a consequence of incomplete job contracts (Borzaga 2000).

A (social) service which is hard to plan, standardize and replicate, and is substantially dependent on the quality and characteristics of individual contributions, allows neither the monitoring of (employee) the worker's effort, nor the monitoring of the relationship between effort and outcome. Opportunistic behaviour is likely to occur as a result. Thus, if control does not work, can it be substituted with an incentive system, and if so, in which way?

In cases where human resources are a critical resource, but at the same time difficult to control, the contractual terms which govern job transactions cannot be restricted to salaried work conditions.[2] It would be more effective to design in a different way how job transactions are governed. This refers to associative contracts which should discipline (1) sharing the right to use the organization (the cooperative); (2) the content of property rights, which would be affected by the profit non-distribution constraint; (3) an incentive set consistent with these rights and conditioned in itself by these rights.

Employee becomes owner, owner is also employee: what should be intrinsic in the role of owner is the incentive to effective performance (Brosio 1995): in other words, where the nature of the performance – both as effort and outcome – makes control unsuitable, it is better to turn the process of monitoring into a process which effectively eliminates goal incongruence between individuals.(Ouchi 1979).

If we focus on the associative contractual features in social cooperatives, we tend to consider its main contents to be the (real) right of organization use, vested in the owner-employee. This right cannot fully correspond to a complete property right, according to the well-established idea of property rights in an economic organization (Hansmann 1996). Following this line of thought, property rights should consist in the right to control and the right to appropriate the firm's profits. The lack of correspondence between property rights in an economic organization and "property rights" in a nonprofit organization – in our case in a social cooperative – is very simple: among the legal prohibitions linked to nonprofit activities prevails the profit non-distribution constraint. The consequence is that in a nonprofit organization, property rights do not include the right to appropriate the residual earnings which should justify and motivate the second element that deals with property rights: the right of control. (Alchian and Demsetz 1973; Coase 1937, 1960) Thus, in social cooperatives control is neither motivated nor, as explained above, feasible. In an effort to give a more coherent content to property rights which could take into account social cooperative features, we have considered two circumstances:

- The particular status of owner-employee.
- The fact that this particular status is prevalently shared by social cooperative members.[3]

With regard to the first circumstance, we have tried to shape property rights in social cooperatives by taking into account both the status of the owner and related incentives as well as the status of employees and related incentives.

---

[2] It cannot be conceived as a mere discipline of the "indifference area" based on the allocation of the right to be paid versus the (not controllable) duty to perform (Simon 1947).

[3] See Article 2512 of the Italian Civil Code (about the *Cooperativa a mutualità prevalente*).

With regard to the second circumstance, we have considered that social cooperatives are places where "communality" rules.[4] Regardless of personal (financial) share, decision rights in fact depend on the "one head-one vote" principle[5]: this underlines how much the personal dimension of property rights is deeply related to the collective dimension. The fact that everyone's contribution is crucial and is thus a critical resource of the social cooperative means that each person is assigned the same power in important decision-making.[6] Property rights should therefore be conditioned by both the role tension between owner and employee and, at the same time, by the strict relationship between the individual dimension and the collective dimension of this role tension.

Thus, in considering the right that should be equivalent in social cooperatives to the right to appropriate residual earnings, our attention is focused on the right to appropriate *ristorni*. Under the heading *ristorni* (very loosely translatable as *rebates*) Italian law refers to a (small) part of the net residual earnings which is possible to distribute to cooperative members in proportion to the amount of effort put into the activity. This particular form of net residual is constrained by a very low variable ceiling percentage of annual profits. The right to appropriate *ristorni* should have, in nonprofit organizations (particularly in social cooperatives) the same role as the right to appropriate residual earnings in for-profit organizations. It is well known that in Italian social cooperatives there is little use of *ristorni*, particularly because there is a strong incentive to declare profits as an indivisible reserve. A significant consequence of the above considerations is that, in order to promote effectiveness, social cooperatives should rebalance incentives toward a greater use of *ristorni*.

In this way *ristorni* constitute additional remuneration for (owner) employees. As a particular (and very limited) form of residual claims in social cooperatives, they have to be consistent with the agent's characteristics, i.e. consistent with the nature of employees. This is the reason why *ristorni* are a surplus on labour income, substantially proportioned to effort and, at the same time, consistent to the nature of the owner.

The distribution criterion of *ristorni* is, however, mainly linked to the factor of production, i.e. labour instead of capital. What can be distributed is prevalently linked, according to the law, with the quantity of work. In contrast to for-profit organizations, the right to appropriate residual earnings is not directly dependent on the factor of production, i.e. capital. It has the nature of an incentive device

[4] With the aim of highlighting phenomena where individual contributions are fused into a common, not-separable contribution, we prefer to use the term "communality" in the strict sense of the etymon i.e. "putting in common".

[5] According to Article 2532 of the Italian Civil Code, in meetings, the people eligible to vote are those who have been enrolled as members for at least 3 years. Each member has one vote, whatever the value of their quota or the amount of shares held.

[6] Schemes of equal representation, not proportionate to contributions, are typical of economic organisations based on equal rights. The actors' contributions towards the collective activity, even when of a different nature, are considered equally indispensable.

directly tied to the single owner-employee's effort and only indirectly to the owner-employees'(collectively considered) effort. We should point out once again that *ristorni* are directly dependent on the single owner-employee's performance and that earnings in general, considered as a limit within which *ristorni* are calculated, that is strictly dependent on the owner-employees' performance. If the right to appropriate *ristorni* can be considered equivalent in nonprofit organizations to the right to appropriate earnings in for-profit organizations, it is nonetheless impossible to find out the right to control (the other owner-employees') performances, since objectively it cannot be activated. In an attempt to define the features of an incentive set based on the quantity of effort put in, it will soon be shown that rather than a right to control, it is possible to talk about an interest in self-controlling. In addition, we will define a further (new) element of the property rights.

3.3 The Janus Face of Social Cooperatives: What to Incentivize

At this stage two sets of questions need to be addressed:

1. Can the link between the *ristorni* and the effort itself, rather than the output of the effort, be an effective choice for the allocation of incentives? Furthermore, can this choice constitute a model on which the entire incentive system could be set up?
2. Who is to provide a definition of the correct measure of the effort necessary to earn, even partially, the *ristorni*? In this way, who has the right to define the nature and kind of incentives?

We will try to answer the first question here and later, in Sects. 3.4 and 3.5, provide some useful ideas to address the second question.

To this end, we need to take into account the agent's role tension and the idea that quantity of work as a point of reference for measuring the *ristorni* emphasizes the status of employee more than the status of owner. It is well known that by definition an employee is a risk-adverse agent. The reason is very simple: job investments cannot usually be diversified and, at the same time, remuneration for the work activity affects to a significant extent the whole level of the employee's wealth (Grandori 1999, 2001). These two circumstances explain why the employee cannot, and does not want to, assume the consequences of the firm's risk, though he does have an interest in receiving a free-from-risk wage. Remuneration that fulfils this expectation has to be independent of uncertainty both in essence and related monetary benefits. This could be satisfied through the design of a remunerative structure that would be totally dependent on the effort itself rather than the outcome of the effort. As we know, outcome of the performance (effort, in other words) is not completely dependent on the agent, as it is usually affected by exogenous factors; an incentive (above all monetary) tied to the outcome of the performance is not free from risk, since "different states of the world" could condition the achievement of the outcome in different ways. According to Article 2545-*sexies* of the Italian Civil Code, the *ristorni* are measured on the basis of the owner-employee's effort, even though control of the effort itself is not easily maintained. Thus, the question – Who is to provide a definition of the correct measure of the effort necessary to earn, even partially, the *ristorni*? – is answered as follows. The only one who can keep the effort under control is the (owner) employee himself. Further observations in this regard are made in Sect. 3.4: the reason for presenting this idea in advance is to point out how ineffective it could be to link the *ristorni* (and, in general, all the incentives) to the outcomes, on the basis of a tenable agency relationship. Above all, setting up an incentive system that uses the outcome of performance as a para-meter when the (owner) employee wants to be provided with incentives for the effort made does not make sense. In the not too distant past, organizational literature noted the underlying inconsistency that characterizes the choice of "rewarding" A when it is fairer to "reward" B (Kerr 1975). Moreover, in using agency mechanisms a further question remains unanswered: what happens if the outcome is not kept under control or if its control, in terms of quality and final outcome of social services, results in excessively high costs?

An answer cannot be provided if we do not accept the idea that control in social cooperatives should be totally replaced with an incentive system, one that has to be designed with the features described below. At this point, consideration of the following example could help to explain the circumstances in which it is possible to replace control with an incentive set.

Hadrian, the Roman emperor, would deploy his armies by positioning his Roman legions in the front line, while the Barbarians captured from conquered villages were forced to fight at the back. In the course of time, he reduced his Roman legions and increased his Barbarian contingents, keeping the same deployment set-up, Romans in progressively reduced numbers in the front line and Barbarians in increasing numbers in the back lines. This begs the following questions: Does control exist in the above situation? Why position the Barbarians at the back?

In normal circumstances Barbarian legions would be expected in the front line, under the control of the Romans. Perhaps this is not necessary if the Barbarians know that their only chance of survival is to follow the Romans. The Barbarian has to survive not only for himself but also for the members of his clan who, in turn, are forced to fight just like him. History teaches us that the practice of forced enlistment in the same family or in the same clan is quite common in building strong armies (the term 'hussar' means twenty, soldiers for instance, from the same village). Thus, although there is no control, there is something else in its place, a powerful force against control, i.e. the incentive to survive. Barbarians follow the front line because they do not possess any strategic ability. They have to follow the front line, otherwise their chances of survival are nil. This incentive for personal survival goes hand in hand with the incentive for collective (communal) survival. They fight beside their brothers, people from the same village. Individual survival is tied to communal survival. The incentive to survive grows in strength if it is not merely a personal matter but a collective concern.

Returning to our topic, can we not recognize a right to survive in the contents of property rights in social cooperatives, too? Is it not also a personal and a communal right at the same time? In our view it is the core of the owner-employee's property right, the element that, unlike the right to *ristorni*, emphasizes the status of the owner more than that of the employee. Briefly, the right to personal survival, closely connected to the right to collective survival, annuls the right to control (apart from a limited form of self-control) according to the following logical path: the right to survive leads to effective performance, i.e. to self-control. Effective performance leads to the opportunity of drawing on an incentive set to which it is linked and measured, not conditioned by exogenous factors but designed to consider the effort put in, and not the output achieved.

We now turn to the twofold dimension of the right to survive. The individual dimension of this *"sui generis"* right involves "the duty to personal survival". It also involves the interest and the will to survive, which is connected to the answer we give to the following question: "How to incentivize?" As will be shown, from the employee's point of view the aim of setting up a system of incentives, especially the extra-monetary elements in it, is to support the interest to become a member of and to work in a social cooperative. Furthermore, there is the communal dimension of the right to survive. Symmetrical to the individual dimension of survival is the communal duty to survive as well as a communal interest in surviving.

The first aspect, the collective duty to survive, is due to the fact that personal survival conditions communal survival, as in the case of the clan, or more so, in families. This idea is based on theorized common feeling which turns into the sharing of values, and which distinguishes, firstly, companies from cooperatives and then, and above all, social cooperatives from cooperatives. What is necessary for the survival of the group is the incentive to put in an effective effort. This is by far the hardest aspect to prove. It is probably easier to think of the clan, wherein the interest for collective survival stems from the common knowledge ("the social memory") of a particular transaction pattern where long-term interaction enables the agent to achieve serial-equity (reciprocity over a longer period of time) rather than requiring immediate or spot equity (Barney and Ouchi 1984, p. 353). "Neutral" common knowledge can be preferred or can, when proved, go together with the sharing of the underlying values. Indeed, it is the incentive set based on the performance and characterized by serial-equity that could provide a model of governance of transactions when performance evaluation is ambiguous, and also local knowledge for the purpose of considering "a general paradigm that helps participants determine collective interest" (Wilkins and Ouchi 1983, p. 108), in our view the interest to survive. The shared *moral standing* (Minkler 2003), typical of nonprofit organizations, underpinning the duty to survive, goes with the sharing of general orientations concerning what is of interest to the collective. The latter should be governed by common rules vested in the group's set of incentives for survival, chief among them the mechanism that measures the relationship between rewards and contribution.

These reflections should be examined in depth, but here they enable the property rights in social cooperatives to be reconsidered in a more complete way. Indeed, if the status of employee legitimizes and defines the right to appropriate *ristorni*, the status of owner enables the right to survive to be designated a means to determine goal congruence between individual goals and collective goals and, at the same time, a means to eliminate control (unfeasible in any case, as already mentioned). Finally, property rights in social cooperatives could be considered as a special right to define and appropriate incentives.

3.4 The Communal Entitlement of the Definition of Incentives: A Possible Model

In an attempt to avoid unrealistic reflections, we propose a possible incentives model that may satisfy all the characteristics described above. It is a remuneration-linked model that can regarded as a pilot model for the entire set of incentives and can also help to solve the problem of free rider effects that might remain in cases where an incentive system substitutes a control system. Further reflections on the use of extra-monetary incentives will be presented in Sect. 3.5. A possible incentive model, such as the distribution of *ristorni*, could be the result of the shared agreement on indicators to be linked to incentives. For example, a mix of the total number of hours and roles performed (to be considered the gamut of shared expectations of specific models of job behaviour), satisfies the requirement to take into account effort (and not output) and to create rules of distributive equity. Obviously, the more the system of roles and mutual expectations of everybody's behaviour is clear and shared, the more it will encourage the forming of homogeneous opinions about the way performances should be realized. This is independent of the value (not controllable) of the work. Furthermore, it is obvious that the existence of a roles system, as opposed to "the open door" principle,[7] implies a condition of double stability: as an attribute for the group's composition and, as far as possible, as an attribute for the group's activity.[8]

The above description raises the following question: In defining an incentive model based on effort which is not controllable but probable according to a series

[7] A typical principle of social cooperatives is "the open door" (Articles 2524 and 2528 of the Italian Civil Code), according to which every person whose interest coincides, in terms of homogeneity, with the founding aim of cooperatives, has the right to membership of the cooperative. It follows that the cooperative association act cannot include exclusion norms that limit membership or that may shift the question of choice into the hands of the board of directors. Neither can the freedom of membership be detached from the common interest. As a consequence capital is variable, since it varies with the number of members. The free will of members to work together constitutes one of the keys of their motivation; this is incompatible with any attempt to impose new members on the cooperative.

[8] The requirement of stability could represent an organisational answer that is irreconcilable with the requirement of the growth of the cooperative. There is therefore an evident trade-off between respecting rules on incentives, such as the ones described above, and the growth in the number of members, sales proceeds, profits and so on.

of indicators, is there not the risk of free rider behaviour? As is already known, scholars in the field (Jensen and Meckling 1976) show how agency theory is suitable in two circumstances, both of which are present in this case, where the performance cannot be kept under control, possibly giving rise to opportunistic behaviour. Again, our reconstruction of property rights can be of help.

1. The individual dimension of the right to survive has two components, both useful to disincentivize opportunistic behaviours. The duty to survive is linked with the status of owner, not with the simple status of employee: in lowering the degree of effort, there will be a negative effect on the profits, particularly if the number of members is not high. This negative effect on the profits will, in turn, have repercussions as a negative effect on *ristorni*. The interest to survive, which is closely linked to the essence of incentives, should exclude any form of indifference as to what the content of the performance is (see above).
2. As previously mentioned, the right to survive in its communal dimension is very close to clan behavioural dynamics. Should a common history, a common aim or a common feeling as the basis of the duty to survive as a group and as a means to disincentivize opportunistic behaviours not exist, it is reasonable to suppose that interest in the group's survival, which requires the acceptance of common roles as a minimum condition, ought to exclude the perception of the individual effort (cost) as higher than the benefits obtainable.

3.5 Incentives Beyond Wages: Bridging the Gap Between Economics and Organization Theory by Using Property Rights

According to the notion of property rights as described above, i.e. the right to define incentives and the right to receive them, the nature of the extra-monetary incentive set has to be analyzed. The aim of this analysis is twofold: (1) the incentive set should be designed to increase the (employee) worker's effort: (2) the incentive set should be designed to foster the (employee) worker's interest to survive both from the individual and communal points of view.

This analysis is important because the way in which the incentive set is designed is fundamental to its own performance. Moreover, its coherence with workers' expectations enhances the effectiveness of governance structures, and in this way triggers a virtuous circle between the incentive structure and the governance structure.

A good starting point is the model in Musella (2003) where the economic ideas on incentives structure coincide with organizational literature. Many empirical studies have found wages not to be enough to justify the higher level of nonprofit workers' satisfaction compared to for-profit organizations. Two hypotheses have been advanced to support this. The first highlights the link between agent and organization, underpinned by individual perception of equity, to explain the empirical findings. (Borzaga 2000) The second deals with the design of the incentive structure shaped in accordance with the idea that to work in the third sector is a way to fulfil a wider set of human needs compared, once again, to the motivation to work in all the other sectors.

There are complementary reflections to be considered; an incentive model which is functional to the right to survive as described above, has to emphasize effort, include a set of rewards (other than the wage), and be perceived as equal. First, let us consider the requirement of extra-monetary incentives; this idea leads to the rejection of traditional economic theory of labour supply in which exchange in the labour market refers exclusively to money *versus* work.

Work as a means to obtain capabilities other than income (according to Sen's line of thought) does not belong to the neoclassical Keynesian and Marxist theories.[9]

The reconstruction of property rights is the meeting point between economic theory, particularly contributions from Sen (1992) and Nussbaum (2002) and organizational theory as in Herzberg (1968) and Maslow (1964), because the model of extra-monetary incentives has to be linked to the interest to survive.

Sen's well-known ideas may be summarized as follows: life is made up of functionings achieved through the use of specific capabilities. Sen (1992, pp. 39–40) wrote: "Living may be seen as consisting of a set of interrelated functionings, consisting of beings and doing. (…) The relevant functionings can vary from elementary things as being adequately nourished, being in good health, avoiding escapable morbidity and premature mortality, etc., to more complex achievements such as being happy, having self-respect, taking part in life of community and so on. (…) Closely related to the notion of functionings is that of the capability to function. It represents the various combinations of functionings that the person can achieve".

Thus, the functionings represent those different dimensions of life that help to achieve well-being or, to use Sen's words, useful to satisfy adequate levels of well-being; in addition, a well-organized classification of functioning has also been put forward by Nussbaum (2002).[10]

The idea that human needs in general give rise to a wider reconstruction of the worker's behaviour in the job stems from the following hypothesis: while work has so far been perceived as being an important functioning, on the other hand it can represent a significant means to achieve those capabilities that give people "the freedom to choose the kind of life they desire". So it has a pivotal role in conditioning people's *well-being*. For us, however, it is more interesting to focus attention on the job as a way to acquire the necessary capabilities to achieve the functioning. From this point of view, the income earned through work is an important capability

---

[9] Mention should be made of the literature on equalizing differences. For a review, along traditional lines, see Rosen (1986).

[10] Nussbaum's list includes: 1. Life. 2. Bodily Health 3. Bodily Integrity 4. Sense, imagination, thought 5. Emotions 6.Practical reason 7. Affiliation 8. Other species 9. Play 10. Control over one's environment.

to achieve essential functionings: in order to obtain "… food, clothing, care, education" people need income and the way to earn it is to work. But it is true, at the same time, that there are other important capabilities obtained by working that are very useful in order to achieve other essential functionings. Organizational theory can make a substantial contribution to enhancing an incentives set that would attach importance to the different ways by which having a job would increase the set of capabilities.

In spite of its well-known limits, Maslow's hierarchy of needs can help us to define some functionings linked to work,[11] while Herzberg's (1968) contribution to the theory of motivation factors can help to study the link between capabilities and incentives.[12] From Herzberg's point of view, in fact, the intrinsic nature of work becomes in itself a capability useful for achieving self-estimation and self-actualization.

The idea to bridge organizational and economic theory arises from the conviction that while Sen's approach represents the foundation for a broader set of incentives, Maslow's and Herzberg's contributions can provide both an accurate hierarchy of human needs and a clear idea of the way to design a good set of incentives based on wages as the primitive determinant of job satisfaction or the only relevant element that workers consider in the situation of low earnings.[13] Furthermore, Herzog's "motivation and hygiene factors" can be viewed most of all as extra-monetary incentives. For example, Herzog's motivation factor encompasses incentives that are useful both for supporting the idea of the relevance of the interest to survive and for building a system of rewards based on effort.

Finally, we turn to the fairness of the set of incentives. According to the literature, the advantages of a set of incentives perceived as fair by the agents are valuable both as a system and for the goals achieved, especially in service organizations, given the immaterial characteristics of the output (Normann 2000). In the same literature it has been emphasized that the perceived fairness of the incentives set of the organization is a strong impulse both to improve the quality of the services and better customer satisfaction. In this category of organizations, social cooperatives are also included and the adoption of a fair set of incentives is therefore of considerable importance for their performance. Moreover, in the social cooperative, that

---

[11] As is known, Maslow's model, which once defined needs as gaps whose lack of satisfaction leads to a rebalancing action, shows the need for design. Maslow's hierarchy of needs is often depicted as a pyramid consisting of five levels: the four lower levels are grouped together as being associated with physiological needs, while the top level is termed as growth needs associated with psychological needs. In particular, the needs are: Safety needs, Social needs, Esteem needs and Self-actualization.

[12] In short, with regard to the factors arising in the labour context, Herzberg's model proposes the distinction between hygiene factors, linked to elements which, although not negative, are unable to motivate workers, and motivation factors that give workers full satisfaction.

[13] On this point, see Borzaga and Musella (2006).

almost always supplies personnel services, there are three further elements that give additional relevance to fairness:

1. Directing output towards social utility. This aspect is linked to the multi-dimensional characteristic of the social cooperatives' output which often means that some aspects of the output, and of the worker's effort, are not easily identifiable or assessable (Borzaga 2003). Often the actual productivity processes are in the hands of the worker, and good quality depends on his/her effort which is not enforceable according to traditional methods of control.
2. There are many dimensions to the relationship between social operators of the cooperative and the customers that affect the perceived quality of the output and its effectiveness (Solari 2003).
3. In this kind of organization the ethical value of the workers and their value system are very significant in terms of the performance of the organization both for workers and for volunteers. The sympathetic relationship within the organization is a very valuable resource for the organization itself; at the same time, its absence, i.e. the adoption of an organizational model that does not fulfil the expectations of the workers and volunteers, can generate a default of the organization. (Solari 2003).

Moreover, a set of incentives for the workers' effort perceived as fair by the stakeholders of the organization could represent, as already mentioned (p.), local knowledge which is socially shared and help people establish collective interest (Wilkins and Ouchi 1983, p. 108) or, using a concept already introduced, a collective interest to survive. In accordance with clan rules, the workers (members) share the rules of the group so as to optimize transactions between each member and the organization.

3.6 Concluding Remarks

The questions we have attempted to answer in this essay are "Why incentivize?", "What to incentivize?" and "How to incentivize?" in social cooperatives. Our answers to the three questions arise from three intertwined issues: the lack of employee's controllability in a delivery service firm, the necessity to build an incentive system that may provide an alternative to a control system, a different reconstruction of property rights which is more consistent both with the characteristics of social cooperatives and with the profit distribution constraint. From those ideas the conclusion follows that, because the employee-owners' motivation is not entirely dependent on remuneration but it is also conditioned by intrinsic incentives as well as the production/consumption of relational goods that go together with the work activity, social cooperatives are an efficient organizational type in the production of social services.

Acknowledgements We are grateful to Sergio Destefanis, who helped us to improve the essay in many points. However, the authors alone remain responsible for errors or omissions

References

Alchian A, Demsetz H (1973) The property right paradigm. Journal of Economic History 33:16–27

Barney JB, Ouchi WG (1984) Information cost and organizational governance. Management Science 10:460–481

Bacchiega A, Borzaga C (2003) The economics of the third sector: a more comprehensive approach. In: Anheier KH, Ben-Ner A (eds) The Study of Non Profit Enterprises: Theories and Approaches. Kluwer, New York

Ben-Ner A (1986) Non-profit organisations: why do they exist in market economies? In Rose-Ackerman S (eds) The economics of non-profit institutions. Oxford University Press, New York

Borzaga C (ed) (2000) Capitale umano e qualità del lavoro nei servizi sociali. Fondazione Italiana del Volontariato, Rome

Borzaga C (2003) L'analisi economica delle organizzazioni non profit: teorie, limiti e possibili sviluppi. In: Borzaga C, Musella M (eds) Produttività ed efficienza nelle organizzazioni non-profit. Edizioni31, Trento

Borzaga C, Musella M (eds) (2003) Produttività ed efficienza nelle organizzazioni nonprofit. Edizioni31, Trento

Borzaga C, Musella M (2006) Sistemi di incentivi e soddisfazione per il lavoro nel settore dei servizi di pubblica utilità: una prospettiva di teoria economica. In: Carpita M, D'Ambra L, Vichi M, Vittadini G (eds) Valutare la qualità. Guerini, Milan

Brosio G (1995) Introduzione all'economia dell'organizzazione. Carocci, Rome

Coase RH (1937) The nature of the firm. Economica 4:386–405

Coase RH (1960) The problem of social cost. Journal of Law and Economics 3:1–44

Eisenhardt K (1985) Control: organizational and economic approaches. Management Science 31:134–139

Frey BS (1997), Not just for money. an economic theory of personal motivation. Edward Elgar, Cheltenham

Grandori A (1999) Organizzazione e comportamento economico. il Mulino, Bologna

Grandori A (2001) Organizzazione e governance del capitale umano. Egea, Milan

Hansmann HB (1996) Too many non-profit organizations? Problems of entry and exit. In: Osservatorio Giordano dell'Amore (ed) Le organizzazioni senza fini di lucro. Giuffrè, Milan

Hart O, Moore J (1990) Property rights and the nature of the firms, Journal of Political Economy 98:1119–1158

Herzberg F (1968) One more time: how do you motivate your employees? Harvard Business Review 46:53–62

Jensen MC, Meckling M (1976) Theory of the firm: managerial behaviour, agency costs and ownership structure. Journal of Financial Economics 3:305–360

Kerr S (1975), On the folly of rewarding A, while hoping for B. Academy of Management Journal, 18:769–783

Kotler P (1983) Principles of marketing. Prentice-Hall, Englewood Cliffs NJ

Maslow A (1964) Motivation and personality. Harper & Row, New York

Minkler L (2003), Managing moral motivation. University of Connecticut Department of Economics Working Paper 2003–06

Musella M (2003) Le caratteristiche dell'occupazione nel settore non profit. In: Borzaga C, Musella M (eds) Produttività ed efficienza nelle organizzazioni nonprofit. Edizioni31, Trento

Normann R (2000) Service management: strategy and leadership in service business, 3rd edn. Wiley, Hoboken NJ

Nussbaum M (2002), Frontiers of justice. Disability, nationality, species membership. The Belknap Press of Harvard University Press, Cambridge MA

Ouchi W (1979) A conceptual framework for the design of organization control mechanism. Management Science 25:833–848

Ortmann A (1996) Modern economic theory and the study of non-profit organizations: why the twain shall meet. Non-profit and Voluntary Sector Quarterly 25:470–484

Rosen S (1986) The Theory of equalizing differences. In: Ashenfelter O, Layard R (eds) Handbook of Labor Economics, vol 1. North Holland, Amsterdam

Rugiadini A (1979) Manuale di organizzazione d'impresa. Giuffrè, Milan

Salamon LM, Aneheier HK (1997) Defining the nonprofit sector: a cross-national analysis. Manchester University Press, Manchester

Simon HA (1947) Administrative behavior. Macmillan, New York

Sen A (1992) Inequality revisited. Oxford University Press, Oxford

Solari L (2003) La relazione tra lavoratore e organizzazione nelle organizzazioni non profit: contratto psicologico ed equità. In: Borzaga C, Musella M (eds) Produttività ed efficienza nelle organizzazioni nonprofit. Edizioni31, Trento

Thompson JD (1967) Organizations in action. Mac Graw-Hill, New York

Wilkins AL, Ouchi W (1983) Efficient cultures: exploring the relationship between culture and organizational performance. Administrative Science Quarterly 28:468–481

Chapter 4
The Supply of Labour and Household Production

João R. Sanson

Abstract Labour supply is seen as an output from household production. Given the physical effort of a person, working in the market also requires specific inputs. This process may be described with the help of a joint-production technology, where at least one of the outputs is labour supply. With the help of a simplified version of the model, the choice among different types of market work is initially discussed. Within this discussion, it is shown how different estimates of the opportunity cost of time naturally appear. Then, the definition of net result of the worker is related to economic rent due to the fact that the consumer–producer cannot alter the time endowment. As a result, the household production model, including labour supply, might be more amenable to integration into general equilibrium theory and microeconomic theory in general.

4.1 Introduction

Labour supply, in standard models, is given by the residual time of the economic agent after the quantity of leisure is chosen. This is generalized in the household production models by defining consumption activities that use, as inputs, purchased goods and own time. Even then, labour supply is modelled in the same way: from total available time in a given period, time in household activities is subtracted so as to get the time sold to the market. An alternative modelling is to have leisure time as a residual.

Another alternative is to have both labour and leisure in the preference function, as in Johnson (1966), Georgescu-Roegen (1968), and Sanson (1987, 1991). Johnson (1966) introduced a model with leisure and labour in the preference function and at

---

J.R. Sanson
Department of Economics, Federal University of Santa Catarina,
88049-970 Florianopolis, SC, Brazil

S. Destefanis and M. Musella (eds.), *Paid and Unpaid Labour in the Social Economy*,
AIEL Series in Labour Economics, DOI: 10.1007/978-3-7908-2137-6_5,

least one input for the production of labour. The paper was highly influential in the literature on urban transportation demand, although gradually superseded by Beckerian models. One important example of this influence was DeSerpa (1971). He included all forms of time use together with the Beckerian commodities in the preference function.

When labour supply is defined as a time residual, a production function for labour is thus explicitly left out. In such a situation, labour time does not appear in the preference function, at least in Walrasian models, one of which is the household production model of Becker (1965). Besides this, Beckerian models define production functions only for the activities that are listed in the preference function. It is true that the household production model can be interpreted as allowing for a linear production function for the labour activity in which time is the only input. As usual, the level of this activity is measured by the amount of time used in it. However, many types of labour may be considered in which this equivalence is not valid. One example would be labour performed and sold by tasks instead of by the hour. Also, there are specific inputs in the productive process of human work. Therefore, a production function that has only time as input does not cover the general case. It amounts to ignoring the productive process for labour.

Many insights on the production of human work exist in the economic literature, although in scattered form. Leontief's closed model, which is related to the *Tableau Économique* of the physiocrats, treats consumers as a sector that specializes in supplying labour. Due to the unrealistic assumption of fixed coefficients for the consumption of final goods, at least from the empiric viewpoint, the more frequently used model in which consumption and labour are exogenous has superseded it.[1]

As in any household productive activity, labour production requires several inputs, some of which have been studied. Singh et al. (1986) and Suen and Mo (1994) present models of productive consumption that include, for example, sleep, nutrition, and health expenditures. An earlier suggestion for treating labour as a household output, as an equal to commodities, appeared in DeSerpa (1971), although the analysis in the paper was made with a fixed supply of labour. Gronau (1986, 1987) treats labour as an activity with its own inputs. However, the analysis is brief and the results are somewhat different from this paper. Human capital theory considers expenditures that increase future capacity for earning income as inputs or, better, as investment. However, such an analysis is done inter-temporally and seems not to include an explicit production function for labour.[2] The literature on collective household production seems to follow Becker's treatment as far as it refers to the production of labour.[3]

[1] See Dorfman et al. (1958, ch. 10) and Pasinetti (1977, chap. 4).

[2] One recent example of this literature is Steger (2002).

[3] For a recent survey of collective household models with emphasis on their econometric implementation, see Vermeulen (2002).

Therefore, it appears that there is some space for a re-discussion of the model in which labour supply is treated as any other output of the household productive process. This paper summarizes and extends research presented by Sanson (1997, 2002).

The present article is restricted to a static situation. In addition, sleep and leisure activities are treated as inputs that are not specific to labour production since they affect the whole productive process of the household. They are among the activities directly included in the preference function.

The paper attempts to design a model of labour supply that should fit in the standard consumer and firm theories. Ideally, the model should also fit in the general equilibrium framework. For this, the endowment treatment is fundamental. We will see that the endowment of work capacity leads naturally to an agent that maximizes rent for the human capital. Currently, the household production theory, despite its growing sophistication, still stays only in the dark alleys of the more popular microeconomics texts, intermediary and advanced. This is inconsistent with the importance of the theme in empirical applications of economics.

The main objective of the article is to formulate a model of household production in which labour is one of the productive activities whose output may be sold in the market. This will be done in the context of Walrasian models, in which the time allocated for work in the market is given as a residual. Section 4.2 covers the notion of time endowment, with emphasis on its interpretation as a period in which the human organism is available for working. This highlights the fact that, in contrast to other types of Walrasian endowments, the time endowment can not be altered. Section 4.3 proposes a Beckerian household production model that has, as a distinguishing characteristic, production functions for different types of labour. Section 4.4 illustrates the general model with the special case of two commodities, where one is a good that does not require time and the other only requires time, being a Beckerian version of the income–leisure model of textbooks. However, the production functions for labour are kept. This model allows for a discussion of the shadow price of time. Finally, Sect. 4.5 adapts the notion of profit or net result, used in models of household production from agricultural economics, to the production of labour.

4.2 The Endowment of Labour

Before the presentation of the labour supply model, it will be necessary to define labour as a result of a productive process. A related question is the definition of the endowment of time for each economic agent. Its interpretation is dependent on the definition of labour, and it implies a modification in the concept of the opportunity cost of time.

The concept of human work presupposes an activity by a person during a time interval.[4] A person, in fact, is a kind of physical capital that renders services during a given period.[5] Thus not only this person has an occupation that may include different kinds of work, but also the number of possible tasks might be infinite. What counts is the combination of personal abilities to be used in each task. The human capital is complemented by different inputs to render different goods and services, not necessarily tied to a paid job. As taught by the theory of household production, work is then one of the many possible outputs from a productive process centred on a person or a family. The organism itself is the basic capital of the person, and to be a worker is to specialize in renting one's own work capacity. The market structure in which this work capacity is rented varies with the type of work. From the view point of the sellers, it goes from quasi-monopolistic markets, in which the labour activity is tied to scarce abilities, to the competitive markets of non-qualified labour.

The second question related to labour production concerns the nature of the endowment of labour force for each person. This endowment is given by Nature, as far as the time interval is considered. Thus, for a given period, the person has a maximum of man-hours during which the organism can be at work, not given by the organism itself but by the time interval. The intensity of work, however, is variable and is dependent on personal limits and the environment in which the organism operates.

Similarly, there are many types of activities that a given person may exercise during the period. Because of this, it is possible to think of a production function for labour in which one of the inputs, the essential one, is the man-hours the person allocates to a given task.[6] A simple example is a gardener who charges for the service by the area covered and then allocates hours of work to the task. From the current viewpoint, the gardener uses, besides the services of gardening physical equipment, the services of the organism itself, treated as capital.

The human organism may be able to perform more than one activity at the same time or at least during the same period. One example is to work on a laptop during

[4]See Debreu (1959, pp. 30–31) and Arrow and Hahn (1971, chap. 4). Whinston (1982, pp. 15–16, 163–164) argues that many textbooks consider time itself as the input. In fact, time only delimits the duration and the direction of the labour process. A favourable interpretation for the textbooks is that an implicit assumption is made. Time is only a short for a number of man-hours of homogeneous human work per period. If every worker delivers the same number of man-hours, then it is enough to count the number of workers. In models of individual supply, the reference to time endowment must be to a number of man-hours. Another semantic question is the use of the words labour and work. In order to avoid a discussion that would easily get into physics, these words are synonymous here.

[5]Walras refers to "… *personal capital* or *persons*, capable of yielding *personal incomes* or *services of persons*, which we shall also call *labour* …" See Walras (1977, p. 215, italics in the original).

[6]This availability of the worker for the execution of alternative tasks may be seen, despite the differences in theoretical paradigms, as the equivalent to the Marxian concept of "abstract human labour". The conversion of abstract labour into different types of labour could be made within the present production function approach. The usual conversion with fixed coefficients would be a special case. An irresistible question is: Would such a solution avoid the aggregation problems that created insurmountable difficulties for the labour theory of value?

a flight, where both activities are related to an occupation.[7] Another example is the leisure of the theory class during academic meetings. This possibility is not considered in the standard models, due to the determination of labour supply as a residual. Therefore, selling labour capacity and using it in unpaid activities are mutually exclusive. Separating the endowment of work capacity from the different types of work that are produced allows for the treatment of this capacity as an input that can be jointly used in the many possible activities of a household.

In terms of the Walrasian treatment of endowments, only the availability of the human capital, measured in man-hours, would be treated as any other good. Labour output, of course, would depend on effort and on the technology implicit in its production function. Arrow and Hahn (1971, pp. 75–76, 165–166) integrate Becker's model of time allocation in their discussion of general equilibrium, in terms of Walrasian endowments. In their solution, they follow a procedure developed by Arrow and Debreu (1954), in which several types of possible endowments of leisure time are considered for each person, although the definition of these endowments is certainly something difficult to do. There is a corresponding set of activities or tasks that require time with fixed coefficients, and the sum of the excess demands for different types of time use cannot be higher than the total endowment of time of the person. There is no restriction on the sign of each excess demand, except for the total available time.

A point that the Walrasian endowment approach brings to the discussion is its fixity. Endowments of goods may be altered, and this is the essence of models of excess demand and reservation prices in general equilibrium analysis. In the case of labour capacity, however, this is not possible. A person may hire external labour in order to substitute for own labour in a given activity, but this does not alter own labour capacity. It just means there is an alternative use for the saved labour capacity.

In the context of household production theory, the endowment of labour capacity may be interpreted as a fixed factor for a firm. Depending on the technology of a firm, a fixed factor has possible uses for the production of different types of goods, and may be used jointly. In household production theory, the decisions about consumption and production are not separable. This can be contrasted to the usual supposition in the theory of the firm, in which there is no interaction between the consumption decisions of the owners of the firm and their decisions on the firm's production. Thus the capacity of labour, as a fixed factor in the household production process, affects simultaneously consumption and production decisions, including labour. The main difference is that this fixed factor, for the worker, is not alterable in the long run. Investments in formal or experience-based education are equivalent to technological progress.

This Walrasian endowment approach in the household production theory results in modifications in the interpretation of the opportunity cost of the labour capacity.

[7] In this example, the service of the organism enters simultaneously in the labour activity, which is an output, and in the transportation activity, which can be a case of an input activity to the work activity being sold.

In the basic income-leisure model, if a person gives up selling part of the labour capacity in the market to consume it, the best alternative wage given up is the opportunity cost. In these models, it is also supposed that there is joint use of the human capital in several activities. This is so because no joint use destroys the one-to-one tradeoff between labour and leisure. With the production function approach for labour supply, a man–hour can have many alternative uses, which include consumption activities or many types of marketable labour. In terms of sacrificed income, now the opportunity cost is given by the best occupation available to the person. However, given the labour supply, there is also an opportunity cost involved in choosing consumption activities. In both situations, it will be seen that the marginal rate of transformation between a pair of activities, associated to a man-hour, as a measure of labour capacity, is now part of the definition of opportunity cost.

4.3 A General Household Production Model

Take a Beckerian model with a given list of commodities with no perfect substitutes in the market.[8] Suppose that any good bought in the market requires some positive amount of man-hours to be consumed, which turns it into a commodity. The person maximizes the preference function

$$u = u(z) \tag{4.1}$$

where z is a vector that represents the quantities of commodities.

Technology is shown by the transformation function

$$F\,(z, y, t) = 0 \tag{4.2}$$

where y is a vector of tradable goods. Inputs are represented by non-positive elements of the vector, with the opposite inequality sign for outputs. One example of output is labour, in fact the tasks performed in a given occupation. Vector t represents the types of labour that the person performs domestically and in the market through different occupations. If the number of commodities and tradable goods is greater than the number of types of work, then there are work activities that are jointly used in several activities of the household. Also, the level of production of a commodity for consumption may affect the productivity of labour activities.[9] This possibility is covered by (4.2), as a general technology of production.

[8] Had the commodities perfect substitutes, it would be necessary to distinguish, for each of them, between what is consumed domestically and what is sold, as done in international trade theory. See Strauss (1986) and Sanson (1997).

[9] This covers the treatment of productive consumption. Suen and Mo (1994) follow a tradition of having a continuum of types of work, given by wage as a function of productive consumption. The present model implies a discrete number of work types. This is more akin to the usual textbook general equilibrium models. However, the present treatment has in common with that followed by Arrow and Hahn (1971) only the limit on total time use, given by Nature. There is no need to define endowments for each type of leisure. Each Beckerian commodity might require work time that will come out from the total work capacity of the person.

The budget restriction is given by

$$p^T y = 0 \tag{4.3}$$

where p is a price vector with the same number of components as y. The only source of income is the sale of outputs from the productive process.[10] As the inputs are negative variables, their costs are being covered by (4.3). In contrast to the usual presentations of household production models, this version treats the goods bought in the market as inputs, which, similarly to the advanced theory of the firm, are treated as negative variables.

The labour restriction[11] is simply the sum of all the possible uses of the total available labour:

$$J^T t = 1 \tag{4.4}$$

where J is the summation vector and the endowment of labour is normalized to unity.

From the Lagrangean function

$$L(z, y, t, \lambda) = u(z) + \lambda_1 F(z, y, t) + \lambda_2 (1 - J^T t) + \lambda_3 p^T y$$

the following first order conditions for a maximum are obtained:[12]

$$\frac{\partial u}{\partial z} + \lambda_1 \frac{\partial F}{\partial z} = 0^T \tag{4.5}$$

$$\lambda_1 \frac{\partial F}{\partial y} + \lambda_3 p^T = 0^T \tag{4.6}$$

$$\lambda_1 \frac{\partial F}{\partial t} - \lambda_2 j^T = 0^T \tag{4.7}$$

The restrictions (4.2), (4.3), and (4.4) should also be listed as part of this matrix equation system. With the appropriate index value, λ_i represents the three Lagrangean multipliers.

---

[10] Income from other sources is supposed to be equal to zero, i.e. $m = 0$. If positive, it would be added to the left-hand side of (4.3).

[11] Calling the usual time restriction a labour restriction is consistent with the argument that a person really has an endowment of labour capacity that the organism may perform during the period under consideration. Walras himself made the suggestion that the labour capacity should be called leisure to differentiate it from market labour, despite the fact that only a fraction of this activity is truly leisure. For simplicity, the inequality conditions on time use are omitted and only interior solutions are considered.

[12] The null vectors may have different dimensions in each equation.

The analytical solution for this model is clearly difficult. But some insights can be gained by opening up some of the equations. From the elements of (4.5), after eliminating the Lagrangean multiplier, it follows that:

$$\frac{\partial u / \partial z_i}{\partial u / \partial z_j} = \frac{\partial F / \partial z_i}{\partial F / \partial z_j} \tag{4.8}$$

This means that the marginal rate of substitution between two commodities is equal to the corresponding marginal rate of transformation. This corresponds to an efficiency condition in the household production process.[13]

From (4.6) and (4.7), by also eliminating the multipliers, it follows that

$$p_i \frac{\partial F / \partial t_i}{\partial F / \partial y_j} = p_j \frac{\partial F / \partial t_i}{\partial F / \partial y_j} \tag{4.9}$$

Consider, for instance, y_j and y_k as types of traded labour. Then it is possible to interpret (4.9) as saying that alternative uses of the labour capacity result in the equality of their values of the marginal products.[14]

An optimal condition for a pair of goods bought from the market follows from (4.6):

$$\frac{\partial F / \partial y_k}{\partial F / \partial y_\ell} = \frac{p_k}{p_\ell} \tag{4.10}$$

Now the marginal rate of technical substitution equals the corresponding input price ratio. This condition is associated to cost minimization.

However, let y_l be interpreted as a given type of traded labour and y_k as an input for this kind of labour. If (4.10) were then rewritten as

$$p_l \frac{\partial F / \partial y_k}{\partial F / \partial y_l} = p_k \tag{4.11}$$

the result would be the equality between the value of the marginal product and the respective price of input y_k used in the production of labour y_l.

Conditions of type (4.10) or (4.11) are familiar from the theory of the firm. However, they cannot, at least for a general model such as this, be solved independently

[13] Paretian efficiency conditions have been explicitly incorporated in modelling collective decisions on consumption and the supply of labour in collective models of household production. See Apps and Rees (1997) and Chiappori (1997).

[14] Since these are implicit derivatives, this interpretation would best be made with negative signs in both sides of (4.9).

of the other equations. The production decisions and the consumption decisions are simultaneously taken.[15]

4.4 A Simple Case with Occupational Choice

A special case of the above model can be cast after the textbook case of income and leisure, although with the supply of two types of labour. In this model, as a simplification, there are only two commodities. The preference function is described by $u(z_1, z_2)$, where z_i represents a commodity. Also for simplification, each unit of z_1 requires one unit of a specific good, x_3, and no man-hours for its consumption. Leisure is also a specialized commodity, requiring only the allocation of some time, t_3, of the total work capacity.[16] Thus the production functions for these commodities are $z_1 = t_3$ and $z_2 = t_3$ and the preference function can be rewritten as $u\,(x_3, t_3)$.[17]

It is supposed that the person has a type of human capital that makes it viable to supply two kinds of market labour. The production function for each labour type is given by $h_j = f_j(x_j, t_j)$, with $j \in \{1, 2\}$ and where x_j and t_j represent specific inputs for the labour activity h_j.[18] The variable t_j shows the duration of the availability of the person's own organism for the labour activity h_j. In fact, this production function reflects the convention that people carry out tasks that require physical effort. With variable coefficients of production, there is the possibility of the substitution between inputs bought and physical effort.

In comparison with the general household production model, presented above, the usual convention of treating all variables as non-negative is here followed, with the negative sign indicating inputs. Therefore, the vector of goods, bought or sold in the market, is given by $y = (-x_1, -x_2, -x_3, h_1, h_2)$. Inputs 1 and 2 are then productive consumption. With this simplified technology, the model focuses on the production and supply of different types of labour.

---

[15] For an early discussion of cases in which recursion of these problems is possible, see Singh et al. (1986).

[16] The reason for the non-coincidence of the indices of commodities and inputs will soon be clear. It has to do with the treatment of the inputs of the occupations.

[17] In $u\,(x_3, t_3)$, the consumer directly values only leisure time, while the other uses of time, in the production of work, will be determined as a residual from the endowment of labour power. As far as the opportunity cost of time is concerned, the individual will only consider the opportunity cost of sacrificing leisure time. DeSerpa (1971) and Pollak and Wachter (1975, p. 271) introduce the time inputs for commodities in the utility function as a way to consider preferences on time use itself. This might be double counting, since a Beckerian commodity is a package that includes the use of own time in its production and consumption. A much older tradition in the literature is to consider the labour supply itself in the preference function, a procedure that seems more related to the present model.

[18] Notice that $f_j(.)$ is being used as a generic symbol for a production function. It should not be taken as a partial derivative.

The income restriction of this worker can be written as

$$p_3 x_3 = w_1 h_1 - p_1 x_1 + w_2 h_2 - p_2 x_2$$

where p_i is the price of goods bought in the market and w_j is the unit wage. This budget restriction may then be interpreted as the equality between the expenditure on the commodity input and the net income from each kind of labour.[19]

The labour capacity restriction, usually referred to as time restriction, is given by $t_l + t_2 + t_3 = 1$ where t_l and t_2 refer to the use of labour capacity in two types of occupations or tasks.

In order to optimize, it is convenient to substitute the production functions for labour in the budget restriction and write the following Lagrangean function:

$$L = u(x_3, t_3) + \lambda_1 [w_1 f_1(x_1, t_1) + w_2 f_2(x_2, t_2) - p_1 x_1 - p_2 x_2 - p_3 x_3] + \lambda_2 (1 - t_1 - t_2 - t_3).$$

Having in mind that $u(x_3, t_3)$ is a function of functions, the first order conditions in relation to x_j's and t_j's are:

$$\frac{\partial u}{\partial z_1} - \lambda_1 p_3 = 0 \tag{4.12}$$

$$\frac{\partial u}{\partial z_2} - \lambda_2 = 0 \tag{4.13}$$

$$\lambda_1 \left(w_j \frac{\partial h_j}{\partial x_j} - p_j \right) = 0; j \in \{1,2\} \tag{4.14}$$

$$\lambda_1 w_j \frac{\partial h_j}{\partial t_j} - \lambda_2 = 0; j \in \{1,2\} \tag{4.15}$$

Eliminating the Lagrangean multipliers and omitting the restrictions, the first order conditions may be rewritten as:

$$\frac{\partial u / \partial z_2}{\partial u / \partial z_1} = \frac{w_1 \partial h_1 / \partial t_1}{p_3} \tag{4.16}$$

[19]Johnson (1966, pp. 142–143) has the trip to work as a time use that should be added to the work time. Also, the cost of the trip should be subtracted from the wage obtained in each trip, although this result is dependent on the transport input being given by a fixed coefficient. The present model could describe this particular case by using a Leontief production function for the labour activity. This production function, in fact, is the one used for each commodity in the first Beckerian models.

$$w_1 \frac{\partial h_1}{\partial t_1} = w_2 \frac{\partial h_2}{\partial t_2} \tag{4.17}$$

$$w_1 \frac{\partial h_1}{\partial t_1} = w_2 \frac{\partial h_2}{\partial t_2}; j = 1,2 \tag{4.18}$$

At least theoretically, these four equations plus the budget restriction, the work restriction, and the two production functions allow for the determination of the values of the following variables: x_1, x_2, x_3, t_1, t_2, t_3, h_1, and h_2.

Equation (4.16) is analogous to (4.8) in the general model, because it involves the marginal rate of substitution for the two commodities. However, the production function of the commodity is extremely simplified, as already noted, since $z_l = x_3$. Thus, instead of a marginal rate of transformation between a pair of commodities, (4.16) shows the ratio between the opportunity cost of the labour capacity used in the leisure activity – measured in terms of the value of the marginal product of labour capacity in the production of labour type 1, i.e. $w_1 dt_1 / dt_1$ - and the price of the good used as input for commodity z_1. Equation (4.16) may be further written as $w_1 \frac{\partial h_1}{\partial t_1} = p_3 \frac{\partial u / \partial z_2}{\partial u / \partial z_1}$.

Now, it may be interpreted as the equality between the value of the marginal product of the labour capacity used in the first occupation and the opportunity cost of leisure time in terms of commodity 1. It is no surprise that the equilibrium conditions of household production recall the conditions for the firm, since consumption and production decisions are interrelated. It also provides, at least in the one commodity model, an alternative estimate for the opportunity cost of leisure.

Equation (4.17) is equivalent to (4.9) and shows that the value of the marginal productivity of labour capacity for each occupation is equal in equilibrium. They are also equal to the opportunity cost of leisure as just seen.[20]

Finally, the equations in (4.18), similar to (4.11), say that the value of the marginal product of each labour input bought in the market is equal to its marginal input cost. If the unit wage for each occupation were isolated in each equation, it would be equal to the corresponding marginal cost of labour. This result is here independent of preferences, as it did in the general model, and is equivalent to the usual price equal to marginal cost in the theory of the firm.

It is also possible to examine the marginal rates of technical substitution in the production of each type of work. They are given by the combination of (4.17) and (4.18), whose result is:

---

[20] This benefit of each unit of work refers only to market revenue. It is a consequence of not considering the preferences of the consumer–producer for the different types of work. Introducing h_j in $u(.)$ could do this. It would extend the labour–leisure models that were referred to in the Introduction.

$$\frac{\partial h_j / \partial t_j}{\partial h_j / \partial x_j} = \frac{w_i \partial h_i / \partial t_i}{p_j}; i \neq j \, and \, i, j = 1,2 \tag{4.19}$$

As expected, the marginal rates of technical substitution between the two inputs for each occupation are equal to a price ratio of inputs. Yet, the labour capacity price is an opportunity cost, given by the revenue that could be obtained by selling that work unit in the market through one of the possible occupations. Equations in (4.19) are also variants of (4.9), now defined for pairs of labour inputs.

These results provide different estimates for the opportunity cost of time, as summarized in the following set of equalities:

$$w_j \frac{\partial h_j}{\partial t_j} = p_j \frac{\partial h_j / \partial t_j}{\partial h_j / \partial x_j} = p_3 \frac{\partial u / \partial z_2}{\partial u / \partial z_1}; j = 1,2 \tag{4.20}$$

There are thus three different ways for estimating the opportunity cost of time: two of them from the productive process of tradable work and one from consumption.[21] In the maximizing position of the consumer–producer, they are all equal. Of course, out of equilibrium they can be different and serve as a guide in decisions on where to better allocate time. In more general models, with production functions also for the Beckerian goods, there will be a greater number of alternative estimates of the opportunity cost of time.

This model relates with others in several ways. First, the person may specialize in one occupation. This may occur due to preferences, technology, relative prices or social rules. Then the model could be specified in non-linear programming terms, with the presence of non-negativity conditions for each variable and inequalities for some of the restrictions.

Second, to obtain the usual income–leisure model, it would be sufficient to suppose a linear production function for labour, with labour supply given by the number of man-hours sold in the market, t_j. The use of other specific inputs in the production of labour would also be ignored.

---

[21] These expressions could serve as a basis for a graphical illustration of the simplified model. With the three alternative uses of the endowment of work capacity, three different individual demand curves could be drawn. The first of them would reflect the demand for leisure and would give the own demand for work capacity. With it, it would be possible to compute a reservation price that could be zero. The other two demand curves would reflect the demand for work capacity as inputs to the production of the two types of market work. The horizontal addition of the three individual demand curves would cross the vertical line at the endowment point that would represent the supply of work capacity, and, there, it would determine the opportunity cost of time for the consumer–producer. Besides, with simple algebraic operations, it can be shown that these expressions for the opportunity cost of time are equivalent to the ratio λ_1/λ_2, widely used in the economics of the allocation of time (Gronau 1986).

In short, the income-leisure model just presented is general enough to also include production functions for labour. It seems to be useful for illustrating the mix of preference and production decisions in the supply of labour. It also seems to give some alternative insights in the discussion of the opportunity cost of time.

As a final characterization of the labour supply, it is useful to discuss a few results in the comparative statics of the specialized model. The study of the compensated demand faces two difficulties. To begin with, the equivalent to the budget restriction is now a non-linear function, when the production functions of labour are substituted in the income restriction. Then, as opposed to the traditional income–leisure model, the elimination of the labour capacity restriction is not simple, so it is kept separate here. The definition of the substitution matrix is now dependent on which exogenous variable and restriction are combined for defining the compensated functions. As usual, the non-labour income from the income restriction will be chosen variable.

In building the Slutsky equations, whether decomposing for commodities, for household outputs or for inputs, it makes a difference. Only commodities enter the utility function, therefore it is natural to interpret a compensated demand as a movement along an indifference curve. Compensated demands for inputs imply movements along isoquants, and the decomposition could be made in terms of substitution and output effects. As for the output, it is unusual to decompose the price effect. Instead, the short-run and long-run supply functions are studied, by distinguishing inputs that are fixed in the short-run. Along these lines, the Slutsky decomposition will be discussed only for the commodities. In the income restriction of the simplified model, the value of non-labour income is given by

$$m = p_1 x_1 + p_2 x_2 + p_3 x_3 - w_1 h - w_2 h_2$$

although it was supposed null above. Minimizing this variable, subject to a given utility level and the remaining restrictions, results in the compensated, or Hicksian, demand functions:

$$x_3^H (p_1, p_2, p_3, w_1, w_3, u) \text{ and } t_3^H (p_1, p_2, p_3, w_1, w_3, u).$$

Establishing the identity between the Marshallian and Hicksian demand functions and applying the Envelope Theorem yield the following Slutsky equations for the commodity z_1:

$$\frac{\partial z_1}{\partial p_i} = \frac{\partial z_1^H}{\partial p_i} - x_i \frac{\partial z_1}{\partial m}; \; i = 1, 2, 3$$

$$\frac{\partial z_1}{\partial w_j} = \frac{\partial z_1^H}{\partial w_j} + h_j \frac{\partial z_1}{\partial m}; \; j = 1, 2$$

The only price that directly acts upon the quantity demanded of this commodity is p_3, even then only if the budget restriction is linearized around the equilibrium position[22]. All the other prices, including wages, act through the non-linear budget, as usual in Beckerian models in which the production functions do not have the property of constant returns to scale. The commodity z_2, being time used outside the market, does not have a price in monetary terms. Here, wage cannot be used as usual. The Slutsky decomposition can then be made only with respect to prices of inputs or wages. The expressions are similar to the ones above, except for the variables in the numerator of each derivative. All the effects work through the non-linear budget function.

4.5 The Net Result from Labour Supply

Provided specific inputs to the productive process of labour are identifiable, it is possible to define gross and net revenue from market work. This recalls farm models in which part of the total income is given by the net result, also called profit, of the goods sold in the market.[23] However, after the above discussion about the endowment of work, which is given by Nature, this net result has the character of an economic rent.

The concept of economic or pure profit in the theory of the firm is clearly defined by the net results obtained over the opportunity cost of own capital applied in the firm. Capital is defined in terms of the market value of the property rights on physical and financial capital. When this capital is fixed in the long run, the pure profit is called economic rent, a concept that follows from a null opportunity cost. However, this absence of opportunity cost is only valid when the owner has no alternative personal use for the resource; said differently, only when the reservation price is zero.

Making an analogy among wages, profits and rent might seem odd, almost a provocation, given the characteristics of the corresponding factor markets. Even

[22]Theorem 6 from Blomquist (1989) considers non-linear budget restrictions in which a term involving a market price and the corresponding good can be additively separated. He then shows how some substitution effects, even so, become predictable. With this theorem, it seems possible to predict that the substitution term $\partial z_1^H / \partial p_3$ is non-positive. For the other terms in the Slutsky decompositions, it would be necessary to deal with a linearized expression of the budget restriction, based on shadow prices for the commodities and the alternative uses of time. For these prices the standard results in comparative statics are valid. But such prices would be functions of the market prices and these indirect effects should be treated separately. General results connecting the prices of goods to commodity demand are unlikely.

[23]See Singh et al. (1986, pp. 18, 71–72). There, the definition is used for farm output and referred to as profit or net result.

neoclassical economists have kept the analysis of each factor separate, in light of the sociological characteristics of each factor market. So, the purpose of the following observations is to find alternative interpretations for the costs of supplying labour. This is, in fact, a practical question in income taxation, where endless discussions occur on what kinds of deductions should be allowed.

The net result for each occupation is equal to $w_j h_j - p_j x_j$ in the model of the previous section. Notice that this is not the profit concept, as just defined, since it does not consider the opportunity cost of using this time in non-market activities or perhaps in a different occupation with a better remuneration. Instead, the net result is equivalent to the concept of quasi-rent, as used in the theory of the firm, being given by the difference between total revenue and variable costs.

The expressions of the net results for the two occupations of the income–leisure model are obtainable from the budget and time restrictions. Initially, multiply both sides of the time restriction by the shadow price of a man-hour, then add the result to the right-hand side of the budget restriction, and finally write:

$$p_3 x_3 + w_1 \frac{\partial h_1}{\partial t_1} t_3 = w_1 \frac{\partial h_1}{\partial t_1} + \sum_{j=1}^{2} \left(w_j h_j - w_1 \frac{\partial h_1}{\partial t_1} t_j - p_j x_j \right) \tag{4.21}$$

The left-hand side of (4.21) shows the expenditures on inputs for the commodities, including the opportunity cost of time dedicated to one of them, leisure. The right-hand side shows the redefined Beckerian full-income, also in terms of the shadow wage. It is given by the value of the endowment of labour capacity plus the economic profit attained in each occupation.

However, this discussion is made in relation to specific inputs for labour. In the case of a firm, the production of tradable goods is supposedly separate from the other activities of the person. It is exactly when consumption and production activities are separable that the idea of firms as a means for the social division of labour can be debated. It is as a consequence of this possibility that the concept of circular flows between firms and consumers may be described.

According to age-old wisdom the supply of labour is different from the supply of other tradable goods and services, especially in the way the person is involved. Suppose a person owns a capital good, such as a lawn mower. This person can use it to sell gardening services or to put it for rent.[24] That is not the case with labour. When a person is hired for work, the organism itself is the source of the service.

[24] Renting a capital good involves a social arrangement with accepted property rights. Even then, there is the work of administrating these property rights or at least of checking the services of those hired to manage these property rights. But the amount of work and the degree of effort required are certainly smaller than the operation of most capital goods, although the stress involved in the uncertainties of returns on financial capital might be high, especially for risk-averse persons.

Thus to separate decisions is impossible, since all consumption that is not specific to work is also consumption by the same organism. The procedure of supposing a specific production function for labour can only capture part of the inputs. It leaves out most of the inputs that are necessary for keeping alive and in good shape the human organism. It seems that the most that can be done by the analyst, in computing the profit from an occupation, is to find the contribution of this output to total income.

Note, however, that the contribution of the net revenue of market work to total income is defined after the equilibrium of the consumer–producer is found. It has the nature of an economic rent, and it defines the net product or *le produit net* of the person, as the physiocrats would say. Perhaps, this can be illustrated by rewriting the above special model in terms of cost functions. Take t_j as given and define the restricted or short-run cost functions, defined without the opportunity costs of time.[25] Minimize $p_j x_j$ subject to $f_j(x_j, t_j) = h_j$ for each kind of market work. This will result in the restricted cost functions $c_j = c_j(h_j, t_j, p_j)$. Now, the budget restriction becomes: $p_3 x_3 = \sum_{j=1}^{2} \left(w_j h_j - c_j\left(h_j, t_j, p_j\right)\right)$. Thus by subtracting variable costs from the total revenue of a given type of market work, the consumer-producer gets the economic rent for a given level of work capacity (time) allocated to that activity. Given (t_1, t_2), the value of the goods used as inputs for commodities has the nature of an economic rent. This is consistent with the Walrasian approach of considering a person as a kind of capital good, as discussed above. A consumer-producer, specialized in selling work and with no income from other property rights, might have a very low level of expenditures on consumption of goods beyond the necessary for working. This would occur with different abilities and for a marginal worker.

However, the real income of a person also involves leisure or, as Becker would put it, commodities that are intensive in the use of time. As seen above, this consumption of leisure is the origin of the opportunity cost of time when this is used as input in order to sell work. This opportunity cost is then the equivalent to a marginal cost of labour. The revenue from work above these variable costs of labour is then the equivalent to an economic net result for the worker and it would be the equivalent to the economic profit for capital goods. People cannot be sold in an economy where slavery is banned. Anyway, if there were slavery, a person would be the equivalent to a capital good for someone else. Thus, for a free person, the present value of the net result that might be obtained along the working life is in fact the value of freedom.

4.6 Concluding Remarks

Time itself is not a productive input in household production. Its role is simply to delimit the interval of time in which production and consumption occur. The true input is the work done during such a time interval or period. However, as a simplification, it is customary to describe labour input by the number of hours during which a

[25] It would be a straightforward extension to use net revenue functions. Nevertheless, cost functions are better suited for the analysis of the returns to human capital.

person exerts such activity. Besides that, the amount of work depends on the level of effort of the person during a given period. Thus, the production of work by a person seems fit for a description by a production function, in which the idea of maximum output for a given set of specific inputs is essential.

A Beckerian model with a technology that includes the possibility of joint production and productive consumption was presented. At least one of the outputs of this productive process is labour, meant to be sold in the market. Implicit in the model is the fact that the effort level depends on attaining the production frontier. With this specification the household production model, including labour supply, might be more amenable for its integration into general equilibrium theory and microeconomic theory in general.

The model is illustrated by the special case of income-leisure, adapted for the inclusion of production functions for two types of labour. With this model, it is possible to get objective estimates for the shadow price of the labour capacity from relations that involve marginal productivities of the inputs in labour output.

Finally, the notion of net result is adapted for the production of labour. Because of the unalterable endowment of labour, the net result is related to economic rent. However, the own use of this endowment creates the equivalent to quasi-rent or economic profit, although this expression is inadequate for a kind of capital that has no market in a modern society, except for its services. From the viewpoint of the consumer–producer, a way to increase the net result is by reducing the costs of producing labour. Investments in technological progress at the domestic factory may reduce these costs. Another form, perhaps with better gains in the long run, is to invest in differentiating the kinds of labour to be offered in the market. It is as if the person tried to become a different type of person as far as the supply of work is concerned. Instead of economies of scale, which is not possible to explore, given the fixity of the time endowment, the consumer-producer creates new outputs, by differentiating the labour supply along Chamberlinian lines.

There are various extensions of the model that could be made. First is the extension to comparative statics, especially with view to econometric work, but also for the purpose of integration of the model in general equilibrium theory. Second, the model could be related to the collective household literature.

Acknowledgments The author thanks Idaleto M. Aued, José Rubens D. Garlipp, Pedro H.V. Mendes, Jean-Luc Rosinger, Joseph Lacey, Luciana T.Sanson, and Fernando Seabra for suggestions during the research. He thanks the National Council for Scientific and Technological Development (CNPq), from Brazil, for a grant that also included research assistance from Michael Ax Wilhelm and Antonio M. Fontoura.

References

Apps PF, Rees R (1997) Collective labour supply and household production. Journal of Political Economy 105:178–190

Arrow KJ, Debreu G (1954) Existence of equilibrium in a competitive economy. Econometrica 22: 265–290

Arrow KJ, Hahn FH (1971) General competitive analysis. North-Holland, Amsterdam
Becker GS (1965) A theory of the allocation of time. Economic Journal 75:493–517
Blomquist NS (1989) Comparative statics for utility maximization models with nonlinear budget constraints. International Economic Review 30:275–296
Chiappori P-A (1997) Introducing household production in collective models of labour supply. Journal of Political Economy 105:191–209
Debreu G (1959) Theory of value. Yale University Press, New Haven
DeSerpa AC (1971) A theory of the economics of time. Economic Journal 81:828–846
Dorfman R, Samuelson PA, Solow R (1958) Linear programming and economic analysis. McGraw-Hill, New York
Georgescu-Roegen N (1968) Utility. In: International encyclopedia of the social sciences, vol 16. Macmillan, New York
Gronau R (1986) Home production: a survey. In: Ashenfelter O, Layard R (eds) Handbook of labour Economics, vol 2. North-Holland, Amsterdam
Gronau R (1987) Value of time. In Eatwell J, Milgate M, Newman P (eds) The New Palgrave: A Dictionary of Economics, vol 4. Macmillan, London
Johnson MB (1966) Travel time and the price of leisure. Western Economic Journal 4:135–145
Pasinetti LL (1977) Lectures on the theory of production. Columbia University Press, New York
Pollak RA, Wachter ML (1975) The relevance of the household production function and its implications for the allocation of time. Journal of Political Economy 83:255–277
Sanson JR (1987) On the labour-leisure model. In: Papers and Proceedings of the 7th Latin American Meeting Of The Econometric Society, vol 4. Fipe/Universidade De São Paulo, São Paulo
Sanson JR (1991) A preferência por trabalho no modelo de produção doméstica (The preference for work in the model of household production). In: Papers and Proceedings of the 13th Brazilian Meeting of Econometrics. Brazilian Society of Econometrics (SBE), Rio De Janeiro
Sanson JR (1997) Uma teoria integrada da produção doméstica e da firma (An integrated theory of household production and the firm). In: Papers and Proceedings of the 25th National Meeting of Economics. National Association of Graduate Centers of Economics (ANPEC), Rio De Janeiro
Sanson JR (2002) A oferta de trabalho como um produto doméstico (The supply of labour as a household output). Textos de Economia 7:11–34
Singh I, Squire L, Strauss J (eds) (1986) Agricultural household models. Johns Hopkins University/World Bank, Baltimore
Steger TM (2002) Productive consumption, The intertemporal consumption trade-off and growth. Journal of Economic Dynamics and Control 26:1053–1068
Strauss J (1986) The theory and comparative statics of agricultural household models: a general approach. In: Singh I, Squire L, Strauss J (eds) Agricultural Household Models. Johns Hopkins University/World Bank, Baltimore
Suen W, Mo PH (1994) Simple analytics of productive consumption. Journal of Political Economy 102:372–383
Vermeulen F (2002) Collective household models: principles and main results. Journal of Economic Surveys 16:533–564
Walras L (1977) Elements of pure economics. Translated by William Jaffé. Augustus MKelley, Fairfield NJ
Whinston GC (1982) The timing of economic activities. Cambridge University Press, Cambridge UK

Chapter 5
Working for Nothing and Being Happy. The Determinants of the Satisfaction of Volunteers and Paid Workers

Miriam Michelutti and Marina Schenkel

Abstract This essay addresses the factors determining the satisfaction that volunteers derive from their own activity, and compares them with those determining the satisfaction of paid workers. The novelty of this approach is that volunteers and paid workers are compared within the same dataset (from Italy), using the same measure of rewards and reported satisfaction for both types of workers. The main findings are that volunteers are individuals who perform an activity which gives them satisfaction for a number of different reasons, and that, while the determinants of satisfaction are not exactly the same for volunteers and paid workers, both of them attach special consideration to the users' well-being.

5.1 Introduction

Why do volunteers consider their activity, namely their direct participation in providing a service, satisfying? Are the determinants of the satisfaction of paid workers in the same services different or similar? It has already been found that volunteers and paid employees have similar job attitudes as far as a number of aspects are concerned (Liao-Troth 2001). Likewise, the hypothesis has been put forward that the determinants of volunteer satisfaction are not dissimilar to those of paid workers (Mosca and Musella 2003). This paper attempts to address both questions; first, to understand the factors determining the satisfaction that volunteers derive from their own activity, and then to compare them with those determining the satisfaction of paid workers, on the basis of empirical results obtained from the FIVOL–FEO survey (Borzaga and Musella 2003).

The novelty of our approach is that we can compare volunteers and paid workers since we have the same measure of the rewards and reported satisfaction for both types of workers. Some inferences on the labour supply in social services could be

M. Michelutti and M. Schenkel (✉)
Department of Economics, University of Udine, Via Tomadini, 30/a, 33100, Udine, Italy

S. Destefanis and M. Musella (eds.), *Paid and Unpaid Labour in the Social Economy*, AIEL Series in Labour Economics, DOI: 10.1007/978-3-7908-2137-6_6,

made from our findings, even though, as will be argued below, the determinants of satisfaction are different from those relating to the labour supply decision.

In the following sections, volunteer work will be defined and the literature on volunteer labour supply will be briefly reviewed in the light of its connection with the issue of satisfaction. The data and some descriptive results on the features and attitudes of volunteers and paid workers will then be presented. Analyses of the determinants of volunteer satisfaction compared to those determining the satisfaction of paid workers will follow. The final section draws some conclusions.

5.2 What is Voluntary Work?

Before proceeding with the empirical analysis, it is necessary to provide a definition of volunteer work that goes beyond the absence of remuneration. This problem, in actual fact, is not a trivial one, since the gratuitous nature of volunteer activities has often been interpreted as the mere absence of pay. However, volunteers can receive other advantages from their activity, such as "psychic income", i.e. the prestige and joy of altruism, the possibility of influencing the composition and allocation of charitable transfers to promote their own welfare, of gathering information on the way their money contributions are employed, of enhancing their job opportunities and their future income, and of encouraging other people to give time and money to services they are interested in (Steinberg 1990). Tschirhart et al. (2001) consider five kinds of volunteer "functions", i.e. multiple possible outcomes of volunteer activity: altruistic (help others), instrumental (help yourself), social (enhance friendship and positive regard by others), self-esteem (feel better about yourself), avoidance (escape alienation, boredom, personal problems).

Since some volunteers expect to receive a tangible reward, including an increase in their future monetary wage, a problem arises. Are they to be considered "true" volunteers, or are they improperly defined as such? Frequent misunderstandings also come from the military origin of the term (Cnaan and Amrofell 1994).

Likewise, the requisite of voluntariness is not problem-free. The absence of remuneration is not sufficient to define an activity as voluntary. Otherwise, for instance, all domestic work would have to be considered volunteer work. Although the family is the primary place where interpersonal relations are characterized by their gratuity, the activities carried out in this area do not seem to reflect the nature of volunteer work, mainly because family relations presuppose the existence of binding social norms. Therefore, not only is volunteer activity without pay, but it is also not imposed by binding social norms (Woolley 2003). In Freeman's (1997) terminology, it is a "conscience good or activity", i.e. "something that people feel morally obligated to do when asked, but they would just as soon let someone else do" (Freeman 1997, p. S140).

Another problem stems from the "work" nature of volunteer activity. According to the standard economic model of labour supply, a necessary (and maybe sufficient) condition for any use of one's time to qualify as work is that it has to be "painful".

In that case the only reason to rationally agree to perform a painful activity is its exchange for a wage. Since volunteering is unpaid, it cannot be painful, so it cannot be defined as work. Rather, it has to be considered a consumption good. However, if work bears some utility, e.g. it is also the consumption of relational goods (Gui 2000), and indeed an activity from which one can receive satisfaction (Lane 1992), besides money and other monetary rewards, volunteering is simply unpaid work.

5.3 The Satisfaction of Volunteers and the Supply of Voluntary Work

Satisfaction is indeed the best proxy measure we have for utility, especially where work is concerned (Clark 1997). It must be remembered, however, that the determinants of satisfaction are related to, but different from, those of the labour supply decision. Satisfaction is a determinant of subsequent behaviour. In the case of paid work, job satisfaction does not coincide with the decision to supply hours of work, or with the decision to stay in one's current position (Lévy-Garboua and Montmarquette 2004). Rather, when workers are asked *ex post* to report upon their level of satisfaction with the job, they are expected to answer to the question, "given what you know about your job outcomes, would you choose the same job again?" (Lydon and Chevalier 2002, p. 15). More generally, one can be happy with the choice one has made for reasons that are different from those that have motivated the decision itself.

Volunteer satisfaction and its determinants have been considered directly in very few works we are aware of. Tschirhart et al. (2001), for instance, found that goals, especially social goals and their achievement, have the greatest influence on satisfaction.

More frequently, a related but different question is posed: What rewards, other than wage, induce volunteers to work without pay? Volunteering is considered a donation of time, and the supply of volunteers' services is explained in the general framework of consumer equilibrium. Reviewing this literature, Schiff and Weisbrod (1993) distinguish four models of volunteer labour supply: demand for charitable output (the "collective goods model"), looking for a return (the "private goods model"), looking for information and influence (the "influence and search model"), and acquiring skills (the "job skills model"). As pointed out by Govekar and Govekar (2002), the last two categories provide further specification of the "private good model".

In most of these models, individuals maximize utility depending on private goods, leisure, and voluntary work; on balance, the marginal utility they get from volunteering is equal to the utility derived from wages or leisure. Models of time allocation are also employed to determine if donations of time and money are complements or substitutes, and whether or not public funding crowds out volunteering.

In other variants of the same ideas, the utility deriving from volunteering is explained indirectly by taking into consideration the goals that the volunteers try to attain. Two types of goals have been identified, "investment" and "consumption". According to the consumption model, time-giving is a normal utility-bearing good, whereas in the investment model, volunteers try to improve their earning opportunities (Menchik and Weisbrod 1987). Both models appear to receive empirical support, and money and time donations appear to be complements. Volunteers tend to be better educated and have higher wages, but the higher the wage the fewer the hours of voluntary work offered. The results are rather mixed as far as the relation between wage and government expenditure is concerned; crowding out seems to exist, but only in some kinds of services (Menchik and Weisbrod 1987; Day and Devlin 1996; Freeman 1997). More recently, Gomez and Gunderson (2003) explain volunteer labour supply in the framework of the household production function, where households produce a charitable activity out of monetary contributions and volunteer time. Obtained from Canadian data, these empirical results indicate that volunteering is positively correlated with income, but higher wages have no significant impact on volunteering, and people of higher status are less likely to volunteer. Moreover, this study underlines the positive correlation of volunteering with religious activity and "the social nature of many family activities" (Gomez and Gunderson 2003, p. 585).

5.4 The Dataset

The data on which this research is based were gathered in a survey carried out in 1998 on social service organizations in Italy, the FIVOL–FEO survey (see, for more details, Borzaga 2000; Depedri 2003). Empirical information was collected on the types and characteristics of the organizations supplying various social services and their workforce. The research focused on the satisfaction of the people working within these organizations, along with their personal features, working conditions and motivation.

The types of services within each province, as well as the provinces themselves, were chosen in an attempt to select a sufficiently representative sample of the organizations' universe. For each type of service, the universe of production units operating in each province was counted, and the chosen organizations were selected from among those providing continuous service provision, that had been established for at least 4 years, and that employed at least three workers. In addition, the sample was drawn ensuring an adequate representation of each type of organization, i.e. public, private for-profit, religious nonprofit, and non-religious nonprofit.

Within each organization, if the number of staff exceeded 20 units, a sample of 10 paid workers and 10 volunteers was selected; otherwise, they were all included in the sample. In the former case, quotas were formed considering profession, tasks, gender and, as far as volunteers were concerned, the continuous or occasional character of their activity.

The research involved 228 organizations operating in 15 northern and southern Italian provinces. Of these organizations, 157 were nonprofit organizations, 54 were public agencies and 17 were for-profit companies. The services provided by them, in the order of importance emerging from the sample, were the following: care and guardianship to elderly people, educational and recreational services, nursing and rehabilitation, job-search assistance for disadvantaged people.

Different questionnaires were distributed to volunteers, paid workers and managers, as well as a questionnaire for each organization. All the questionnaires were self-completed, whenever possible, at the place of work, and in the presence of a trained interviewer. A total of 730 interviews conducted on volunteers and 2,066 on paid labourers were collected and analyzed.

5.5 The Features of Volunteers and Paid Workers

Volunteers were present in 65.5% of the organizations included in the research. On average, 74.5% of those interviewed volunteered on a regular basis. 78.4% of volunteers worked in nonprofit organizations; the rest worked in the public sector. Paid workers in nonprofit organizations accounted for less than two thirds of the total and, like the volunteers, were mainly working in non-religious organizations. Although the average age was around 40, young (under 30), followed by older people (over 50) formed the two largest groups. On average, paid workers were only slightly younger (the average age was 37), while the presence of young people (under 25) and of people about to retire was limited. Women were in a slight majority among paid workers. More often than paid workers, volunteers were single and with a high level of education. More than 58% of the interviewees declared they belonged to categories outside the labour force, and only 30% said that they were employed. In northern and central Italy students, retired and employed people, mainly among white-collar professions, prevailed, while in the south the percentage of unemployed people was higher.

The interviewees said they carried out their activities on average for 10h per week on a regular basis, half of which were in direct contact with the people they assisted. In some organizations they held managerial positions, and many of the managers interviewed had previously been volunteers.

Their service is highly valued by managers, above all because they help to lower costs, improve the quality of services, and better understand the needs of consumers. The other workers and the volunteers themselves hold the same opinions. In particular, the activity they are engaged in leads to an increase in the overall motivation of workers, and the cost reduction brought about by their presence makes it possible to introduce new services and to innovate.

The interviews conducted with organizations allow for further investigation into some peculiarities of volunteer work. It should be noted that the total number of hours reported by the organizations is noticeably inferior to what volunteers themselves reported. On average the volunteers donated 15h of work per month, except in the public sector where they worked on average almost twice as much, i.e. 24h. It is interesting to note that even paid workers donate work without pay in the form of hours of overtime that were not remunerated. This practice is most frequent among nonprofit religious organizations (31.7% of workers) and in social cooperatives (19.3% of workers). These two organizational types also those make the greatest use of overtime work. On average almost 2h per week in the first case, and little more than an hour and a half for the second.

5.6 Comparing Volunteers' and Paid Workers' Motivations, Attitudes and Satisfaction

Among the set of questions posed to the volunteers and paid workers, the responses concerning their attitudes towards work and the qualitative aspects of their activity are particularly interesting for the study of the determinants of satisfaction. The expectations that both types of workers have towards their activity, and above all their values and desires, are essential in determining the satisfaction they obtain from it, and will be described in this section.

A well-known result of Thompson and Bono (1992), starting from a Marxist perspective on paid labour as "alienation, self-estrangement, result[ing] from individuals engaging in activities for extrinsic rather than intrinsic rewards" (Thompson and Bono 1992, p. 121), is that volunteer firefighters were motivated by the need to struggle against alienated social relations. We found instead that both intrinsic and extrinsic aspects are important in attitudes towards work, without substantial differences between volunteer and paid workers (see Table 5.1). Among volunteers, intrinsic motivations towards work, and above all the desire for self-fulfilment (mean value of 5.53 points, on a scale from 1, not important to 7, very important), achieved the higher consensus. Extrinsic motivations immediately followed in order of importance, especially those related to primary socio-economic needs (work was felt as a means to sustain oneself and his or her family). The relational goal received a considerable score (4.87). For paid workers the extrinsic motivations obviously have the greatest importance, since work is firstly regarded as "a means to earning a living" and "a duty". The intrinsic and relational motivations follow thereafter.

Table 5.1 Attitudes towards work

(1: do not agree – 7: Agree)

	Volunteers			Paid workers		
	Rank	Mean	Variance	Rank	Mean	Variance
Work is self-fulfilment	1	5.53	2.97	3	5.57	2.90
Work is a means to earning a living	2	5.27	3.71	1	5.71	2.77
Work is a way to give financial help to the family	3	5.16	3.78	4	5.38	3.61
Work is a duty	4	5.18	3.51	2	5.64	2.83
Work is an occasion for external relations	5	4.87	2.68	5	4.85	3.38
Work is a contribution to improving society	6	4.79	3.45	6	4.34	4.08
Work is a way to be successful and renowned	7	2.76	3.78	8	2.65	3.70
Work is a means to earning as much as possible	8	2.69	3.31	7	2.97	4.23
Work is a pastime	9	2.27	2.72	9	2.13	2.83

Another similarity between volunteers and paid workers was found in the reasons why they have chosen the organization (see Table 5.2). For the volunteers, the reasons are as follows in decreasing order of importance: (1) agreement with the way of interacting with users (5.43 points, again on a scale from 1, not important, to 7, very important); (2) the sector in which the organization operates (5.33); (3) the capacity of the organization to meet the needs of the volunteer (4.59). Paid workers also value the coherence between their studies and their job, but otherwise their motivations are about the same.

The level and aspects of satisfaction that volunteers and paid workers get from their activity are compared in Table 5.3. Volunteers generally felt more than satisfied with the activity they performed (5.66), above all for the following factors: relations with other volunteers (6.15), with managers (5.72), and with their paid colleagues (5.49); coherence with their own ideals (6.13); usefulness of their contribution to users (5.50); recognition for the activity carried out (5.25). As for paid workers, however, the primary sources of satisfaction arise from their relations with colleagues and the recognition of their role towards recipients.

Table 5.2 Motivations for choosing the organization

(1: not important – 7: very important)

	Volunteers			Paid workers		
	Rank	Mean	Variance	Rank	Mean	Variance
The worker/volunteer approves the organization behaviour towards recipients	1	5.43	3.63	4	4.41	5.11
Interest in the organization's activity	2	5.33	3.68	1	5.39	4.04
Organization capacity to meet the workers'/volunteers' needs	3	4.59	4.59	2	4.52	4.93
Knowledge of people involved in the organization	4	4.36	5.13	8	3.22	5.22
Paid workers and volunteers are deeply involved in internal decisions	5	4.16	4.67	7	3.54	4.72
Knowledge of organization's recipients	6	2.85	4.44	10	2.23	3.44
This organization was almost the only one which offered me a job (paid workers)/the opportunity to volunteer (volunteers)	7	2.65	4.39	6	3.60	5.88
Wage and career (paid workers)/ enrolment (volunteers) opportunity	8	1.69	2.10	9	2.33	3.18
Coherence between the job and educational attainment (paid workers only)[a]	–	–	–	3	4.50	5.53
Job security (paid workers only)[a]	–	–	–	5	4.20	5.63

[a]Question addressed to paid workers only

Table 5.3 Aspects of satisfaction

	Volunteers			Paid workers		
(1: dissatisfied – 7: very satisfied)	Rank	Mean	Variance	Rank	Mean	Variance
Coherence between his/her activity and ideals (volunteers only)[b]	1	6.13	1.23	–	–	–
Relation with volunteer colleagues (volunteers only)[b]	2	6.15	1.28	–	–	–
Relation with the managers	3	5.72	2.09	4	5.17	2.96
Job satisfaction	4	5.66	1.31	3	5.27	2.03
Recognition of the help given to the recipients	5	5.50	1.76	2	5.31	2.22
Relation with paid workers' colleagues	6	5.49	2.44	1	5.51	2.14
Activity recognition.	7	5.25	2.31	8	4.54	3.13
Physical working environment	8	5.00	2.51	10	4.48	3.44
Activity's variety and creativity	9	4.88	2.18	7	4.63	3.15
Professional enrichment	10	4.85	2.37	9	4.50	3.31
Decisional autonomy	11	4.66	2.85	11	4.36	3.27
Chances of future career advancement (paid workers)/enrolment (volunteers)	12	2.91	3.34	14	2.93	3.40
Work time (paid workers only)[a]	–	–	–	5	4.81	3.06
Job security (paid workers only)[a]	–	–	–	6	4.70	3.69
Wage (paid workers only)[a]	–	–	–	12	4.07	3.31
Career advancement (paid orkers only)[a]	–	–	–	13	3.10	3.74

[a] Question addressed to paid workers only
[b] Question addressed to volunteers only

The satisfaction of volunteers is generally higher than that of paid workers, both in general and for each single item. Volunteers are not satisfied as regards the prospect of being hired by the organization (2.91). Similarly, paid workers are not satisfied with their own career opportunities (2.93). It could, in fact, be concluded that rather than being dissatisfied, volunteers are simply not interested in the prospect of being recruited, whereas paid workers are not interested in career advancement, as is evident from the answers to the above-mentioned questions on motivation.

The satisfaction of volunteers does not seem to differ according to the type of organization. Loyalty towards volunteering and the organization is very high, albeit slightly lower among nonprofit religious groups.

We now turn our attention to some questions only addressed to volunteers (whose answers are not reported in tables). Volunteers were also asked about their attitudes to volunteering in addition to those towards work. Above all, they consider volunteering an enriching experience on a human level (6.58), an opportunity for helping others (6.45), an occasion for establishing new and deeper human relationships (5.89), a chance to act coherently with one's own values (5.88), and a moral duty (4.64), while it is not considered a way to improve one's work skills (2.26), nor a way to fill free time (2.63).

As far as the role of volunteers within the organizations is concerned, it appears that they believe that the development of volunteering is something positive (6.56);

they consider their own activity important for temporarily filling a lack of resources in the organization (5.3); they perceive their activity as support to workers (5.12); a good means for networking between users and the local community (5); a source of innovation in the provision of services (4.84).

According to the interviewees, the working environment in which they operated was characterized fundamentally by good communication of the tasks to be carried out (5.5); good capacity to offer opportunities to better oneself and to recognize one's merits (5.1); a good degree of openness towards new ideas and suggestions from volunteers (5); a fair capacity to offer opportunities for professional growth (4.57); a reduced level of stress (2.5).

Notwithstanding a general satisfaction with the capacity of the working environment to recognize one's own merits, on average the interviewees would have worked harder if only they had received more recognition for the work done (3.21 was the average score).

For the volunteers, it is of primary importance that users get the maximum benefit from the services provided (6.52), are directly involved in their work (5.46), and in the activity of the organization (4.55). They do not maintain, however, that the needs of users should be cared for to the detriment of their own needs and rights (1.86), nor do they consider the users merely customers requesting a certain service (1.79).

The volunteers agreed on the following features of the relations they maintained with paid workers: full respect and acceptance (5.7); recognition of the work done by volunteers as a support activity for workers (5.54); easing of relations between the two categories (5.35); parity of treatment within the organization (4.92); complementariness of the tasks of volunteers and the workers (4.8).

The volunteers felt that their work was done fundamentally in the interest of users (6.45), of the local community (5.27), of society at large (5.1), and also in that of other volunteers (4).

All the scores related to volunteers' involvement in various aspects of control are lower than 5. Among these, the highest score is given to the quality of relations with users (4.87), followed by quality control of services (4.87), and that of relations among people in the organization (4.28).

5.7 Ordered Logit Analysis: The Determinants of Volunteers' and Paid Workers' Satisfaction

We now proceed to an econometric analysis of the determinants of job satisfaction for volunteers and paid workers. This has been done by estimating some "ordered logit" models, taking the overall reported satisfaction of paid workers and volunteers as a dependent variable.

The choice of this technique was determined by the nature of the dependent variable, which is a discrete variable of seven categories (expressing an increasing degree of satisfaction: from 1 – not satisfied, to 7 – fully satisfied).

According to the ordered logit model:

$$y_{ij} = \begin{cases} 1 \; \textit{if respondent i declares satisfaction j} \\ 0 \; \textit{otherwise} \end{cases} \tag{5.1}$$

where i=1,….N, j=1, … 7.
It is then assumed that there is a latent variable y^*, which can be modelled as: $y^* = b'x + \theta \sim$ Logistic ($\theta = 1$), that is, y* can be explained by the k independent variables contained in x, and the logistic distribution with mean 0 has the following probability density function:

$$f(x) = \frac{1}{\theta} \frac{\exp(x/\theta)}{[1+\exp(x/\theta)]^2} \tag{5.2}$$

The parameters of the model are then estimated using a maximum likelihood technique.

The same model was applied to volunteers and paid workers separately using the hypothesis of independence between the two equations.[1] The estimates of a satisfaction equation can suffer from endogeneity bias, since some unknown variable can jointly determine, for example, the job choice and the on-the-job satisfaction. We think that on the whole this problem is attenuated in our case, since many variables have been included in both the satisfaction equations. We therefore assume that the correlation between the errors of each satisfaction equation, and another hypothetical equation explaining the choice of working in a social service organization with or without pay, is low. In interpreting the estimates, we have to remember that since volunteers and paid workers self-select themselves, the two samples are not randomly chosen. So it would be incorrect to say that *per se* volunteering is a more satisfying activity than paid work, since we do not know the level of satisfaction of volunteers if instead they were paid workers, and vice-versa. If the previous assumption is correct, however, it is possible to find whether or not the same variables have a roughly similar effect on the satisfaction of the volunteers and paid workers. If this is not the case, our results clearly cannot hold. It must be remembered, nonetheless, that most empirical literature on job satisfaction based on detailed information about workers and firm characteristics makes the same assumption implicitly (see for instance Depedri 2003; Tortia 2007 and Chap. 6 in this book) or explicitly (Bauer 2004; Origo and Pagani 2006).

In Tables 5.4 and 5.5, the results of two models are presented. Together with a set of other common control variables, attitudes to work in the first model, and reasons

[1]The same set of independent variables were used for both volunteers and paid workers, with the following exceptions: a) wage in the volunteer equation; b) motivations for choosing the organization included only in the volunteers' or paid workers' questionnaires; c) volunteers' civil status due to the high number of missing cases affecting the variable.

Table 5.4 Ordered logit: impact of attitudes towards work on job satisfaction

Dependent variable: Job satisfaction (1: dissatisfied – 7: very satisfied)

	Volunteers[a]		Paid workers[b]	
Female	0.1177	–	–0.1051	–
Age	0.1819	**	–0.6385	***
Age squared	–	–	0.8569	***
Marital status				
Single	–	–	0.1277	–
Separated/divorced	–	–	–0.2466	**
Widow	–	–	0.3210	*
Married (base-line)	–	–	–	–
Educational attainment				
Vocational qualification	0.6522	–	–0.1137	–
High school	0.2488	–	–0.1186	–
Three-year degree	–0.2178	–	–0.2311	*
Four/five year degree	–	–	–0.3392	**
No qualification or primary school (base-line)	–	–	–	–
Previous (paid workers)/current (volunteers') condition				
Employed	0.2996	*	0.9339	–
Student	–0.4193	–	–0.9189	–
Housewife	–0.4684	–	0.6100	–
Compulsory military service	0.5689	–	–	–
Unemployed, retired (base-line)	–	–	–	–
Wage and work time				
Log wage	–	–	0.3452	**
Log wage squared	–	–	–0.1239	
Full time worker (paid worker) regular volunteer (volunteers)	–0.2794	**	–0.2196	–
Type of activity				
Manager	0.4069	–	0.3558	***
Provision of the service (in direct contact with recipients)	0.3096	**	0.2553	–
Support activity (not in direct contact with recipients)	0.4729	***	–0.2717	–
Other	0.6443	***	–0.1034	–
Administration/Accountancy (base-line: paid workers only)	0.1884	–	–	–
Personnel development and management (base-line: paid workers only)	0.6119	–	–	–
Attitudes towards work				
Work is self-fulfilment.	0.9462	***	0.1612	***
Work is an occasion for external relations.	–0.7053	**	0.5891	***
Work is a contribution to improve society.	0.1246	***	0.4224	***
Work is a means to earning a living	0.2724	–	–0.5799	***

[a]N: 466; Log likelihood function: –659.9784; Restricted log likelihood function –684.3783; Chi-squared: 48.79990; Degrees of freedom 26; Significance level: 0.0043
[b]N: 1,560; Log likelihood function: –2471.696; Restricted log likelihood function: –2596.584; Chi-squared: 274.0195; Degrees of freedom: 31; Significance level: 0.0000
The symbols ***, **, * denote significance at the 1, 5 and 10% levels respectively

for choosing the organization in the second model have been used as explanatory variables. We have chosen to estimate two different equations on the assumption that the two sets of variables have a separate effect on satisfaction. This makes the interpretation and comparison of the estimates easier. For each equation we present the

Table 5.5 Ordered logit: impact of motivations for choosing the organization on job satisfaction

Dependent variable: Job satisfaction (1: dissatisfied – 7: very satisfied)				
	Volunteers[a]		Paid workers[b]	
Female	0.1316	–	–0.2670	–
Age	0.1874	***	–0.3960	***
Age squared	–	–	0.5786	***
Marital status				
Single	–	–	–0.1940	–
Separated/divorced	–	–	–0.2543	**
Widow	–	–	0.5182	**
Married (base-line)	–	–	–	–
Educational Attainment				
Vocational Qualification	0.1054	–	–0.1137	***
High school	0.4894	*	–0.1186	***
Three-year degree	–0.9392	–	–0.2311	**
Four/five year degree	–	–	–0.3392	***
No qualification or primary school (base-line)	–	–	–	–
Previous (paid workers)/current (volunteers') condition				
Employed	0.2419	–	0.1574	–
Student	–0.5112	*	–0.9908	–
Housewife	–0.3944	–	0.4394	–
Compulsory military service	0.4005	–	–	–
Unemployed, retired (base-line)	–	–	–	–
Wage and work time				
Log wage	–	–	0.4275	***
Log wage squared	–	–	–0.1909	**
Full time worker (paid worker) regular volunteer (volunteers)	–0.2435	*	–0.1838	–
Type of activity				
Manager	0.1364	–	0.2572	***
Provision of the service (in direct contact with recipients)	0.3843	***	–0.9980	–
Support activity (not in direct contact with recipients)	0.4311	***	–0.2489	**
Other	0.5149	***	–0.2049	*
Administration/Accountancy (base-line: paid workers only)	0.1083	–	–	–
Personnel development and management (base-line: paid workers only)	0.5072	–	–	–
Motivations for choosing the organization				
Interest in the organization's activity	0.1081	***	0.1130	***
Knowledge of people involved in the organization	–0.3916	–	0.1818	–
Personal knowledge of organization recipients	0.2591	–	–0.4219	**
The worker/volunteer approves the organization's behaviour towards recipients	0.7066	**	0.7121	***
Coherence between the job and his/her educational attainment (paid workers only)	–	–	0.5518	***
Organization capacity to meet the workers'/volunteers' needs	0.2767	–	0.3772	–
This organization was almost the only one which offered me a job (paid workers only)/the opportunity to volunteer (volunteers)	–0.9876	–	–0.1182	–
Wage and career (paid workers)/enrolment (volunteers) opportunity	–0.6868	**	0.2649	–

(continued)

Table 5.5 (continued)

Dependent variable: Job satisfaction (1: dissatisfied – 7: very satisfied)				
	Volunteers[a]		Paid workers[b]	
Job security (paid workers only)	–	–	−0.1326	–
Paid workers and volunteers are deeply involved in internal decisions	0.4621	*	0.9368	***
Type of organization				
Public organization	–	–	−0.1517	–
Nonprofit non-religious organization	0.1052	–	−0.9921	–
Nonprofit religious organization	0.6209	–	0.7497	–
For-profit organization (base-line)	–	–	–	–

[a]N: 466; Log likelihood function: −653.1463; Restricted log likelihood function: −684.3783; Chi-squared: 62.46412; Degrees of freedom: 25; Significance level: 0.0000
[b]N: 1,500; Log likelihood function: −2286.758; Restricted log likelihood function: −2475.780; Chi-squared: 378.0435; Degrees of freedom: 33; Significance level: 0.0000
The symbols ***, **, * denote significance at the 1, 5 and 10% levels respectively

odds ratios for all explanatory variables. The symbols ***, **, * denote significance at the 1, 5 and 10% levels respectively.

As for individual features, age has a negative effect on the satisfaction of paid workers, but a positive one on the satisfaction of volunteers. More educated paid workers are less satisfied. However, educational level does not have a significant effect on the satisfaction of volunteers.

Remuneration (only up to a given threshold) has a positive influence on paid workers' satisfaction, and work time has a negative influence on volunteers' satisfaction. The type of organization has no influence, either on paid workers' or volunteers' satisfaction.

As for the kind of activity performed, whilst being a manager has a positive effect on the satisfaction of paid workers, being engaged in support activities, but without any contact with users has a negative effect. The most satisfied volunteers are, on the other hand, those working in contact with users and those engaged in support activities.

Results are rather mixed where the attitudes towards work and the motivations in choosing the organization are concerned. Believing that work is self-fulfilment and that it contributes to improving society enhances the satisfaction of both, while believing that work is an occasion for external relations has a positive influence on workers' satisfaction, but a negative influence on that of volunteers. Moreover, thinking that work is a means to earning a living has a negative impact on paid workers' satisfaction, and is not significant for volunteers' satisfaction.

Having chosen the organization they work for on the basis of their interest in a particular sector has a positive influence on the satisfaction of both paid and volunteer workers. Paid workers, whose choice was influenced by the fact that they knew a customer of the organization, have a higher chance of being disappointed, but the same is not true for volunteers. The expectation of being hired by the organization seems to have a strong negative influence on volunteers' satisfaction.

5.8 Concluding Remarks

The economic literature has broadly explored the field of volunteer labour supply, while less attention has been devoted to the subject of the present article, namely the analysis of volunteer satisfaction. As far as we know, this is the first attempt to compare volunteers with paid workers from the point of view of the degrees and determinants of the satisfaction that both obtain from their activity.

The empirical analysis has shown that volunteers and paid workers have different levels of satisfaction and display both differences and similarities as far as the determinants of satisfaction are concerned. The hypothesis that the determinants of satisfaction in volunteers and paid workers are similar is neither completely rejected, nor confirmed. In addition, to understand if there is a distinct behavioural pattern in the supply of labour between volunteers and paid workers, research specially devoted to this aim is needed.

Volunteers seem not only to give considerable importance to users' needs, an attitude which they share with paid workers, but seem to be particularly satisfied if they personally donate their service, while the same is not true for paid workers.

The most frequent motivations indicated by paid workers and volunteers are their interest in the organization's sector of activity, and their approval of the work modalities in favour of users.

Thus, from our findings, volunteers can be described as individuals who perform an activity which gives them satisfaction, for a number of different reasons. Some determinants are the same for both volunteers and paid workers, others are not, but what both especially appreciate is mainly connected to their interest in the users' well-being. Hence, some results of previous research (Borzaga et al. 1995), which had hypothesized that volunteers have a special taste for working with the disabled or needy people can also be extended to paid workers.

Acknowledgments We thank the participants to the 2006 AIEL Conference in Udine, and Marco Musella, Sergio Destefanis, Enrico Rettore, Guido Masarotto for their comments. The usual disclaimer applies.

References

Bauer T (2004) High performance workplace practices and job satisfaction: evidence from Europe. RWI Mitteilungen 54/55:57–85

Borzaga C (ed) (2000) Capitale umano e qualità del lavoro nei servizi sociali. Fondazione Italiana del Volontariato, Rome

Borzaga C, Musella M (2003) (eds) Produttività ed efficienza nelle organizzazioni nonprofit. Edizioni31, Trento

Borzaga C, Gui B, Schenkel M (1995) Disoccupazione e bisogni insoddisfatti: il ruolo delle organizzazioni non-profit. Quaderni di Economia del lavoro 50:100–129

Clark AE (1997) Job satisfaction and gender: why are women so happy at work? Labour Economics 4:341–372

Cnaan RA, Amrofell L (1994) Mapping volunteer activity. Nonprofit and Voluntary Sector Quarterly 23:335–351

Day KM, Devlin RA (1996) Volunteering and crowding out: Canadian econometric evidence. Canadian Journal of Economics 39:37–53

Depedri S (2003) Le determinanti della soddisfazione dei lavoratori: un'analisi per tipologie organizzative. In: Borzaga C, Musella M (eds) Produttività ed efficienza nelle organizzazioni nonprofit. Edizioni31, Trento

Freeman R (1997) Working for nothing: the supply of volunteer labor. Journal of Labor Economics 15:S140–S166

Gomez R, Gunderson M (2003) Volunteer activity and the demands of work and family. Relations Industrielles/Industrial Relations 58:573–589

Govekar PL, Govekar MA (2002) Using economic theory and research to better understand volunteer behavior. Nonprofit Management and Leadership 13:33–48

Gui B (ed) (2000) Special Issue on "Economics and interpersonal relations". Annals of Public and Cooperative Economics 71(2)

Lane RE (1992) Work as 'disutility' and money as 'happiness': cultural origins of a basic market error. Journal of Socio-Economics 21:43–65

Lévy-Garboua L, Montmarquette C (2004) Reported job satisfaction: what does it mean? Journal of Socio-Economics 33:135–151

Liao-Troth M (2001) Attitude differences between paid workers and volunteers. Nonprofit Management and Leadership 11:423–442

Lydon R, Chevalier A (2002) Estimates of the effect of wages on job satisfaction. CEP Discussion Paper 531

Menchik P, Weisbrod BA (1987) Volunteer labor supply. Journal of Public Economics 32:159–183

Mosca M, Musella M (2003) Le relazioni tra salari, *fairness* ed *effort* nelle organizzazioni nonprofit. In: Borzaga C, Musella M (2003) (eds) Produttività ed efficienza nelle organizzazioni nonprofit. Edizioni31, Trento

Origo F, Pagani L (2006) Is work flexibility a stairway to heaven? The story told by job satisfaction in Europe. University of Milano Bicocca Department of Economics Working Paper 97

Schiff J, Weisbrod B (1993) Competition between for-profit and non-profit organizations. In: Ben-Ner A, Gui B (eds) The non-profit sector in the mixed economy. University of Michigan Press, Ann Arbor

Steinberg R (1990) Labor economics and the nonprofit sector. A literature review. Nonprofit and Voluntary Sector Quarterly 19:2–19

Thompson AM III, Bono BA (1992) Alienation, self-actualization and the motivation for volunteer labor. Review of Radical Political Economics 24:115–123

Tortia E (2007) Worker well-being and perceived fairness: survey-based findings from Italy. Journal of Socio-Economics 37:2080–2094

Tschirhart M, Mesch D, Perry JL, Miller T, Lee G (2001) Stipended volunteers: their goals, experiences, satisfaction and likelihood of future service. Nonprofit and Voluntary Sector Quarterly 31:422–443

Woolley F (2003) Social cohesion and voluntary activity: making connections. In: Osberg L (ed) The Economic Implications of Social Cohesion. University of Toronto Press, Toronto

Chapter 6
Perceived Fairness and Worker Well-Being in Public, For-Profit and Nonprofit Firms: Evidence from the Italian Social Service Sector

Ermanno Tortia

Abstract This essay analyzes the links between workers' fairness concerns and job satisfaction in different ownership and organizational forms of the Italian social service sector. Social cooperatives emerge as the organizational form that best sustains the perception of procedural fairness. On the other hand, the public sector shows the most serious weaknesses. A clear difference emerges between the public and the private sector in general, with the former at a disadvantage. Given the very significant role of procedural fairness in influencing job satisfaction, social cooperatives turn out as an innovative and successful organizational form, at least as far as labour relations are concerned, the difficulties in retaining their more educated and skilled workforce notwithstanding.

6.1 Introduction

The Italian social service sector presents an interesting case of institutional and organizational plurality since it encompasses markedly different ownership and organizational forms. The sector is dominated by nonprofit organizations which, as a whole, represent about 70% of the total number of organizations.[1]

[1]Data are taken from the FIVOL-FEO survey. The 2001 ISTAT Italian Census on Industry and Services recorded 1,401,481 workers employed in the health care and social service sector at the national level. Since a census of social services alone did not exist in Italy at the time the research was performed (1998), one was carried out directly on the basis of administrative sources in the ex-ante selected 15 provinces (out of a total of 107), which were representative of the different social and economic conditions of the country. Two different services were selected for each province and organizations were drawn at random from the census. The sampling procedure seems sound, since the social service sector alone can be estimated to employ about 500,000 workers nationally. Also the distribution of ownership forms in the FIVOL–FEO sample fairly well reflected the national distribution, even though for-profits were over-represented in order to allow meaningful comparisons.

E. Tortia
Department of Economics, University of Trento and European Institute for Cooperative and Social Enterprise, Via Inama 5, 38100 Trento, Italy

S. Destefanis and M. Musella (eds.), *Paid and Unpaid Labour in the Social Economy*, AIEL Series in Labour Economics, DOI: 10.1007/978-3-7908-2137-6_7,

Also with regard to nonprofits, variety is the dominant feature since they are sorted into social cooperatives and traditional nonprofits (associations and foundations), which are partly religious and partly non-religious. Introduced in Italy in 1991 (Law 381/1991), social cooperatives are still a young and growing organizational form and represent an interesting case of institutional hybridization since they pertain to the law on cooperative enterprises but retain many of the features of nonprofit organizations, such as non-distributable and mission-devoted assets with an explicit social aim. They are also allowed to operate as multi-stakeholder organizations controlled by representatives of different patrons, such as volunteers, workers, and customers.

The public sector provides an important, but not dominant, share of social services, while for-profit firms are mainly concentrated in activities requiring relatively high capital intensity (like residential homes). Such an institutional variability is not so common in contemporary market economies since most sectors are dominated either by for-profit firms or by publicly-owned organizations. Various theories have been set forth concerning the reasons why social and welfare services are observed in many countries to embrace a significant share of nonprofit organizations (Weisbrod 1977, 1988; Hansmann 1996; Borzaga 2003). Even nowadays market imperfections in the form of internal and external agency problems continue to provide the basis for an explanation to this evidence. However, a growing number of articles is no longer satisfied with this traditional neo-institutionalist explanation and endeavours to introduce new arguments in a more evolutionary and developmental fashion. More democratic, socially oriented and inclusive organizational forms, often embedded at the local level, would be better suited to engender a high degree of procedural fairness because of the different objectives, financial structure, and less costly incentive mix used to motivate workers (Borzaga and Tortia 2007a, b, 2008). The objectives are no longer defined in terms of maximizing the expected financial value of the organization, but rather in terms of satisfying specific needs that can be private, but also social, and correspond to the production of community interest goods and services. Finally, the incentive mix used to motivate workers takes into account not only self-interested motivation of an economic and monetary type, but also relational, process-related and other relevant motivations (Borzaga and Mittone 1997; Ben-Ner and Putterman 1999; Bacchiega and Borzaga 2001, 2003). This specific organizational setting would, in turn, be particularly suitable to produce services requiring a high content of trust and good relations between users and firms. In this research stream, institutional evolution is a key issue in explaining the ability of different organizational forms to adapt to the surrounding economic environment. New institutional tools, such as mission-oriented multi-stakeholdership correspond to the satisfaction of specific needs.

This study concentrates on the comparative analysis of the determinants of worker well-being, which is indexed by job-satisfaction and loyalty to the organization. Special attention will be given to the role of workers' fairness perceptions in distributive and procedural terms as determinants of well-being. Our analysis may be considered the continuation of a previous work (Tortia 2007) dealing with the overall impact of fairness on worker well-being as compared with wage and effort. The comparative analysis is explored in greater depth by introducing descriptive statistics for all the five organizational forms existing in the sector, and by running separate regressions for each organizational form in order to highlight the different composition and weight of the determinants of well-being in different institutional contexts. Furthermore, job satisfaction, described in terms of satisfaction with fourteen different aspects of the job, is sorted into two components, representing the "material" and the "non-material" aspects. Separate regressions will be run for the two components in order to highlight how they are influenced by different features of workers and of the work environment. It will be seen that fairness, mainly of a procedural kind, represents a transversal determinant of well-being, impacting heavily on all the components of satisfaction as well as on loyalty. In this regard, it can be said that the fairness of procedures emerges as an intrinsic workers' need to seek fulfilment in organizations, whatever the ownership and the organizational form. However, different forms clearly appear to sustain markedly different degrees of fairness. Social cooperatives are best able to guarantee a high degree of procedural fairness, while many critical aspects emerge in the public sector. By guaranteeing better relations on the job and fairer procedures, nonprofits in general are able to offset other weaknesses that have to do mainly with weaker monetary and material incentives.

This paper is organized as follows: Sect. 6.2 presents the descriptive analysis of the variables involved focussing predominantly on the comparison between different perceptions of distributive and procedural fairness in the five organizational forms. Section 6.3 introduces the econometric analysis where the factors influencing overall material and non-material job-satisfaction, together with loyalty to the organization, will be introduced and studied. Section 6.4 discusses the main results and conclusions.

6.2 The Descriptive Analysis of Procedural and Distributive Fairness

The statistics displayed in this section are reduced to the essential since a more in-depth descriptive analysis of the same variables can already be found in Borzaga and Depedri (2005), Borzaga and Tortia (2006), and Tortia (2007). These articles also present a detailed description of the characteristics of the workforce which will not be repeated here. Hence, only the average indexes of satisfaction, loyalty and fairness, as they are used in the econometric analysis, are displayed.

The number of organizations and workers included in the FIVOL–FEO survey (for more details on this survey, see Borzaga 2000; Depedri 2003) is shown in Table 6.1. Nonprofits as a whole represent about 70% of the organizations and 60% of workers. Among nonprofits, social cooperatives are the most distinct typology, representing almost one third of the whole sample of organizations and almost 30% of workers. The public sector represents about one fourth of the nonprofits sector in terms of number of organizations and almost 30% of the workforce. For-profit firms make up 10% of the workforce.

Job satisfaction is measured using different indexes (Table 6.2). The first indicator is synthetic and corresponds to the single item in the question on job satisfaction

Table 6.1 Organizational types and their workers

	Organizations		Workers	
	N	%	N	%
Public ownership	54	23.7	616	29.8
For-profit	17	7.5	204	9.9
Social cooperatives	74	32.5	588	28,5
Other non-religious nonprofits	51	22.4	440	21.3
Religious nonprofits	32	14.0	218	10.5
Total	228	100	2,066	100

Table 6.2 Job satisfaction, loyalty and effort

	Social cooperatives	Other non-religious nonprofits	Religious nonprofits	Public ownership	For-profit firms	Total
Job satisfaction (general)[a]	5.38	5.25	5.25	4.99	5.38	5.27
Job satisfaction (average)[a]	4.66	4.50	4.86	4.19	4.50	4.50
Material satisfaction[a]	4.10	4.06	4.53	3.74	4.20	4.06
Non-material satisfaction[a]	5.09	4.84	5.10	4.53	4.71	4.84
Loyalty[b]	4.05	3.94	4.21	3.78	3.93	3.97
Effort[c]	1.44	1.06	1.98	1.31	0.74	1.32
Hourly wage	4.96	5.74	4.97	5.85	5.19	5.43

[a]Values ranking from 1 (minimum) to 7 (maximum)
[b]The values, ranking from 1 (minimum) to 5 (maximum), represent in ascending order: leave as soon as possible; looking for a job in a different sector; looking for a job in the same sector; stay at least for some years; stay as long as possible
[c]Effort (or stress) is measured as the difference between contractual work-hours and effective work-hours

which asked "What is your overall satisfaction with the job?" This is followed by the general average of all the fourteen specific items enclosed in the same question, subdivided into its material and non-material components. (Tortia 2007). Material satisfaction concerns the work environment, pay, working hours, job security, previous career advancement and future career advancement. Non-material satisfaction concerns professional development, recognition of one's contribution, decision-making autonomy, variety and creativity on the job, usefulness of the job for beneficiaries, relations with superiors, relations with colleagues, and relations with volunteers. This grouping was not done exclusively on an *ex ante* basis, but subsequent to the results of the categorical principal component analysis (CatPCA) performed on the items of satisfaction.[2]

[2]The relational items have been moved from one component to the other and considered part of non-material satisfaction even though the analysis grouped them in the material component. This ad hoc modification was suggested by the results of the econometric analysis which followed the CatPCA. The component coefficients are displayed in Table 6.4.

Nonprofit organizations in general satisfy workers best, though the difference with for-profit firms is negligible. The scores concerning nonprofits and for-profit firms are very similar when material satisfaction is considered, while nonprofits show an advantage in terms of non-material satisfaction. Conversely, the public sector shows a disadvantage on all the components of satisfaction and the gap with the average total value is greater for the non-material than for the material component.[3] This is true even though the public sector exhibits the highest wage level, while social cooperatives and religious nonprofits show a conspicuous disadvantage in terms of monetary incentives. Loyalty is represented by workers' willingness to stay with the organization. Workers were asked how long they predicted they would stay with their organizations and the five mutually exclusive options representing the increasing strength of the linkage between the worker and the organization were ranked from 1 to 5.[4] As is apparent in Table 6.2, workers in nonprofit organizations are more loyal than workers in the public sector and for-profit firms, although the data are not complete in terms of the level of turnover and the intentions of workers that had already left in the past. Effort is represented by the excess of effective work-hours in relation to contractual work-hours, which is an imperfect proxy for effort whose meaning is nearer to stress on-the-job than to effort itself, but it is the only one available in this dataset.[5]

When fairness is taken into consideration (Table 6.3), it is immediately apparent that nonprofit organizations in general show a significant advantage on almost all dimensions, which are sorted into distributive and procedural aspects. Distributive fairness refers exclusively to individual and non-relational dimensions, hence to the equity of the wage in relation to the level of job responsibility, training, experience, effort, stress and the organization's ability to pay. It is does not, therefore, refer to a comparison of wages with those of other workers and managers. Religious nonprofits score highest on almost all dimensions, the low level of wages notwithstanding, and this can testify to a better ability to accommodate and satisfy the distributive expectation of a workforce that shows a relatively low level of education.[6] It should also be noted, however, that workers in social cooperatives recognize more than all the others the equity of distribution when the organization's ability to pay is considered. The more inclusive organizational models allow workers to be aware of the financial limitations of their firm and this may be one

[3]The public sector obtains relatively high scores for some items in the material component, like professional growth and job security.

[4]The five mutually excluding options are "stay as long as possible", "stay at least for some years", "look for a job in the same sector", "look for a job in a different sector", "leave as soon as possible".

[5]The tension in the meaning of the proxy for effort is highlighted in the econometric analysis where it is clear that effort measured as excess work-hours has contrasting effects in different organizational forms.

[6]Religious nonprofits show the lowest percentage among all the five organizational forms in terms of workers that accomplished a university degree or a secondary school diploma (Borzaga and Tortia 2006).

Table 6.3 Distributive and procedural fairness (average scores)[a]

	Social cooperatives	Other non-religious nonprofits	Religious nonprofits	Public ownership	For-profit	Total
Distributive fairness						
Responsibility	4.0	4.2	4.6	3.6	3.9	4.0
Training	4.1	4.2	4.4	3.6	3.8	4.0
Experience	4.1	4.1	4.3	3.6	4.0	4.0
Effort	4.0	4.0	4.3	3.4	3.7	3.8
Quality of the work	4.0	4.0	4.5	3.5	3.8	3.9
Stress and tension	3.6	3.6	3.8	3.0	3.3	3.4
Economic resources of the organization	5.0	4.4	4.5	3.5	3.7	4.2
Average score	4.11	4.07	4.30	3.46	3.74	3.90
Procedural fairness						
Incentives to contribution balance	3.5	3.0	3.3	2.5	3.3	3.1
Communication	5.0	4.2	4.8	3.9	5.0	4.5
Being listened to	4.7	4.1	4.4	3.3	4.2	4.1
Professional growth and career	4.0	3.2	3.2	2.2	3.0	3.1
Growth of skills and capabilities	4.7	4.2	4.5	3.3	3.9	4.1
Transparency of promotions	3.6	3.0	3.2	2.1	3.0	3.0
Average score	4.25	3.62	3.90	2.88	3.73	3.65

[a]Values ranking from 1 (minimum) to 7 (maximum)

reason why they are willing to accept such a low wage level. Public organizations obtain the lowest scores on all dimensions, while for-profit firms remain in-between nonprofit and public ownership.

Procedural fairness is intended to express workers' judgements concerning some of the main organizational routines dealing with communication, being listened to, career advancement, development of skills and capabilities, and transparency of promotions. A first general result is that average scores are lower than in the case of distributive fairness and in the case of job satisfaction. This may indicate an increased difficulty for organizations to accomplish satisfactory results when procedures and not exclusively outcomes are considered (Benz and Stutzer 2003; Benz et al. 2004; Benz 2005). On the other hand, there is a clear need for proper institutional tools to manage the relation between workers and the organization, since some organizational forms perform better than others.

Social cooperatives are able to respect workers' rights and to fulfil their expectations as to how industrial relations should be properly managed and human resources dealt with. When this result is seen in the light of our econometric estimates which, as will be seen, show that procedural fairness is the most significant determinant of workers' well-being in terms of job satisfaction and willingness to stay with the organization, it becomes clear that social cooperatives represent a new and interesting system of industrial relations that is less centred around monetary incentives, and more around democratic management, inclusiveness, and fair procedures.

Beside social cooperatives, all the other organizational forms can be divided into private and public. Traditional nonprofit organizations (associations and foundations) and for-profit firms receive similar evaluations, while the public sector appears to undergo serious shortcomings, mainly as far as professional growth and career, transparency of promotions and the balance of incentives to contributions are concerned. Indeed, the transparency of promotions is the only item that receives an evaluation below the median score in all organizational forms and can be considered the most critical procedural aspect in the management of the firm. The strongly relational nature of this aspect of procedural fairness (i.e. the fairness of one's promotion is evaluated in relation to the fairness of the promotion of other workers) highlights the intrinsic difficulty to build up proper routines that do not violate workers' expectations. This is well-known to scholars of labour relations (Lazear 1995). However, the weak improvements observed when switching from one ownership form to the other indicate that institutional change and evolution does play a role in the growth of the acceptance of managerial decisions concerning career advancement (Table 6.4).

Table 6.4 Grouping the items of satisfaction (categorical principal components analysis)

	1	2	3
	Relational and extrinsic component	Intrinsic component	Economic component
Professional development		0.664	
Decision-making autonomy		0.712	
Recognition of one's contribution		0.688	
Variety and creativity of the job		0.713	
Working environment	0.568		
Social usefulness of the job		0.486	
Salary	0.485		0.494
Working hours	0.636		
Previous career advancements			0.842
Future career advancements			0.833
Job security	0.694		
Relations with superiors	0.639		
Relations with colleagues	0.647		

Rotation Method: Varimax with Kaiser Normalization. Rotation converged in 5 iterations

6.3 The Influence of Procedural and Distributive Fairness on Worker Well-Being

The econometric analysis can shed new light on the influence of workers' fairness concerns and other personal and organizational variables of on-the job well-being both in terms of satisfaction with the job and in terms of loyalty. While the same analysis concerning the whole sample of firms can be found in Tortia (2007), here are presented the comparative results concerning the five different organizational forms. Public organizations, non-religious nonprofits and social cooperatives are introduced explicitly, together with the total of traditional nonprofits.[7] The analysis is supposed to bring out statistical correlations more than causal relations since the study is carried out in a cross-section environment.

Starting with satisfaction, three sets of linear regressions were run taking as dependent variables average, material and non-material satisfaction, as shown in Tables 6.5–6.6. Average satisfaction in general is strongly influenced by fairness concerns mainly of a procedural kind (see Table 6.5). This is true in all organizational forms, and the same results will be found also in the case of material and non-material satisfaction, and of loyalty. In non-religious nonprofit organizations an increase from low to high (from 1 to 7) of procedural fairness corresponds on average to an increase of 2.75 points in satisfaction (which is also measured on the 1–7 Lickert scale), while the same measure is equal to 1.05 for distributive fairness. This variation equals about 60% of the average value of satisfaction, which is 4.5. While the direct comparison of the coefficients across organizational forms is problematic given the different dimension of the samples, it is possible to compare the impact of procedural vs. distributive fairness. The former shows a much stronger influence than the latter, since the coefficient is almost three times as great for most organizational forms. The only exception is represented by social cooperatives that show a ratio slightly higher than two. We found that social cooperatives show the highest degree of procedural fairness. Hence the evidence may support the idea that the variation corresponds to decreasing marginal variations of well-being since its impact appears stronger in the contexts where workers' judgments are less favourable. On the other hand, the influence of distributive fairness does not vary significantly across organizational forms, hence its relation with worker satisfaction is more likely to be linear.

As for the other covariates, there is fairly strong evidence that women are more satisfied than men, but only in traditional nonprofits, both religious and non-religious, while the effect is absent in social cooperatives and the public sector.

---

[7] The total of traditional nonprofits is the sum of religious and non-religious nonprofits. The explicit analysis of religious nonprofits and for-profit firms was excluded since the low number of cases (235 in the case of religious nonprofits and 180 in the case of for-profit firms) does not yield clear results beyond the influence of fairness concerns, which is common with all the other organizational forms.

Table 6.5 Average satisfaction (OLS)

	Public	Non-religious nonprofits	All nonprofits	Social Cooperatives
Gender	0.078	0.195**	0.141**	0.081
	0.094	*0.077*	*0.070*	*0.068*
Age (years)	0.010**	0.001	0.002	0.005
	0.004	*0.004*	*0.003*	*0.004*
High school diploma	−0.027	0.052	0.031	0.180**
	0.087	*0.102*	*0.077*	*0.074*
University degree	−0.138	−0.033	−0.057	0.214**
	0.125	*0.115*	*0.093*	*0.096*
Specific training	−0.195**	0.100	0.000	−0.259**
	0.091	*0.080*	*0.073*	*0.072*
Open-ended contract	−0.072	0.088	0.103	0.106
	0.076	*0.080*	*0.071*	*0.068*
Log Size	−0.147**	−0.022	−0.029	−0.048**
	0.036	*0.027*	*0.026*	*0.024*
Effort	−0.015	−0.027**	−0.016**	0.014**
	0.009	*0.007*	*0.005*	*0.007*
Hourly wage	0.037	0.013	0.006	0.004
	0.022	*0.016*	*0.017*	*0.015*
Distributive fairness	0.157**	0.174**	0.163**	0.169**
	0.024	*0.029*	*0.024*	*0.025*
Procedural fairness	0.421**	0.458**	0.427**	0.350**
	0.027	*0.032*	*0.025*	*0.026*
Constant	2.724**	1.481**	1.962**	2.417**
	0.353	*0.311*	*0.284*	*0.264*
N	582	378	611	580
R^2	0.508	0.606	0.544	0.499

Note: Regression coefficients in plain text, standard deviations in *italics*. The symbol ** denotes coefficients significant at the 5% level. Size of the organization is proxied by the number of employees. Effort is proxied by the number of extra hours worked

The gender effect seems to be linked to the material component of satisfaction (Table 6.6), averaging about 7% of the total in non-religious nonprofits (the mean value of satisfaction in these organizations is about 4.2) and is likely to be due to better employment possibilities and flexible labour hours for women in nonprofit organizations. Age is positively related with satisfaction only in the public sector. The public sector and social cooperatives are characterized by a negative impact of specific training. Its justification is to be found in non-material satisfaction more than in the material component (Table 6.7). Hence, the frustration of the expectations of specifically trained workers is likely to be due to a lack of autonomy and creativity in the tasks that they are asked to perform, more than to a lack of monetary incentives, though this second effect is also seen in the public sector. Effort in terms of extra hours worked has a negative effect only in traditional nonprofit organizations (both religious and non-religious).

A clearly distinctive model of industrial relations can be found at work in social cooperatives, the only organizational typology where higher education increases

Table 6.6 Material satisfaction (OLS)

	Public	Non-religious nonprofits	All nonprofits	Social Cooperatives
Gender	0.098	0.289**	0.202**	0.074
	0.110	*0.100*	*0.090*	*0.089*
Age (years)	0.006	0.001	–0.002	–0.003
	0.005	*0.005*	*0.004*	*0.005*
High school diploma	–0.184	–0.148	–0.112	–0.049
	0.101	*0.133*	*0.100*	*0.097*
University degree	–0.397**	–0.227	–0.290**	–0.044
	0.145	*0.150*	*0.121*	*0.126*
Specific training	–0.057**	0.208**	0.037	–0.138
	0.106	*0.104*	*0.094*	*0.095*
Open-ended contract	0.265**	0.192	0.329**	0.339**
	0.089	*0.104*	*0.093*	*0.089*
Log Size	–0.142**	0.004	–0.011	–0.043
	0.042	*0.035*	*0.033*	*0.031*
Effort	–0.037**	–0.040**	–0.025**	0.004
	0.010	*0.009*	*0.007*	*0.010*
Hourly wage	0.066**	0.030	0.017	0.014
	0.025	*0.021*	*0.022*	*0.020*
Distributive fairness	0.224**	0.236**	0.205**	0.224**
	0.028	*0.038*	*0.031*	*0.033*
Procedural fairness	0.349**	0.461**	0.451**	0.372**
	0.032	*0.041*	*0.822*	*0.034*
Constant	1.526**	0.274	0.822**	1.205**
	0.411	*0.403*	*0.368*	*0.347*
N	582	378	611	580
R^2	0.446	0.532	0.479	0.423

Note: see note to Table 6.5

satisfaction even though only in its non-material component. The effect is also quantitatively non-negligible, since the accomplishment of a university degree increases general satisfaction by 4% (the mean for social cooperatives is 5.2) and its non-material component by 8% on average (the mean is 4.7). The same result is found in the case of extra hours worked, which is positively connected with non-material satisfaction with work. Here it is possible to hypothesize a mechanism of inverse causation: higher non-material satisfaction is likely to induce workers to work overtime. The picture concerning social cooperatives is completed by the negative impact of specific training and dimension. The former, as already stated, is linked to the non-material component of satisfaction, which is decreases by about 7% on average. The interpretation of this effect may not be free of controversy. Many workers in social cooperatives would rather work in the public sector given the higher wage and job security, and this is all the more true when they are specifically trained, since this is often a precondition to being employed in the public sector. This does not seem to be the correct explanation, however, since the impact concerns only non-material satisfaction. A second possible explanation

Table 6.7 Non-material satisfaction *(OLS)*

	Public	Non-religious nonprofits	All nonprofits	Social Cooperatives
Gender	0.051	0.127	0.094	0.047
	0.114	*0.087*	*0.078*	*0.077*
Age (years)	0.012**	0.002	0.005	0.009**
	0.005	*0.004*	*0.004*	*0.004*
High school diploma	0.094	0.240**	0.165**	0.387**
	0.105	*0.115*	*0.086*	*0.084*
University degree	0.032	0.149	0.139	0.416**
	0.151	*0.129*	*0.105*	*0.108*
Specific training	−0.282**	0.009	−0.037	−0.358**
	0.110	*0.090*	*0.081*	*0.082*
Open-ended contract	−0.296**	0.006	−0.067	−0.062
	0.092	*0.090*	*0.080*	*0.077*
Log Size	−0.153**	−0.030	−0.035	−0.050
	0.044	*0.030*	*0.029*	*0.027*
Effort	0.002	−0.017**	−0.009	0.021**
	0.011	*0.008*	*0.006*	*0.008*
Hourly wage	0.019	0.000	−0.004	−0.011
	0.026	*0.019*	*0.019*	*0.017*
Distributive fairness	0.093**	0.138**	0.136**	0.107**
	0.029	*0.033*	*0.026*	*0.028*
Procedural fairness	0.450**	0.446**	0.403**	0.334**
	0.033	*0.036*	*0.028*	*0.030*
Constant	3.692**	2.326**	2.785**	3.513**
	0.426	*0.349*	*0.318*	*0.298*
N	582	378	611	580
R^2	0.387	0.496	0.433	0.382

Note: see note to Table 6.5

concerning social cooperatives, which does not apply to the public sector, refers to the relatively low percentage of specifically trained workers who find it more difficult to interact with unskilled workers and reach the expected degree of self-fulfilment. This is one of the few limitations found in the organizational model characterizing social cooperatives and may indicate the need to better define a role for specialized workers, though this objective may be difficult to achieve given the higher degree of participation in decision-making and inclusion of the unskilled. Finally, the negative impact of dimension is non-linear given the use of the log of dimension as covariate. It means that small cooperatives show a higher degree of satisfaction, while the negative relation disappears as dimension grows.

The distinctive effects of social cooperatives give rise to positive relations in most cases and seem to correspond to a model of "community enterprise" (Borzaga and Tortia 2007a, b) in which the small dimension is combined with a good set of non-monetary incentives, such as better on-the-job relations based on trust, procedural fairness, and a strong motivational content linked to local embeddedness (Granovetter 1985). The peculiar incentive mix is able to foster happiness even for educated workers and in the presence of weak monetary incentives.

When the material component of satisfaction is considered in isolation (Table 6.6), over and above the effects already underlined in previous paragraphs, a negative impact of higher education is detected in the public sector and in traditional nonprofits. The effect is strong in public organizations since it reaches 11% when measured against the average value of material satisfaction (which is 3.6), whereas it equals approximately 7% in nonprofits. Specific training shows a weak negative impact in the public sector, while it has a significant positive impact (about 5%) in non-religious nonprofits, which are the only organizational form where this positive impact emerges. Hence, they are likely to represent the work environment most suited to accommodating the aspirations of workers with a specific professional background. A long-term contractual relation with the firm shows a general positive impact on material satisfaction, and this is quite a reasonable result since long-term relations usually imply more job security, higher wages and faster career progression. While the size of the organization reduces material satisfaction only in the public sector, a weak but widespread negative impact of extra hours worked is recorded in all organizational forms with the exception of social cooperatives where, conversely, extra hours worked show a positive impact on non-material satisfaction. Wage increases material satisfaction only in the public sector, though on average the effect is lower than 2%. This result may support the idea that the organizational model in the public sector is more centred around monetary and extrinsic incentives which, given the very low degree of procedural fairness, are likely to represent an unsuccessful substitute for more transparent and equitable procedures and outcomes. Finally, it is worth emphasizing that the dimension of the impact of distributive fairness is generally higher for the material component of satisfaction than for the non-material one, though procedural fairness is still more important even in the case of material satisfaction. This result is intuitively sound since distributive fairness refers specifically to pay issues and has linkages with non-material satisfaction only insofar as professional development and the recognition of one's contribution are concerned.

The influence of procedural fairness is dominant on non-material satisfaction, while in this case the linkage with distributive fairness is much weaker. An increase from low to high in procedural fairness increases non-material satisfaction by 2.7 points in publicly-owned organizations. This, again, confirms the non-linear relation between procedural fairness and worker well-being. On the contrary, the effect of the same increase in distributive fairness is only equal to 0.6 on average. The other specific effects concerning non-material satisfaction (Table 6.7) are found in a positive impact of age in the public sector and in social cooperatives, while no effect is found in nonprofits in general. A high school diploma increases satisfaction in both nonprofits and social cooperatives. Hence, it emerges that education in general is conducive to higher non-material satisfaction, but is detrimental to satisfaction in terms of wage, job security and career advancement. This ambivalent effect is generalized and concerns all organizational forms except social cooperatives. Jobs in social services seem to satisfy educated workers, but not in relation to material incentives. The latter effect can be cast in terms of comparison income related to reference groups outside the organization and the social service sector, or be due to the insufficient purchasing power of the salary in comparison with the cost of living in general. More recent data concerning social cooperatives in 2005 (see the Special Issue of Impresa Sociale 2007 No. 3) strongly support these possibilities since the appropriateness of the wage in relation to the cost of living turns out to be quite low in social cooperatives and represents one of the main factors detrimental to worker well-being.[8] Long-term contractual relations damage non-material satisfaction only in the public sector. This finding represents a new critical aspect concerning the public sector and can be explained in terms of deterioration of workers' intrinsic, procedural and relational motivations in this context. It appears to be particularly serious since the stability of employment is one of the hallmarks of the Italian public sector. The size of the organization is detrimental to non-material satisfaction, probably due to the more formal and impersonal relations, and to more standardized procedures in larger organizations. This effect is statistically significant only in the public sector, however. Finally, the negative impact of extra hours worked is confirmed only in non-religious nonprofits.

Overall, it can be said that various critical elements emerge in the public sector while, at the other extreme, social cooperatives seem characterized by a virtuous circle. Traditional nonprofit organizations do not present markedly positive or negative features. However, they represent the only organizational model able to valorize specific training in terms of monetary remuneration and career advancement.

Worker well-being can also be measured indirectly on the basis of the intention to stay with the organization which can be interpreted in terms of loyalty. Willingness to stay can be considered a proxy for worker well-being, since it can be presumed that workers dissatisfied with their contractual relation tend more often to be willing to quit either as soon as possible or in a reasonable span of time.[9] However, it is not obvious that the determinants of loyalty are the same as the determinants of satisfaction. Indeed, a worker may prefer to quit even though s/he enjoys her/his contractual relation, for example because s/he has more than one outside option or because pay is too low. Vice versa, s/he may be willing to stay even though s/he is not satisfied because s/he does not have other opportunities or because of higher monetary incentives. If happiness and loyalty do not exactly overlap, there may be a shift in the determinants, and it will be seen that this is indeed the case. A limitation of the analysis is that there is an obvious process of self-selection of more loyal workers since workers not willing to stay are more likely to have already quit.[10] This is confirmed by the positive effect of age as a determinant of loyalty in all organizational forms and by the significance of being on open-end contract, which at any rate is high only in nonprofit organizations (Table 6.8).[11] This may be due, on

[8] Indeed, it is likely to have a relevant impact on worker well-being in all sectors of the economy.

[9] When they are willing to quit when a new job opportunity comes, the desire to stay in the same sector means that there are elements of dissatisfaction with the specific organization in which they work. If instead they want to change sector of activity, dissatisfaction with some aspects of the job presumably concerns the sector as a whole.

[10] Unluckily, the measurement of turnover cannot be ascertained as control variable in this database.

[11] A second limitation of the analysis is that regional rates of unemployment are lacking, and they may have had an impact on loyalty since they represent a negative index of the availability of outside options.

Table 6.8 Loyalty *(ordered logit)*

	Public	Non-religious nonprofits	All nonprofits	Social Cooperatives
Gender	1.118	1.189	1.167	1.039
	0.245	*0.279*	*0.230*	*0.197*
Age (years)	1.031**	1.048**	1.053**	1.023**
	0.010	*0.013*	*0.010*	*0.011*
High school diploma	0.748	0.669	0.769	0.591**
	0.161	*0.212*	*0.169*	*0.128*
University degree	0.458**	0.671	0.870	0.564**
	0.133	*0.238*	*0.228*	*0.160*
Specific training	1.286	1.061	0.950	0.631**
	0.275	*0.250*	*0.188*	*0.125*
Open-ended contract	0.703	1.929**	1.811**	0.763
	0.130	*0.441*	*0.348*	*0.146*
Log Size.	0.860	1.001	1.034	0.847**
	0.072	*0.077*	*0.072*	*0.054*
Effort	0.954**	0.990	1.000	1.022
	0.020	*0.018*	*0.014*	*0.021*
Hourly wage	0.958	0.926	0.910**	1.066
	0.044	*0.042*	*0.041*	*0.073*
Distributive fairness	1.338**	1.229**	1.237**	1.249**
	0.079	*0.108*	*0.083*	*0.089*
Procedural fairness	1.130	1.502**	1.543**	1.586**
	0.074	*0.148*	*0.115*	*0.120*
N	582	378	611	580
Pseudo-R^2	0.561	0.879	0.096	0.102

Note: odds ratios in plain text, standard deviations in italics. The symbol ** denotes odds ratios significant at the 5% level. Otherwise see note to Table 6.5

the one hand, to the tendency of many workers in social cooperatives to be willing to quit even though they are on open-end contract in order to get a better-paid job in the public sector, and, on the other hand, to a general tendency of workers in the public sector not to have a strong attachment to their job.[12]

Education has a strong negative impact on loyalty in social cooperatives, despite their workers demonstrating one of the highest levels of education.[13] Having a university degree increases the odds of being more willing to quit by a factor of about 1.8, while the effect is just slightly weaker in the case of a high school diploma. The former effect is still stronger in public organizations which show a level of education below social cooperatives, since the same factor is equal to 2.2. The reasons why graduate workers may be so willing to quit is likely to be different in social cooperatives and the public sector. In the former case, it is clear that young and educated workers enjoy more job opportunities and may prefer to look for more

[12] This evidence is shown in Borzaga and Depedri (2005) and Borzaga and Tortia (2006).

[13] See Borzaga and Tortia (2006).

remunerative work. In the latter case, graduate workers may not be satisfied with the job and its remuneration, but often they would rather stay in the public sector by switching to a different activity. Specific training is conducive to unwillingness to stay only in social cooperatives and this again may be due to either a general tendency of workers in cooperatives to look for a better-remunerated job in the public sector, or to the inability of social cooperatives to valorize a specific professional background. The size of the organization has a negative impact on social cooperatives and this confirms the result found in the case of satisfaction. Finally, the negative influence of effort is very weak but still statistically significant in the public sector and wage has a negative impact on loyalty in traditional nonprofits. This last effect is linked to the answers given by workers in religious nonprofits and most likely refers to the difficulty of finding a different job for workers on low income ladders.

Distributive and procedural fairness again have a positive impact on loyalty, but this time the relative weight of the effect is different since distributive fairness weighs almost as much as procedural fairness in influencing the willingness to stay. The odds ratios of being more willing to stay are increased by a factor similar for both indexes of fairness in all ownership forms, though the effect of procedural fairness is still slightly stronger in nonprofits and cooperatives, while in the public sector only the effect of distributive fairness is statistically significant. In the public sector procedural fairness is extremely relevant in influencing satisfaction, mainly in its non-material component, while it does not have a relevant impact on loyalty. Indeed, in the public sector procedures are felt to be particularly unfair, causing dissatisfaction, but when it comes to loyalty only outcomes are relevant; this confirms that workers in the public sector show outcome-oriented preferences which induce them to switch to other jobs when they are not satisfied with their wage, even though the unfairness of procedures reduces their on-the-job well-being too.

It is also interesting to examine in greater depth the picture emerging from the analysis of social cooperatives. While this organizational model appeared the strongest when satisfaction, especially in its non-material component, was considered, it shows various weaknesses when the determinants of loyalty are analyzed. The most serious worries emerge from the apparent difficulty of social cooperatives to retain educated workers, probably due, in many cases, to low job security and wages. However, these negative results concerning loyalty seem to be linked also to the young age of the organizational model at the time of the research, since the new data gathered on social cooperatives in 2006 show a markedly higher degree of willingness to stay also by educated workers (Depedri 2007). Hence, the development of this model from its early stages at the beginning of the 1990s seems to be leading to more structured and effective solutions, since in many cooperatives employment relations have only reached stability over the last decade.

The overall results concerning loyalty seem to clearly point out that outcomes are more important with regard to willingness to stay than to satisfaction as already stated in previous works (Tortia 2007). Workers are satisfied with their job when material and non-material incentives are adequate (Borzaga and Tortia 2006), the environment is fair, and relations with colleagues and superiors are good (Borzaga and Depedri 2005). However, when considering whether quitting the organization is a desirable perspective, they take into consideration more seriously monetary incentives and distributive fairness (which in these data refers exclusively to the individual wage, but that may be imagined (and proved with new data available) to be relevant also in terms of wage comparison and the cost of living. Too low wages in the presence of a high cost of living may be a strong enough reason to convince many workers to quit even though they enjoy the work environment.

6.4 Concluding Remarks

The foregoing analysis has brought to light the crucial role that fairness concerns, largely those of a procedural nature, play in influencing worker well-being. This is true for all organizational forms which, however, differ in their ability to provide adequate levels of fairness. A clear divide emerges between the public and the private sector in general, since the former is at a disadvantage at the level of both worker well-being and perceived fairness. While for-profit firms and nonprofit organizations show similar levels of job-satisfaction, both material and non-material, religious nonprofits best guarantee distributive fairness and social cooperatives score highest when procedural fairness is considered. Given the more significant role of procedural fairness in influencing worker well-being, it would seem safe to state that social cooperatives represent an innovative and successful organizational form, at least as far as labour relations are concerned, the difficulties in retaining their more educated and skilled workforce notwithstanding. This conclusion is also justified by the virtuous circle existing between higher education, long-term contractual relations and workers' satisfaction which is generally high in its non-material component and which may induce workers to work more than required by the contract.

Essentially, the root of this success may be found in three elements. First, the democratic scheme of governance in cooperatives in general, and in worker cooperatives more specifically, guarantees more autonomy to workers and provides them with the opportunity to have their say even with regard to managerial decisions, in a manner that is absent in other organizational forms. Second, the multi-stakeholder scheme of governance guarantees a more inclusive organizational environment for all the actors involved, incorporating various external effects and contractual imperfections, namely those linked to asymmetric information. For instance, better information flows concerning the financial limitations of the organization are likely to improve the perception of distributive fairness even if wages are low. This is likely to improve relations and procedures in general, and hence labour relations. Third, the social role of the organization, which is often embedded at the local level and satisfies local needs, is closely interconnected with those personal relations forming the basis of the activity. Higher procedural fairness and well-being can also be linked to the specific vocational activity, since personal relations and local embeddedness are conducive to strengthened trust relations and more equitable procedures. By contrast, the many critical elements emerging in the perception of public sector workers seem to be linked mainly to a particularly low level of procedural fairness and of intrinsic and relational motivations, which are not made up by higher monetary incentives. These results can give a convincing explanation of the low efficiency levels, mainly due to higher costs, of public bodies.

Future work on these issues will need to concentrate more on the institutional factors that are more conducive to generating fairness of procedures, for example taking into account the degree and features of inclusiveness and worker participation in decision-making and in the activity of the firm. A second field of enquiry concerns the relation between perceived fairness and the presence of the organization's objectives besides the maximization of economic surpluses. Third, it would appear essential to further develop the relationships between local embeddedness, worker motivations and the quality of procedures in order to underscore a possible local and relational component in the perception of procedural fairness. Finally, what also remains unexplored is the impact of distributive and procedural fairness on the quality of the services delivered.

Acknowledgements I thank Carlo Borzaga for his precious comments. Of course, the standard disclaimer applies.

References

Bacchiega A, Borzaga C (2001) Social enterprise as an incentive structure. In: Borzaga C, Defourny J (eds) The emergence of social enterprise. Routledge, London

Bacchiega A, Borzaga C (2003) The economics of the third sector: toward a more comprehensive approach. In: Anheier HK, Ben-Ner A (eds) The study of the nonprofit enterprise. Theories and approaches. Kluwer, New York

Ben-Ner A, Putterman L (1999) Values and Institutions in economic analysis. In: Ben-Ner A, Putterman L (eds) Economics values and organization. Cambridge University Press, Cambridge UK

Benz M (2005) The Relevance of procedural utility for economics. Institute for Empirical Research in Economics University of Zurich, Working Paper 26

Benz M, Stutzer A (2003) Do workers enjoy procedural utility? Applied Economics Quarterly 49:149–172

Benz M, Frey B, Stutzer A (2004) Introducing procedural utility. Journal of Institutional and Theoretical Economics 160:377–401

Borzaga C (ed) (2000) Capitale umano e qualità del lavoro nei servizi sociali. Fondazione Italiana del Volontariato, Rome

Borzaga C (2003) L'analisi economica delle organizzazioni nonprofit: teorie, limiti e possibili sviluppi. In: Borzaga C, Musella M (eds) Produttività ed efficienza nelle organizzazioni nonprofit. Edizioni31, Trento

Borzaga C, Depedri S (2005) Interpersonal relations and job satisfaction: Some empirical results in social and community care services. In: Gui B, Sugden R (eds) Economics and social interaction: accounting for interpersonal relations. Cambridge University Press, Cambridge UK

Borzaga C, Mittone L (1997) The multi-stakeholders versus the nonprofit organizations. University of Trento Department of Economics Discussion Paper 7

Borzaga C, Tortia E (2006) Worker motivations, job satisfaction and loyalty in public and non-profit social services. Nonprofit and Voluntary Sector Quarterly 35:225–248

Borzaga C, Tortia E (2007a) Social economy organizations in the theory of the firm. In: Clarence E, Noya A (eds) The social economy. Building inclusive communities. OECD, Paris

Borzaga C, Tortia E (2007b) The growing social content of cooperative firms: an evolutionary interpretation. 1st CIRIEC Research Conference on the Social Economy. Victoria, Canada

Borzaga C, Tortia E (2008) Social enterprises and local development: an evolutionary approach. Mimeo, University of Trento, Department of Economics

Depedri S (2003) La ricerca: metodologia campione e principali risultati. In: Borzaga C, Musella M (eds) Produttività ed efficienza nelle organizzazioni nonprofit. Edizioni31, Trento

Depedri S (2007) Livelli di soddisfazione e fedeltà dei lavoratori. Impresa Sociale 17:193–211

Granovetter M (1985) Economic action and social structure: the problem of embeddedness. American Journal of Sociology 91:481–510

Hansmann H (1996) The ownership of enterprise. The Belknap Press of Harvard University Press, Cambridge MA

Lazear EP (1995) Personnel Economics, MIT Press, Cambridge MA

Tortia E (2007) Worker well-being and perceived fairness: survey-based findings from Italy. Journal of Socio-Economics 37:2080–2094

Weisbrod BA (1977) The voluntary nonprofit sector. Lexington Books, Lexington MA

Weisbrod BA (1988) The nonprofit economy. Harvard University Press, Cambridge MA

Chapter 7
Wage Effects of Recruitment Methods: The Case of the Italian Social Service Sector

Michele Mosca and Francesco Pastore

Abstract This essay analyzes the role of different recruitment channels, and of informal networks in particular, on wage structures across various organization types in the Italian social service sector. While the impact of recruitment methods on wages has been addressed in several previous contributions, none of them focuses on social services. Comparison of outcomes across organization types within the same sector is in itself another novelty, as compared to previous studies that generally focus on differences across sectors or, more recently, across countries. The main findings are that nonprofit organizations prefer informal recruitment methods to better select the most motivated workers, namely those workers who share the nonprofit mission. Furthermore the impact of informal contacts on the wage structure explains much of the unobserved wage differentials across organization type.

7.1 Introduction

In recent years, several scholars, policy makers and opinion leaders have raised a number of criticisms on the nature of the expansion of private organizations in the social service sector in Italy. It has often been claimed that private, especially nonprofit, organizations have played a marginal role in terms of employment growth and, furthermore, that they have tended to employ unskilled workers to supply services of low quality. Hiring their personnel through informal recruitment channels would be essential to the survival strategy of nonprofits since they supposedly belong to and depend financially on political lobbies. Because of the widespread use of referrals in the recruitment process, skill mismatch would be frequent,

M. Mosca and F. Pastore (✉)
Department of Economic Theory and Applications, University of Napoli Federico II, Via Rodinò 22, 80138 Napoli, Italy

S. Destefanis and M. Musella (eds.), *Paid and Unpaid Labour in the Social Economy*, AIEL Series in Labour Economics, DOI: 10.1007/978-3-7908-2137-6_8,

amounting to one of the main explanations of the low returns to education in these organizations (see, among others, Carinci 2001).

This paper attempts to address such criticisms in two ways. First, it analyzes the returns to education in the social service sector. The econometric analysis is based on the FIVOL–FEO data and includes information on public, private for-profit and private nonprofit organizations. This allows us to assess whether nonprofit organizations employ lower productivity workers and pay them less than other types of organizations within the sector. Previous contributions have studied the determinants of the nonprofit wage gap (see, for instance, Preston 1989; Leete 2000, 2001; Ruhm and Borkoski 2003; Pestana Barros 2006; Mosca et al. 2007) leaving aside the issue of the possible differences in returns to human capital across organization types. Second, the paper aims to assess the relative impact of different recruitment channels, and of informal networks in particular, on wage structures across organizations in the social service sector. While the impact of recruitment methods on wages has been addressed in several previous contributions, none of them focuses on social services. Comparison of outcomes across organization types within the same sector is in itself another novelty, as compared to previous studies that generally focus on differences across sectors or, more recently, across countries.

This paper is organized as follows. Section 7.2 reviews the theoretical and empirical literature on wage effects of informal networks. Section 7.3 presents the methodology used to estimate the wage equations and the impact of hiring and job search methods. Section 7.4 illustrates some features of the FIVOL–FEO dataset, while Sects. 7.5 and 7.6 report our empirical results. Section 7.7 provides a joint discussion of the results and concludes.

7.2 Theoretical and Empirical Evidence on Informal Networks

Theoretical reasoning predicts that informal networks, here intended as the help of friends and relatives[1] in finding a job, exert two main effects on labour markets. First, they increase the probability of being hired and, second, they produce a positive effect on earnings (Montgomery 1991; Mortensen and Vishwanath 1994). Informal contacts are supposed to be able to signal the right worker for the right job, thereby increasing his/her probability of being employed. Also, by reducing the ex ante information asymmetry between employer and employee, job referral mechanisms allow for the selection of a more productive workforce and consequently the payment of higher wages.

[1] In fact, the early literature on informal networks has focused on professional ("old boys"), rather than family networks (see, for instance, Saloner 1985; Simon and Warner 1992). Some recent empirical literature distinguishes the relative impact of these two types of networks, finding a positive wage effect in the former case and a negative one in the latter case (Sylos Labini 2004a; Antoninis 2006; Datcher Loury 2006).

The empirical evidence is unanimous in confirming the expected impact of informal networks on the probability of job finding, but is at variance with theoretical predictions when assessing their impact on earnings. Empirical studies show that informal networks increase the number of offers per contact, which explains also why 30 through 60% of all employed workers found their job through friends and relatives (Holzer 1987, 1988; Roper 1988; Blau and Philip 1990; Osberg 1993; Sylos Labini 2004b; Goos and Salomons 2007).[2] Nonetheless, employees hired through informal contacts not only declare a lower level of job satisfaction (Addison and Portugal 2002), but also have lower wages as compared to those hired through other entry channels.

Indeed, in contrast with the theoretical predictions, and with a few exceptions relating mainly to Anglo-Saxon countries and high-skill labour markets (Simon and Warner 1992; Marmaros and Sacerdote 2002; Kugler 2003 for the USA; Goos and Salomons 2007 for the UK), the available empirical evidence concurs and reaches the conclusion that the wage effect of informal channels is neither positive nor constant across sectors and countries (see, among others, Collier and Garg 1999; Pistaferri 1999; Margolis and Simonnet 2003; Pellizzari 2004; Bentolila et al. 2009; Meliciani and Radicchia 2005; Antoninis 2006; Datcher Loury 2006; Delattre and Sabatier 2007; Weber and Mahringer 2008; Pastore, 2008).[3]

A wage penalty is invariably found in all studies concerning Italy. Using the 1991 and 1993 waves of the SHIW dataset collected by the Bank of Italy, Pistaferri (1999) finds a negative coefficient (–0.046) of informal networks as compared to any other job search method. The coefficient shrinks to –0.031 when controlling for low-skill sectors and occupations. Sylos Labini (2004a) confirms this result for 1998 using the same data. He finds a wage penalty of –0.025 when there is no control for the type of referral. The wage penalty associated with family and friends' referrals becomes –0.047 when controlling for the presence of a network of colleagues, which yields a wage premium of 0.025. Meliciani and Radicchia (2005) use data collected by ISFOL in 2003. They find a wage penalty of –0.037 for workers hired using informal networks as compared to those hired through public competitions, direct applications, direct experience on the job and referrals through school.

The main explanation for these contrasts between theory and evidence is that informal networks are more common among unskilled workers, whose labour market is less affected by asymmetric information problems. In these markets, informal networks represent a negative, not a positive, signal for employers. This does not need to mean, though, that referrals are only due to unobserved job characteristics that might cause compensating wage differentials. This reverse causality-hypothesis is ventilated in Ioannides and Datcher Loury (2004) and

[2] For the sake of brevity, the following discussion focuses on wage effects. See Ioannides and Datcher Loury (2004) for a more comprehensive review of the literature on employment effects.

[3] Table 7.11 (in the Appendix) reports in some detail various features of these studies.

Datcher Loury (2006). Pistaferri (1999) and particularly Delattre and Sabatier (2007) conclude that their IV-based findings can be interpreted as lending support to the hypothesis that users of informal networks have unobserved attributes, negatively correlated with wages.

Pellizzari (2004) brings to the fore a different explanation of the cross-country differences in the wage effect of referrals. A negative wage effect would be typical of labour markets where formal recruitment methods are more common, as is the case especially in the public sector of most European countries, including Italy. In this case, informal channels are generally considered a cheap selection device. In fact, informal channels are commonly considered a way for lobbies to affect the employer's hiring decision, as in Goldberg's (1982) model of nepotistic firms, rather than an instrument to gather information on job applicants.

The case of social services is interesting inasmuch as informal channels of recruitment are, according to several authors (see, e.g. Carinci 2001), more common than in other sectors. Nonprofit organizations are inclined to use informal networks more often than other types of organizations as a tool to achieve political and financial support, as in Goldberg (1982). Based on this prediction, informal search methods should be associated with lower wages. Implicit in this first interpretation is the assumption that informal recruitment methods are less able than the formal ones to solve the ex ante information asymmetries. This paper proposes a different interpretation based on previous research on nonprofit organizations.

Some authors (see, e.g. Preston 1989) claim that workers in nonprofit organizations would also incorporate the satisfaction of social needs in their subjective utility function and would be willing to be paid less to achieve their social aims. In a similar vein, Mosca et al. (2007) suggest a theoretical framework to explain the nonprofit wage gap where, as in Akerlof (1984), the worker's effort correlates not only with wages but also with non-monetary compensations. These take the form of relational goods and services by-produced in the delivery of particular services. As formalized in Handy and Katz (1998), by paying lower pecuniary compensations (but higher non-pecuniary compensations), the nonprofit sector is able to attract similarly skilled, but intrinsically more motivated, workers able to provide, in principle, a higher level of effort than their counterparts in the for-profit sector.

More specifically, the information content of informal contacts might be different from that of formal selection methods, since such individual characteristics as work ethic and motivation might not be easy to assess through answers to tests or direct interviews. Consequently, different organization types might choose different recruitment strategies. As DeVaro (2005) notes too, nonprofit organizations might prefer informal methods which are aimed not only at assessing the productivity level in candidates, often better assessed with more formal methods, but also their degree of motivation and compatibility with the ideological aims and the mission of nonprofit organizations.

7.3 Aims and Econometric Methodology

We aim to extend previous research by testing: (a) whether hiring and job-search methods differ across organizations; (b) whether such differences may contribute to explaining cross-organization wage differentials. The underlying hypothesis is that search methods cannot be ranked according to their different ability to obtain the same set of information as hypothesized in the previous literature on informal networks, but that they satisfy different informational needs.

In order to estimate the returns to education across organizations and the wage effects of recruitment methods we adopt the standard Mincerian approach. The equilibrium condition of the present value of the (expected) income in a certain year is equal to the cost of the investment. It can be proven that the internal rate of return to schooling can be approximated by the difference in the logarithm of wages between leaving education in a given year and leaving it in the previous year. The augmented or 'extended' version of the earnings equation is:

$$In\ w_i = \alpha_i + rs_i + Dx_i + Gx_i^2 + u_i \tag{7.1}$$

where w_i is the net hourly earnings for an individual i, s_i represents a measure of his/her schooling, x_i is a measure of work experience and u_i is the usual disturbance term, assumed independent of x_i, that represents other elements the model does not directly capture. Squared work experience is used to capture the concavity of the earnings profile. The term r reflects the private financial return to schooling as well as being the proportionate effect on wages of an increment to s. Expression (7.1) represents a log-linear transformation of an exponential function and can be estimated by OLS. The coefficients have a semi-elasticity interpretation: they measure the ceteris paribus percentage change in the dependent variable for any unit change in any independent variable.[4]

The wage effect of informal networks can be estimated by augmenting equation (7.1):

$$In\ w_i = \eta IN_i + rs_i + Dx_i + Gx_i^2 + u_i \tag{7.2}$$

where *IN* is a dummy equal to 1 if individual i has used informal networks to find her/his current job. The coefficient of *IN* is the estimated value of the wage effect of informal networks. The FIVOL–FEO dataset also allows controlling for different

[4] When treating independent dummy variables, such as being a woman, the semi-elasticity interpretation is flawed and Halvorsen and Palmquist (1980) propose the following formula: (eβ–1)*100. It measures the percentage change in the median wage, which is less influenced by outliers. It is possible to interpret the estimated coefficient of dummy variables directly as semi-elasticity if the estimated coefficient is close to zero.

recruitment methods (RM), as detailed in the next section. To take these into account, (7.1) is then further augmented:

$$In\ w_i = \eta IN_i + \psi RN_i + rs_i + Dx_i + Gx_i^2 + u_i \tag{7.3}$$

As Pellizzari (2004) notes, informal networks could just signal above/below average skills in candidates. In other words, the wage effect associated with informal networks could not be due to informal networks themselves, but rather to the skill level of those who use this job-search method. IV estimates might be used to test for endogeneity of informal networks. However, datasets do not readily provide suitable instruments to implement IV estimation procedures and hence, it is useful to adopt an indirect approach to the endogeneity issue based on the following line of reasoning.

If informal networks are not just a signal of skills, but rather an independent factor causing a wage penalty/premium, this wage premium/penalty should disappear with tenure time. According to a first interpretation, jobs obtained through informal networks could be associated with unobserved job specific characteristics; in this case, wage penalties (or wage premiums) would compensate for non-monetary benefits related to the job, such as job security and stability, responsibility or effort. In the case of nonprofit organizations operating in the provision of social services, lower wages might be compensated by better relations among colleagues, sharing the organization's aims and so on. Alternatively, wage differentials could depend on job-worker mismatches. Empirically, wage differences linked to compensating differentials should not vanish with job tenure. On the contrary, differences due to a mismatch between jobs and workers should disappear once workers move to a better job. To test these two alternative hypotheses, (7.4) modifies (7.3) by introducing interactions of dummies for informal networks and recruitment methods with other dummies for short and long job tenure:

$$\begin{aligned} In\ w_i = {} & [\eta IN^*\ ShortTenure + \eta IN^*\ LongTenure] + \\ & + [\psi RM^*\ ShortTenure + \psi RM^*\ LongTenure] + \\ & + rs_i + Dx_i + Gx^2_i + u_i \end{aligned} \tag{7.4}$$

If the coefficients of the two interactions are statistically different from each other, then one can infer that informal networks are an independent factor of wages. On the other hand, if they are not, we can conclude that informal networks are a signal of skill.

A job tenure of more than 2 years is considered to be long in this paper, since 2 years are deemed necessary for workers and firms to understand whether informal networks have led to some form of worker-to-job mismatch. In addition, workers need sufficient time to implement their 'job shopping' activity successfully and firms to adjust wages to the real skill level of their workers.

7.4 Data and Variables

The empirical analysis is based on the FIVOL–FEO survey conducted in the first semester of 1998 on Italian public, for-profit and nonprofit organizations operating in the supply of such social services as care and guardianship, nursing/rehabilitation, educational, cultural, recreational, school and school-to-work guidance, job-search assistance and others (see Borzaga 2000; Depedri 2003 for further details on the survey).

The survey was carried out in fifteen provinces,[5] mainly concentrated in the Northern regions, where nonprofit organizations are more numerous. 724 voluntary workers, 2,066 (out of 9,226) paid workers, 228 organizations, divided into 268 units, and 266 managers filled in the questionnaires. About 61.7% of paid workers in the sample are employed in the nonprofit organizations, of which 33% are in non-religious nonprofits, 29.3% in public organizations and 9.0% in for-profit organizations. The data set provides detailed information on educational attainment, work experience, wages, satisfaction linked to wages, jobs, organization and relations among colleagues, as well as on hiring and job-search methods.

The natural logarithm of net hourly wages, $Ln(w_h)$, obtained by dividing the declared average monthly wage after tax[6] by contractual hours, is the dependent variable in estimates of earnings equations.[7] The independent variables can be grouped into individual characteristics, environmental variables, and, at a later stage, job search and hiring methods.

Individual characteristics include a gender dummy variable for men and two dummy variables for civil status (singles and divorced/widowed). Various forms of human capital endowment are considered. Schooling is measured in years of completed education, according to the Italian education system: primary school (5 years), lower secondary school (8), professional qualification (11), upper secondary school (13), bachelor's degree (16) and the traditional university degree (18).[8]

---

[5]From North to South: Trento, Gorizia, Pordenone, Trieste, Udine, Venezia, Cuneo, Torino, Brescia, Firenze, Napoli, Salerno, Catanzaro, Reggio Calabria and Messina.

[6]Interviewees were asked: "Could you please indicate the average net monthly wage you received in recent months (exclusive of extra-work pay, wage arrears and so on)?"

[7]A small number of sampled individuals (9.5%) did not declare either their monthly wage (6.8%) or their contractual hours (4.1%). As an experiment, missing observations have been replaced by mean values of the variable distinguished by organisation type. The pre and post transformation average wages differ only by less than 1%. However, results based on estimates of the same equations on the original and on the transformed dependent variable show that the results are not robust to the change in the dependent variable. As a consequence, the transformed wages are discarded.

[8]The statutory years for the traditional university degree vary from 4 (in general) to 5 years (for Engineering and Medical sciences). Nonetheless, the average actual years of attendance necessary to gain a university degree is over 7–8 years depending on the type of degree. This implies that the estimated returns to a year of education overestimate the true returns. A reform implemented in the second half of the 1990s has brought in a new type of University degree that can be gained in three years. This second type of degree is here called the bachelor's degree.

In most estimates, education is measured in terms of educational qualifications above the compulsory level, rather than in terms of years of schooling, to test for non-linearity in returns to educational attainment levels (Psacharopoulos 1994).

Moreover, following a standard procedure, potential work experience is computed as age minus years of schooling minus six (age of first year of school). The extensive length of time individuals have to devote to job searching in order to find a job in Italy would suggest that this variable overestimates the return to a year of work experience. The hypothesis of non-linearity of returns to work experience is tested including a quadratic term. Job-specific work experience is captured by the declared tenure as measured in years since the respondent started to work in the current job.

A variable measuring the age of the organization is used to test whether old organizations, considered more stable, pay higher wages. In fact, this variable can also be considered a proxy for the firm's size.

Dummies for groups of regions are included in the estimates. One would expect that wages paid by organizations operating in the less developed South to be lower than in Centre-Northern regions, considering the lower cost of living of the former.[9]

Organizations are divided into public (G), for-profit (FPs) and nonprofit organizations (NPs). The latter include social cooperatives, religious and non-religious institutions. Social cooperatives were legally recognized in 1991 (Law 381/1991) and can be of two types: Type A provide health, social or educational services, while Type B integrate disadvantaged people into the labour market and at least 30% of their members must be from the disadvantaged target groups. The categories of disadvantage in the latter target group may include physical and mental disability, drug and alcohol addiction, developmental disorders and problems with the law. They do not include other factors of disadvantage such as race, sexual orientation or abuse. Non-religious and religious organizations differ in the aims they pursue: religious institutions tend to pursue aims similar to the social cooperatives. These differences within the NPs could clearly also affect the mechanism of wage determination. Therefore, we group together social cooperatives and religious nonprofits (NP1) to distinguish them from non-religious nonprofits (NP2).

Environmental factors include sector, occupation, professional qualification and type of contract. The questionnaire distinguishes eight sectors, which have been aggregated into four to have larger cell sizes: nursing services, recreational services, training and school-to-work services, home care. All the other services are used as baseline. These variables allow us to also control the firm's size and skill level differences across sub-sectors.

The number of occupations considered in the questionnaire is ten, of which only six had a sufficient number of observations to be considered in the estimates: home carer, (legally qualified) social worker, general and professional nurse, social therapist and educator/teacher. The rest (9.1%) are pooled together with

[9] We experimented with variables for the effect of the higher cost of living in big cities. However, these variables turned out to be statistically insignificant and were excluded from the estimates.

the large group of those not answering the question (41.7%), thus forming the baseline occupation.

Control variables include dummies for part-time and temporary work, having a professional qualification to work in NPs and holding a particular type of contract. To capture the possible effect of union membership, a dummy is included for those who always go on strike when requested by the unions.

A particularly interesting feature of the FIVOL–FEO data is that they allow hiring *and* job-search methods to be controlled. With regard to hiring methods, the questionnaire asked respondents whether their job was obtained through public competitions or direct hiring. In the latter case, respondents were asked whether they were hired after some form of selection or without any selection. A specific dummy was included for those who did not declare their method of selection. Information on hiring channels is important for two reasons. First, it allows three different levels of selection to be distinguished. Second, it allows the joint effect of hiring and job-search methods to be assessed and thus the hypothesis to be tested that the wage effect of informal networks is greater if hiring methods are less formal (Pellizzari 2004). This is also possible because different organization types adopt different hiring methods.

In addition, the questionnaire reports information on the following job-search methods that workers adopt to find their current job: (a) having a previous relationship of professional collaboration with the organization, (b) having an affiliation to an association or group (religious or not) to which the organization is connected; (c) having previously been on duty for the voluntary service within the organization; (d) having previously been a customer (or customer's relative) of the services the organization delivers; (e) having previously been signalled by friends or relatives; (f) having previous direct knowledge of the organization because it operates in the residential area of the interviewee; (g) having acted as a volunteer within the organization; (h) having answered a job advertisement published in specialized newspapers; (i) having contacted the public or a private employment office; (j) having used other methods. Only one option is given to respondents. Option (j) is chosen as baseline. Unfortunately, the FIVOL–FEO data does not allow us to distinguish professional networks (the 'old boys') from networks of family and friends.

7.5 Wage and Human Capital Differentials by Organization

Descriptive analysis of the FIVOL–FEO sample (see Table 7.1) shows that public organizations pay higher wages compared to their private for-profit and nonprofit counterparts. Among private organizations, wage differences are by and large statistically not significant, although for-profits and NP2s pay on average higher wages than NP1s. If workers in NPs were significantly less skilled than average, this would already explain wage differences across organizations. However, this does not seem to be the case.

Table 7.1 Average monthly and hourly wages by type of organization

All workers (monthly wages)	G	FP	NP	NP2	NP1
G					
FPs	9.6				
NPs	16.2	6.0			
Social cooperatives (NP1)	22.7	12.0	5.6		
Non-relig. organizations (NP2)	7.0	−2.3	−7.8	−12.8	
Religious organizations (NP1)	17.8	7.5	1.4	−4.0	10.0
Full-time workers (monthly wages)	G	FP	NP	NP2	NP1
G					
FPs	12.4				
NPs	13.1	0.6			
Social cooperatives (NP1)	16.8	3.9	3.3		
Non-relig. organizations (NP2)	5.5	−6.2	−6.7	−9.7	
Religious organizations (NP1)	18.2	5.2	4.5	1.2	12.1
Part-time workers (hourly wages)	G	FP	NP	NP2	NP1
G					
FPs	−12.2				
NPs	2.3	16.6			
Social cooperatives (NP1)	10.5	25.9	8.0		
Non-relig. organizations (NP2)	−9.6	3.0	−11.6	−18.2	
Religious organizations (NP1)	4.1	18.6	1.7	−5.8	15.2

Note: each figure in the table shows the difference between column (j) and row (i): w_j/w_i. Therefore a positive sign indicates a premium in favour of the organization type shown in the column
Source: own elaboration on FIVOL–FEO data

As shown in Table 7.2, workers in NPs and in public organizations have slightly more years of education than average. Those employed in NPs have 12 and NP2s, in particular, have 12.9 years of education on average, corresponding to upper secondary education attainment. Almost the same applies to public organizations (11.5 years). Workers in FPs have on average fewer years of education (10.8). Differences in educational levels are therefore not stark, but tend to be in favour of NPs. In addition, workers in public organizations have a significantly higher level of work experience (21.1 years) than workers in FPs (19.8) and in NPs (18.2). In NP2s the average level of work experience is 19.1 years. Job tenure of workers in NPs (6.7 years) and FPs (6.8) is lower than that in public organizations (9.6). However, the years of job tenure in NP2s (8.7) is close to that in the public sector. Overall, the longer work experience of workers in governmental organizations might partly explain the G/NP, but not the NP/FP, pay gap.

Table 7.3 reports the results of augmented earnings functions by organization type. Overall, the adj. R^2 is higher in FPs and in the public sector, suggesting that there is a lower degree of heterogeneity in these types of organization. Returns to education are low in the entire social service sector, regardless of the type of organization. Mosca et al. (2007), Table 6 estimated a private annual rate of return to education of about 2.9% in basic earnings equations and of 2.0% when adding all the control variables contained in Table 7.3. These figures are lower than those found for the entire economy in previous studies (6.6% for men and 7.7% for women, according to Brunello et al. 2000). For-profit organizations pay a

Table 7.2 Workers characteristics by sector and type of organization

Variables	Type of organization				
	G	FP	NP	NP1	NP2
Age (years)	38.6	36.5	36.2	35.3	38.0
Education (years):	11.5	10.8	12.0	11.6	12.9
No qualification (%)	0.2	–	–	0.5	–
Primary school (%)	4.2	12.0	4.8	5.3	3.8
Lower secondary school (%)	18.6	27.4	21.1	24.7	13.9
Vocational secondary school (%)	32.3	20.0	13.7	15.0	10.9
Upper secondary school (%)	34.0	26.9	40.5	38.5	44.7
University degree (%)	4.0	9.7	8.7	7.5	11.4
Postgraduate (%)	6.7	4.0	10.7	8.4	15.4
Work experience (years)	21.1	19.8	18.2	17.7	19.1
Tenure (years)	9.6	6.8	6.7	5.8	8.7
Age of organization (years)	88.0	13.4	22.1	20.3	25.7
Women (%)	84.4	88.0	72.1	73.9	68.4
Civil status:					
Single (%)	24.6	32.0	36.1	37.3	33.8
Married (%)	65.4	53.7	58.6	54.3	56.8
Divorced (%)	7.9	9.1	7.2	6.8	7.8
Widow (%)	2.1	5.1	1.6	1.6	1.5
Macro-regions:					
North-West (%)	41.8	68.6	32.5	39.3	18.7
North-East (%)	48.8	9.7	38.1	34.7	44.9
Centre (%)	1.2	5.7	7.8	7.7	8.1
South (%)	8.2	16.0	21.6	18.4	28.3
Part-time (%)	14.0	14.3	25.3	25.6	24.8
Sector:					
Care and guardianship (%)	52.1	77.1	45.9	49.1	39.5
Nursing and rehabilitation (%)	8.6	21.7	7.9	5.1	13.7
Educational (%)	34.2	–	22.9	27.5	13.7
Cultural (%)	–	–	–	–	0.8
Recreational (%)	4.6	–	1.8	1.7	2.0
School and school-to-work guidance (%)	0.5	–	–	–	9.9
Job-search assistance (%)	–	–	12.2	15.9	4.8
Other services (%)	–	1.1	5.7	0.7	15.7
Occupation:					
Home carer (%)	14.9	1.7	12.4	14.2	8.8
Social worker[10](%)	1.9	6.9	2.1	1.5	3.3
Social worker (%)	17.9	22.4	12.0	13.4	9.1
Educator (%)	33.6	5.2	28.8	28.0	30.3
General nurse (%)	1.6	4.0	0.8	0.9	0.5
Professional nurse (%)	4.0	9.8	3.5	4.1	2.3
Medical doctor (%)	1.6	–	–	–	–
Therapist–Psychologist (%)	1.4	9.2	5.1	2.7	9.8
Sociologist (%)	0.2	–	0.2	0.1	0.3
Other (%)	10.9	27	12.8	12.9	12.4

Source: own elaboration on FIVOL–FEO data

[10]These respondents qualified themselves as social worker, but were not legally qualified social workers.

Table 7.3 Augmented Mincerian earnings equations by type of organization. OLS coefficients

Variables	All	G	FP	NP	NP1	NP2
Male	0.010	−0.030	−0.055	0.037**	0.035	0.043
University degree and above	0.237***	0.285***	0.340***	0.234***	0.193***	0.218***
Bachelor's degree	0.160***	0.068	0.114*	0.206***	0.190***	0.175**
Upper secondary school	0.100***	0.075***	0.024	0.125***	0.089***	0.148***
Professional qualification	0.049***	0.048*	0.030	0.046***	0.027	0.092
Work Experience	0.014***	0.006*	−0.008	0.019***	0.015***	0.019***
Squared work experience	0.000***	0.000	0.000	0.000***	0.000***	0.000***
Tenure	0.003***	0.002	0.002***	0.003*	0.003**	0.003
North-East	0.065***	0.130***	0.287*	0.045	0.013	0.043
North-West	0.009	0.100**	0.155**	−0.005	−0.010	−0.030
Centre (Florence)	−0.012	0.362***	0.144	−0.026	−0.010	−0.062
Singles	−0.019	−0.007	−0.077**	−0.015	−0.020	−0.035
Divorced/widowed	−0.003	0.023	0.037	−0.011	0.012	−0.056
Part-time worker	0.099***	0.080***	0.167***	0.110***	0.117***	0.127***
Coordinator	0.028	0.076	−0.066	0.017	0.049	−0.021
Care and guardianship	−0.039***	−0.032	−0.373***	−0.038**	−0.011	−0.090***
Home and social care	−0.016	−0.054*	−0.107**	0.005	0.011	−0.006
General/ professional nurse	0.146***	0.111***	0.067	0.180***	0.208***	0.092
Social worker	−0.030	−0.073***	−0.079**	0.002	0.021	−0.034
Teacher /Educator	0.014	0.081***	0.191***	−0.020	−0.040	0.031
Therapist	0.209***	0.300***	0.027	0.193***	0.338***	0.085
Work and training contracts	−0.198***	−0.420***	−0.136	0.016	0.063	0.055
Temporary worker	0.051**	0.015	0.055	0.057*	0.082**	0.040
Occasional worker	0.139***	−0.005	0.109	0.149***	0.116***	0.141**
Union contract	0.047***	0.077***	0.041	0.033*	0.012	0.055
Often going on strike	0.037	0.037	0.087	−0.023	−0.056	0.050
FP	−0.048**					
NP1	−0.120***	−0.120***				
NP2	−0.083***					
Constant	8.965***	8.980***	9.372***	8.794***	8.851***	8.851***
N	1946	570	175	1201	805	396
Adj. R^2	0.24	0.37	0.58	0.20	0.18	0.22

Note: *, **, *** denote significance levels of 10, 5 and 1% respectively
The Huber/White/sandwich estimator of variance is used to correct for heteroskedasticity
The natural log of hourly wages is the dependent variable. The benchmark variables are married women with lower secondary education or below, working in a full-time permanent contract job in public organizations located in southern regions, operating in any service but care and guardianship, and without a specific type of occupation, not willing to always go on strike

slightly higher than average annual premium to education (4%) in basic earnings equations, but lower than average annual premium (1.5%) in augmented equations. Indeed, profit-seeking firms are more common than public and nonprofit organizations in nursing/rehabilitation, where the annual rate of return to education is higher than average.

The private annual rate of return to university education is higher in FPs and in public organizations (3.2% for workers in public organizations and 3.7% for workers in for-profit organizations, vs. 2.6% in nonprofits), but the rate of return to other post-compulsory education degrees is higher in NPs. The return to work experience and job tenure is very low in general, but higher in NPs.

After controlling for individual and environmental characteristics of workers within the sector, the conditional wage gap across organizations reduces considerably, but is still statistically significant. The G/FP gap shrinks from 0.096 (unconditional) to 0.048 (conditional).[11] The G/NP1 gap shrinks from 0.145 to 0.120. The G/NP2 gap increases from 0.034 to 0.083. This last result would suggest that NP2s have higher productivity characteristics than workers in the state sector, but these characteristics are paid less. Omitted results of an Oaxaca and Ransom (1994) type of decomposition analysis suggest that the share of the wage gap between nonprofit organizations and their public and profit-seeking counterparts explained by the equations of Table 7.3 is around 40%. Explaining the rest of these differentials across organizations in terms of the hiring and job-search methods adopted is the main aim of the next section.

7.6 Wages and Hiring and Job-Search Methods

Are hiring and job-search channels different across organizations? Which recruitment methods would nonprofit organizations prefer and why? Can hiring and job-search methods be ranked in terms of their performance? Or, rather, can different methods allow access to different types of information on candidates?

Table 7.4 reports the distribution of workers by hiring method and organization type in the social service sector. On average, public organizations use public competitions more frequently for recruiting their employees: 46.1% of their employees have been hired through public competitions (caption 1 of Table 7.4). This should come as little surprise, since every job in the public sector should be assigned through public competitions according to the Italian Constitution. Nonetheless, the state still hires a large number of employees without public competitions. Public organizations, FPs and NP1s tend to implement some form of selection for about a quarter of their personnel, a percentage which goes down to only 19.4% for NP2s (caption 2 of Table 7.4).

[11] Considering the low coefficients, the Halvorsen and Palmquist (1980) correction of coefficients of dummy variables will be ignored. In fact, in this case, the values are roughly the same.

Table 7.4 Hiring methods (in percentage)

1. Public competition	G	FP	NP1	NP2	Total
No	53.9	100.0	97.9	95.0	84.6
Yes	46.1	0.0	2.1	5.0	15.4
2. Direct hiring with selection from among more candidates	G	FP	NP1	NP2	Total
No	77.4	73.1	76.7	80.6	77.5
Yes	22.5	26.9	23.3	19.4	22.6
3. Direct hiring without selection	G	FP	NP1	NP2	Total
No	68.4	28.6	26.1	26.5	38.8
Yes	31.6	71.4	73.9	73.5	61.2
N	570	175	805	396	1946

Source: own elaboration on FIVOL–FEO data

Table 7.5 Job search methods (in percentage)

Contact	G	FP	NP1	NP2	Total
Previous relationship of professional collaboration with the organization	6.0	9.7	9.3	15.4	9.6
Affiliation to an association or group (religious or not) to which the organization is connected	1.6	1.7	5.3	5.6	4.0
Civil service in the organization	0.2	0.0	1.9	1.8	1.2
Customer (or customer's relatives) of the services supplied by the organization	1.9	4.0	3.0	6.6	3.5
Signalling of relatives and friends	12.8	29.1	33.3	27.3	25.7
I have known the organization because it operates in the territorial area in which I live	9.5	21.1	17.9	13.9	14.9
Experience of voluntary work in the organization	2.8	0.6	8.2	6.6	5.6
Job vacancies published in specialized newspapers or publications advertizing public competitions	39.3	8.0	2.5	3.0	13.9
Employment office (or similar structure)	12.3	12.6	2.2	2.3	6.1
Other	13.7	13.1	16.4	17.7	15.6
N	570	175	805	396	1946

Source: own elaboration on FIVOL–FEO data

Table 7.5 shows that informal networks of family and friends are the most common job search method used in the social service sector.[12] Informal networks are more common among workers of NPs (respectively 33.3% for NP1s and 27.3% for NP2s) and FPs (29.1%) than those in the state sector (12.8%).

[12]Even if data are difficult to compare due to the different number of options given to respondents, the share of workers using informal networks as their preferred job search methods is in the social service sector lower than the country's average. Using SHIW data, Pistaferri (1999) finds a share of about 47% in 1991 and 38% in 1993. Using the European Community Household Panel, Pellizzari (2004) finds an average share of individuals in the sample using informal networks of 25.5% in 1996.

To sum up, the evidence available on the distribution of hiring and job search methods suggests that nonprofit organizations use formal recruitment methods to obtain information on job candidates less frequently. The question then arises as to why this is the case. The first possible answer is that public organizations tend to select their personnel better than NPs and also profit-seeking organizations. The alternative answer is that informal recruitment methods allow for a better selection of workers who are more interested in non-pecuniary than in pecuniary compensations. In turn, if this is the case, it might also be possible that in nonprofit organizations informal networks bring with them a wage premium rather than a wage penalty.

Table 7.6 reports results of Mincerian earnings equations allowing for hiring methods (but not for job-search methods). Workers hired through a public competition are in the baseline. In the entire sample, being hired through public competitions brings with it a wage premium of about 10% compared to hiring without selection, of just less than 7% compared to hiring with some form of selection and about 20% for those who did not answer the relevant question. In addition, the returns to education are slightly reduced in all sectors.

The impact of public competitions is different across organizations. The greatest impact is not in the public sector, but in NP2s where it yields a wage premium of about 16% compared to those undergoing no selection and about 9% to those undergoing some form of selection. Those not declaring their hiring method experience

Table 7.6 Mincerian equations augmented with hiring methods. OLS coefficients

Variable	All	G	FP	NP1	NP2
Male	0.0147	−0.0281	−0.0502	0.0370	0.0514
Degree	0.2224***	0.2630***	0.3347*	0.1929***	0.2074***
Bachelor's degree	0.1481***	0.0395	0.1106	0.1878***	0.1704***
General Secondary	0.0931***	0.0573*	0.0202	0.0882**	0.1463***
Vocational Secondary	0.0444**	0.0318	0.0197	0.0264	0.0961
Pot. work exp.	0.0132***	0.0048	−0.0077	0.0151***	0.0185***
Pot. work exp. ^2	−0.0002***	−0.0001	0.0001	−0.0003**	−0.0003***
Job tenure	0.0028**	0.0026*	0.0026	0.0029*	0.0038
FP	−0.0051				
NP1	−0.0787***				
NP2	−0.0410*				
Hiring with no selection	−0.1009***	−0.0867***		−0.0284	−0.1623***
Hiring with selection	−0.0680***	−0.0189	0.0587	−0.0322	−0.0886*
Hiring missing	−0.2042**	0.0270		−0.1243	−0.3212**
Constant	9.0309***	9.0421***	9.3411***	8.8826***	9.0017***
N	1946	570	175	805	396
Adj. R^2	0.26	0.42	0.67	0.20	0.29

Note: see the notes under Table 7.3. The coefficients of civil status, regional, industry, occupation and union membership are omitted. In addition, the benchmark group is further restricted to those individuals who have been hired through public competition. No employee in the FPs has been hired through public competition and only very few do not respond to the question on the hiring method adopted. In this case, the baseline is 'hiring with no selection or missing observation on hiring'

a wage penalty of over 30% of their wages. The impact of hiring methods is statistically insignificant in FPs and NP1s.

Table 7.7 reports the results of earnings equations augmented with both hiring and job-search methods. The wage effect of hiring methods is now reduced by the introduction of controls for job-search methods, whereas the coefficients of organizations' dummies remain substantially unchanged. In other words, job-search methods capture part of the impact of hiring methods, but not that on wage differentials across organizations. There is apparently some relationship between hiring and job search methods. Public organizations use more formal hiring methods and, hence, also more formal job search methods (answering advertisements in newspapers and so on). Consequently, the wage effect of being hired through

Table 7.7 Mincerian equations augmented with hiring and job-search methods. OLS coefficients

Variable	All	G	FP	NP1	NP2
Male	0.0217	−0.0305	−0.0427	0.0451	0.0583
Degree	0.2119***	0.2601***	0.3523**	0.1869**	0.1935***
Bachelor's degree	0.1381***	0.0563	0.1165	0.1825***	0.1511**
General Secondary	0.0917***	0.0590*	0.0150	0.0841**	0.1463***
General Secondary	0.0917***	0.0590*	0.0150	0.0841**	0.1463***
Pot. work exp.	0.0123***	0.0046	−0.0068	0.0143***	0.0165***
Pot. work exp. ^2	−0.0002***	−0.0001	0.0001	−0.0003**	−0.0003***
Job tenure	0.0028**	0.0029*	0.0023	0.0024	0.0043
Hiring with no selection	−0.0711***	−0.0789**		−0.0363	−0.1377**
Hiring with selection	−0.0445*	−0.0098	0.0398	−0.0429	−0.0630
Hiring missing	−0.1779*	0.0248		−0.1000	−0.3241**
FP	−0.0073				
NP1	−0.0772***				
Previous professional collaboration	0.0984***	0.0089	−0.0813	0.1561***	0.1486***
Affiliation to an association	0.0173	0.0085	−0.0714	0.0550	0.0738
Civil service in the organization	−0.1494*			−0.1312	−0.0386
Customer	0.0426	0.0586	−0.1196	0.1468**	0.0181
Relatives and friends	0.0139	−0.0652*	−0.0178	0.0632*	0.0166
Co-resident of the organization	0.0105	−0.0104	−0.0488	0.0266	0.0468
Previously Volunteer	−0.0272	−0.0418		0.0375	−0.0124
Job vacancies published in newspapers	0.0602**	−0.0099	0.0533	0.0627	0.0922*
Employment office	−0.0097	−0.0274	−0.0009	−0.0452	0.0301
Constant	8.9925***	9.0622***	9.3729***	8.8474***	8.9524***
N	1946	570	175	805	396
Adj. R^2	0.28	0.43	0.68	0.23	0.32

Note: see the notes under Table 7.6. In addition, the benchmark group is further restricted to those individuals who have been hired through public competition and have used 'other job search methods'

a public competition reduces now from 10 to 7% for those hired with no selection, from 6.8 to 4.5% for those hired with some form of selection and from 20 to 18% for those who did not declare their entry channel.

Interestingly, family and friends bring with them a statistically significant and negative wage effect (–6.5%) in the public sector where public competitions are common, whereas they yield a statistically significant and positive wage effect (6.3%) in social cooperatives and religious nonprofit organizations. This would confirm the hypothesis, already formulated above, that job search methods have a different function and therefore yield a different impact on wages in different organization types. In the public sector, where formal methods are considered necessary to assess the productivity level in candidates, being hired through informal networks is seen as a sign of low productivity. Conversely, in nonprofit organizations, informal networks are seen as the best way to assess not only the productivity level, but also the degree of ideological motivation and, hence, yield a positive wage effect.

Other job-search methods also affect wages. Having had previous professional collaboration with the organizations generates a wage premium of about 10% in all sectors. This result is especially due to workers employed in nonprofit organizations, where the wage premium of previous professional collaborations rises to about 15%. This result is stable across different specifications and confirms the importance of direct knowledge of workers in the sector in general and in NPs in particular. Again, this would confirm the importance of knowing the candidate personally to assess such characteristics as motivation that cannot be assessed using formal selection methods.

Table 7.8 summarizes the coefficients of organizations' dummies in different specifications of the earnings function. Having controlled for hiring methods, wage differentials across organizations are substantially reduced or, in the case of for-profit organizations, turn to statistical insignificance. This suggests that the positive wage gap between Gs and FPs is entirely explained by hiring methods. Even the coefficient of the dummy for NP2s shrinks by a half compared to that obtained in augmented earnings equations and reduces its significance level. The coefficient for NP1s shrinks by about 30% (from –0.120 to –0.079), but remains statistically significant.

Table 7.8 Wage differentials across organizations after controlling for recruitment methods. OLS coefficients

	(1)	(2)	(3)	(4)	(5)
NP2	–0.095***	–0.048**	–0.005	–0.007	–0.027
NP1	–0.145***	–0.120***	–0.079***	–0.077***	0.093***
FPs	–0.034*	–0.083***	–0.041*	–0.043*	–0.060**

Note: the public sector is the baseline. The columns mean: (1) Unconditional regression; (2) Augmented earning equation (Table 7.3); (3) Augmented earning equation with hiring methods (Table 7.6); (4) Augmented earning equation with hiring and job-search methods (Table 7.7); (5) Augmented earning equation with job-search methods only (results available upon request)

Table 7.9 summarizes estimates for the coefficients of informal networks with and without controls for hiring methods. This is done for comparative purposes, since previous research has used this variable without controls for other job-search methods. The informal network coefficient is statistically significant only for public organizations, where it is negative. Having been hired through informal networks yields a wage penalty of almost 6% if one controls for hiring methods and 8% without controls for hiring methods. The informal network coefficients for the public sector are similar to those in Table 7.7.

On the other hand, unlike in Table 7.7, the informal network coefficients for NP1s are not statistically significant. This finding is a warning against the use of informal networks without controls for other job-search methods. The range of answers available in the questionnaire might drive the results when estimating the wage effect of informal networks.

Are informal networks an exogenous determinant of wages? Or are they a signal of workers' ability? Previous studies find much evidence that in Italy low-skilled workers use informal networks more frequently. Informal networks are also common in markets for high-skilled workers. This might suggest that informal networks may just signal above/below average skills in candidates. Owing to the lack of suitable instruments, we adopt an indirect approach to this issue. If informal networks are not just a signal of skills but, rather, an independent factor causing a wage penalty/premium, this wage premium/penalty should disappear with time. In fact, as soon as workers understand that their wages are lower/higher than they should be, based on their skills, then, in the event of a wage penalty, workers will leave the firm in search for higher wages and, in the case of a wage premium, firms will understand the real skill level of workers and adjust wages to it. Vice versa, if informal networks were just a signal of skills, then the wage penalty/premium associated with it should continue over time; in this case, workers would indeed have no reason to move to seek wage improvements, in the event of a wage penalty, and firms would have no reason to reduce wages, in the case of a wage premium. To test these alternative hypotheses, we allow for informal networks interacted with tenure and check whether the coefficients in (7.4) are statistically different from each other.

Table 7.9 The role of informal networks (in absence of other job-search methods). OLS coefficients

	All	G	FP	NP1	NP2
	Controlling for hiring methods				
Relatives and friends	−0.004	−0.057*	0.009	0.022	−0.031
	No controls for hiring methods				
Relatives and friends	0.011	−0.081**	0.009	0.022	0.037

Note: the estimates refer respectively to an augmented earning equation allowing for all hiring methods and only relatives and friends as job-search method, and to an augmented earning equation not including hiring methods and allowing for only relatives and friends as job-search method (all results available upon request)

Table 7.10 Informal networks and tenure profile. OLS coefficients

Variables	All	G	FP	NP1	NP2
In basic earnings equations					
Family and friends* 2 years of tenure	0.0429	−0.2897**	0.0886	0.1485*	−0.0503
Family and friends* more years of tenure	−0.0025	−0.0939*	−0.0576	0.0637*	−0.0271
Wald-test of H_0: b_1-b_2=0	1.14	3.95**	2.27	2.05	0.10
In augmented earnings equations					
Family and friends* 2 years of tenure	0.0238	−0.1655*	0.0591	0.0922	−0.0034
Family and friends* more years of tenure	0.0110	−0.0506	−0.0388	0.0532	0.0211
Wald-test of H_0: b_1-b_2= 0	0.11	2.62	0.85	0.53	0.13

Note: basic earnings equations include only human capital variables, whereas augmented earnings equations include all the variables of Table 7.7

Table 7.10 reports the coefficients of the dummies for informal networks interacted with tenure and the results of the test of equality of coefficients. The differences in coefficients are sizeable in the two cases in which informal networks are statistically significant, namely in the estimates relating to governmental organizations and NPls. The difference in coefficients is about 50% or more. However, the test of equality of coefficients suggests rejecting the null hypothesis in one case only, namely for basic earnings equations relating to public organizations. Two years of job tenure is a reasonable assumption in the social service sector in Italy, where labour legislation is particularly binding. Furthermore, unreported sensitivity analysis experimenting with different job tenures does not seem to change the results very much.

We also implemented the same type of test for public competitions interacted with years of job tenure (estimates are not reported, but are available on request). It is worth recalling from the beginning of this section that public competitions are used almost exclusively in the state sector and in NP2s. The results allow the null of equality of coefficients to be rejected in the case of governmental organizations, but not in the case of NP2s. This might suggest that public competitions yield a specific wage premium only in the former case.

7.7 Concluding Remarks

According to an unsympathetic interpretation, in recent years nonprofits have substituted the good jobs typical of the state sector with low-quality jobs. From this it follows that nonprofits would prefer informal recruitment methods because these methods would serve the aim of hiring low-skill protégés of political lobbies to obtain financial support. This paper addresses these criticisms in two ways. First, it looks at the quality of employment and at the returns to education across organization types operating in the social service sector. Second, it tests whether differences in the choice of recruitment channels across organization types may explain at least in part the negative nonprofit wage gap of social cooperatives and religious nonprofit against profit-seeking and, to a greater extent, governmental organizations within the sector.

We provide evidence that public organizations pay higher wages than their private for-profit and nonprofit counterparts, while workers in NPs are *not* significantly less endowed with human capital. Turning to hiring and job-search methods, informal networks are more common in nonprofit than in public organizations, but are as common as in for-profit organizations. The difference between public and private organizations is to be found first and foremost in the former's legal obligation to hire through formal recruitment methods, especially public competitions. Irrespective of the organization type, being hired through public competitions brings with it a substantial wage premium (ranging from 7 to 32%). Controlling for methods in the selection of personnel (public competition, some form of selection, no selection, do not answer), informal networks bear a wage penalty (with a coefficient of –0.065) in the state sector, and a wage premium (+0.063) in social cooperatives and religious institutions. They are not significant determinants of earnings for workers in for-profit and non-religious nonprofit organizations. This could imply that the information content of informal networks is higher when formal recruitment methods are not common (especially in the public sector). All in all, the differences in hiring and job-search methods between state and private organizations explain 50–100% of the conditional wage differential across organizations.

Our interpretation of these findings is that nonprofit organizations prefer informal recruitment methods to better select the most motivated workers, namely those workers who share the nonprofit mission. In principle, these findings can be interpreted in two alternative ways.

First, in following the previous literature on the wage impact of hiring and job-search methods (see, among others, Montgomery 1991; Ioannides and Datcher Loury 2004), one could conclude that the higher the degree of formality of recruitment methods adopted, the higher is also the ability of these methods to solve the ex ante asymmetric information problem that employers have to face when recruiting their employees. This would explain the wage premium attached to jobs accessed through formal recruitment methods. This interpretation would lend support to the view that nonprofits hire low-productivity workers through informal methods, bearing a cost in terms of lower productivity and quality of the services provided, because they favour political and social lobbies. In turn, these lobbies would ensure the–inefficient – survival of nonprofits.

The alternative explanation is that the degree of formality of hiring and job-search methods is not so important in terms of the quantity of the information achieved, but rather of its quality. More specifically, while both formal and informal methods would equally allow the productivity level of workers to be assessed (the level and quality of human capital, in fact, are signalled also by academic qualifications and credentials and can therefore be known also through informal methods), informal methods would also enable the degree of motivation in candidates to be assessed, in addition to their work ethic, sharing of aims and mission of the organization, and so on.

The overall evidence provided in this paper, as well as in some previous literature, would suggest that the latter interpretation of our findings is to be preferred. Indeed, if public competitions were a better hiring method, as suggested in the first interpretation, then workers employed in public organizations should be better endowed with human capital and supply their services more efficiently. This, however, seems not to be the case in our sample. Human capital endowments are not in favour of the state sector. In addition, using the same dataset, Mosca et al. (2007) found that the degree of motivation and job satisfaction is much higher for workers employed in the nonprofit than in the state sector, despite the wage gap in favour of the latter. Furthermore, relying on the organizations' questionnaire of the same dataset, Destefanis and Maietta (2003) showed that including the degree of motivation of employees in the production function has a positive and significant impact on the G–NP gap in terms of technical efficiency, at least in Nursing/Rehabilitation. When the degree of motivation of employees is not controlled for, there are no statistically significant efficiency differences between public organizations and NPs. Destefanis and Maietta interpret this finding as evidence that a relatively lower degree of worker motivation reduces technical efficiency in the state sector. In terms of our analysis, this result may suggest that informal recruitment methods are at least equally able to detect the human capital level and, at the same time, are better suited to hiring motivated candidates.

Furthermore, if informal methods are less effective than formal ones, as suggested in the first interpretation, they should entail a wage penalty not only in the state sector, but also in nonprofit organizations. However, there is a wage *premium* in social cooperatives and religious nonprofit organizations. This finding might be consistent with firms preferring informal recruitment methods when they aim to assess not only the level and quality of human capital, but also the degree of motivation in potential candidates.

From a policy perspective, this paper suggests that different recruitment methods are necessary to reduce the *ex ante* information asymmetries existing between employers and employees across different types of organizations. In particular, formal hiring and job-search methods need not necessarily be the best instrument to select the most skilled among otherwise identical individuals, as traditional wisdom would suggest. When ideological motivation is an important quality in candidates, informal recruitment methods may be better suited.

Acknowledgments A previous, longer, version of this Chapter has been published as IZA discussion paper n. 3422. We thank Sergio Destefanis and Valentina Meliciani for useful suggestions on former drafts. However, the responsibility of any errors remains only ours.

Appendix

Table 7.11 Survey of previous findings on hiring and job search methods

Authors	Data bank	Country and years	Estimation method	Control for hiring methods	Impact on wages
Simon and Warner (1992)	Survey on Natural and Social Scientists and Engineers	USA: 1972	OLS	No	Workers hired through the old-boy networks earn higher initial salaries (from 0.034 to 0.087), experience lower wage growth on the job and stay on the job longer than otherwise comparable workers hired from outside the network
Pistaferri (1999)	SHIW	Italy: 1991, 1993	OLS, IV	No	Negative and statistically significant coefficient: –0.046. When controlling for low wage sectors and occupations: –0.031. OLS underestimates wage effects, which become: –0.071 and controlling for firm size –0.039
Collier and Garg (1999)	Living Standards Survey	Ghana: 1989	OLS with Heckman-Lee correction	No	Wage premium for kinship equals 25 per cent.
Marmaros and Sacerdote (2002)	Survey of Dartmouth College Seniors	USA: 2001	OLS	No	Informal networks significantly affect the probability to access high paying jobs
Kugler (2003)	National Longitudinal Survey of Youths (NLSY) and Current Population Survey (CPS)	USA: 1982 (NLSY) and 1984 (CPS)	OLS	No	Statistically significant wage premium: 0.04. Controlling for tenure: –0.01

Margolis and Simonnet (2003)	Youth and Career Survey by Institut National de la Statistique et des Études Économiques	France: 1997	OLS	Yes	Individuals who found their 1997 job via informal contacts earn significantly more than those who found their job by any other method (16 per cent more than market methods, 34 per cent more than intermediaries and 13 per cent more than other methods)
Pellizzari (2004)	European Community Household Panel (ECHP) and National Longitudinal Survey of Youths (NLSY)	EU (ECHP): 1994–1999; USA (NLSY): 1979–1999	OLS	No	Large cross-country and cross-industry variation in the wage differentials
Sylos Labini (2004a)	Survey on university to job transition, ISTAT	Italy: 1998	OLS	Yes	Wage penalty for all informal networks (–0.025). Networks of family and friends yield a wage penalty (–0.047), whereas networks of colleagues yield a wage premium (0.025)
Meliciani and Radicchia (2005)	Data provided by ISFOL	Italy: 2003	OLS, Probit and IV	Yes	Informal contacts generates a wage penalty of –0.037 with respect to public competitions, direct applications, direct experience on the job and schools
Antoninis (2006)	Personnel files of a manufacturing firm	Egypt: 2000	OLS	No	No wage effect in general. When controlling for source of referrals, skilled jobs have not statistically significant penalty (–0.055) for families and friends and significant premium for old colleagues (0.347); for unskilled jobs a significant penalty for family and friends (–0.140) and not statistically significant premium for old colleagues (0.114)

(continued)

Table 7.11 (continued)

Authors	Data bank	Country and years	Estimation method	Control for hiring methods	Impact on wages
Datcher Loury (2006)	National Longitudinal Survey of Youths (NLSY)	USA: 1982–2003	OLS	No	Wage penalty for men relying on female contacts (–0.066); wage premium for men relying on male contacts (0.151); wage premium for women relying on male contacts (0.129); not significant effect for women relying on female contacts
Delattre and Sabatier (2007)	French Longitudinal Survey: 'Trajectoires des Demandeurs d'Emploi et Marchés Locaux du Travail' by Direction de l'Animation et de la Recherche, des Études et des Statistiques	France: 1995	OLS, IV and switching regression model	No	No statistical significant wage effect (OLS and IV); informal networks yield a statistically significant wage penalty of 7 per cent in the case of Switching regression models
Goos and Salomons (2007)	Quarterly Labour Force Survey	UK: 2001–2006	OLS	Yes	Men (0.053) receive higher average referral wage premium than women (0.015). Referral wage premium for men and women increases with years of education. Networks explain a significant part of the gender wage gap for newly hired workers

Weber and Mahringer (2008)	Ad hoc survey of successful job seekers	Austria: 2004	OLS, IV	No	OLS estimates yield no statistically significant effect of informal networks. IV estimates yield a not statistically significant wage penalty
Pastore (2008)	School-to-Work Survey	Mongolia: 2006	OLS	No	Not statistically significant wage penalty for the entire sample: (−0.1134). Statistically significant penalty for young people aged 25–29 (−0.1706) and for men (−0.1990)
Bentolila et al. (2009)	Multi-city Study of Urban Inequality (MCSUI) and European Community Household Panel (ECHP)	USA (MCSUI): 1992–1994; EU (ECHP): 1994–1998	OLS	No	Social contacts reduce the time to wait by 1–2 months, but lead to individual wage discounts of 5 –7%

These respondents qualified themselves as social workers, but were not legally qualified social workers.

References

Addison JT, Portugal P (2002) Job search methods and outcomes. Oxford Economic Papers 54:505–533

Akerlof GA (1984) Gift exchange and efficiency wage theory: four views. American Economic Review 74:79–83

Antoninis M (2006) The wage effects from the use of personal contacts as hiring channels. Journal of Economic Behavior and Organization 59:133–146

Bentolila SC, Michelacci C, Suàrez J (2009) Social contacts and occupational choice. Economica 76:forthcoming

Blau DM Philip RK (1990) Job search outcomes for the employed and unemployed. Journal of Political Economy 98:637–55

Borzaga C (ed) (2000) Capitale umano e qualità del lavoro nei servizi sociali. Fondazione Italiana del Volontariato, Rome

Brunello G, Comi S, Lucifora C (2000) The returns to education in Italy: a new look at the evidence. IZA Discussion Paper 130

Carinci F (2001) Questioni giuslavoristiche in tema di organizzazioni di volontariato e di cooperative sociali. Italian Labour Law E-Journal 3(3). http://www.dirittodellavoro.it/public/current/ejournal/

Collier P, Garg A (1999) On kin groups and wages in the Ghanaian labour market. Oxford Bulletin Of Economics and Statistics 61:133–151

Datcher Loury L (2006) Some contacts are more equal than others: informal networks, job tenure and wages. Journal of Labor Economics 24:299–318

Delattre E, Sabatier M (2007) Social capital and wages: an econometric evaluation of social networking's effects. Labour 21:209–236

Depedri S (2003) La ricerca: metodologia campione e principali risultati. In: Borzaga C, Musella M (eds) Produttività ed efficienza nelle organizzazioni nonprofit. Edizioni31, Trento

Destefanis S, Maietta OW (2003) La determinazione dell'efficienza produttiva nel settore nonprofit. In: Borzaga C, Musella M (eds) Produttività ed efficienza nelle organizzazioni nonprofit. Edizioni31, Trento

DeVaro J (2005) Employer recruitment strategies and the labour market outcomes of new hires. Economic Enquiry 43:263–282

Goldberg M (1982) Discrimination, nepotism and long-run wage differentials. Quarterly Journal of Economics 97:307–319

Goos M, Salomons A (2007) Dangerous liaisons: a social network model for the gender wage gap. University of Leuven CES Discussion Paper 07.22

Halvorsen R, Palmquist R (1980) The interpretation of dummy variables in semilogarithmic equations. American Economic Review 70:474–475

Handy F, Katz E (1998) The wage differential between nonprofit institution and corporations: getting more by paying less? Journal of Comparative Economics 26:246–261

Holzer HJ (1987) Job search by employed and unemployed youth. Industrial and Labor Relations Review 40:601–611

Holzer HJ (1988) Search method use by unemployed youth. Journal of Labor Economics 6:1–20

Ioannides YM, Datcher Loury L (2004) Job information networks, neighborhood effects and inequality. Journal of Economic Literature 42:1056–1093

Kugler AD (2003) Employee referrals and efficiency wages. Labour Economics 10:531–556

Leete L (2000) Wage equity and employment motivation in nonprofit and forprofit organisations. Journal of Economic Behavior and Organization 43:423–446

Leete L (2001) Whither the nonprofit wage differential? Estimates from the 1990 Census. Journal of Labour Economics 19:136–170

Margolis DN, Simonnet V (2003) Educational track networks and labor market outcomes. IZA Discussion Paper 699

Marmaros D, Sacerdote B (2002) Peer and social networks in job search. European Economic Review 46:870–879

Meliciani V, Radicchia D (2005) Returns to education in Italy: the role of labour market recruitment channels. XX AIEL Conference, University of Rome "La Sapienza"

Montgomery J (1991) Social networks and labor market outcomes. American Economic Review 81:1408–1418

Mortensen D, Vishwanath T (1994) Personal contacts and earnings. It is who you know! Labour Economics 1:187–201

Mosca M, Musella M, Pastore F (2007) Relational goods monitoring and non-pecuniary compensations in the nonprofit sector: the case of the Italian social services. Annals of Public and Cooperative Economics 78:55–86

Oaxaca R, Ransom M (1994) On discrimination and the decomposition of wage differentials. Journal of Econometrics 61:5–21

Osberg L (1993) Fishing in different pools: job-search strategies and job-finding success in Canada in the early 1980s. Journal of Labor Economics 11:348–386

Pastore F (2008) School-to-work transition in Mongolia employment. International Labour Office Working Paper 2008/14

Pellizzari M (2004) Do friends and relatives really help in getting a good job? CEP Discussion Paper 623

Pestana Barros C (2006) Earnings, schooling and social capital of cooperative managers. Annals of Public and Cooperative Economics 77:1–20

Pistaferri L (1999) Informal networks in the Italian labor market. Giornale degli Economisti e Annali di Economia 58:355–375

Preston AE (1989) The nonprofit worker in a forprofit world. Journal of Labor Economics 7:438–463

Psacharopoulos G (1994) Returns to investment in education: a global update. World Development 22:1325–1343

Roper S (1988) Recruitment methods and vacancy duration. Scottish Journal of Political Economy 35:51–64

Ruhm C, Borkoski C (2003) Compensation in the nonprofit sector. Journal of Human Resources 38:992–1021

Saloner G (1985) Old Boy networks as screening mechanisms. Journal of Labor Economics 3:255–267

Simon C, Warner J (1992) Matchmaker, matchmaker: the effect of Old Boy networks on job match quality earnings and tenure. Journal of Labor Economics 10:306–30

Sylos Labini M (2004a) Social networks and wages: it's all about connections! Sant'Anna School of Advanced Studies, Lucca, LEM Working Paper 10

Sylos Labini M (2004b) Job search methods and outcomes for the employed and unemployed: an empirical investigation. Mimeo, Sant'Anna School of Advanced Studies, Lucca

Weber A, Mahringer H (2008) Choice and success of job search methods. Empirical Economics 35:153–178

Chapter 8
The Productivity of Volunteer Labour: DEA-Based Evidence from Italy

Sergio Destefanis and Ornella Wanda Maietta

Abstract This paper analyzes the relatively novel concept of a downward-sloping demand for volunteer labour, using data from the Italian social services sector. Both descriptive and econometric evidence shows that the price of volunteer labour (proxied by its shadow price obtained through DEA) is negatively related to the number of volunteer hours. Furthermore, the demand for volunteer labour is higher in areas relatively well endowed with social capital, where there is also evidence that organizations refrain from substituting volunteers for paid workers when the latter become more expensive. According to our results, the productivity of voluntary labour is higher in social capital-rich regions, where more motivated and skilful volunteers are drawn from a relatively larger pool.

8.1 Introduction

The number, characteristics and economic weight of private nonprofit organizations (NPs) is increasing fast in the OECD economies. In the US, it is estimated (2002 data from the US Census Bureau) that over 1.5 million NPs account for 6.8% of total national income, and 11.4% of total employment (including voluntary workers). In Europe the nonprofit sector is still less developed than in the US but is growing fast, especially in the field of social utility services (see the figures quoted in the Introduction and in Chap. 1 of this book).

NPs are private firms characterized by the non-distribution of profits[1] which produce goods or services of collective interest (non-distribution means that

[1]Pure NPs are at the extreme end of a spectrum including, besides pure forprofit firms at the other end, all the organizations (cooperatives, associations of mutual character) constrained in some way in the distribution of their profits. According to Borzaga (2003), the strength of these constraints allies such organizations to NPs.

S. Destefanis (✉)
Department of Economics and Statistics and CELPE, University of Salerno,
Via Ponte Don Melillo, 84084, Fisciano (SA), Italy

S. Destefanis and M. Musella (eds.), *Paid and Unpaid Labour in the Social Economy*,
AIEL Series in Labour Economics, DOI: 10.1007/978-3-7908-2137-6_9,

profits can be made, but not distributed). NPs are often chosen by altruistic or ideology-minded entrepreneurs, who may also come from religious, trade-union or political groups, depending on the form that best suits the intrinsic character of the services provided, as well as the promotion of a set of values across society and the acquisition of new backers (Young 1983; James 1989; Rose-Ackerman 1996). One of the most distinguishing features of NPs is that they often aim to reform the distribution of opportunities in a given society according to the preferences of the founding group (Borzaga 2003). Since this redistributive task often means providing goods and services at a very low or zero price, it follows that a basic condition for the survival and growth of these organizations is the capability to attract donors and workers who agree to supply their resources at a very low or zero cost.

Non-paid labour can take the form of either volunteer labour or extra effort from paid workers. This implies that NPs must rely on the selection of workers ready to share the *mission* of the organization (Besley and Ghatak 2005) and on the utilization of other non-monetary incentives. While there already exists a number of studies on the relationships between the selection procedures of paid workers in NPs, the utilization of non-monetary incentives and workers' satisfaction (see on this, for instance, Borzaga and Depedri 2005), the characteristics of volunteer labour have attracted considerably less attention, especially inasmuch as the productivity of this kind of labour is concerned. Now, while trends are hard to identify and good practices are difficult to pin down, it is at any rate clear that NPs look for skilled, conscientious and compassionate labour. One of the main challenges of the nonprofit sector is indeed to use volunteer labour, this valuable but unwieldy resource, to its fullest.

It is our belief that analysing the relationships between marginal productivity and hours of volunteer labour can shed new light on the above issues. In this paper we attempt to do this by drawing on evidence from the FIVOL-FEO survey on Italian NPs and other organizations providing social utility services, and relying on measures of marginal productivity obtained through DEA (Data Envelopment Analysis). In Sect. 8.2 we provide a survey of literature on the productivity of volunteer labour. We single out some key questions and suggest ways in which novel evidence can be brought to bear upon these issues. The basic empirical approach is described in Sect. 8.3, while Sect. 8.4 presents some descriptive evidence from the FIVOL-FEO survey, mainly comparing measures of the marginal productivity of volunteer labour with analogous indicators for paid labour. Section 8.5 provides some econometric evidence on the relationships between marginal productivity and hours of volunteer labour, in the spirit of Emanuele (1996) and Handy and Srinivasan (2005). Finally, some concluding remarks are offered in Sect. 8.6.

8.2 The Productivity of Volunteer Labour: A Survey

Throughout the OECD, the growth of the nonprofit sector mainly relates to the field of social utility services. The development of NPs is closely related to the reduction in the impact of the government in the economy. In the USA, the National Commission on Philanthropy and Civic Renewal, established in 1996, aimed to respond to the "end of the Interventionist State". In Europe, while public administration is often still the main provider of social utility services, a growing unease concerning the quality and efficiency of publicly provided services has led to some important reforms that attempt to redesign the incentives within this field and broaden the field of action for NPs. Implicit in the belief that NPs can provide services ranging from school lunches to welfare, is the assumption that a readily available source of volunteer labour can be easily matched with NPs' productive needs.

The importance of volunteer labour for many NPs and, more in general, for the economy has been highlighted in a number of studies (Salamon and Anheier 1998; Toppe et al. 2002; Weitzman et al. 2002). A recent study found that 80% of US charities use volunteers (Hager 2004). In Canada (Statcan 2004) 93% of all volunteers are engaged by 161,000 nonprofit organizations (NPs). In Italy, according to ISTAT, as of 2001 there were over 3 million volunteers in nonprofit organizations. A strong demand thus appears to exist for volunteer labour, supposedly because of its relatively low cost and the abundance of individuals willing to supply unpaid labour. However, while a number of studies examine the supply of volunteer labour and determine why and how individuals give their time without remuneration (Vaillancourt and Payette 1986; Menchik and Weisbrod 1987; Smith 1994; Freeman 1997), fewer studies examine the demand for volunteer labour and its productive use (Emanuele 1996; Handy and Srinivasan 2005).

A very important reflection on these issues, giving rise to the premise that volunteer labour cannot be modelled as a free input, was perhaps first provided in Steinberg (1990). Steinberg argues first that paid labour is needed to train and supervise volunteers and, more generally, to operate a volunteer programme. Second, volunteers may use resources that might otherwise be used by paid workers. Indeed, some volunteers are paid a stipend to cover their living expenses during the time they spend volunteering. Finally, the recruitment itself of additional volunteers is a process likely to consume time and money. Given the existence of these costs, organizations will probably be unable to accept all of the volunteers who wish to enter, but will instead choose how many (and which) volunteers to employ. This choice, which implies weighing the cost of volunteer labour against the costs of paid labour and/or other inputs, entails the existence of a downward sloping demand curve for volunteer labour.

Emanuele (1996) considers whether organizations that use volunteer labour show evidence of possessing a demand curve for volunteer labour that is consistent over time. In order to analyze this issue, Emanuele relies upon US data from the Nonprofit Sector Project (NSP), collected by the Urban Institute in a two-stage survey in the early 1980s. While these data do not contain direct information on the cost of volunteer labour, they can be used to deduce relevant information on that variable. In the 1982 stage of the NSP survey, organizations were asked: 'During the past year, has your organization made any of the following *management changes?*' (italics in original survey), one of these possible changes being 'placed greater reliance on volunteers'. Note that this question did not ask whether more volunteers offered to donate more time, but rather if the organization *chose* to place a greater reliance on volunteers. This is likely to imply that organizations possess a demand curve for volunteer labour. The 1984 stage of the survey included questions on the change in the use of volunteer labour between 1983 and 1984. Hence Emanuele tests the null hypothesis that there is no relationship between placing greater reliance on volunteers in the years before 1982 and requesting considerably more volunteer labour in the years between the two stages of the survey. The null is comfortably rejected, suggesting that the organizations are demanding volunteer labour in a behaviourally consistent manner. Due to data limitations, however, Emanuele (1996) is not able to specify and estimate a standard demand curve for volunteer labour.

Handy and Srinivasan (2005) also challenge the assumption that organizations are accepting all the volunteer labour offered to them. Furthermore, they carry out an econometric analysis of the demand of volunteer labour by hospitals in the Toronto area, showing that the number of volunteer hours requested has a decreasing function in their costs. Handy and Srinivasan use data generated from a questionnaire given to the CEOs of 28 hospitals in Toronto, and model the demand for volunteer hours as a function of:

1. Cost/hour: CEOs were asked for the amount of the volunteer administration budget, including the salaries and operating costs of coordinating and managing volunteer labour; this amount was then divided by the number of volunteer hours. Handy and Srinivasan expected a negative relationship between this variable and the number of volunteer hours used by the hospital
2. The donation that the CEO was willing to trade for 1 h of volunteer labour, i.e. the trade-off between time donations and money donations. This productivity proxy is supposed to affect positively the demand for volunteer labour
3. CEO satisfaction with volunteers: this is another subjective proxy of productivity
4. The number of beds at the hospital: this is an output proxy, expected to increase the demand for volunteer labour
5. The existence of a trade union in the hospital, expected to deter the demand for volunteer labour

A linear regression of volunteer hours on these variables provides some support for the a priori expectations. Volunteer labour in hospitals is negatively related to the costs per volunteer hour and positively related to measures of productivity and output. On the other hand, the presence of a union actually encourages the use of volunteers. While this is interesting evidence of the demand for volunteer hours, there are problems with the rather small number of observations made by Handy and Srinivasan (28), as well as with the subjective nature of some of their indicators.

More in general, there are various ways in which novel evidence can be brought to bear upon these issues. First, it would be interesting to have a quantitative comparison, drawing from the same dataset, of the productivity of volunteers and paid workers. Such a simple and direct evaluation of the value of volunteer labour is still missing from the literature. Secondly, there is the issue of complementarity among different kinds of labour. Paid workers may view volunteers in certain areas, such as education and hospitals, as replacements for paid labour (Macduff 1997; Zahnd 1997). Some US evidence, however, suggests that public employee unions may not resist the use of volunteer labour because their introduction offers unions the opportunity to firm up labour contracts and protect paid positions (Brudney and Kellough 2000). Preston (2007) proposes a simple test of this hypothesis. Volunteers become substitutes for paid labour if an increase in the cost of paid labour leads to more volunteers being used. Alternatively, they become complements for paid labour if an increase in the cost of paid labour leads to a decrease in the number of volunteer hours being used. Direct evidence on this issue is again missing.

Finally, volunteer labour resources are far from being a monolithic concept. Handy and Brudney (2007) suggest that there are four important types of volunteering differing in terms of costs, productivity, and externalities that can extend to the larger society: mandated (e.g. conscientious objectors, likely to be the most expensive to the organization, as well as the least productive), episodic (likely to be very cheap, but also relatively unproductive), traditional (the closest in character to paid labour), and virtual (consisting of the supply of non-paid labour through ICT means). In Italy, it has often been suggested that volunteer characteristics are influenced by the territorial endowment of what Putnam (1993) defines as social capital. The larger this endowment, the more skilled and conscientious volunteers are likely to be, and hence the greater the demand for volunteer labour. More trivially, it would also be interesting to see whether volunteer productivity differs across sectors, as social utility services of a different nature may attract people with different skills.

8.3 The Empirical Approach

In this work, we intend to provide evidence on the relationships between (marginal) productivity and hours of volunteer labour by drawing upon data from the FIVOL-FEO survey carried out on Italian NPs and other organizations providing social utility services (see for more details: Borzaga 2000; Depedri 2003). The crucial (and novel) feature of our evidence is that we rely upon DEA, a non-parametric approach to the measurement of productive efficiency in order to obtain measures of the marginal productivity of volunteer (and paid) labour.[2]

DEA allows the calculation not only of technical (and allocative) efficiency, but also of output and input shadow prices. The latter are measures of the input marginal products. Formally, the postulates utilized to build the production possibility set $Z_{BCC}(Z^{\circ})$ are:

1. Strong free input and output disposal;
2. Convexity:

[2] A complete introduction to DEA is given in Cooper et al. (2000).

$$\forall \ (\mathbf{x}_i, \mathbf{y}_i) \ e \ (\mathbf{x}_j, \mathbf{y}_j) \in \ Z_{BCC}(Z°),$$

$$\forall \ 0 \leq \alpha \leq 1, \quad \begin{pmatrix} \mathbf{x} \\ \mathbf{y} \end{pmatrix} = \alpha \begin{pmatrix} \mathbf{x}_i \\ \mathbf{y}_i \end{pmatrix} + (1-\alpha) \begin{pmatrix} \mathbf{x}_i \\ \mathbf{y}_i \end{pmatrix} \in \ Z_{BCC}(Z°)$$

3. The vector $\mathbf{0} \notin Z_{BCC}(Z°)$.

The production possibility set is defined by:

$$\hat{Z}_{DEA-V}(Z°) = \{(x, y) \in R^{N+M} :$$
$$y \leq \sum_{j=1}^{N} \gamma_j y_j; \, x \geq \sum_{j=1}^{N} \gamma_j x_j; \ \sum_{j=1}^{N} \gamma_j = 1; \ \gamma_j \geq 0, \ j = 1, \ldots, N\}$$

and its frontier is characterized by variable returns to scale. The *input-saving* efficiency measure DF_I of the i-th observation, λ_i, is obtained from the *input-oriented* model Bcc_P-I (x_i, y_i):[3]

$$\min_{\lambda_i, \, \gamma_j} \ \lambda_i$$

$$s.t.$$

$$y_{mi} \leq \sum_j \gamma_j \ y_{mj}, \qquad m = 1, \ldots, M$$

$$\lambda_i x_{ki} \geq \sum_j \gamma_j \ x_{kj}, \qquad k = 1, \ldots, K$$

$$\lambda_i \geq 0, \quad \sum_j \gamma_j = 1, \qquad j = 1, \ldots, N$$

Usually, observations are dominated by convex combinations of efficient observations situated on the frontier. The identification problem has been formulated above in its *envelopment form*. The dual expression, the *multiplier form*, is:

$$BCC_D^I(x_i, y_i):$$

$$\max_{\mu_i, \nu_i, \omega_i} \ \mu_i y_i + \omega_i$$

$$\nu_i x_i = 1$$

$$\mu_i y_i - \nu_i x_i + \omega_i \leq 0$$

$$\mu_i \geq 0, \nu_i \geq 0$$

[3]Formally, an output-oriented model can be set up, and output-increasing efficiency measures obtained. However, in the present context we need be interested only in the input-oriented model.

providing information on the shadow prices ν_i and μ_i; the ratios among the latter are the input and output marginal rates of substitution. The shadow prices ν_i measure the marginal products of inputs x_i. Under the hypothesis of allocative efficiency, the ν_i's also measure the prices of inputs x_i. In the following sections, we will first compare the shadow prices of paid and volunteer labour in order to provide descriptive evidence on the productivity of volunteer labour. Then, using the shadow price of volunteer labour as a proxy of its actual price, we specify and estimate a demand curve for volunteer labour.

In order to provide econometric evidence on the relationships between marginal productivity and hours of volunteer labour, we estimate a demand for volunteer labour specified as follows:

$$x_{Vi} = \beta_0 + \beta_1 \omega_{Vi} + \omega_i \beta_2 + y_i \beta_3 + I_i \beta_4 + S_i \beta_5 + \varepsilon_i$$

where subscript *i* refers to operating units (OUs) *i*, the β's are coefficients and ε_i is a zero-mean residual. The dependent variable, x_{Vi}, is the natural log of volunteer work-hours; α is a constant term, ω_{Vi} is the natural log of the shadow price of volunteer labour, ω_i is a vector of input prices, y_i is a vector of output quantities. I_i is a vector including, first of all, the binary variables FP_i e *G*, respectively equal to one if the organization is for-profit or public. These variables will be significant if the demand of these organizations differs from the demand of nonprofit organizations (the reference category). Furthermore, I_i includes an indicator relative to the OUs located in Putnam's regions (denoted Putnam).

Vector S_i includes structural variables that can affect the demand for volunteer labour. They may refer to:

1. Environmental or technological heterogeneities: age, territorial location, size of the area served, number of services provided, presence of more than one OU in the organization, length of the user-organization relationship, care for the user, human capital of paid workers (unfortunately, no measure is available for the human capital of volunteers)
2. Factors related to the motivation of managers and workers: the type of user participation in the organization's life, the hiring criteria for paid workers, the hiring procedures for paid workers
3. The socio-demographic composition of the labour force: share of female paid workers, share of organization members among paid workers, share of part-timers among paid workers, share of project workers among paid workers. Critically, our dataset also includes variables relating to the composition of non-paid labour: share of female volunteers, share of organization members among volunteers, share of permanent volunteers, share of occasional volunteers, share of mandated volunteers (conscientious objectors), share of users among volunteers. The analysis in Preston (2007) suggests that the share of organization members among volunteers can be a proxy of (organization-specific) human capital

Note that although we specify our equation as a demand function, what is actually observed is the equilibrium result of the interplay of demand *and* supply of volunteers. In other words, there exists what is known in econometrics as an identification problem. Nevertheless, the adoption of IV estimation techniques can provide unbiased coefficient estimates, provided that appropriate instruments can be found. These techniques can also be useful because the shadow price of volunteer labour is a good proxy of its actual price only if the hypothesis of allocative efficiency holds true. The adoption of IV procedures can provide unbiased coefficient estimates even if this hypothesis does not hold true and the price of volunteer labour is consequently measured with error.

8.4 Some Descriptive Evidence

In this work we use data from the FIVOL-FEO survey on Italian NPs and other organizations providing social utility services (care and guardianship, nursing and rehabilitation, educational, cultural, recreational, school and school-to-work guidance, job-search assistance, others). This dataset is described in greater detail in Borzaga (2000) or in Depedri (2003). It relates to a sample of 228 Italian organizations, with 268 OUs involved in the provision of social utility services. In our empirical work we will concentrate on the OUs because they are more numerous and contain more disaggregate information. For organizational reasons, data could be gathered only in ten North-Centre provinces and in five Southern provinces. It is, however, believed that the dataset offers a sufficiently accurate image of the population of organizations as far as territorial distribution, type of service provided and institutional category are concerned.

The majority of OUs in the sample belong to nonprofit organizations, while not very many of them belong to for-profit organizations (the latter are concentrated in the provision of care and guardianship, nursing and rehabilitation). Paid workers are evenly distributed across OUs belonging to different categories. On the other hand, volunteer labour mostly belongs to nonprofit organizations (93% of religious nonprofit organizations, 71% of non-religious nonprofit organizations, 61% of social cooperatives have non-paid workers), but is also present in public administration (40% of the OUs belonging to public administration have non-paid workers, basically conscientious objectors).

Perhaps of paramount importance among the prerequisites of DEA is the comparability of the units being examined, which must have sufficiently similar technology, input and output composition. This requirement is certainly relevant here as OUs may provide widely different mixes of social utility services. Efficiency has to be measured across OUs characterized by a sufficiently similar service-mix, bearing in mind that the number of observations for our dataset is relatively low. This means that our sample can be divided in two, at most three, more homogeneous sub-groups. In other works (Destefanis and Maietta 2001, 2003) we have considered this issue in some detail. Suffice it to say here that three homogeneous sub-groups tend to emerge in our sample:

(a) OUs providing the elderly with care and guardianship, nursing and rehabilitation, *mainly* on a residential basis
(b) OUs providing educational, cultural, recreational, school and school-to-work guidance, *mainly* on a day-care basis, to users from risk areas, young people, immigrants/homeless, people with family problems
(c) OUs providing job-search assistance, mainly on a day-care basis, to drug addicts, AIDS sufferers, alcoholics, people with mental illnesses, detainees and former detainees

While the latter group is rather small and cannot be used for estimation purposes, the other two groups are sufficiently large. Here we will focus on a group A of 95 OUs providing care and guardianship, nursing and rehabilitation, *exclusively* on a residential basis and on a group B of 98 OUs providing educational, cultural, recreational, school and school-to-work guidance, *exclusively* on a day-care basis.

In order to define the production set, we rely on the literature relating to health or education services. Inputs include hours of paid workers, volunteers and either number of beds for group A, or the surface of buildings for group B. For both groups, we take as outputs the number of service users and the number of hours dedicated on average to each user. For a given service, the latter can be considered a proxy of the service quality. In our dataset there are missing values for some of these variables, particularly for the surface of buildings and number of hours devoted on average to each user. These values have been imputed using the *Ice* routine of *Stata* 9.2, which implements the *MCMC* algorithm (Cameron and Trivedi 2005).

As *DEA* is rather sensitive to the existence of outliers in the production set, we searched for these observations through the procedure suggested in Tørgersen et al. (1996). This has implied the exclusion of four outliers from group A and three from group B, yielding two final samples of 91 and 95 observations respectively.

In Table 8.1 we provide, for both groups A and B, some descriptive evidence for the relationship between volunteer labour, paid labour and their marginal productivities. For group A, it is clear that marginal productivities are inversely related to the relative quantities of their input amounts, while in group B the inverse relationship between marginal productivities and input amounts is less marked, especially in NPs. In Tables 8.2 and 8.3, we relate, respectively, ω_V and ω_L, to the scale of production.[4] An inverse relationship between the latter and marginal productivities clearly shows up in both tables.

This descriptive evidence suggests the existence of a downward sloped demand for volunteer labour which, unlike previous evidence, is based upon a quantitative measure of marginal productivity. In the following section we provide further evidence on this relationship through econometric analysis.

[4]In Tables 8.2 and 8.3 we proxy the scale of production with volunteer work-hours. Results using paid work-hours, available upon request, are much the same.

Table 8.1 Marginal productivities and input quantities

Type	X_V(h's)	X_V(n's)	X_L(h's)	X_L(n's)	ω_V	ω_L	
Group A: Residential (care and guardianship, nursing and rehabilitation) services							
NP	339.9	25	1,182.1	38	0.0129153	0.0007864	Mean
N=54	102	15	597.5	18	0.0009955	0.0003585	Median
FP	19.8	2	1,579.7	44	0.1143078	0.0007492	Mean
N=13	0	0	864	31	0.055430	0.000415	Median
G	261.1	21	1,680.1	50	0.0238737	0.0005401	Mean
N=24	142	6	956	28	0.0015445	0.0001905	Median
Total	273.4	21	1,370.2	42	0.0302901	0.0007161	Mean
N=91	100	8	650	21	0.0015470	0.000309	Median
Group B: Non-residential (day-care) services							
NP	163.8	18	454.2	22	0.0078076	0.0056141	Mean
N=67	60	7	202	6	0.0019530	0.0037880	Median
FP	1	5	274	12	0.0127540	0.0072270	Mean
N=2	1	5	274	12	0.0127540	0.0072270	Median
G	212.3	10	643.3	18	0.0089337	0.0022615	Mean
N=26	0	0	486	14	0.0039785	0.0020300	Median
Total	173.6	16	502.2	21	0.0082199	0.0047305	Mean
N=95	20	3	252	8	0.0021620	0.0023810	Median

Note: X_V(h's), X_V(n's), X_L(h's), X_L(n's) are respectively volunteer work-hours, volunteer workers, paid work-hours, paid workers; ω_V is the shadow price of volunteer work-hours, ω_L is the shadow price of paid work-hours

Table 8.2 Scale of production and ω_V

	Five quantiles of X_V(h's)						
Type	1	2		4	5	Total	
Group A: Residential (care and guardianship, nursing and rehabilitation) services							
NP	0.0572883	0.0270712	Mean	0.0009405	0.0004119	0.0129153	Mean
	0.0061490	0.0031460	Median	0.0006420	0.000161	0.0009955	Median
	7	9	N	11	13	54	N
FP	0.1480658	0.002465	Mean	0.0004130	–	0.1143078	Mean
	0.0680510	0.002465	Median	0.0004130		0.055430	Median
	10	2	N	1	–	13	N
G	0.0779027	0.004918	Mean	0.0007473	0.0001034	0.0238737	Mean
	0.0730830	0.004918	Median	0.000479	0.000117	0.0015445	Median
	7	2	N	6	5	24	N
Group B: Non-residential (day-care) services							
NP	0.0247462	–	0.0033233	0.0022126	0.0005889	0.0078076	Mean
	0.0083920	–	0.0035385	0.001446	0.0001625	0.0019530	Median
	17	–	16	18	16	67	N
FP	0.018883	–	0.006625	–	–	0.012754	Mean
	0.018883	–	0.006625	–	–	0.012754	Median
	1	–	1	–	–	2	N
G	0.0108741	–	0.002242	0.001347	0.0001107	0.0089337	Mean
	0.0084720	–	0.002242	0.001347	0.0000000	0.0039785	Median
	21	–	1	1	3	26	N

Note: X_V(h's) are volunteer work-hours; ω_V is the shadow price of volunteer work-hours

Table 8.3 Scale of production and ω_L

	Five quantiles of X_V(h's)						
Type	1	2	3	4	5	Total	
Group A: Residential (care and guardianship, nursing and rehabilitation) services							
NP	0.0006177	0.0009274	0.0005494	0.0015835	0.0003602	0.0007864	Mean
	0.0008060	0.000690	0.0002245	0.000373	0.0002840	0.0003585	Median
	7	9	14	11	13	54	N
FP	0.0009021	0.001445	–	0.0004290	–	0.0007492	Mean
	0.0007010	0.0001445	–	0.0004290	–	0.0004150	Median
	10	2	–	1	–	13	N
G	0.0007614	0.000198	0.0001827	0.0002017	0.0010592	.0005401	Mean
	0.0008940	0.000198	0.0001435	0.000177	0.000155	.0001905	Median
	7	2	4	6	5	24	N
Group B: Non-residential (day-care) services							
NP	0.0049814	–	0.0050430	0.0059596	0.0064688	0.0056141	Mean
	0.0023010	–	0.005476	0.003528	0.0036860	0.003788	Median
	17	–	16	18	16	67	N
FP	0.002120	–	0.012334	–	–	0.007227	Mean
	0.002120	–	0.012334	–	–	0.007227	Median
	1	–	1	–	–	1	N
G	0.0021982	–	0.006633	0.002508	0.001165	0.0022615	Mean
	0.002032	–	0.006633	0.002508	0.001369	0.002030	Median
	21	–	1	1	3	26	N

Note: X_V(h's) are volunteer work-hours; ω_L is the shadow price of paid work-hours

8.5 Some Econometric Evidence

In this section we provide some econometric evidence on the relationships between marginal productivity and hours of volunteer labour, in the spirit of Emanuele (1996) and Handy and Srinivasan (2005). In order to gain some information about the robustness of our evidence, we present estimates from a wide array of specifications.

1. The baseline specification: age, territorial location (Putnam's areas, that is Firenze and Trento, the North-East and South), size of the area served, number of services provided, presence of more than one OU in the organization, length of the user-organization relationship, care for the user, for-profit organizations, public organizations
2. Baseline plus human capital of paid workers
3. Baseline plus human capital of paid workers and share of female paid workers
4. Baseline plus human capital of paid workers and share of non-organization members among paid workers
5. Baseline plus human capital of paid workers and share of part-timers among paid workers, share of project workers among paid workers

6. Baseline plus human capital of paid workers and the type of user participation in the organization's life
7. Baseline plus human capital of paid workers and the hiring procedures for paid workers
8. Baseline plus human capital of paid workers and the hiring criteria for paid workers
9. Baseline plus human capital of paid workers and share of female volunteers
10 Baseline plus human capital of paid workers and share of non-organization members among volunteers
11. Baseline plus human capital of paid workers and share of permanent volunteers
12. Baseline plus human capital of paid workers and share of occasional volunteers
13. Baseline plus human capital of paid workers and share of mandated volunteers (conscientious objectors)
14. Baseline plus human capital of paid workers and share of users among volunteers.

In Tables 8.5 and 8.8 in Appendix we report estimates from an OLS model for coefficients on the shadow price of volunteer labour (to provide evidence on a downward sloping curve for volunteer labour), wage (to provide evidence on complementarity of paid and volunteer labour), and on territorial and institutional variables. In Tables 8.6 and 8.9 in Appendix, the same specifications are estimated through an IV procedure. The instruments used are the profits at t-1, profits at t-2, the presence of an executive board, the participation of members in the organization's decisions (these IVs pass both relevance and over-identification tests, available upon request).

Finally, we suppose that in Putnam's areas there may be not only less difficulty in recruiting skilled and conscientious volunteers, thereby enhancing the demand for volunteers, but also less opportunistic behaviour from the organization in substituting more volunteers for paid workers when wages increase. We put this hypothesis to the test by including in the specifications presented in Tables 8.7 and 8.10 in Appendix a variable interacting wages with the dummy for Putnam's areas.

The tables always include the number of observations and the adjusted R square. The t-ratios (in italics) are always obtained for robust estimates of the variance-covariance matrix. Obviously, specifications (9)–(14), including the structural characteristics of volunteers, are estimated only for organizations which have a non-zero number of volunteers, as these variables are not available for the rest of the sample.[5]

The econometric evidence supports the existence of a downward-sloping curve for volunteer labour, especially if one considers the sample with organizations which have a non-zero number of volunteers. This makes sense since DEA provides shadow

[5]In group A, there are 9 nonprofits (on 54) with no volunteers, 10 FPs (on 13), 7 Gs (on 24). In group B, the numbers are 16 nonprofits on 67, 1 FP on 2, and 6 Gs on 26.

prices of volunteer labour also for organizations with no volunteers, but the inclusion of these organizations in the estimates (with shadow prices varying for no volunteers) is likely to cloud the functional relationship between the variables of interest.

As far as the other variables are concerned, the demand for volunteers is obviously lower in for-profits, while the dummy for Putnam's areas warrants further discussion. In both groups, it is significant and positive if the sample excludes organizations with no volunteers. This evidence, according to which the productivity of volunteers is higher in areas well endowed with social capital has interesting relationships with the findings of Fiorillo in Chap. 9 of this book, to the effect that people who live in regions relatively well endowed with social capital are more likely to provide volunteer labour. It would appear that, in social capital-rich regions, more motivated and skilful volunteers can be drawn from a relatively larger pool of potential applicants.

In group B, if no allowance is made for the interaction between wages and the Putnam dummy, the dummy is hardly significant even in the smaller sample. However, it becomes significant and positive in the interactive specification, though not in the larger sample. The interaction term is fairly significant in the sample excluding organizations with no volunteers.[6] In non-Putnam areas, organizations tend to substitute volunteers for paid workers when the latter become more expensive, but this is not true in Putnam's areas, thereby confirming expectations about a less opportunistic behaviour in these regions.

Finally, in Table 8.4 we highlight some evidence (from the interactive specification) about the structural characteristics of volunteers.

Table 8.4 Evidence for the structural characteristics of volunteers from the interactive specification in Tables 8.7 and 8.10

	Residential services	Non-residential services
Share of female volunteers	0.33	0.26
	0.52	*0.44*
Share of non-organization members among volunteers	0.10	–0.59
	0.15	*–1.12*
Share of permanent volunteers	0.25	0.25
	0.47	*0.40*
Share of casual volunteers	–0.06	–0.51
	–0.11	*–0.80*
Share of mandated volunteers	–1.52	–0.61
	–1.97	*–0.90*
Share of users among volunteers	1.94	1.23
	3.50	*1.52*

Note: OLS coefficients in plain text, t-ratios in italics

[6]Actually, the estimates in Tables 8.7 and 8.10 relate to a dummy that interacting wages with Putnam's areas and nonprofits. Similar results are obtained, however, if the dummy only interacts wages with Putnam's areas, while a dummy interacting wages with nonprofits only is considerably less significant.

In group A there is evidence of a significantly lower demand the higher the share of mandated volunteers, and the lower the share of users among volunteers. Evidence broadly in agreement with the latter finding also comes from group B. In substantial disagreement with the expectations of Handy and Brudney (2007), other characteristics of the volunteer labour force do not seem to matter very much.

8.6 Concluding Remarks

In this paper we analyze the relationships between marginal productivity and hours of volunteer labour, drawing evidence from the FIVOL-FEO survey and relying on measures of marginal productivity obtained through DEA. Both our descriptive and econometric evidence show that the prices of volunteer labour (as proxied by its shadow price) is negatively related to the number of volunteer hours. Further, the demand for volunteer labour is higher in Putnam's areas, where there is also evidence that organizations refrain from substituting volunteers for paid workers when the latter become more expensive.

Insofar as the employment of volunteers is demand- rather than supply-constrained, policies promoting the provision of social utility services should focus on facilitating the incorporation of volunteer labour rather than increasing its supply. For instance, financial help for organizations that employ volunteers should be channelled towards adopting professional management techniques, as well as rationalizing the recruitment and training of volunteers.[6]

Acknowledgements We gratefully acknowledge financial support from the Italian Ministry of Education, University and Research (PRIN 2005) and from the DISES, University of Salerno.

Appendix

Table 8.5 OLS estimates (residential services)

Variable	(1)	(2)	(3)	(4)	(5)	(6)	(7)	(8)	(9)	(10)	(11)	(12)	(13)	(14)
ω_V	–7.67	–5.38	–5.27	–5.32	–5.06	–5.35	–6.53	–4.87	–25.13	–23.77	–24.00	–23.96	–23.72	–24.42
	–2.09	*–1.44*	*–1.41*	*–1.41*	*–1.32*	*–1.45*	*–1.72*	*–1.23*	*–2.82*	*–2.67*	*–2.94*	*–2.84*	*–3.44*	*–3.32*
w	0.20	0.18	0.16	0.19	0.16	0.17	0.26	0.13	0.15	0.14	0.15	0.15	0.13	0.13
	1.76	*1.65*	*1.64*	*1.73*	*1.35*	*1.33*	*2.59*	*1.17*	*2.04*	*1.98*	*1.84*	*1.87*	*1.71*	*1.55*
Putnam	1.14	0.89	0.89	0.87	0.82	0.62	1.55	0.88	1.24	1.26	1.26	1.29	1.21	1.39
	1.31	*1.08*	*1.07*	*1.02*	*0.99*	*0.71*	*1.88*	*0.92*	*2.06*	*2.12*	*2.25*	*2.24*	*2.07*	*2.40*
North East	1.46	0.93	1.07	0.92	0.95	0.80	0.94	0.68	–0.05	0.00	0.11	0.04	–0.21	–0.25
	2.97	*1.85*	*2.02*	*1.85*	*1.81*	*1.48*	*1.74*	*1.19*	*–0.11*	*0.01*	*0.24*	*0.09*	*–0.41*	*–0.58*
South	0.29	–0.61	–0.48	–0.67	–0.57	–0.32	–0.48	–1.18	–0.01	0.01	0.19	0.06	–0.03	–0.27
	0.25	*–0.53*	*–0.41*	*–0.58*	*–0.48*	*–0.23*	*–0.45*	*–1.07*	*–0.01*	*0.01*	*0.24*	*0.07*	*–0.03*	*–0.34*
FP	–2.26	–2.32	–2.35	–2.43	–2.26	–2.14	–2.53	–2.04	–1.45	–1.32	–1.44	–1.31	–1.56	–1.05
	–2.53	*–2.62*	*–2.62*	*–2.61*	*–2.54*	*–2.41*	*–3.14*	*–2.02*	*–1.48*	*–1.48*	*–1.68*	*–1.54*	*–1.81*	*–1.33*
G	–0.65	–0.91	–0.95	–0.97	–0.81	–0.73	–1.49	–0.74	–0.12	–0.08	–0.08	–0.13	0.21	–0.14
	–1.12	*–1.64*	*–1.74*	*–1.73*	*–1.45*	*–1.29*	*–1.83*	*–1.1*	*–0.30*	*–0.19*	*–0.20*	*–0.31*	*0.52*	*–0.34*
N	91	91	91	91	91	91	91	91	65	65	65	65	65	65
Adj. R^2	0.37	0.41	0.41	0.40	0.39	0.41	0.44	0.41	0.36	0.35	0.36	0.35	0.44	0.45

Table 8.6 IV Estimates (residential services)

Variable	(1)	(2)	(3)	(4)	(5)	(6)	(7)	(8)	(9)	(10)	(11)	(12)	(13)	(14)
ω_V	−16.31	−14.23	−13.89	−14.42	−14.36	−12.02	−13.44	−15.98	−36.16	−34.52	−29.52	−31.52	−28.93	−26.88
	−2.10	*−1.79*	*−1.74*	*−1.81*	*−1.67*	*−1.52*	*−2.24*	*−2.01*	*−1.92*	*−1.89*	*−1.89*	*−1.97*	*−1.85*	*−2.12*
w	0.25	0.23	0.22	0.24	0.22	0.20	0.30	0.20	0.14	0.13	0.14	0.14	0.13	0.13
	2.29	*2.14*	*2.20*	*2.24*	*1.86*	*1.77*	*3.48*	*1.97*	*2.07*	*1.97*	*2.04*	*1.99*	*1.89*	*1.84*
Putnam	1.06	0.92	0.92	0.90	0.92	0.71	1.62	1.03	1.17	1.18	1.23	1.25	1.18	1.38
	1.38	*1.23*	*1.23*	*1.19*	*1.21*	*0.92*	*2.34*	*1.20*	*2.12*	*2.17*	*2.45*	*2.44*	*2.29*	*2.76*
North East	1.55	1.24	1.36	1.24	1.24	1.09	1.16	1.03	−0.14	−0.06	0.08	0.00	−0.24	−0.27
	2.86	*1.93*	*2.07*	*1.92*	*1.92*	*1.65*	*2.03*	*1.48*	*−0.36*	*−0.16*	*0.21*	*0.00*	*−0.58*	*−0.74*
South	0.21	−0.30	−0.19	−0.33	−0.27	−0.03	−0.20	−0.66	−0.06	−0.04	0.17	0.04	−0.04	−0.28
	0.20	*−0.27*	*−0.17*	*−0.29*	*−0.24*	*−0.02*	*−0.20*	*−0.61*	*−0.08*	*−0.06*	*0.26*	*0.05*	*−0.07*	*−0.42*
FP	−1.08	−1.22	−1.27	−1.26	−1.20	−1.30	−1.80	−0.61	−1.55	−1.34	−1.46	−1.33	−1.58	−1.06
	−0.85	*−0.99*	*−1.03*	*−0.96*	*−0.97*	*−1.07*	*−1.98*	*−0.44*	*−1.87*	*−1.90*	*−2.10*	*−1.96*	*−2.24*	*−1.62*
G	−0.55	–	−0.75	−0.74	−0.70	−0.57	−1.57	−0.57	−0.20	−0.14	−0.11	−0.18	0.18	−0.15
	−1.08	–	*−1.47*	*−1.35*	*−1.41*	*−1.11*	*−2.20*	*−0.96*	*−0.55*	*−0.41*	*−0.31*	*−0.49*	*0.54*	*−0.43*
N	91	91	91	91	91	91	91	91	65	65	65	65	65	65
Adj. R^2	0.29	0.33	0.34	0.32	0.31	0.36	0.39	0.28	0.33	0.32	0.35	0.34	0.43	0.45

Table 8.7 OLS estimates, interactive specification (residential services)

Variable	(1)	(2)	(3)	(4)	(5)	(6)	(7)	(8)	(9)	(10)	(11)	(12)	(13)	(14)
ω_V	−7.67	−5.34	−5.14	−5.28	−4.94	−5.28	−6.52	−4.70	−26.82	−25.99	−25.51	−25.84	−25.45	−26.25
	−2.08	*−1.44*	*−1.44*	*−1.41*	*−1.32*	*−1.48*	*−1.70*	*−1.22*	*−3.01*	*−2.95*	*−3.06*	*−3.05*	*−3.62*	*−3.57*
w	0.20	0.18	0.16	0.18	0.15	0.16	0.26	0.13	0.16	0.15	0.16	0.16	0.14	0.14
	1.74	*1.62*	*1.55*	*1.69*	*1.25*	*1.22*	*2.55*	*1.06*	*2.33*	*2.29*	*1.99*	*2.25*	*1.97*	*1.82*
w*Putnam*NP	0.00	0.05	0.12	0.05	0.08	0.09	0.01	0.10	−0.23	−0.23	−0.24	−0.23	−0.20	−0.21
	0.02	*0.30*	*0.74*	*0.29*	*0.45*	*0.55*	*0.07*	*0.53*	*−3.17*	*−3.39*	*−2.99*	*−3.35*	*−2.70*	*−2.85*
Putnam	1.13	0.59	0.12	0.57	0.34	0.07	1.49	0.27	2.78	2.82	2.71	2.82	2.54	2.81
	0.66	*0.37*	*0.08*	*0.35*	*0.20*	*0.04*	*0.97*	*0.15*	*4.22*	*4.39*	*3.91*	*4.37*	*3.99*	*4.05*
FP	−2.26	−2.29	−2.26	−2.39	−2.19	−2.08	−2.53	−1.99	−1.43	−1.30	−0.11	−1.33	−1.54	−1.07
	−2.53	*−2.61*	*−2.62*	*−2.60*	*−2.51*	*−2.41*	*−3.15*	*−2.09*	*−1.51*	*−1.50*	*−0.23*	*−1.59*	*−1.82*	*−1.39*
G	−0.64	−0.84	−0.78	−0.90	−0.69	−0.61	−1.48	−0.56	−0.45	−0.44	0.19	−0.43	−0.11	−0.45
	−1.08	*−1.44*	*−1.39*	*−1.53*	*−1.13*	*−1.03*	*−1.75*	*−0.77*	−1.06	−1.04	0.23	−1.00	−0.26	−1.03
N	91	91	91	91	91	91	91	91	65	65	65	65	65	65
Adj. R^2	0.36	0.40	0.41	0.39	0.39	0.40	0.43	0.40	0.40	0.40	0.40	0.40	0.47	0.49

Table 8.8 OLS estimates (non-residential services)

Variable	(1)	(2)	(3)	(4)	(5)	(6)	(7)	(8)	(9)	(10)	(11)	(12)	(13)	(14)
ω_V	−30.04	−30.03	−23.55	−28.77	−33.73	−30.71	−21.92	−21.36	−480.02	−488.75	−470.46	−481.13	−468.93	−456.67
	−1.69	*−1.67*	*−1.31*	*−1.62*	*−2.08*	*−1.85*	*−1.52*	*−1.42*	*−5.47*	*−5.95*	*−5.13*	*−5.23*	*−5.30*	*−5.13*
w	0.05	0.05	0.03	0.04	−0.01	0.01	0.05	0.05	0.15	0.14	0.14	0.13	0.13	0.14
	0.55	*0.55*	*0.39*	*0.45*	*−−0.07*	*0.17*	*0.59*	*0.44*	*1.12*	*1.38*	*1.10*	*1.10*	*1.06*	*1.18*
Putnam	−2.09	−2.09	−2.07	−2.23	−2.19	−1.75	−2.07	−2.10	0.39	0.38	0.40	0.48	0.27	0.51
	−2.28	*−2.25*	*−2.24*	*−2.39*	*−2.13*	*−2.11*	*−1.92*	*−1.80*	*0.61*	*0.58*	*0.61*	*0.70*	*0.41*	*0.77*
North East	−1.75	−1.76	−1.91	−1.81	−1.62	−1.44	−1.53	−1.50	0.54	0.39	0.54	0.61	0.34	0.58
	−2.53	*−2.51*	*−2.71*	*−2.49*	*−2.38*	*−1.84*	*−1.73*	*−1.88*	*1.03*	*0.76*	*1.03*	*1.22*	*0.60*	*1.13*
South	−1.83	−1.84	−2.05	−2.00	−1.62	−1.73	−2.46	−2.15	−0.30	−0.45	−0.31	−0.18	−0.44	−0.06
	−1.65	*−1.59*	*−1.70*	*−1.73*	*−1.19*	*−1.73*	*−1.88*	*−1.68*	*−0.28*	*−0.48*	*−0.29*	*−0.18*	*−0.41*	*−0.06*
FP	−0.88	−0.89	−0.57	−1.11	−0.44	−1.79	1.66	−1.03	0.75	1.72	0.91	1.26	0.58	1.11
	−0.92	*−0.94*	*−0.54*	*−1.02*	*−0.38*	*−1.45*	*1.01*	*−0.66*	0.46	1.23	0.59	0.90	0.37	0.73
G	−1.29	−1.29	−0.98	−1.42	−0.98	−1.37	−0.30	−1.03	1.35	1.51	1.38	1.35	1.36	1.25
	−1.62	*−1.55*	*−1.03*	*−1.55*	*−0.95*	*−1.70*	*−0.21*	*−0.99*	*1.30*	*1.62*	*1.37*	*1.38*	*1.33*	*1.28*
N	95	95	95	95	95	95	95	95	58	58	58	58	58	58
Adj. R^2	0.31	0.30	0.31	0.29	0.31	0.35	0.35	0.33	0.54	0.57	0.53	0.54	0.54	0.54

Table 8.9 IV estimates (non-residential services)

Variable	(1)	(2)	(3)	(4)	(5)	(6)	(7)	(8)	(9)	(10)	(11)	(12)	(13)	(14)
ω_V	−70.78	−71.68	−67.92	−73.67	−57.44	−53.77	−61.77	−60.05	−516.89	−348.27	−497.12	−518.04	−485.87	−442.50
	−2.91	*−2.95*	*−2.33*	*−2.92*	*−2.44*	*−1.90*	*−2.26*	*−2.30*	*−2.47*	*−2.54*	*−2.75*	*−3.22*	*−2.75*	*−2.20*
w	0.08	0.08	0.08	0.09	0.00	0.03	0.08	0.08	0.15	0.14	0.14	0.13	0.14	0.14
	0.96	*1.00*	*0.97*	*1.04*	*0.01*	*0.39*	*1.01*	*0.85*	*1.38*	*1.67*	*1.37*	*1.38*	*1.32*	*1.47*
Putnam	−1.31	−1.29	−1.30	−1.22	−1.74	−1.27	−1.29	−1.56	0.51	−0.07	0.48	0.60	0.32	0.47
	−1.43	*−1.40*	*−1.39*	*−1.22*	*−1.89*	*−1.46*	*−1.34*	*−1.50*	*0.66*	*−0.12*	*0.66*	*0.86*	*0.45*	*0.63*
North East	−1.64	−1.64	−1.71	−1.62	−1.54	−1.40	−1.60	−1.31	0.57	0.28	0.57	0.64	0.36	0.56
	−2.51	*−2.46*	*−2.53*	*−2.27*	*−2.44*	*−2.01*	*−2.14*	*−1.92*	*1.38*	*0.65*	*1.38*	*1.64*	*0.79*	*1.35*
South	−0.78	−0.76	−0.87	−0.67	−0.95	−1.15	−1.54	−1.21	−0.27	−0.56	−0.28	−0.13	−0.42	−0.07
	−0.62	*−0.59*	*−0.64*	*−0.49*	*−0.73*	*−1.01*	*−1.24*	*−0.92*	*−0.31*	*−0.71*	*−0.34*	*−0.17*	*−0.49*	*−0.08*
FP	−0.99	−0.99	−0.87	−0.93	−0.46	−2.01	1.90	−0.48	0.76	1.49	0.93	1.32	0.60	1.10
	−1.25	*−1.29*	*−1.06*	*−1.04*	*−0.48*	*−1.94*	*1.34*	*−0.38*	*0.58*	*1.27*	*0.75*	*1.14*	*0.47*	*0.92*
G	−1.10		−0.98	−1.05	−0.85	−1.39	−0.10	−0.71						
	−1.44	.	*−1.07*	*−1.16*	*−0.90*	*−1.95*	*−0.08*	*−0.72*						
N	95	95	95	95	95	95	95	95						
Adj. R^2	0.22	0.21	0.22	0.19	0.28	0.32	0.27	0.25						
G	1.49	0.95	1.48	1.49	1.42	1.19								
	1.61	*0.99*	*1.77*	*1.89*	*1.74*	*1.38*								
N	58	58	58	58	58	58								
Adj. R^2	0.53	0.52	0.53	0.53	0.54	0.54								

Table 8.10 OLS estimates, interactive specification (non-residential services)

Variable	(1)	(2)	(3)	(4)	(5)	(6)	(7)	(8)	(9)	(10)	(11)	(12)	(13)	(14)
ω_V	−30.20	−30.18	−24.32	−28.82	−33.63	−32.13	−21.16	−21.88	−599.00	−591.83	−597.32	−608.58	−592.35	−582.49
	−1.77	*−1.75*	*−1.39*	*−1.68*	*−2.11*	*−2.07*	*−1.52*	*−1.51*	*−6.03*	*−6.28*	*−5.98*	*−6.15*	*−5.88*	*−5.88*
W	0.02	0.02	0.02	0.01	−0.03	−0.04	0.02	0.02	0.29	0.27	0.28	0.28	0.28	0.29
	0.23	*0.21*	*0.19*	*0.11*	*−0.24*	*−0.40*	*0.21*	*0.18*	*2.95*	*3.10*	*3.01*	*3.07*	*2.88*	*3.06*
w*Putnam*NP	0.09	0.09	0.06	0.09	0.07	0.13	0.10	0.07	−0.33	−0.30	−0.34	−0.34	−0.33	−0.34
	0.75	*0.74*	*0.49*	*0.76*	*0.54*	*1.14*	*0.78*	*0.56*	*−2.24*	*−2.16*	*−2.42*	*−2.50*	*−2.26*	*−2.37*
Putnam	−2.81	−2.82	−2.51	−2.99	−2.74	−2.69	−2.91	−2.67	3.91	3.53	4.01	4.09	3.80	4.08
	−1.84	*−1.81*	*−1.76*	*−1.90*	*−1.61*	*−2.12*	*−1.71*	*−1.48*	*2.18*	*2.16*	*2.33*	*2.45*	*2.11*	*2.35*
FP	−0.65	−0.66	−0.46	−0.90	−0.28	−1.72	1.57	−0.84	0.06	0.70	1.04	0.49	−0.08	0.32
	−0.61	*−0.63*	*−0.41*	*−0.77*	*−0.22*	*−1.29*	*0.97*	*−0.51*	*0.04*	*0.46*	*1.94*	*0.34*	*−0.05*	*0.21*
G	−0.72	−0.71	−0.66	−0.85	−0.55	−0.73	0.11	−0.65	1.08	1.20	0.99	1.08	1.09	0.98
	−0.57	*−0.55*	*−0.52*	*−0.64*	*−0.37*	*−0.66*	*0.07*	*−0.45*	*0.98*	*1.21*	*0.84*	*1.07*	*0.99*	*0.95*
N	95	95	95	95	95	95	95	95	58	58	58	58	58	58
Adj. R^2	0.31	0.30	0.30	0.29	0.30	0.36	0.35	0.32	0.61	0.62	0.61	0.62	0.61	0.62

Legend of Tables 8.5–8.10: variable acronyms are defined in the text. Estimates include an unreported constant term. Regression coefficients are in plain text, t-ratios in *italics*

References

Besley T, Ghatak M (2005) Competition and incentives with motivated agents. American Economic Review 95:616–636
Borzaga C (ed) (2000) Capitale umano e qualità del lavoro nei servizi sociali. Fondazione Italiana del Volontariato, Rome
Borzaga C (2003) Effort, fedeltà, soddisfazione dei lavoratori. In: Borzaga C, Musella M (eds) Produttività ed efficienza nelle organizzazioni nonprofit. Edizioni31, Trento
Borzaga C, Depedri S (2005) Interpersonal relations and job satisfaction: Some empirical results in social and community care services. In: Gui B, Sugden R (eds) Economics and Social Interaction: Accounting for Interpersonal Relations. Cambridge University Press, Cambridge UK
Brudney JL, Kellough JE (2000) Volunteers in state government: involvement, management, and benefits. Nonprofit and Voluntary Sector Quarterly 29:111–130
Cameron AC, Trivedi PK (2005) Microeconometrics: methods and applications. Cambridge University Press, New York
Cooper WW Seiford LM, Tone K. (2000) Data envelopment analysis. Kluwer, New York
Depedri S (2003) La ricerca: metodologia campione e principali risultati. In: Borzaga C, Musella M (eds) Produttività ed efficienza nelle organizzazioni nonprofit. Edizioni31, Trento
Destefanis S and Maietta OW (2001) Assessing the productive efficiency of non-profit organisations: a comparative analysis. CELPE Discussion Paper 63
Destefanis S, Maietta OW (2003) La determinazione dell'efficienza nel settore nonprofit. In: Borzaga C, Musella M (eds) Produttività ed efficienza nelle organizzazioni nonprofit. Edizioni31, Trento
Emanuele R (1996) Is there a (downward sloping) demand curve for volunteer labor? Annals of Public and Cooperative Economics, 67:193–208
Freeman RB (1997) Working for nothing: the supply of volunteer labor. Journal of Labor Economics 15:S140–S166
Hager MA (2004) Volunteer management capacity in America's charities and congregations. Urban Institute, Washington DC. http://www.urban.org/url.cfm?ID=410963.
Handy F, Brudney J (2007) When to use volunteer labor resources? An organizational analysis for nonprofit management. Vrijwillige Inzet Onderzocht 4:91–100
Handy F, Srinivasan N (2005) The demand for volunteer labor: a study of hospital volunteers. Nonprofit and Voluntary Sector Quarterly 34:491–509
James E (1989) The nonprofit sector in international perspective. Oxford University Press, New York
Macduff N (1997) Solving the hazards of unions and volunteer relations in government organizations. Journal of Volunteer Administration 14:34–39
Menchik PL, Weisbrod BA (1987) Volunteer labor supply. Journal of Public Economics 32:159–183
Preston AE (2007) Volunteer resourcesYoung DR(ed) Financing nonprofits. Putting theory into practice. Rowman Altamira, Walnut Creek CA
Putnam R (with Leonardi R, Nanetti R) (1993) Making democracy work. Princeton University Press, Princeton
Rose-Ackerman S (1996) Altruism, non profit and economic theory. Journal of Economic Literature 34:701–728
Salamon LM, Anheier HK (1998) The emerging sector revisited; a summary. Center for Civil Society Studies, Johns Hopkins University, Baltimore
Smith DH (1994) Determinants of voluntary association participation and volunteering: a literature review. Nonprofit and Voluntary Sector Quarterly 23:243–263
Statcan (2004) Cornerstones of community: highlights of the national survey of nonprofit and voluntary organizations. Statistics Canada, Ottawa
Steinberg R (1990) Labor economics and the nonprofit sector. A Literature review. Nonprofit and Voluntary Sector Quarterly 19:151–169

Toppe CM, Kirsch AD, Michel J (2002) Giving and volunteering in the United States 2001: Findings from a national survey. Independent Sector, Washington DC

Tørgersen AM, Førsund FA, Kittelsen SAC (1996) Slack-adjusted efficiency measures and ranking of efficient units. Journal of Productivity Analysis 7:379–398

Vaillancourt F, Payette M (1986) The supply of volunteer work: the case of Canada. Journal of Voluntary Action Research 15:45–56

Weitzman MS, Jalandoni NT, Lampkin LM, Pollak TH (2002) The new nonprofit almanac and desk reference: the essential facts and figures for managers, researchers, and volunteers. Wiley, Hoboken NJ

Young D (1983) If not forprofit for what? Lexington Books, Lexington MA

Zahnd L (1997) Volunteer staff relationships in a unionized environment. Journal of Volunteer Resources Management 6:8–9

Chapter 9
Volunteer Labour Supply: Micro-econometric Evidence from Italy

Damiano Fiorillo

Abstract This essay examines the evidence in favour of different motivations for unpaid labour supply in volunteer service associations, using an Italian micro dataset which allows use of a measure of household income to test the consumption against the investment hypothesis. The main finding is that the donation of unpaid activity to a volunteer service association is determined both by the consumption and the investment motivation, confirming the evidence of studies for the US, Canada and the UK. Interestingly, however, regional patterns of volunteer labour reflect the pattern of participation described in the social capital literature. People who live in regions relatively well-endowed with social capital do significantly more volunteer labour.

9.1 Introduction

The supply of unpaid labour within social organizations expanded considerably during the 1990s in a number of Western countries. Comparing findings of the World Values Survey for 1990 and 1999 we see that the fraction of people performing volunteer work within a formal organization increased by 95% in the United Kingdom, 74% in Canada, 51% in the United States, 43% in the Netherlands and Sweden, 42 % in Denmark, 33% in Belgium, 19% in Ireland, 18% in Italy and 12% in France. These increments widened the existing difference between the US and Canada on the one hand and Europe on the other; and within Europe, between the high-participation countries (Sweden and the Netherlands) and the low (France and Italy); see Table 9.1.

Understanding the motivations for people's active participation in volunteer-work social organizations in Italy is important for two reasons. First, as a consequence of the welfare reforms that have constricted public spending, volunteer work has

D. Fiorillo
Department of Economics, University of Napoli Parthenope, Via Medina, 40, Napoli, 80133, Italy

S. Destefanis and M. Musella (eds.), *Paid and Unpaid Labour in the Social Economy*, AIEL Series in Labour Economics, DOI: 10.1007/978-3-7908-2137-6_10,

Table 9.1 Volunteer labour in selected developed countries (percentage of population)

	1999	1990
Belgium	0.27	0.36
Denmark	0.26	0.37
France	0.23	0.26
Ireland	0.26	0.31
Italy	0.22	0.26
Netherlands	0.35	0.50
Sweden	0.39	0.56
United Kingdom	0.22	0.43
United States	0.45	0.68
Canada	0.43	0.75

Source: Own elaboration on 2000 World Values Survey data

become a vital production input for nonprofit organizations supplying social, educational, cultural, recreational and other services. Second, as the social-capital literature suggests, volunteer labour in Italy (the first country in which the effects of social capital have been studied analytically) would appear to contribute to regional economic growth by making public institutions and markets more efficient (Putnam 1993; Beugelsdijk and Van Schaik 2005).

Economics posits two rational motivations for individuals to perform volunteer labour: the consumption motivation and the investment motivation (Menchik and Weisbrod 1987). On the consumption hypothesis, volunteer work serves the individual's own purposes, and hence is a factor in his utility function. In the investment model, it enhances the volunteer's human capital, improving employability and future earnings prospects. Empirical studies of volunteer work, mostly American, have not provided decisive results for determining which motivation prevails.

This essay contributes to the literature by examining the evidence for the consumption and the investment motivation for voluntary work in two types of solidarity association: volunteer service associations proper and 'other associations', the latter defined as organizations that are not officially classed as volunteer service but that the members consider to be such. We use an Italian public database published by ISTAT: the *Indagine Multiscopo sulle Famiglie, Aspetti della Vita Quotidiana*, 1997 (multipurpose survey of households and daily life, *Multiscopo* for short). To my knowledge this is the first empirical analysis based on Italian data to use a measure of household income to test the consumption against the investment thesis. The study focuses on these two types of organization because the literature on social capital classes 'volunteer service associations' and other associations as Putnam-type organizations, i.e. groups that pursue social objectives.[1]

The essay is organized as follows. Section 9.2 sets out the theoretical hypotheses for empirical analysis and Sect. 9.3 briefly surveys the empirical literature on the

[1] See Knack and Keefer (1997), Knack (2003), Beugelsdijk and Van Schaik (2005).

consumption and investment motivations. Section 9.4 describes the dataset and presents some descriptive statistics. Section 9.5 sets out the econometric strategy followed and the results obtained. Section 9.6 concludes.

9.2 The Empirical Hypotheses

In the private consumption model, the volunteer's utility derives directly from the volunteer act, per se. It is volunteer work itself and the related rewards that motivate people to donate their labour. These rewards include self-integration, social status, satisfaction from the work itself or from the strengthening of ethical or social norms, or maybe just what has been called the 'warm glow' from having done a good deed (Andreoni 1990; Ziemek 2006). In this model, then, the unpaid activity is an argument of the volunteer's utility function, and assuming that it is a normal good the individual's decision varies directly with overall income.[2] Also, unpaid activity should vary inversely with *labour income*, which represents the opportunity cost of volunteer work. Two hypotheses follow:

- *Consumption model 1:* The sign of the coefficient of labour income should be negative.
- *Consumption model 2:* The expected sign of the coefficient of total income should be positive.

In the investment model, the volunteer worker forgoes present earnings for higher future income. As part of the organization, the volunteer gets three potential advantages: (1) training and new skills; (2) useful contacts and personal relations; (3) signalling his capability to potential employers. This may enable the volunteer to get a better, higher-paying job than otherwise (Menchik and Weisbrod 1987; Duncan 1999; Prouteau and Wolff 2004; Ziemek 2006). Unpaid work for a social organization has been considered as social capital.[3] In the 'economic approach to social capital' (Glaeser et al. 2002), passive or active membership in a social organization is treated as an investment in social skills by means of which a person can get market and non-market returns from relations with other people. The basic idea is that an individual invests in social skills in order to improve his or her income prospects (market returns).

In this approach, the investment in volunteer activity should decline as earned income increases; it should be less in older age-groups, because the period during which the investment will produce market returns is shorter. In several different investment models (Menchik and Weisbrod 1987, p. 177; Glaeser et al. 2002, p. F447), unpaid activity should trace an inverted *U*-curve over the life cycle. Thus the investment model, in

---

[2] For a formal analysis see Menchik and Weisbrod (1987) and Freeman (1997).

[3] See Costa and Khan (2003), Beugelsdijk and Van Schaik (2005), Bjørnskov (2006). According to Bourdieu (1986), social capital has two elements: the social network that gives individuals access to resources and the ability to obtain resources by virtue of participation in the social network (Portes 1998, pp. 3–5).

addition to a hypothesis equal to hypothesis 1 under the consumption model (volunteer activity decreases as labour income increases), implies another hypothesis:

- *Investment model 3:* The expected shape of the unpaid activity investment curve is an inverted *U* over the life cycle.

That is, both the consumption and the investment models predict a negative correlation between the opportunity cost of time, labour income, and voluntary service activity. The main distinction between the two concerns that effect of total income and that of age. The private consumption model predicts that unpaid activity will increase with total income, while the investment model does not posit such a correlation. As to age, the consumption model does not imply any variation while the investment model predicts an inverted *U*-curve.

9.3 The Empirical Literature

Mueller (1975) and Schram and Dunsing (1981) analyze women's voluntary labour supply postulating a consumption motivation and an investment motivation. Mueller uses OLS estimates for the United States and finds no statistically significant link between income and the number of hours of volunteer work. Schram and Dunsing, doing the same, find that the probability of married women's being volunteers is correlated negatively with age.

Menchik and Weisbrod (1987) apply a Tobit model to US data and show that voluntary service increases as its opportunity cost (hourly wages) decreases and as total income increases; on a life-cycle basis, they find a peak at age 43. They argue that these results are evidence for both the consumption and the investment motivation. Brown and Lankford (1992) also use a Tobit model for the United States and find that more education and lower opportunity cost increase the number of hours of volunteer work. They too find a life-cycle peak in the 30–40 age-group, though it is not statistically significant. The authors suggest that this may indicate not an investment motivation, as Menchik and Weisbrod contend, but involvement in unpaid work in connection with their own children's activities.

Vaillancourt (1994) and Day and Devlin (1996) have done empirical work on Canadian data. Using Probit models, both studies show that the probability of being a volunteer is affected positively both by educational level and by household income (consumption motivation). As to age, the two studies' findings differ. Day and Devlin show a peak in the probability of volunteer work at age 55–64, whereas Vaillancourt finds that younger people participate more than older. Both sets of evidence are consistent with the investment motivation (the accumulation of human capital).

Freeman (1997) has run another empirical test of the private consumption model for the United States, examining both the decision to perform volunteer service and the decision to donate a given number of hours. On the first of these decisions, the volunteer workers display characteristics associated with a higher value of time: higher hourly earnings and household income, greater age and more education. The author suggests a social factor as the cause: people become volunteers when this is requested by the work environment: "You are more likely to accede to personal requests than to telephone or written requests; to requests from employers, colleagues, and the like, than to requests from strangers" (Freeman 1997, p. S164). Carlin (2001) studies volunteer work by married women in the United States, getting results in line with Freeman's. Using Probit specifications with sample selection, he shows that an increase in labour income prompts a small reduction in women's active participation and an increase in the number of hours worked. Active participation, moreover, increases with non-labour incomes, suggesting that the decision to do volunteer work is a normal good.

The consumption hypothesis is tested for Italy in two studies in particular. Cappellari and Turati (2004) apply the same analytical structure as Frey and Götte (1999) to the role of extrinsic and intrinsic motivations in explaining the decision to do volunteer work.[4] In a theoretical structure of simultaneous investigation of both types of motivation, the authors apply Probit equations to samples of Italian workers and show that the proxies for extrinsic motivations reduce the likelihood of volunteer work, while those for intrinsic motivations increase it. Cappellari et al. (2007) take up the consumption hypothesis in a labour supply model that can simultaneously explain both a donation of time and a donation of money, considering also the supply of paid labour and the time dedicated to housework. Intrinsic preferences are attributed to three factors: 'warm glow', 'social prestige' and altruism (the individual's propensity to contribute to the provision of impure public goods). Simultaneous estimation of this model using the data for the year 2000 of the *Multiscopo* survey shows that the proxies for intrinsic preferences are important determinants of donations.

Here, we consider both types of motivation, as in Mueller (1975), Schram and Dunsing (1981), Menchik and Weisbrod (1987), Vaillancourt (1994) and Day and Devlin (1996). Like Cappellari et al. (2007), we use the *Multiscopo* dataset, but the present work differs from that study and from Cappellari and Turati (2004) in testing the consumption hypothesis with a direct estimate of total household income instead of proxies for extrinsic motivations and household economic resources.

9.4 The Data

ISTAT initiated its new series of multipurpose household surveys in 1993. Every year a representative sample of some 20,000 households (60,000 individuals) is surveyed on key aspects of daily life and behaviour. Though it is annual, it is not a panel survey; it does not follow any cross-section of respondents over time. Among the mass of information provided, there are data on unpaid activities, personal characteristics and household income. In the present work, the unit of analysis is the individual. The survey asks respondents whether they have performed unpaid activity during the past year in either of two types of social organization: 'volunteer service' and 'other' associations, which the survey defines as associations that are

[4] A person is said to have an "intrinsic" motivation when there is no apparent reward other than the activity itself; that is, when conduct is determined by ethical and moral considerations (Frey 1992).

not officially classed as 'volunteer service' but that the respondents consider to be such. On the basis of the answers, I create two dummies for unpaid activity, *Avol* (official volunteer service associations) and *Aass* (other associations), which take the value of 1 for a positive response, 0 for a negative.[5]

Table 9.2 gives names and definitions of all the variables. In addition to age and total income, these variables include sex, marital status, number of children, education, family size, health, home ownership, newspaper reading, and church-

Table 9.2 Variable names, definitions and sources

Variable	Description
Avol	Dummy, 1 if unpaid activity for official volunteer service associations; 0 otherwise
Aass	Dummy, 1 if unpaid activity for other associations; 0 otherwise
Female	Dummy, 1 if female; 0 otherwise
Married	Dummy, 1 if married; 0 otherwise
Age 14–19	Dummy, 1 if age is between 14 and 19; 0 otherwise
Age 20–34	Dummy, 1 if age is between 20 and 34; 0 otherwise
Age 35–44	Dummy, 1 if age is between 35 and 44; 0 otherwise. Reference group
Age 45–54	Dummy, 1 if age is between 45 and 54; 0 otherwise
Age 55–64	Dummy, 1 if age is between 55 e 64; 0 otherwise
Age 65+	Dummy, 1 if age is equal to 65 and above; 0 otherwise
No education	Dummy, 1 if no education; 0 otherwise
Compuls. ed	Dummy, 1 if compulsory education, 0 otherwise
High school	Dummy, 1 if high school graduate, 0 otherwise. Reference group
University	Dummy, 1 if university degree and doctorate; 0 otherwise
Children0_5	Dummy, 1 if there are in the household children aged between 0 and 5; 0 otherwise
Children6_15	Dummy, 1 if there are in the household children aged between 6 and 15; 0 otherwise
Famcomp	Number of people who live in family
Goodhealth	Dummy, 1 if the individual sees himself in a good state of health; 0 otherwise
Homeowner	Dummy, 1 if the individual owns the house where s/he lives; 0 otherwise
Churchgoer	Dummy, 1 if the individual goes to church at least once a week; 0 otherwise
Newspapers	Dummy, 1 if the individual reads newspapers every day of the week; 0 otherwise
Ln (HI)	Natural logarithm of total monthly household income, see text for details
Employed	Dummy, 1 if the individual is employed; 0 otherwise
Employee	Dummy, 1 if the individual is employed as an employee; 0 otherwise
Privserv	Dummy, 1 if individual is employed in private services; 0 otherwise
Grandparent	Dummy, 1 if the individual is a grandfather/mother; 0 otherwise
Micro-crime	Dummy, 1 if the individual has suffered pickpockets; 0 otherwise
Parking	Dummy, 1 if the individual declares that there is not difficulty in parking in the area where s/he lives; 0 otherwise
Traffic	Dummy, 1 if the individual declares that there is not traffic in the area where s/he lives; 0 otherwise
Pollution	Dummy, 1 if the individual declares that there is not pollution in the area where s/he lives; 0 otherwise

[5]The *Multiscopo* data on unpaid activity for each type of organization have 2 per cent missing values; the simplest solution is adopted, namely eliminating the missing values and analyzing only the sample with complete observations.

going. I also analyze variables relating to work status, job type and sector, which are especially relevant when the dependent variable is represented by 'other' associations. The *Multiscopo* survey is the source of all the variables.

The variables concerning home ownership and newspaper reading are included as indicators of attachment to the local community that are available in the *Multiscopo* survey. In the social capital literature, DiPasquale and Glaeser (1999) maintain that home owners have an incentive to improve the community in order to safeguard their real estate investment, and because home ownership is a barrier to mobility. Glaeser et al. (2002) contend that in order to increase the value of their local property home owners have an incentive to invest in forms of capital that are complementary to residential capital, such as civic organizations. Putnam (1993, p. 109) argues that newspapers are the most effective means of disseminating information on local events and problems, especially in Italy. Readers are better informed than non-readers and therefore better prepared to participate in decisions that affect the community. The literature on volunteer work has treated church-going and religious participation in general both as a 'taste' (Menchik and Weisbrod 1987; Vaillancourt 1994; Day and Devlin 1996) and as a proxy for altruistic behaviour (Cappellari et al. 2007).

The survey does not give data on respondents' labour income; for the year 1997 only it gives data on the household's total monthly income, divided into sixteen categories, the lowest being the equivalent of less than Euros 155, the highest of more than Euros 4,131. Following Freeman (1997), I take the mean for each category as the measure of household income. The lack of data on individual income prevents estimation of a complete structural model in which individual income and volunteer work are endogenous. So in line with most of the literature - Menchik and Weisbrod (1987), Day and Devlin (1996), Freeman (1997) – and the social capital literature – Alesina and La Ferrara (2000) and Glaeser et al. (2002) – I take household income as an exogenous variable.

Table 9.3 reports descriptive statistics and some correlations for the sample, for 1997, the year for which the income variable is available. The most common type of unpaid activity is for a volunteer service association (8%), twice as frequent as for 'other' associations (4%). Note that the variables for active participation in a social organization are positively correlated with one another.

9.5 The Econometric Strategy

This section performs an empirical test of the hypotheses presented in Sect. 9.2. First, we jointly estimate the equations for *Avol* and *Aass*, using a bivariate Probit model that considers the correlation between the errors of the two probit equations.

$$V_1^* = \boldsymbol{\beta}_1' \mathbf{X}_1 + \varepsilon_1,\ V_1 = 1 \text{ if } V_1^* > 0,\ 0 \text{ otherwise} \tag{9.1}$$

$$V_2^* = \boldsymbol{\beta}_2' \mathbf{X}_2 + \varepsilon_2,\ V_2 = 1 \text{ if } V_2^* > 0,\ 0 \text{ otherwise}$$

with error terms

Table 9.3 Sample descriptive statistics and correlations

Panel A. Descriptive statistics

	N	Mean	Std. Dev.	Min	Max
Avol	48,960	0.08	0.27	0	1
Avol	48,960	0.08	0.27	0	1
Aass	48,921	0.04	0.19	0	1
Female	49,917	0.52	0.50	0	1
Married	49,917	0.59	0.49	0	1
Age14–19	49,917	0.08	0.28	0	1
Age20–34	49,917	0.27	0.44	0	1
Age45–54	49,917	0.16	0.37	0	1
Age55–64	49,917	0.14	0.34	0	1
Age65+	49,917	0.16	0.37	0	1
Children0_5	49,917	0.14	0.40	0	4
Children6_15	49,917	0.33	0.64	0	5
Compul. ed	49,917	0.06	0.24	0	1
High school	49,917	0.57	0.49	0	1
Univ.	49,917	0.07	0.25	0	1
Famcomp	49,917	3.27	1.28	1	10
Goodhealth	49,383	0.46	0.50	0	1
Homeowner	49,667	0.74	0.44	0	1
Churchgoer	49,211	0.27	0.44	0	1
Newspapers	49,217	0.25	0.43	0	1
Ln (HI)	48,329	14.67	0.58	12.61	15.89
Employed	49,917	0.43	0.49	0	1
Employee	49,917	0.31	0.46	0	1
Privserv	49,917	0.16	0.37	0	1

Panel B. Correlations

	Avol	AAass
Avol	1.0000	
Aass	0.2727**	1.0000

Note. The *Multiscopo* sample survey on unpaid activity consists of perons at least 14-years-old. The variables are described in Table 9.2. Panel A gives the descriptive statistics, Panel B the correlations between the volunteer service activities. ** denotes significance at 5% level

$$\begin{pmatrix}\varepsilon_1\\ \varepsilon_2\end{pmatrix} \sim N_2, \left[\begin{pmatrix}0\\0\end{pmatrix}\begin{pmatrix}1\rho_{12}\\ \rho_{21}1\end{pmatrix}\right]$$

distributed as a normal bivariate, each with mean of zero and a variance-covariance matrix with values equal to 1 on the main diagonal and to the ρ correlations elsewhere. V_i is the dummy for unpaid activity, X_i the vector of age, household income, the other individual characteristics, the factors of attachment to the local community and the regional dummies, associated with the vector of the β coefficients. ϕ is the cumulative normal standard density function. The estimate of the β coefficients is intended to confirm the determinants of the decision to donate unpaid work to a social organization and verify hypotheses (1)–(3) set forth in Sect. 9.2.

As the *Multiscopo* dataset does not give individual respondents' incomes, to get some evidence on the role of this factor hypothesis (1) is also estimated separately for the sub-samples of employed and non-employed persons. The results of the estimate of (9.1) for the entire sample are given in Table 9.4, which shows the marginal effects and their significance levels (in brackets).

First we find that total household income is an important factor in the decision to give one's time to a volunteer service association or other association. The positive

Table 9.4 Bivariate Probit estimates of the probability of performing unpaid labour for a solidarity association. Marginal effects

	Avol	Aaas
	−0.0174***	−0.0126***
Female	(0.0026)	(0.0012)
	−0.0165***	−0.0037**
Married	(0.0036)	(0.0015)
	−0.0126**	0.0058
Age14–19	(0.0053)	(0.0035)
	−0.0073*	−0.0021
Age 20–34	(0.0040)	(0.0028)
	0.0031	0.0009
Age 45–54	(0.0035)	(0.0022)
	−0.0188***	−0.0039
Age 55–64	(0.0035)	(0.0037)
	−0.0655***	−0.0237***
Age 65+	(0.0047)	(0.0044)
	−0.0108***	−0.0014
Children0_5	(0.0034)	(0.0020)
	0.0075***	0.0026**
Children6_15	(0.0028)	(0.0013)
	−0.1134***	−0.0598***
Compuls. ed.	(0.0195)	(0.0067)
	−0.0347***	−0.0182***
High school	(0.0041)	(0.0015)
	0.0241***	0.0100***
University	(0.0044)	(0.0024)
	0.0007	−0.0008
Famcomp	(0.0015)	(0.0009)
	−0.0093***	−0.0059***
Goodhealth	(0.0035)	(0.0022)
	0.0094***	0.0044***
Homeowner	(0.0026)	(0.0015)
	0.0263***	0.0069***
Churchgoer	(0.0044)	(0.0020)
	0.0123***	0.0047***
Newspapers	(0.0034)	(0.0018)
	0.0086***	0.0064***
Ln (HI)	(0.0034)	(0.0024)
	−0.0073	0.0026

(continued)

Table 9.4 (continued)

	Avol		Aass
	(0.0043)		(0.0023)
	−0.0032		−0.0050**
Employee	(0.0041)		(0.0025)
	−0.0052**		−0.0021
Privserv	(0.0026)		(0.0023)
N		46 625	
Log Likelihood		−17 964	
LLR test of significance		300.123	
(χ^2)		(0.000)	
		0.5591	
ρ_{21}		(0.002)	
		24.22	
LLR test for Ln (HI)		(0.000)	
LLR test for age dummies		247.01	
		(0.000)	
LLR test for education dummies		508.18	
		(0.000)	

Note. The dependent variable is 1 if the person has performed unpaid labour in the past 12 months for a volunteer service association or 'other association'. All specifications include regional dummies. The variables are described in Table 9.2. The estimates are marginal effects calculated on the sample means of the independent variables. Standard errors (in brackets) are corrected for heteroskedasticity and the clustering of residuals at regional level. The symbols ***, **, * denote significance at the 1, 5 and 10% levels respectively. ρ_{21} is the correlation coefficient between the errors of the *Avol* and *Aass* equations

correlation between the probability of being a volunteer worker and household income validates the consumption model for these organizations and is consistent with the findings of Menchik and Weisbrod (1987), Vaillancourt (1994), and Day and Devlin (1996).

Second, the coefficients of the age dummy indicate a non-linear relationship between age and unpaid activity for a volunteer service association. The probability of working for an *Avol* increases with age up to the 45–54 group, then declines. The age estimates do not change when a dummy regressor corresponding to year of birth is added (these coefficients are not shown). Nor does the decline among older people depend on health effects. Including a dummy for those who say their health is good, the decline remains. The evidence that volunteer work decreases with age would appear to support the investment model. For volunteer organizations proper (*Avol*), this result is consistent with Menchik and Weisbrod (1987) and Day and Devlin (1996). For *Aass* the results are less significant, but here too, consistent with the investment motivation, unpaid activity is less common in the oldest age-group.

The probability of being a volunteer increases with education. People with no more than compulsory schooling (junior high school) do significantly less volunteer work than high school graduates, and university graduates do significantly more. The positive correlation between education and volunteer work can be thought of as one of the positive externalities of formal schooling (Day and Devlin 1996, p. 44).

For the dummies *Children 0–5* and *Children 6–15* too, the coefficients are in line with the American evidence; however, in contrast with the US, in Italy women are less likely than men to be volunteers.

Let us turn to local roots. For both volunteer work and other associations, unpaid activity is likely to come from people who own their own homes and read the daily newspaper. The coefficients of *Homeowner* and *Newspapers* are positive and highly significant. This evidence supports the predictions of Putnam (1993) and the findings of DiPasquale and Glaeser (1999) and of Glaeser et al. (2002). The coefficient of *churchgoer* is positive and significant for both types of association. If we take religious participation as a proxy of altruistic motivation, the evidence is that altruism is a causal factor in the decision to perform unpaid work for a volunteer service or other association. This would appear to support the evidence cited by Cappellari et al. (2007).

The regressors include eighteen regional dummies (Val d'Aosta is aggregated with Piedmont), whose marginal effects are shown in Table 9.5. People who live in the regions of central and northern Italy do significantly more volunteer work for both types of association. These regional patterns reflect the well-known pattern of passive participation described in the social capital literature (Putnam 1993; Forni and Paba 2000).

Note further that the covariances of the two cross-section equations are positively and significantly correlated. This is evidence that at least as far as unobserved aptitudes are concerned the two types of unpaid activity are not in competition but rather tend to concur.

Work status and sector are important determinants of volunteer working. Being employed reduces work for volunteer work associations, as those who are employees donate less unpaid work to other associations. So in order to get more information on the role of *labour income* the following discussion uses sub-samples of employed and non-employed persons. An additional robustness check is performed in two successive steps.

One might presume that the evidence in Table 9.4 on the older age-groups reflects the fact that in Italy more than elsewhere grandparents take care of their grandchildren, leaving them no time for volunteer work. If this were so, less volunteer work by the elderly could be connected with care of grandchildren. Thus I use the 1997 *Multiscopo* survey to construct a *grandparents* dummy taking value 1 if the respondent is a grandparent and 0 otherwise. A negative coefficient for this variable would capture the grandchild-care thesis. As further controls I consider dummies for environmental effects in the respondent's place of residence. The intuition here is that these factors may affect the pattern of active participation. The variables considered are: street crime, parking, traffic and pollution. For a description, see Table 9.2. The grandparent and *environment* dummies are added to vector **X** in equation 9.1.

Table 9.5 Bivariate Probit estimates of the probability of performing unpaid labour for a solidarity association. Regional marginal effects

	Avol	Aass
Piedmont+VdA	0.0004	0.0014***
	(0.0005)	(0.0003)
Trentino-AA	0.0651***	0.0251***
	(0.014)	(0.0007)
Veneto	0.0208***	0.0133***
	(0.0007)	(0.0004)
Friuli-VG	0.0104***	0.0149***
	(0.0005)	(0.0005)
Liguria	−0.0168***	−0.0096***
	(0.0012)	(0.0006)
Emilia-R	0.0056***	0.0064***
	(0.0008)	(0.0003)
Tuscany	0.0025***	0.0042***
	(0.0006)	(0.0003)
Umbria	−0.0238***	−0.0015***
	(0.0009)	(0.0005)
Marche	−0.0265***	−0.0043***
	(0.0006)	(0.0005)
Lazio	−0.0508***	−0.0135***
	(0.0012)	(0.0007)
Abruzzi	−0.0291***	−0.0054***
	(0.0011)	(0.0007)
Molise	−0.0434***	−0.0146***
	(0.0015)	(0.0011)
Campania	−0.0602***	−0.0122***
	(0.0017)	(0.0013)
Puglia	−0.0299***	−0.0098***
	(0.0019)	(0.0013)
Basilicata	−0.0447***	−0.0127***
	(0.0020)	(0.0013)
Calabria	−0.0491***	−0.0073***
	(0.0017)	(0.0011)
Sicily	−0.0561***	−0.0150***
	(0.0018)	(0.0013)
Sardinia	−0.0120***	0.0061***
	(0.0020)	(0.0010)

Note: Lombardy is the reference region. Otherwise, see note to Table 9.4

The marginal effects are shown in Table 9.6 for the employed and Table 9.7 for the non-employed. Since the point is to test the hypotheses of Sect. 9.2, I report only the estimates for age, education, total income and *grandparent*.

Among the employed, let us first consider the education dummy. Volunteer labour increases with education. Starting from the sample mean, an increase of one standard deviation in educational level implies an increase of 1% in unpaid labour for volunteer service organizations and of 0.5% for other associations.

Table 9.6 Marginal bivariate Probit effects for the employed

	Avol		Aass
Age14–19	−0.0423***		−0.0194*
	(0.0129)		(0.0103)
Age20–34	−0.0145**		−0.0041
	(0.0065)		(0.0043)
Age45–54	−0.0031		−0.0004
	(0.0057)		(0.0035)
Age55–64	−0.0300***		0.0006
	(0.0098)		(0.0075)
Age65+	−0.0520*		−0.0365**
	(0.0304)		(0.0143)
Grandparent	0.0065		0.0099
	(0.0508)		(0.0272)
Compuls. ed.	−0.0991***		−0.4290***
	(0.0337)		(0.0082)
High school	−0.0385***		−0.0227***
	(0.0071)		(0.0032)
University	0.0326***		0.0162***
	(0.0074)		(0.0039)
Ln (HI)	0.0007		0.0042
	(0.0052)		(0.0043)
N		19 982	
Log Likelihood		−9 169	
LLR test of significance (χ^2)		151.060	
		(0.000)	
ρ_{21}		0.5471	
		(0.035)	

Note. The dependent variable is 1 if the person has performed unpaid labour in the past 12 months for a volunteer service association or 'other association'. The estimator is Maximum Likelihood. The unreported regressors are those specified in Table 9.2 plus the *grandparent* and *environment* dummies. All specifications include regional dummies. The variables are described in Table 9.2. Marginal effects calculated on the sample means of the independent variables. Standard errors (in brackets) are corrected for heteroskedasticity and the clustering of residuals at regional level. The symbols ***, **, * denote significance at the 1, 5 and 10% levels respectively. ρ_{21} is the correlation coefficient between the errors of the *Avol* and *Aass* equations

This evidence confirms the view of volunteer work as a positive externality of education and excludes the interpretation that it proxies for the opportunity cost of time, by virtue of the discussion, further on, of total household income.

As to the age dummy, a one-standard-deviation increase for the younger age-groups (under 35) reduces work for formal volunteer organizations by 1.2% points; for the older groups (over 55), it reduces it by 1.3 points. That is, the evidence confirms the inverted U-curve, and hence the investment model, owing among other things to the fact that the *grandparent* variable is not significant. The latter variable is equally insignificant as regards work for other associations: employed people older than 65 donate less unpaid labour than the reference group, as do employed people 19 or younger. Specifically, a one-standard-deviation increase in the dummy reduces the supply of volunteer labour by about 0.2% points. But this evidence, combined with the non-significance of the other age dummies, confirms the investment model for other associations only in the broadest sense.

For both types of organization, total household income of the employed is not a significant factor. The following argument may apply. The lack of significance of total household income for the sub-sample of the employed, by contrast with its significance for the entire sample, suggests that the time opportunity cost effect is stronger among these respondents, which implies a labour income substitution effect. This powerful labour income substitution effect, for the employed, offsets the effect of non-labour income, making the coefficient for total income insignificant. The performance of the education dummies supports this argument. If education were a proxy for labour income, it would follow that labour income and non-labour income would be complements, as both would increase the supply of volunteer labour. This implies a positive and highly significant effect of total income on volunteer labour, but this is rejected by the probit analysis. This argument for a labour income substitution effect would thus imply support for the consumption and investment motivations both for formal volunteer service associations and for other associations.

Turning to the non-employed (Table 9.7 in Appendix), we find that for the volunteer service associations proper, education retains its link with unpaid activity. An increase of one standard deviation in educational level increases volunteer labour by 0.4%. For other associations, though, better education is not statistically significant. As to the age dummies, for the former type of organization the coefficients, where significant, have the sign predicted by the investment hypothesis. Grandparent status also plays a role in reducing volunteer labour for these organizations: increasing the dummy by one standard deviation reduces unpaid activity by 0.5% points. This tells against the investment model. For other associations too, the positive sign of the 14–19 age dummy, together with the non-significance of the other age dummies, raises doubts as to the validity of the investment model, at least in its canonical form.

The positive and significant coefficient of total income with respect to both types of association is evidence for the consumption motivation. Increasing household income by one standard deviation induces an increase of 0.7% points for volunteer service associations proper and 0.3 points for other associations.

One more check for robustness, finally, considers household equivalent income. As we know, purchasing power varies in non-linear fashion with the number of household members, thanks to economies of scale. In order to compare the economic situation of households that differ in size and composition, therefore, total household income is divided by 'equivalent household size' using the OECD's modified scale of household equivalence (assigning a weight of 1 to the first adult, 0.5 to every additional member aged 14 or more, and 0.3 to every member younger than 14). Household equivalent income is the ratio of household income to number of adult-equivalents. The estimates using equivalent income (not shown but available from the author) confirm the earlier results.

9.6 Concluding Remarks

The difficulty of research on the determinants of volunteer labour in Italy can certainly be blamed on lack of data. This essay uses ISTAT's 1997 *Indagine Multiscopo sulle Famiglie, Aspetti della Vita Quotidiana* (multipurpose survey of households and daily life) to test the consumption and investment motivations for volunteer work empirically. The study takes as the dependent variable the fact of having performed unpaid labour for a social organization (a formal volunteer service association or another association) in the 12 months preceding the interview, applying a bivariate probit.

For the entire sample it is found that the donation of unpaid activity to a volunteer service association (or other association) is determined both by the consumption and by the investment motivation. This confirms the evidence of studies for the US, Canada and the UK, and in particular Menchik and Weisbrod's conclusion that "Not surprisingly, there is evidence that both consumption and investment motivations influence the supply of volunteer labour" (Menchik and Weisbrod 1987, p. 180). The overall results are basically confirmed by analysis of sub-samples of the employed and the non-employed. For the employed, we find evidence of a powerful labour income substitution effect, consistent with the predictions of both the consumption and the investment model. For the non-employed, the evidence is most favourable to the consumption hypothesis, although here too there is some evidence of an investment motivation.

As to the empirical literature on Italy, the present study confirms Cappellari et al. (2007) in finding evidence of the consumption motivation but not the conclusions of Cappellari and Turati (2004), stressing the active role of extrinsic (or investment) motivations in the decision to donate unpaid labour to a volunteer work or other association.

Acknowledgements My thanks to Sergio Destefanis, Carlo Borzaga, Luigi Bonatti, Gilberto Turati, Federica Origo, Matteo Lippi Bruni, Lorenzo Cappellari, Bruna Bruno, Fernanda Mazzotta, Adriana Barone and the participants at the 21st AIEL conference, and of seminars at the universities of Bergamo and Bologna for helpful comments and suggestions. For any errors and omissions, as always the author alone is responsible.

Appendix

Table 9.7 Marginal bivariate Probit effects for the non-employed

	Avol		Aass
Age14–19	−0.0031		0.0071*
	(0.0074)		(0.0040)
Age20–34	0.0004		0.0003
	(0.0073)		(0.0044)
Age45–54	0.0140**		0.0038
	(0.0063)		(0.0038)
Age55–64	−0.0050		−0.0023
	(0.0065)		(0.0036)
Age65+	−0.0405***		−0.0149***
	(0.0049)		(0.0041)
Grandparent	−0.0337**		−0.0033
	(0.0133)		(0.0085)
Compuls. ed.	−0.0954***		−0.0442***
	(0.0075)		(0.0043)
High school	−0.0304***		−0.0149***
	(0.0034)		(0.0013)
University	0.0231***		0.0046
	(0.0054)		(0.0043)
Ln (HI)	0.0114***		0.0059**
	(0.0362)		(0.0023)
N		26 184	
Log Likelihood		−8 549	
LLR test of significance (χ^2)		480.214	
		(0.000)	
ρ_{21}		0.5716	
		(0.019)	

Note. See note to Table 9.6

References

Alesina A, La Ferrara E (2000) Participations in heterogeneous communities. Quarterly Journal of Economics 115:847–904

Andreoni J (1990) Impure altruism and donations to public goods: a theory of warm-glow giving. Economic Journal 100:464–467

Beugelsdijk S, van Schaik T (2005) Social capital and growth in European regions: an empirical test. European Journal of Political Economy 21:301–324

Bjørnskov C (2006) The multiple facets of social capital. European Journal of Political Economy 22:22–40

Bourdieu P (1986) The forms of capital. In Richardson J (ed) Handbook of theory and research for the sociology of education. Greenwood Press, Westport CT

Brown E, Lankford H (1992) Gifts of money and gifts of time: estimating the effects of tax prices and available time. Journal of Public Economics 47:321–341

Cappellari L, Turati G (2004) Volunteer labour supply: the role of workers' motivations. Annals of Public and Cooperative Economics 74:619–643
Cappellari L, Ghinetti P, Turati G (2007) On time and money donations. CESifo Working Paper 2140
Carlin PS (2001) Evidence on the volunteer labour supply of married women. Southern Economic Journal 67:801–824
Costa DL Kahn ME (2003) Understanding the decline in social capital 1952–1998. Kyklos 56:17–46
Day KM Devlin RA (1996) Volunteerism and crowding out: Canadian econometric evidence. Canadian Journal of Economics 29:37–53
DiPasquale D, Glaeser EL (1999) Incentives and social capital: are homeowners better citizens? Journal of Urban Economics 45:354–384
Duncan B (1999) Modeling charitable contributions of time and money. Journal of Public Economics 72:213–242
Forni M, Paba S (2000) The sources of local growth: evidence from Italy. Giornale degli Economisti e Annali di Economia 59:1–49
Freeman R B (1997) Working for nothing: the supply of volunteer labour. Journal of Labor Economics 15:S140–S166
Frey BS (1992) Tertium datur: pricing regulating and intrinsic motivation. Kyklos 45:161–184
Frey BS, Götte L (1999) Does pay motive volunteers? University of Zurich Institute for Empirical Research in Economics Working Paper 7
Glaeser EL, Laibson D, Sacerdote B (2002) An economic approach to social capital. Economic Journal 112:F437–F458
Knack S (2003) Groups, growth and trust: cross-country evidence on the Olson and Putnam hypotheses. Public Choice 117:341–355
Knack S Keefer P (1997) Does social capital have an economic payoff? A cross country investigation. Quarterly Journal of Economics 112:1251–1288
Menchik PL, Weisbrod BA (1987) Volunteer labour supply. Journal of Public Economics 32:159–183
Mueller MW (1975) Economic determinants of volunteer work by women. Signs 1:325–338
Portes A (1998) Social capital: its origins and applications in modern sociology. Annual Review of Sociology 24:1–24
Prouteau L Wolff FC (2004) Relational goods and associational participation. Annals of Public and Cooperative Economics 75:431–463
Putnam R (with Leonardi R, Nanetti R) (1993) Making democracy work. Princeton University Press, Princeton
Schram VR Dunsing MM (1981) Influences on married women's volunteer work participation. Journal of Consumer Research 7:372–379
Vaillancourt F (1994) To volunteer or not: Canada 1987. Canadian Journal of Economics 27:813–826
Ziemek S (2006) Economic analysis of volunteers' motivations. A cross-country study Journal of Socio-Economics 35:532–555

Chapter 10
Voluntary Associations and Trustworthiness: An Empirical Examination at Italian Regional Level

Giacomo Degli Antoni

Abstract This essay studies the level of trustworthiness across Italian regions in relation to three variables: membership in cultural and recreational associations; membership in ecological, civil rights and peace associations; unpaid participation in voluntary service associations (solidarity associations). Two main results emerge: a positive and significant effect of unpaid participation in solidarity associations on the regional level of trustworthiness, and a negative, if not always significant, effect of membership in environmental associations. Consequently, it is unpaid labour of solidarity associations that crucially contributes to the creation of propitious conditions for the diffusion of trustworthy behaviour throughout the community.

10.1 Introduction

There is a long tradition of scholarship on the possible contribution of voluntary associations to social and economic development. Tocqueville (1840) described the propensity to form associations as an essential characteristic of people living in democratic societies and stressed the role of voluntary associations in allowing people to achieve their common purposes through cooperation. Along Tocqueville's lines, Putnam (1993) emphasized that "Internally, associations instill in their members habits of cooperation, solidarity and public-spiritedness. [...] participation in civic organization inculcates skills of cooperation as well as a sense of shared responsibility for collective endeavors". Putnam states also that "a dense network of secondary associations both embodies and contributes to effective social collaboration" (Putnam 1993, pp. 89–90). An opposing view is espoused by Olson (1965), 1982), who highlights the presumed role of associations in pursuing the private interests of their members and in relegating the collective interest to a minor role. From this perspective, associations do not help to create a social fabric of trust and trustworthiness but instead exacerbate divisions and self-interest.

G. Degli Antoni
Centro interuniversitario EconomEtica, University of Milano-Bicocca,
Edificio U9, Viale dell'Innovazione 10, 20126 Milano, Italy

S. Destefanis and M. Musella (eds.), *Paid and Unpaid Labour in the Social Economy*, AIEL Series in Labour Economics, DOI: 10.1007/978-3-7908-2137-6_11,

A number of studies, some designed expressly to inquire into the difference of approach between Putnam and Olson, have run empirical checks on the effects of associations: on the general level of trust (Knack and Keefer 1997; Brehm and Rahn 1997; Stolle and Rochon 1998; Claibourn and Martin 2000; Knack 2003; Mayer 2003); on civicness (Knack and Keefer 1997; Mayer 2003; Wollebæck and Selle 2003); on trust in public institutions (Brehm and Rahn 1997; Stolle and Rochon 1998; Mayer 2003; Wollæbaeck and Selle 2003); and on tolerance, free riding and optimism (Stolle and Rochon 1998). Ordinarily, then, the extent of associative movements is studied as a determinant of some of the intangible factors of development, such as trust and civicness, that have been shown to foster economic growth (Knack and Keefer 1997; Helliwell and Putnam 2000; Zak and Knack 2001).

This essay offers an empirical analysis, for the different regions of Italy, of the effect of association membership on the level of opportunism. Here, opportunistic behaviour is defined as the betrayal of trust in a situation in which cooperation between individuals is needed. Suppose that two agents (A and B) have initiated a cooperative process in the framework of which each believes he can trust the other to honour the agreements made. Both A and B, under the acceptation of 'trust' that we use here,[1] assign a high probability to observance of the cooperative agreement. In what follows we define as 'trustworthy' (or non-opportunistic) the conduct of an agent who, in such a context, honours his commitments and does not betray the trust placed in him. The inquiry into the effects of association membership on trustworthy conduct is an original approach - while many studies (cited above) have produced empirical examinations of the role of associations in generating trust, their impact on trustworthiness has gone basically unexplored.

Although some studies have shown a strong correlation between trust and trustworthy behaviour (Knack and Keefer 1997; Glaeser et al. 2000),[2] the two concepts do not coincide. Experimental economic analyses have highlighted some unclear aspects of the correlation between a person's trust in reciprocally honest conduct by another and the actual realization of that behaviour. In an investment game framework, for instance, the empirical results do not conclusively demonstrate the existence of an increasing relation between the amount of money the trustor sends, which can range from 0 to the entire amount, and the amount returned by the trustee, who gets three times the amount sent (Berg et al. 1995). In their seminal studies, Berg et al. (1995) conducted an investment game by implementing two different treatments: a baseline treatment, where a standard investment game was played, and a 'social

[1](Gambetta 1988, p. 217) observes: "There is a degree of convergence in defining trust which can be summarized as follows: trust is a particular level of the subjective probability with which an agent assesses that another agent or group of agents will perform a given action".

[2]Knack and Keefer (1997) correlate an index of generalized trust at national level with an index based on an experiment run by *Reader's Digest* (reported in *The Economist*, 22 June 1996). The experiment consisted in leaving wallets containing $50.00 and the name and address of the "owner" on the street in various cities and countries. The correlation between the national index of trust and the percentage of wallets returned in the various countries was 0.67. Glaeser et al. (2000) used an experimental approach to show that people's evaluations of their trust in others mirror their own tendency to be trustworthy.

history' treatment, where players were informed about the decision made by other subjects who had played in the previous no history treatment. In the no history treatment, there is not a significant correlation between the amount sent by trustors and the amount returned by trustees, while in the social history treatment the correlation is significant and equal to 0.34.

Essentially, without trust no cooperative relationship is formed; but it is trustworthy behaviour that makes the success of cooperation and the generation of reciprocal advantage for both participants possible.

If trust and trustworthiness do not refer to precisely the same phenomenon, then an express examination of the latter is economically relevant. Lack of opportunism lowers transaction costs and favours cooperative agreements. The variable we use here as a measure of regional trustworthiness is positively correlated with the growth of per capita GDP (Degli Antoni 2006).

We study the level of trustworthiness in the Italian regions in relation to three variables gauging the extent of diffusion of three types of association: membership in cultural and recreational associations; membership in ecological, civil rights and peace associations; and unpaid participation in voluntary associations formally regulated in Italy for the first time in 1991 by Law 266/1991. The latter are nonprofit associations, characterized by solidarity aims and democratic structure and their members are for the most part voluntary workers. In order to stress that (according to Law 266/1991) these associations must be characterized by aims of solidarity, we will name them 'solidarity associations'. That is, we focus on associations whose social purposes should make them least oriented to the pursuit of individual self-interest and most capable of stimulating the propensity to cooperate within the communities in which they operate. However, as we shall see, there are significant differences among the three types of association, bound up with their specific objectives and their primary activities, which justify differential analysis of their effects on the overall level of trustworthiness.

Our estimates control for the possible effects on trustworthiness of the main socio-economic factors considered in the literature: per capita GDP, educational levels, the Gini index of income concentration, and the employment rate.

This essay is organized as follows. Section 10.2 presents the data and describes the methodology for our empirical analysis. Specifically, it describes the peculiarities of the measure of trustworthiness adopted. Section 10.3 gives the main results of our econometric test. Section 10.4 offers an interpretation of these results and some concluding considerations.

10.2 Empirical Analysis: Data and Methodology

10.2.1 A Methodological Introduction

Our empirical analysis must overcome two essential methodological obstacles.

The first is the possible distortion of the estimates owing to the difficulty of making allowance for cultural variables relating to the society under study, which may theoretically affect the degree of trustworthiness. These factors are hard to measure, and if they cannot be taken account of in the estimate they may be significant omitted variables. Typically, the level of trustworthiness in the various regions of Italy may also be related to long-term factors involving history and tradition.[3] The database created and used in this work covers all twenty regions and eight time periods. This makes it possible to use econometric techniques that can deal with the problem of the possible omission of significant time-invariant variables.

The second is the possible endogeneity of the extent of association membership with respect to the dependent variables considered. There may well be reciprocal causality between the extent of social and cultural associations and the degree of trustworthiness.

In theory, according to Putnam and Olson, the effect of associations on trustworthy behaviour may be positive or negative. In the light of the ambiguous results of such works as Knack and Keefer (1997) on the effect on the social fabric of membership in Putnam-type associations, aggregated into a single index, in the present study we have kept the different types of association distinct.[4] That is, we track the effects on trustworthiness deriving, separately, from cultural and recreational associations; environmental, civil-rights and peace associations; and solidarity associations.

As to reverse causation, running from trustworthiness to the extent of association membership, it can be argued that the lower probability of being the victim of opportunistic behaviour may heighten people's propensity to join associations for two main reasons.

1. First, in a social environment marked by lack of opportunism, one imagines there is a greater likelihood that an association's activities will successfully achieve their purposes. This may be both because within the associations the individual members themselves can be trusted to carry out their commitments and reliably perform their assigned tasks and because associations encounter more cooperation in the community as a whole and with public institutions for the achievement of goals that should be recognized as socially desirable. This type of environment, by fostering the success of the associations, should also be an incentive for their formation and for membership.

[3] Putnam (1993) suggests an explanation of the level of social capital in the North and the South of Italy based on the different course of history in the two areas.

[4] Knack and Keefer (1997) examine the effect of associations on the general level of trust in different countries. They distinguish between "Putnam" associations (cultural, artistic or musical, sports, etc.) and "Olson" associations (trade unions, political parties or groups, and business associations). Their results on the role of the different types of association are surprising. Overall, association membership has a positive but not statistically significant effect on trust. Distinguishing between "Putnam" and "Olson" associations, they unexpectedly find a negative though not significant effect of the former and a positive effect of the latter.

2. Second, recent work (Uhlaner 1989; Gui 1994, 2002) has shown how certain behaviours on the part of economic agents can be interpreted in the light of 'relational goods', which can be produced (and at the same time consumed) exclusively by the interaction of two or more persons. Relational goods comprise such things as social approval, friendship, the pleasure of conversation with a brilliant man or woman. In some cases, the production of relational goods is the prime purpose of the encounter between agents. That is, certain interactive contexts would appear to be 'designed' for the creation of relational goods. "If you think of a recreational club meeting, you spontaneously imagine that the main output is mutual entertainment, 'company': an intangible output that is 'consumed' by the participants who, because they bring the human resources employed in the process generating this good, are also the producers" (Gui 2002, p. 38 - our translation). We believe that relational goods play an important role in the associations considered here. The decision to join is often dictated by the desire to enjoy time spent in the company of other people sharing the same aims. In an environment in which opportunistic behaviour is relatively rare, it is less probable that the encounter with others will be disappointing in relational terms. Thus association membership, where its purpose is effectively the enjoyment of relational goods, may be fostered by the absence of opportunism.

In order to deal with the possible endogeneity between trustworthiness and association membership, in our empirical test we employ a two-stage least-squares estimation procedure.

10.2.2 Data and Methodology

We use regional panel data (from 1995 to 2002) taken from the *Indagine Multiscopo sulle Famiglie-Aspetti della Vita Quotidiana* (multipurpose survey of households and daily life), a survey published by ISTAT. The total sample consists of 160 observations (8 years for each of the twenty regions). The dependent variable is the index of trustworthiness, which is designed to measure 'the probability of observing, within a given community, non-opportunistic behaviour in response to the actions of agents who expect such non-opportunistic conduct'. The index is the simple arithmetic mean of three appropriately standardized indicators:

1. The number of proceedings brought concerning labour, social security and compulsory assistance per 1,000 persons employed
2. The number of protests of bills and personal cheques per 1,000 population
3. The number of persons brought to court by the law enforcement forces per 1,000 population

The formula used to standardize the three indicators is:

$$1-\frac{x_{ic}^{t}-\min(x_{i}^{t})}{\max(x_{i}^{t})-\min(x_{i}^{t})}$$ where x_{ic}^{t} is the value of the indicator i in region c at time t.[5]

The composite index resulting from this formula increases as the values of the individual simple indicators decrease. That is, it is a measure of the absence of opportunism. The three indicators pick up opportunistic behaviour in several contexts.

The first refers to labour conflict. The number of initial proceedings in matters of work, social security and compulsory assistance proxies opportunism in relations between workers and employers. Such disputes may arise when one party feels that an employment agreement has been violated. And this may naturally be affected by individuals' propensity for opportunistic behaviour. Obviously there are also other variables that can affect this indicator, such as the characteristics of the labour market (above all unionization) and confidence in the judicial system. The presence of strong unions may prompt workers to turn to the courts to settle some disputes, both because they feel better protected when there is a union and because the union is likely to inform workers of possibilities they would otherwise be unaware of. As to the judicial system, it is evident that if someone does not believe that a complaint can be settled quickly or cheaply enough, he may elect not to lodge it in the first place.

The second indicator picks up opportunistic behaviour between debtors and creditors. A protest means that the debtor has not acted in accordance with the expectations of the creditor. This may reflect opportunism on the part of someone who decides not to discharge his payment obligation, and may thus be an index of (lack of) trustworthiness. The number of protests can also be determined by purely economic contingencies, such as recession, that affect the possibility of actually effecting the payment.

The third indicator does not refer, at least in most cases, to specific economic or social relations between two or more agents. It reflects the betrayal of a community's general trust in law-abiding conduct. The indicator may be significantly influenced by the efficiency of law enforcement. Unlike the number of labour and social security suits brought to court, it does not depend on confidence in the judicial system, in that crime reports are recorded automatically by the police forces.

An examination of the three indicators that go into our composite index shows that each of them is affected by a number of different factors, but the only one that appears to affect all three is individuals' tendency to act opportunistically.[6]

---

[5] The source for the data for the dependent variable is ISTAT's statistical yearbook, *Annuario Statistico Italiano*. All three indicators refer to the calendar year. The simple arithmetic mean used to aggregate the three simple standardized indicators is appropriate given the strong initial correlation between them (Saisana and Tarantola 2002). The procedure yields standardized indicators with the same range, from 0 to 1. This procedure is therefore more robust than possible alternative techniques in the presence of outliers (Saisana and Tarantola 2002, p. 11).

[6] For a more detailed description of the factors that may influence each of the simple indicators and the arguments for using them to produce the trustworthiness index, see Degli Antoni (2006).

This is why the average of the three simple indicators can be read as a good proxy of trustworthiness in each region.

The most interesting explanatory variables for our purposes are those of membership in the three different types of association. The first variable, *Cultu*, is membership in cultural and recreational associations, gauged as the percentage of the population aged 14 or more who have attended at least one meeting of a cultural, recreational or other similar association in the last 12 months. The second, *Eco*, is the percentage of the population aged at least 14 who have attended at least one meeting of an environmental, civil rights or peace association in the last 12 months. The third, *Volo*, is the percentage of the population aged 14 or more who have performed some unpaid activity for a solidarity association in the last 12 months.

The index of trustworthiness is then related to a series of variables which, consistent with the economic literature, might explain the presence of a social fabric based on relations of trustworthiness. Apart from *Cultu*, *Eco* and *Volo*, our model's regressors are:[7]

- *Edu_1*: Percentage of the population aged 15–19 with at least a junior high school diploma
- *Edu_2*: Percentage of the population aged 20–24 with at least a high school diploma
- *GDP*: Per capita GDP
- *Gini*: Gini's income concentration index
- *Empl*: Employment rate (per cent) for population aged 15–64

As to the estimation methodology, it is designed to deal with two essential problems (see Sect. 10.2.1). One is the possibility of specific regional characteristics, perhaps depending on history and tradition, that may affect the degree of trustworthiness. To overcome this difficulty, we estimate region fixed effects for a model such as:

$$Trustworthiness_{\mathrm{it}} = \beta_1\, Cultu_{\mathrm{it}} + \beta_2\, Eco_{\mathrm{it}} + \beta_3\, Volo_{\mathrm{it}} + \sum\nolimits_{j=1}^{s} \beta_{\mathrm{j}} X_{\mathrm{jit}} + \eta_{\mathrm{i}} + \varepsilon_{\mathrm{it}}$$

where *i* and *t* are region and time period, *Cultu, Eco* and *Volo* are the three variables relating to association membership, X_{it} is the set of other explanatory variables described above, η_{i} is the regional fixed effect and $\varepsilon_{\mathrm{it}}$ the error term.

[7]Except for the Gini index, taken from Cannari and D'Alessio (2003), all the variables used in this study are constructed from ISTAT data. *Cultu, Eco* and *Volo* in particular are based on data from ISTAT, *Indagine Multiscopo sulle famiglie "Aspetti della vita quotidiana" - Cultura socialità e tempo libero* (1996–2003). Per capita GDP uses data from ISTAT, *Annuario Statistico Italiano* (1996–2003). *Edu_1* (at least compulsory - junior high school - education) comes from ISTAT's quarterly labour force survey, *Rilevazione trimestrale sulle forze del lavoro. Edu_2* (high school education) and *Empl* (employment rate) come from ISTAT's continuous labour force survey, *Rilevazione continua sulle forze di lavoro*. The descriptive statistics for all the variables are given in the Appendix (Table 10.3).

The second potential problem is reciprocal causality between level of trustworthiness and association membership. Here, we have performed two-stage estimates, considering two instrumental variables.[8] One, designated *Pol*, stands for political involvement and is defined as the percentage of people who talk about politics at least once a week. The other, *Spett*, refers to participation in theatrical or musical events and is defined as the number of tickets to such events sold per 100 inhabitants. The idea is that these two variables do not affect trustworthiness directly but only through their impact on the decision to join an association, as they are the sign of a degree of civic spirit. The Sargan test supports their validity in the estimates made using them.

To assess the possibility that associations affect trustworthiness with a lag due to the time needed for membership to influence individuals' propensity to cooperate, we have performed our estimations:

- First, taking both the dependent variable (trustworthiness) and the regressors in the same year
- Second, taking the average of the values of the regressors for 2-year and 3-year periods and relating those averages to trustworthiness at the end of the period. This lagged structure averaging several years instead of considering single years, seems to be less ad hoc and more consistent with the nature of the independent variables

10.3 The Empirical Results

The estimates in Table 10.1 are simultaneous, i.e. the dependent variable and the regressors all refer to the same time period. Table 10.1 presents region fixed effects estimates with the level of trustworthiness as the dependent variable.

The first three regressions are for each of the three types of association individually; the fourth includes all three. Only unpaid participation in solidarity associations (*Volo*) has a statistically significant positive correlation with the region's level of trustworthiness. *Cultu* and *Eco* show a negative, but not significant, relation. This result is not totally surprising in view of Knack and Keefer (1997), which found a negative but not significant relation between the index of trust based on World Values Survey data and an index for Putnam-type association membership.

These initial results – which our other, subsequent regressions confirm – suggest, interestingly, that on these data not all the associations ordinarily defined as 'Putnam-type' actually bear out Putnam's thesis that association membership strengthens real social cooperation. At least in Italy and for the types of association used here, this potential would seem to depend on the number of people who engage in unpaid voluntary service in solidarity associations.

[8]These instrumental variables are used only in relation to *Volo*. As the next section shows, this is the variable that leads to the creation of trustworthiness.

Table 10.1 Association membership and trustworthiness (region fixed effects method)

Equation	*1*	*2*	*3*	*4*	*5*	*6 (IV)*
Volo	0.014**			0.021***	0.012*	0.040*
	(0.007)			(0.007)	(0.006)	(0.022)
Cultu		−0.003		−0.009		
		(0.005)		(0.006)		
Eco			−0.017	−0.021		
			(0.015)	(0.016)		
GDP	−0.000	−0.000	−0.000	−0.000**		
	(0.000)	(0.000)	(0.000)	(0.000)		
Edu_1	0.007	0.007	0.007	0.008		
	(0.008)	(0.008)	(0.008)	(0.008)		
Edu_2	0.010***	0.009***	0.009***	0.008***	0.006***	0.005***
	(0.002)	(0.003)	(0.003)	(0.003)	(0.001)	(0.002)
Empl	0.000	0.002	0.003	0.001		
	(0.008)	(0.008)	(0.008)	(0.008)		
Constant	−0.451	−0.338	−0.324		0.102	−0.031
	(0.757)	(0.769)	(0.766)		(0.094)	(0.143)
Sargan Test						0.144
R^2						
within	0.202	0.177	0.183	0.229	0.186	0.078
between	0.002	0.267	0.229	0.112	0.598	0.639
overall	0.001	0.161	0.133	0.033	0.518	0.578

Note: variable names are defined in the text. Least squares coefficients in plain text. Standard errors in brackets. Significance at the 1, 5, and 10 per cent level is indicated respectively by ***, ** and *. The Sargan test shows a chi-square distribution with one degree of freedom under the null hypothesis that the instruments are valid. The number of observations in the sample is 160.

Of the other regressors, per capita GDP has a negative coefficient, a result not found in the international literature, but it is not significant. The variables reflecting educational attainment have positive coefficients, but the only one that is statistically significant is that for high school graduation. The employment rate shows a positive correlation, indicating a possible connection between employment and an easing of social friction, but in many cases it is not significant.

Finally, a standard deviation increase in *Volo* is associated with an increase in trustworthiness of 0.351 standard deviation (regression 4, including all the explanatory variables). Regression 5 is obtained from regression 4, eliminating the least significant variables one-by-one. Here, *Volo* remains significant with a probability of 5.6%. The sixth regression is designed to gauge the possibility of endogeneity between solidarity association membership and trustworthiness, applying instrumental variables to the same specification as regression 5. Both variables (*Pol* and *Spett*) are strongly correlated with *Volo* (64.6 and 57.0% respectively), and the Sargan test confirms their validity. The results using these instrumental variables confirm the effect of volunteer associations on regional trustworthiness. Regression 6 puts the increase in trustworthiness at 0.669 standard deviations for a 1-standard-deviation rise in *Volo*.

The estimates of Table 10.1 are subject to some qualifications, however. They fail to consider a variable that is generally related to trust and trustworthiness, namely income inequality. Our Gini index of income concentration is an average for the period 1995–2000. In order to include another socio-economic factor likely to affect the degree of social conflict, therefore, we elected to consider the employment rate in our region fixed effects regressions. This choice seems appropriate, in that the Ramsey test of correct specification does not reject the null hypothesis that no relevant variables are omitted. Nevertheless, in order to consider the Gini index of income concentration and also greatly increase degrees of freedom, we have performed random effects estimates adding income concentration to the explanatory variables in Table 10.1. The results do not differ substantially; they show a negative effect of income inequality on trustworthiness.

As we have seen, the estimates presented in Table 10.1 are simultaneous, i.e. the regressors and the dependent variable all refer to the same time period. Yet association membership might affect trustworthiness with a lag, the time needed to alter individuals' propensity to cooperate. To account for this possibility, as far as the data allow, we performed another set of regressions, taking the average values of *Cultu*, *Eco* and *Volo* over 2- and 3-year periods and that of trustworthiness in the second or third year. The 2-year averages are for 1995–1996, 1997–1998, 1999–2000, 2001–2002, the dependent variable and the other regressors are respectively for 1996, 1998, 2000 and 2002. The 3-year averages are for 1995–1997 and 1998–2000, the dependent variable and the other regressors for 1997 and 2000.

The results are given in Table 10.2. Regressions 1 and 2 were for the 2-year periods, regressions 3 and 4 for the 3-year. The initial independent variables considered were *Volo*, *Cultu*, *Eco*, *Per capita GDP*, *Edu_1*, *Edu_2*, *Empl* and *Gini* for the random effects estimates; the least statistically significant were then eliminated one by one.[9]

The above table is interesting for two main reasons. The results confirm the positive effect of unpaid voluntary service in solidarity associations in forming a spirit of cooperation, and they show a more significant negative effect particularly of membership in environmental, civil rights or peace associations (*Eco*).

10.4 Concluding Remarks

The aim of the paper was to run an empirical test of the effect of association membership in helping to form a society with greater trustworthiness, a factor that is commonly seen as playing a major role in explaining such essential economic variables as the rate of per capita GDP growth.

Our dependent variable was a measure of the society's degree of trustworthiness, designed to pick up the probability that agreements for cooperation between two or more agents will be honoured. The causal variables postulated were the extent of membership in various types of association. Panel data for the Italian

[9]The variables eliminated were not significant at the 10% level.

Table 10.2 Association membership and trustworthiness (two- and 3-year periods)

Equation	*1(FE)*	*2(RE)*	*3(FE)*	*4(RE)*
Volo	0.038***	0.032***	0.065*	0.049***
	(0.014)	(0.009)	(0.033)	(0.010)
Cultu	−0.031***			
	(0.011)			
Eco	−0.087**	−0.109***	−0.202**	−0.138**
	(0.036)	(0.034)	(0.092)	(0.066)
GDP			−0.000*	
			(0.000)	
Edu_1				
Edu_2				
Empl		0.014***		
		(0.004)		
Gini				−2.727***
				(0.747)
Constant	0.767	−0.167	1.514	1.251
	(0.137)	(0.174)	(0.695)	(0.256)
R^2				
within	0.314	0.265	0.371	0.216
between	0.010	0.731	0.268	0.790
overall	0.007	0.679	0.188	0.738
Sample size	80	80	40	40

Note: variable names are defined in the text. Least squares coefficients in plain text. Standard errors in brackets. Significance at the 1, 5 and 10 per cent level is indicated respectively by ***, ** and *. Regressions 1 and 3 apply region fixed effects; 2 and 4, random effects

regions were estimated employing several econometric techniques: region fixed effects, random effects, and two-stage estimates with instrumental variables. Two main results emerge:

1. A positive and statistically significant effect of unpaid participation in solidarity associations (our *Volo* variable) on the regional level of trustworthiness
2. A negative if not always statistically significant effect of membership in environmental, civil rights and peace associations (*Eco*) and in cultural and recreational associations (*Cultu*), which are generally considered as Putnam-type groups

There are substantial differences between the three types of association, which may explain our results. They differ both in purpose and in their main activities. Participation in the type of association measured by *Volo* is generally intended to produce services that do not go solely to the organization's own members (as those of cultural and recreational associations do) and that are highly personalized (which is not generally the case of the advocacy groups captured by our *Eco* variable).

For the most part, the services provided by volunteer workers in voluntary solidarity associations go to the neediest, such as the elderly or the poor, and they reflect a strong spirit of solidarity. These people's unpaid work may strengthen their conviction that it is possible to join together in voluntary associations and cooperate to produce benefits for persons who are not members. Moreover, not infrequently this work puts the volunteers in direct contact with people who have relational difficulties. This implies the need for the association members to develop special communications skills and relational capabilities in general. So in many of these organizations the service itself is founded upon the establishment of a direct, continuous cooperative relationship between provider and beneficiary, in which both can see that efficacy depends on success in creating real cooperation. This may be what makes solidarity associations, under the Putnam approach, real 'gymnasiums' for ingraining the habit of cooperation.

Neither advocacy groups (represented here by the *Eco* variable) nor cultural and recreational organizations (*Cultu*) are intended chiefly to provide services for the disadvantaged. The former are founded mainly in order to mobilize the community's attention to issues and problems that the members consider significant. The latter generally serve to satisfy the recreational or cultural 'needs' of their own members, who have joined together for this purpose (organizing events, exhibits, etc.). Thus it is quite possible that both *Eco* and *Cultu* associations serve purposes that if not necessarily 'self-interested' are in any case not directly addressed to outsiders.

The motivations of solidarity association members, then, are clearly different from those of advocacy or cultural groups. They are motivated by the desire to cooperate in order to serve non-members, whereas the members of other associations seek objectives that are more or less closely related to their own 'special' interests, which may potentially be in conflict with those of other associations. Essentially, the members of these latter groups may tend to form bonding relationships (Narayan 1999), closed to widespread cooperation. Thus the net impact of *Eco* and *Cultu* on trustworthiness will be a sort of resultant of two contrasting factors:

1. The positive effect that should derive from the presence among them of groups who pursue their own objectives while also favouring other community purposes, thereby fostering cooperation between their members and other organizations and public institutions
2. The negative effect that may stem from the presence of organizations whose members' interests may 'clash' with those of other groups or the community institutions, and which may seek to promote their own association at the expense of others

Our empirical analysis, finding a negative correlation of the variables *Eco* and *Cultu* with trustworthiness, suggests that the second of these effects prevails. Consequently, what really counts is the unpaid work in solidarity associations. It is their activity that seems to create propitious conditions for the diffusion of trustworthy behaviour throughout the community. These organizations operate directly, in a framework of solidarity, for socially valuable purposes, providing services to the neediest (the elderly, the ill, the poor), who are most vulnerable to social exclusion. Moreover, they appear to be capable of raising the level of trustworthiness of the community as a whole, helping to forge a social fabric that a broad consensus now sees as conducive to economic growth.

Acknowledgements I would like to thank Carlo Borzaga, Paolo Buonanno, Sergio Destefanis, Gianluca Grimalda, Benedetto Gui, Lorenzo Sacconi and Stefano Zamagni for their useful suggestions. My thanks go also to the Provincia Autonoma di Trento for financially supporting the project 'Social capital, corporate social responsibility and local economic development'. Remaining errors are solely my own.

Appendix

Table 10.3 Summary statistics (variable names are defined in the text)

Variable	N	Mean	Std. Dev.	Min	Max
Trustworthiness	160	0.629	0.229	0.012	1
Volo	160	8.075	3.831	3.100	22.100
Edu_1	160	95.609	1.392	91.100	98.700
Edu_2	160	66.194	7.390	45.500	83.300
GDP[a]	160	16769.95	4265.69	9729.53	23882.95
Gini	160	0.280	0.039	0.228	0.378
Cultu	160	9.337	3.942	3.700	24.500
Eco	160	1.767	0.583	0.700	4
Empl	160	54.314	8.023	39.456	69.527
Pol	160	33.081	5.521	23.300	47.200
Spett	160	50.044	21.438	9.700	120.500

[a]Thousands of € - 1995 prices

References

Berg J, Dickhaut J, McCabe K (1995) Trust, reciprocity and social history. Games and Economic Behaviour 10:122–142

Brehm J, Rahn W (1997) Individual-level evidence for the causes and consequences of social capital. American Journal of Political Science 41:999–1023

Cannari L, D'Alessio G (2003) La distribuzione del reddito e della ricchezza nelle regioni italiane. Banca d'Italia Tema di Discussione 482

Claibourn MP, Martin PS (2000) Trusting and joining? An empirical test of the reciprocal nature of social capital. Political Behavior 22:267–291

Degli Antoni G (2006) Capitale sociale e crescita economica: una verifica empirica a livello regionale e provinciale. Rivista Italiana degli Economisti 3:363–393

Gambetta D (1988) Can we trust trust? In Gambetta D (ed) Trust: making and breaking cooperative relations. Blackwell, Oxford

Glaeser E, Laibson D, Scheinkman J, Soutter C (2000) Measuring trust. Quarterly Journal of Economics 115:811–846

Gui B (1994) Interpersonal relations: A disregarded theme in the debate on ethics and economics. In: Lewis A, Warneryd KE (eds) Ethics and economic affairs. Routledge, London

Gui B (2002) Più che scambi, incontri. La teoria economica alle prese con i fenomeni interpersonali. In Sacco PL, Zamagni S (eds) Complessità relazionale e comportamento economico. il Mulino, Bologna

Helliwell JF, Putnam R (2000) Economic growth and social capital in Italy. In: Dasgupta P, Serageldin I (eds) Social capital: a multifaceted perspective. World Bank, Washington DC

Knack P (2003) Groups, growth and trust: cross-country evidence on the Olson and Putnam hypotesis. Public Choice 117:341–355

Knack S, Keefer P (1997) Does social capital have an economic payoff? A cross country investigation. The Quarterly Journal of Economics 112:1251–1287

Mayer N (2003) Democracy in France: do associations matter? In: Hooghe M, Stolle D (2003) (eds) Generating social capital. Civil society and institutions in comparative perspective. Palgrave Macmillan, Basingstoke
Narayan D (1999) Bonds and bridges: social capital and poverty. World Bank Policy Research Working Paper 2167
Olson M (1965) The logic of collective action. Harvard University Press, Cambridge MA
Olson M (1982) The rise and decline of nations. Yale University Press, New Haven
Putnam R (with Leonardi R, Nanetti R) (1993) Making democracy work. Princeton University Press, Princeton
Saisana M, Tarantola S (2002) State-of-the-art report on current methodologies and practices for composite indicator development. European Commission Joint Research Centre, Brussels
Stolle D, Rochon T (1998) Are all associations alike? Member diversity, associational type and creation of social capital. American Behavioral Scientist 42:47–65
Tocqueville A (1840) De la démocratie en Amérique. English translation, Democracy in America. Chicago University Press, Chicago2000
Uhlaner CJ (1989) Relational goods and participation: incorporating sociability into a theory of rational action. Public Choice 62:253–285
Wollebæck D, Selle P (2003) The importance of passive membership for social capital formation. In Hooghe M, Stolle D (2003)Generating social capital. Civic society and institutions in comparative perspective. Palgrave Macmillan, Basingstoke
Zak PJ, Knack S (2001) Trust and growth. Economic Journal 111:295–321

Chapter 11
A Comparison of Wage Inequality in For-Profit, Nonprofit and Local Government Organizations: Nursing Homes in the Midwestern US

Avner Ben-Ner, Ting Ren, and Darla Flint Paulson

Abstract This essay is devoted to investigate ownership-related wage differentials, distinguishing between nonprofit, for-profit and local government organizations, within a sample of US nursing homes. It focuses on within-organization across-occupation wage dispersion. The results do not support widespread opinions about wage dispersion across the three ownership types. Neither the intrinsic motivation perspective's prediction of less inequality among employees in nonprofit and government sectors, nor the agency theory prediction that higher level employees will use their influence to increase their own well-being without increasing the well-being of others, are supported.

11.1 Introduction

Are employees in for-profit firms paid better than in nonprofit and local government organizations? Are nonprofit and local government organizations more egalitarian in their compensation practices than for-profit firms? Popular opinion seems to suggest an affirmative answer to both questions. The research literature provides a mixed answer. It has been suggested that because of the donation of labour by nonprofit employees (Preston 1989, cross-industries), the sorting of intrinsically-motivated employees into the nonprofit sector (Steinberg 1990, review of literature; Handy and Katz 1998, theoretical analysis), and the compensating differentials favouring for-profit workers (Weisbrod 1983, study of lawyers; Frank 1996, cross-occupations), nonprofit workers will have lower compensation than their for-profit counterparts. Other authors claim the opposite, suggesting that nonprofit organizations pay higher wages than for-profit firms for philanthropic or charitable reasons

A. Ben-Ner (✉)
Carlson School of Management, University of Minnesota,
Minneapolis, Minnesota, 55455, USA

S. Destefanis and M. Musella (eds.), *Paid and Unpaid Labour in the Social Economy*,
AIEL Series in Labour Economics, DOI: 10.1007/978-3-7908-2137-6_12,

(Feldstein 1971, the hospital industry), because of the attenuated property rights (Borjas et al. 1983; nursing homes; Preston 1988, the day care industry), and their use of efficiency wages to elicit employees' effort, especially for high-skill workers (Ito and Domian 1987, symphony orchestras; Holtmann and Idson 1993, nursing homes). Yet others argue that observed pay differentials across sectors may be attributed to a variety of observable and unobservable differences in organizational characteristics, workers and jobs rather than any systematic differences between sectors (Leete 2006, review of the literature). Indeed, empirical studies have suggested that there exists no economy-wide wage differential between nonprofit and for-profit organizations, after occupation and industry heterogeneity is taken into account (Leete 2001, cross-industries; DeVaro and Brookshire 2007, cross-industries). However, other studies have suggested that nonprofit organizations may go beyond wages and offer a higher total compensation package to attract intrinsically-motivated employees (Mocan and Tekin 2003, child care centres; Mosca et al. 2007, social services). Most of this literature, with the exception of Mosca et al. 2007, has focused on comparing wages in for-profit to nonprofit firms, excluding local government organizations.

Regarding within-organization wage inequality, it has been argued that with a more intrinsically-motivated workforce nonprofit organizations will prefer more wage equity between different levels of employees than do their for-profit counterparts (Leete 2000). Preston (1989) found in multi-industry data that although low-level employees are paid similar wages, high-level nonprofit employees earn less. Supporting this finding, studies of the hospital industry also show that at the managerial and high-skill levels nonprofit employees earn less than their counterparts in for-profit firms (Preyra and Pink 2001; Roomkin and Weisbrod 1999; Ballou and Weisbrod 2003), although these studies did not investigate the wages of low-skill employees. Empirical evidence based on 1990 Census data found lower wage dispersion among employees in nonprofit organizations than their counterparts in the for-profit organizations (Leete 2000). However, this finding may be a result of the concentration of nonprofit and government organizations in industries where for various reasons pay dispersion is lower.

The literature thus provides an incomplete answer to our two leading questions. The purpose of the present study is to investigate ownership-related wage differentials and within-organization across-occupation wage dispersion using a sample of nursing homes with data on the average wage of the main groups of nursing employees. We can distinguish among nonprofit, for-profit and local government organizations, as well as control for important factors that may affect wages and their dispersion. Although our sample is not representative of the population of for-profit, nonprofit and local government organizations, in it we can isolate the impact of ownership on wages and wage inequality in the context of an industry where all organizations produce the same narrowly-defined service, employ key employees with three job titles from the same narrowly-defined occupations, compete in the same labour markets, and face the same regulatory environment. In addition, thanks to the detailed nature of our data (based on an original survey as well as information drawn from regulatory enforcement reports) we are able to control for various organizational characteristics, such as the medical condition of nursing home residents, the unionization status of different groups of employees, and the level of competition in the local market, variables that may affect wage levels and dispersion. The analysis of our data does not support the popular opinion regarding comparative wage levels and dispersion across the three sectors.

The remainder of the paper is organized as follows. Section 11.2 develops the conceptual framework for the analysis of the comparison of wage inequality across sectors, integrating the intrinsic-motivation and agency-theoretic perspectives, and proposes key testable hypotheses. Section 11.3 describes the dataset and methodology used for the empirical investigation. Section 11.4 reports the empirical results, and Sect. 11.5 provides discussion of the findings in light of the theoretical framework, and concludes.

11.2 Theory and Hypotheses

In this section we discuss the factors that affect wage levels and inequality within-organization and between sectors, using the perspectives of intrinsic motivation and agency theories. Table 11.1 summarizes the current debate on the issues between the two theoretical perspectives and the consequent predictions, and will be referred to in the following discussion. We then integrate the insights derived from these perspectives and generate a set of empirically testable hypotheses. It is important to remember that wages are determined primarily through the competitive market mechanism, implying that sectoral differentials will be generally small or even non-existent (Ruhm and Borkoski 2003); hence for the hypotheses developed below, the null hypothesis is that of 'no difference.'

11.2.1 The Intrinsic Motivation Perspective

It has been argued that in the presence of informational asymmetry between an organization and its consumers, nonprofit status serves as a signal of trustworthiness to customers that their well-being will not be compromised by the organization's pursuit of profit (e.g. Arrow 1963; Hansmann 1980; Steinberg 1987; Hirth 1999). Nonprofit status can also serve as a signal to employees with high levels of intrinsic motivation that they can safely engage effort levels for the sake of the 'cause,' trusting that the extra effort will not be exploited for the owners' gain (Rose-Ackerman 1996). In addition, since for-profit organizations have a measurable outcome, profitability, employees in such organizations may be rewarded for this observable outcome,[1] possibly helping create a culture in the organization where

[1] We develop this argument below, when we discuss agency theory.

Table 11.1 Summary of hypotheses of differences in wages and wage inequality among For-profit (FP), Nonprofit (NP) and Local Government (G) organizations

Theory	Dimension of theory	Wages of NP and G workers relative to their FP counterparts	Within-firm across-occupation wage inequality in NP and G organizations relative to FP counterparts
Intrinsic motivation perspective	NP and G donate labour	– (Because NP and G workers are more intrinsically motivated)	– (Because higher level employees are more likely to offer donation)
	FP employees are paid a compensating differential	– (Because FP executives are more likely to ask employees to perform work that is out of line with their values)	– (Because higher level employees are more likely to need a compensating differential)
	NP and G employees are more inequality averse	None	– (Because intrinsically motivated workers value fairness over proprietary gain)
	Concern for customer well-being leads to the careful selection of intrinsically motivated workers	+ (Because NP and G offer higher salaries in order to have greater choice among applicants and to attract people who believe in the mission of the organization)	+ (Because the selection of managerial staff is relatively more important for quality of care than the selection of lower-level staff)
	Less reliance on incentives in NP and G since they crowd out intrinsic motivation	– (Because FP have to pay higher wages to compensate risk averse agents for greater use of variable pay)	– (Because NP and G use fewer tournament wage schemes)
	NP and G managers care more about employee well-being than do FP managers	+ (Because NP and G are more likely to believe that it is ethical to share financial resources with employees)	– (Because NP and G believe it is more ethical to raise wages of workers close to the poverty line than the wages of better-off employees)
Agency theory	Principals are less interested in monitoring performance in NP and G than in FP	+ (Because NP and G have extra decision-making latitude that can be used to enhance their compensation and the compensation of their subordinates)	+ (Because the NP and G staff with the most decision-making influence are at the higher levels of the organization and may increase their own compensation more than the compensation of lower level employees)
	Objectives in NP and G are more complex and harder to quantify than objectives in FP	+ (Because the performance of NP and G is more difficult to monitor, efficiency wages may be used)	+ (Efficiency wages are likely to be higher in managerial positions)
	Less reliance on incentives in NP and G because the goals of the organization are harder to quantify	– (Because FP have to pay higher wages to compensate risk averse agents for greater use of variable pay)	– (Because NP and G use fewer tournament wage schemes)
	FP employees are paid a compensating differential	– (Because higher level employees are more likely to need a compensating differential)	– (Because FP is more likely to ignore unobservable quality forcing employees in allocating time and energy in a way they may not prefer)

less measurable outcomes, such as interpersonal treatment of vulnerable customers, are neglected. Intrinsically motivated employees who care about customer well-being may therefore migrate to the nonprofit sector, where tangible results are less likely to be rewarded and employees are more likely to be able to distribute their effort according to their values.

If employees who self-select into nonprofit organizations derive their well-being from serving the mission of the nonprofit sector rather than the organization's and the employees' gains, they will be willing to accept lower wages than their counterparts working in for-profit organizations. The lower pay is essentially the monetary donation the employees make to the organization for providing certain public goods (Preston 1989; Leete 2006). Nonprofit organizations use lower wages to sort-out employees with higher commitment to the organization's mission. By doing so, they are able to reduce monitoring and increase efficiency (Steinberg 1990; Handy and Katz 1998). This phenomenon is believed to be particularly salient for employees at the managerial and professional levels (Weisbrod 1983; Preston 1989; Handy and Katz 1998). Indeed, Mirvis and Hackett (1983) found that nonprofit managers are more likely than their for-profit counterparts to report that their work is more important than the money they earn.

Compensating differentials may be a reason why for-profit organizations pay higher wages than nonprofit organizations when perfect matching between employees according to their levels of intrinsic motivation and types of organization does not occur (Frank 1996). In industries where employees are intrinsically motivated to serve customers, employees may be less willing to work for an organization that compromises their values by putting the profit motive above customer care. Intrinsically-motivated employees, such as many nurses in a nursing home, may have to be paid a compensating differential to work in an emotionally challenging cost-cutting environment where they are asked to provide a service that is of lower quality than what they would be able to provide if the organization did not pursue profit.

The intrinsic motivation perspective suggests that within-organization wage dispersion may be lower in nonprofit organizations because employees are motivated by factors other than wages, and are believed to find merit in the perception of fairness of pay (Leete 2000). Intrinsic motivation is fragile, and can be ruined by perceptions of injustice (Frey 1993). Managers of nonprofit organizations seek to maximize the intrinsic motivation of their staff in order to ensure quality, and so may provide fixed wage rates and equal pay to employees so as not to harm intrinsic motivation. This argument applies both to wage dispersion within and across occupations.

Another reason for a more compressed wage structure in nonprofit organizations is that, as noted above, managers and professional employees are more likely to donate labour than lower-level employees. This is because they are better able to see how their actions have an impact on the mission of the organization. For example, while a nurse can see the connection between his or her duties and patient well-being, clerical employees are less able to see the connection.

11.2.2 *The Agency Theory Perspective*

The severity of the agency problem differs across organizational types. Nonprofit and local government organizations are likely to suffer from more difficult agency problems for two major reasons (Ben-Ner 2006; Steinberg 2008). First, because control over these organizations is not linked to claims on profits or equity, principals may be less interested in monitoring the performance of the organization. The ultimate legal decision-making power in most nonprofit organizations rests with a volunteer board of directors, which is usually selected by top management or by representatives of another nonprofit organization that owns it (e.g. a church-related association owning a nonprofit nursing home). In local government-owned organizations, ultimate control is held by a city or county. The representatives of such entities act as principals on behalf of the citizenry in their jurisdiction and are generally not rewarded directly for the achievements of the organization over which they have control. The principals in both nonprofit and local government organizations cannot be held accountable the way representatives of for-profit owners are, and furthermore, there are only weak mechanisms for holding them accountable. Principals in nonprofit organizations are therefore likely to be less interested in the daily operation of the organization than are principals in their for-profit counterparts, *unless* the dedication (intrinsic motivation) of these principals, or the dedication of the management of the organizations which they control, compensate for their lack of accountability or profit motive. The contract failure arising from the agency problems in nonprofit and local government organizations can therefore be more severe than that in their for-profit counterparts (Fama and Jensen 1983).

Second, the objectives of nonprofit and local government organizations are multifaceted, complex, difficult to articulate and hard to quantify. Accordingly, accountability for the attainment of goals is hard to establish. For example, the commonly-stated goal of maximizing the well-being of an organization's customers raises questions about the definition of the well-being of different groups of customers and the appropriate course of action; most problematic is the difficulty to assess the degree of the organization's compliance with this stated goal. This leaves room for management and key employees in these organizations to attain greater control over their organizations and run them according to their own interests (Pauly and Redisch 1973; Glaeser 2003), which may include increasing their own wages (Hansmann 1980). Due to the lack of specifically defined organizational goals and corresponding reward metrics such as performance-based incentives, nonprofit and local government organizations need to provide other forms of rewards, such as efficiency wages, to maintain the loyalty of employees. For example, Ito and Domian (1987) found that nonprofit orchestras paid musicians higher wages than their for-profit counterparts, and explained the difference as an efficiency wage due to less measurable outcomes in nonprofits. Therefore, actual wages may be higher for managers and employees in nonprofit and local government organizations than that in for-profit ones.

To align employees' effort with organizational goals, organizations often rely on various incentive mechanisms. For-profit firms, guided by the profit-maximization objective and being more able to derive employee goals that can be assessed from their contribution to the firm objectives, are more able to implement financial incentives than nonprofit or local government organizations. Furthermore, research has shown that external interventions such as reward and incentive schemes can reduce individuals' intrinsic motivation based on dispositional states such as self-perceptions of value, good will, trust, and reciprocity (Frey 1998; Prendergast 1999; Deci et al. 1999). As noted earlier, employees in nonprofit and local government organizations may have relatively high intrinsic motivation and therefore monetary incentives should be limited in these organizations. Indeed, Roomkin and Weisbrod (1999) found that for-profit hospitals used bonuses and performance-contingent pay to a greater extent than nonprofit hospitals.

The effects of concentrating on measurable outcomes are illustrated by Gass (2004), in a book about his experiences working in a for-profit nursing home. Gass argues that the way the nursing home and the residents looked and the measurable outcomes sought by regulators were more important than how the residents felt. The primary problem, from the residents' perspective, was that they were lonely and in pain, and needed comfort and attention, yet in the chronically understaffed nursing home, physical needs alone were attended to and residents were often treated as if they were a 'sack of potatoes.'[2] What this suggests is that there are different dimensions of quality in nursing homes, and given that nonprofit organizations exist for customer well-being, it is more likely that the less observed dimension of quality will be a goal in these homes. The cultures of nonprofit, local government and for-profit organizations differ even within the same narrowly defined industry. With this argument, even agency theory suggests that for-profits will have to pay a compensating differential to employees, at least to employees who care about customer well-being.

Differentiation in pay according to differentiation in performance results, of course, in wage inequality. Hence the prediction that nonprofit and local government organizations will rely less on rewarding performance than for-profit firms implies that they will have less inequality in compensation of similar workers. If the for-profit organization creates extrinsic incentives via the use of pay for performance, within-occupation wage inequality will be greater in for-profit organizations. If for-profit organizations instead use tournaments, where higher-level positions are paid more in an effort to incentivize lower level employees to compete for them (e.g. Lazear and Rosen 1981), then across-occupation wage inequality will differ by sector.

[2]In Gass' own words: "Aides do not gain points for doing these tasks [the regulations]; they only lose points for not doing them. We have a schedule to maintain — prescribed routines to follow and tasks to perform and record. All the other stuff, what I would consider our real purpose, is officially just by-product. All the affection, all the consoling, all the filling of emotional holes and the tidying up of frayed feelings are invisible to the owners, to the administration, and to the regulators." (Gass 2004; p. 114)

11.2.3 Hypotheses

We now develop a series of central hypotheses, based on the theoretical perspectives developed above. We start with hypotheses concerning the type of pay in different types of organizations, followed by a hypothesis regarding the comparative pay level, and conclude with a hypothesis comparing within-organization across-occupation pay inequality across sectors.

Extrinsic rewards are more effective in some contexts than others. For example, performance-based pay is less effective the less measurable are outcomes because the performance on which to base compensation or promotion decisions becomes more noisy and subjective, hence more prone to error and less likely to be perceived by employees as instrumental or fair. Second, performance-based compensation is ineffective when employees are intrinsically motivated, because, as noted earlier, extrinsic motivation may crowd out intrinsic motivation. Third, merit-based pay is ineffective in situations where there is interdependent work, because it can undermine cooperation and lead to difficulties in assessing who is responsible for the performance. In the context of sectoral comparison, agency theory suggests that outcomes are less measurable in nonprofit and local government organizations than in for-profit ones and the intrinsic motivation perspective clearly states that nonprofit employees are more intrinsically motivated; therefore both theoretical perspectives suggest that extrinsic rewards would be used more in the for-profit sector.

It is important to note that nursing home employees have interdependent work, so that the individual contribution to the overall quality of care given to residents is difficult to observe and measure. In this type of team production (Alchian and Demsetz 1973), pay-for-performance incentive should not be prevalent because it is difficult to determine the party responsible for the result, so the for-profit nursing homes may not use it either (Shaw et al. 2002). Instead of direct pay-for-performance incentive schemes, broader measures of linking pay to performance such as merit-based pay raises are likely to be used in the for-profit sector. Tournaments may also be used, but in the nursing-home industry they are less likely to be effective due to educational barriers across organizational–occupational levels.

- Hypothesis 1. For-profit organizations are more likely to provide merit-based incentives to their employees than their nonprofit and local government counterparts.

The more limited reliance on merit-based incentives does not imply lesser compensation in nonprofit and local government organizations, for the predictions of various aspects of the intrinsic motivation perspective and agency theory are conflicting with respect to wage levels (see Table 11.1 for a summary of predictions). While for-profit employees will need additional compensation to compensate for the risk they take with merit-based pay schemes, we believe that nonprofit and local government organizations might have incentive to compensate employees better overall. The donative labour hypothesis suggests that nonprofits and local government organizations will search for intrinsically-motivated employees with lower compensation, but this could backfire if it attracts applicants of low quality, who cannot be distinguished from the intrinsically-motivated ones. They may instead search for intrinsically-motivated employees through social networks of current employees whose values are likely to be more congruent with the mission of the organization (Ben-Ner and Ren 2008), and be willing to pay higher wages to such workers in order to attract them; this argument applies primarily to professional staff and managers. Nonprofit managers may also choose to compensate employees more because it is easier to deal with employees who are paid well relative to the market (an agency problem). From a different perspective, emphasis on quality service to customers may call for paying higher compensation in order to attract better employees, or to elicit better effort from employees in the efficiency-wage fashion (Ito and Domian 1987). The argument that key employees in nonprofit and local government organizations have more decision-making power than their for-profit counterparts because of more severe agency problems suggests that such employees in nonprofit and local government organizations will also earn more than for-profit employees in similar positions. The fact that these key employees in nonprofit and local government organizations are likely to be intrinsically motivated increases the likelihood that they are other-regarding, and increases the probability that they will also increase the well-being of lower-level employees.

The agency problem is more severe the greater the extent of asymmetric information between the principal and the agents in the organization. Asymmetric information is especially prevalent in care-giving industries because medical staff know more about adequate care options than do patients. For this reason, we expect the agency problem to be particularly severe in nursing homes,[3] and therefore the importance of selecting intrinsically motivated employees who will not abuse their informational advantage is especially high, increasing the likelihood of using efficiency wage packages, especially among employees with the highest decision-making latitude. These efficiency wages may take the form of straight pay, fringe benefits, or other perquisites. We therefore expect that nonprofit and local government employees in the nursing home industry earn more than their for-profit counterparts.

The hypothesized existence of differences in wage structures or wage levels across sectors presupposes that organizations have flexibility in determining their wage structures. If ownership-related wage premiums exist, the type of organization that provides the premium must have corresponding surpluses from its operation to serve as the source of the premium. We suggest that nonprofit and local government organizations have these premiums. In nonprofits, these sources may include tax benefits and donations. In nonprofit and local government organizations, sources of higher productivity may include employees' extra effort driven by concern for others (customers, the mission of the organization, or the

[3]In nursing homes, this is compounded by the fact that residents are vulnerable adults, who often have decisions made on their behalf by family members who are rarely present in the home to observe the care. The residents themselves may have difficulty communicating their treatment to their family members or to other home employees due to their health problems, deepening the information asymmetry.

society at large), and some employees' willingness to receive lower compensation for a given level of effort. In local government organizations, political relationships could be used to generate the surpluses necessary to pay the hypothesized efficiency wages.

- Hypothesis 2. Nonprofit and local government organizations are likely to offer more fringe benefits to their employees than their for-profit counterparts.
- Hypothesis 3. Nonprofit and local government organizations are likely to pay higher wages to their employees, especially to the higher-level employees, than their for-profit counterparts.

We recognize that our hypothesis of higher wages to employees, especially the key professional employees, is not supported by some of the past empirical studies (e.g. Roomkin and Weisbrod 1999), and suggest that this is for one of three reasons. First, employees may ease the demands of their jobs rather than their compensation in order to enhance their well-being. Second, the principals may be highly motivated, perhaps because they are customers of the organization or ideologues who are passionate about their cause, and monitor the agents more extensively than agency theory would suggest. Third, the principals may have succeeded in attracting mission-committed agents who do not exploit their informational advantage to enhance their material well-being because their self-interest is the well-being of the customers. While we have no means of controlling for the motivation of the principals since our survey was completed by agents (executives), we do control explicitly for the workload and value congruence of key employees in our analysis. This will help us to determine whether holding constant mission commitment, nonprofit managers are likely to increase their employees', especially the key professional employees, and their own compensation relative to the compensation of their for-profit counterparts. We also control for observable human capital to rule out the possibility that higher wages in one sector are due to the observable quality of workers. Notably, we are unable to control for differences in the quality of workers that are unobservable, but do conduct a robustness check with an employee level dataset to control more carefully, at the individual unit of analysis, for human capital. To summarize, the combination of Hypotheses 2 and 3 suggests that nonprofit and local government organizations indeed offer a higher level of *compensation* to their employees, in comparison to their for-profit counterparts.

Consider next pay dispersion. Table 11.1 shows also the inconsistency of predictions from both the intrinsic motivation perspective and agency theory regarding within-firm across-occupation wage inequality, so the relative strength of each of these arguments will determine differences in wage inequality across sectors. We do not believe that the use of tournaments is likely in nursing homes because, as noted, the move across organizational levels within the nursing occupation is tied (through state licensing requirements) to educational accomplishments. We have argued above about the relative merits of other predictions, and it follows from Hypothesis 3 that nonprofit and local government organizations will experience greater across-occupation wage inequality than for-profit firms.

- Hypothesis 4. Within-firm across-occupation wage dispersion in nonprofit and local government organizations is higher than in their for-profit counterparts.

11.3 The Empirical Methodology

This section describes the dataset and methodology used for the empirical investigation.

11.3.1 The Data

We test the theoretical predictions in the nursing home context in the state of Minnesota of the United States. The data for the current empirical analysis come from three sources. (1) The OSCAR (Online Survey, Certification and Reporting) database contains data for all Medicare eligible nursing homes in the United States about their ownership type, capacity, nursing inputs, violation of regulations, health condition of residents, and more; the data are collected in accordance with federal laws and regulations, supplemented by Minnesota laws and regulations. For the current study, we obtained information on nursing home characteristics from this database. (2) A nursing home quality database constructed and maintained by the state Department of Health and the Department of Human Services (MDH and DHS). For the current study we obtained a variable on nursing homes' case mix to capture the overall health condition of each home's residents. (3) The Minnesota Nursing Homes Employer Survey (MNHES) filled out by the nursing home's administrator or top human resources manager, which contains information about incentive pay scheme implemented in the home, and the average wages and fringe benefits for different job titles. We administered the survey to all 409 nursing homes identified in the OSCAR database in late 2005, with follow-up surveys mailed to non-respondents twice in the spring of 2006. We received 121 responses for a response rate about 30%, which compares favourably to other organizational surveys that measure human resource practices (e.g. Freeman and Kleiner 2000; Sesil 2006). Our effective sample size is a little smaller due to missing data.

Although for-profit homes are under-represented among respondents in our sample (the state ownership distribution of all the nursing homes is about 60% nonprofit homes, 13% government homes, and 27% for-profit homes, whereas among survey respondents are about 61% nonprofit, 17% local government, and 22% for-profit), these differences are not of great concern because our sample contains substantial variation that allows us to capture the relationships between the key variables of interest. Non-parametric Mann-Whitney tests show that respondents are similar to non-respondents in the key home characteristics such as total number of residents, chain status, hospital affiliation, proportion of Medicare residents and resident case mix.

11.3.2 Variables and Empirical Specification

Detailed variable descriptions, sources, and summary statistics are presented in Table 11.2. Here we explain briefly the dependent variables and the key independent variables. All dependent variables were obtained from the organizational survey, separately for each of the three groups of nursing staff: registered nurses, licensed practical nurses, and certified nursing assistants.

The merit-based pay dummy variable was derived from a survey question asking to list three key elements that determine the pay raise for employees. If merit is indicated as one of the top two determinants, the variable is coded 1, otherwise 0. Average hourly wages for the three types of nursing staff are reported by survey respondents. The fringe benefits variable is a count of the number of fringe benefits (pension plan, health insurance, paid vacation leave and paid sick leave) that are provided to each employee group. The wage dispersion variable is the ratio of the highest-level nurses (registered nurses) average wage to the lowest-level nursing staff (certified nursing assistants) average wage; we also use the ratio of licensed practical nurses (below the level of registered nurses, but above nursing assistants) average wage to certified nursing assistants average wage.

The key independent variables are dummy variables for nonprofit organizations, local government organizations and for-profit firms; in all analyses for-profit is the excluded category. We control for various nursing home, employee and environmental characteristics that may be associated with the level or structure of wages in nursing homes. The home-level control variables are size (total number of residents in the home), a dummy variable indicating the home's chain status (1 if operated by a parent organization as one of multiple facilities, and 0 if an autonomous stand-alone organization), a dummy variable indicating whether the home is affiliated with a hospital, and a case mix index measuring the severity of the medical condition of the residents, where higher numbers indicate the need for more intensive care. Each of these variables may have an impact on compensation in familiar ways from the literature: for example, larger firms pay better wages, chains may pay less, hospitals pay higher wages than other facilities employing nurses, and greater severity requires higher skills which command better pay. We also control for some aspects of the environment: level of market competition in the county area (measured by Herfindahl-Hirschmann index), and per capita income in the ZIP code area where the nursing home is located; both are often found to be associated with wage levels. Employee–related control variables are tenure of service in the home, job complexity, union representation, workload and value congruence; again, the literature has findings that associate all of these variables with wages except for the last one, which is rarely included in wage estimations. For the estimation of adoption of merit-based pay scheme, we also include supervisor's ability to evaluate employees' work as a control variable.

For the estimation of implementation of merit-based pay, we used a probit model with robust standard errors. We applied OLS, also with robust standard errors, to the estimations of wage equations, fringe benefits and within-sector wage dispersion. The results are robust to alternative methods (such as ordered logit for fringe benefits).

Table 11.2 Variable descriptions, sources and summary statistics

Variables	Description	Mean (std. dev.)	Min	Max	Data source
Organizational types					
Nonprofit	1– Nonprofit	0.61	0	1	OSCAR
Local government	1– Local government	0.17	0	1	OSCAR
For-profit	1– For-profit	0.22	0	1	OSCAR
Dependent variables					
Merit as basis for pay raise for registered nurses (RNs)	1 If merit ranks as one of the top two criteria for determining individual RN's pay raise; 0 otherwise	0.28	0	1	MNHES
Merit as basis for pay raise for licensed practical nurses (LPNs)	1 If merit ranks as one of the top two criteria for determining individual LPN's pay raise; 0 otherwise	0.23	0	1	MNHES
Merit as basis for pay raise for certified nursing assistants (CNAs)	1 If merit ranks as one of the top two criteria for determining individual CNA's pay raise; 0 otherwise	0.28	0	1	MNHES
Wage of RNs	Average hourly wage for RNs in the nursing home (NH) ($)	22.46 (3.63)	17	35	MNHES
Wage of LPNs	Average hourly wage for LPNs in the NH ($)	16.17 (2.08)	12.5	21.25	MNHES
Wage of CNAs	Average hourly wage for CNAs in the NH ($)	11.11 (1.48)	8	15.45	MNHES
Fringe benefits for RNs	Number of fringe benefits (pension plan, health insurance, paid vacation leave and paid sick leave) received by most RNs	3.54 (0.89)	0	4	MNHES
Fringe benefits for LPNs	Number of fringe benefits (pension plan, health insurance, paid vacation leave and paid sick leave) received by most LPNs	3.53 (0.88)	0	4	MNHES
Fringe benefits for CNAs	Number of fringe benefits (pension plan, health insurance, paid vacation leave and paid sick leave) received by most CNAs	3.51 (0.87)	0	4	MNHES
Wage ratio of RNs' to CNAs'	RNs' average wage divided by CNAs' average wage	2.03 (0.35)	1.54	4.38	MNHES
Wage ratio of LPNs' to CNAs'	LPNs' average wage divided by CNAs' average wage	1.46 (0.14)	1.2	2	MNHES
Control variables					
Home size	Total number of residents in the NH	80.18 (46.43)	5.5	300	OSCAR
Chain status	1 If the NH belongs to a chain operation; 0 if independent	0.50	0	1	OSCAR
Case mix index	Intensity of care and services provided to residents in each NH	1.00 (0.09)	0.65	1.26	MDH and DHS

(continued)

Table11.2 (continued)

Variables	Description	Mean (std. dev.)	Min	Max	Data source
Hospital affiliation	1 If the facility reports affiliation with a hospital; 0 otherwise	0.15	0	1	OSCAR
Degree of market competition	Herfindahl–Hirschmann Index = 100 (N residents in NH_i/N residents in county's NHs)^2	2.42 (1.65)	0.28	10	OSCAR and ZIP code
Per capita income	Per capita income in the ZIP code area 1999	20.107 (4.93)	9.821	45.402	US 2000 Census and ZIP code
Average tenure of RNs	RNs' average length of service (in years) in the NH	7.77 (4.54)	<1	20	MNHES
Average tenure of LPNs	LPNs' average length of service (in years) in the NH	8.00 (4.28)	<1	22	MNHES
Average tenure of CNAs	CNAs' average length of service (in years) in the NH	5.78 (4.19)	<1	35	MNHES
Job complexity of RNs	Average score of the following two items: 1. Extent to which the tasks performed by RNs are complex (1– not at all, 5 – extreme); 2. Extent to which the tasks performed by RNs are routine (1– not at all, 5– extreme; reverse scoring)	3.30 (0.59)	1	5	MNHES
Job complexity of LPNs	Average score of the following two items: 1. Extent to which the tasks performed by LPNs are complex (1– not at all, 5 – extreme); 2. Extent to which the tasks performed by LPNs are routine (1– not at all, 5 – extreme; reverse scoring)	2.94 (0.55)	1	4.5	MNHES
Job complexity of CNAs	Average score of the following two items: 1. Extent to which the tasks performed by CNAs are complex (1– not at all, 5 – extreme); 2. Extent to which the tasks performed by CNAs are routine (1– not at all, 5 – extreme; reverse scoring)	2.41 (0.61)	1	4	MNHES
RNs' belief in nursing home mission	Average score of the following two items: 1. Most of our RNs believe in the mission of our organization (1– strongly disagree, 5 – strongly agree); 2. For most of our RNs working here is just a job (1– strongly disagree, 5 – strongly agree; reverse scoring)	4.22 (0.56)	2.5	5	MNHES

LPNs' belief in nursing home mission	Average score of the following two items: 1. Most of our LPNs believe in the mission of our organization (1– strongly disagree, 5 – strongly agree); 2. For most of our LPNs working here is just a job (1– strongly disagree, 5 – strongly agree; reverse scoring)	4.07 (0.58)	2	5	MNHES
CNAs' belief in nursing home mission	Average score of the following two items: 1. Most of our CNAs believe in the mission of our organization (1– strongly disagree, 5 – strongly agree); 2. For most of our CNAs working here is just a job (1– strongly disagree, 5 – strongly agree; reverse scoring)	3.85 (0.67)	2	5	MNHES
Unionization of RNs	1 If the nursing home reports unionization of RNs; 0 otherwise	0.17	0	1	MNHES
Unionization of LPNs	1 If the nursing home reports unionization of RNs; 0 otherwise	0.29	0	1	MNHES
Unionization of CNAs	1 If the nursing home reports unionization of RNs; 0 otherwise	0.29	0	1	MNHES
Workload of RNs	How demanding is RNs' workload (1 – very low, 5 – very high)?	4.19 (0.74)	2	5	MNHES
Workload of LPNs	How demanding is LPNs' workload (1 – very low, 5 – very high)?	3.95 (0.76)	2	5	MNHES
Workload of CNAs	How demanding is CNAs' workload (1 – very low, 5 – very high)?	4.09 (0.74)	2	5	MNHES
supervisor's ability to tell how well RNs carry out their tasks	Extent to which supervisors are able to tell how well a RN carries out his or her tasks (1– not at all, 5 – extreme)	3.97 (0.66)	2	5	MNHES
supervisor's ability to tell how well LPNs carry out their tasks	Extent to which supervisors are able to tell how well a LPN carries out his or her tasks (1– not at all, 5 – extreme)	3.94 (0.66)	2	5	MNHES
supervisor's ability to tell how well CNAs carry out their tasks	Extent to which supervisors are able to tell how well a CNA carries out his or her tasks (1– not at all, 5 – extreme)	3.90 (0.82)	2	5	MNHES

MNHES – Minnesota Nursing Homes Employer Survey; available at http://webpages.csom.umn.edu/hrir/abenner/web/papers/work–surv/Nursing-homes-survey.pdf

OSCAR – Online Survey, Certification and Reporting data of nursing facilities (Centers for Medicare and Medicaid Services). http://www.cms.hhs.gov/NursingHomeQualityInits

MDH and DHS – Minnesota State Departments of Health and Human Services; details available at http://www.health.state.mn.us/nhreportcard

11.4 Results

Table 11.3 shows the estimation of the implementation of merit-based pay. The equations are fairly well determined overall (with R^2s around 0.2). Nonprofit and local government organizations are less likely than for-profit firms to provide merit-based pay to all their nursing employees. The comparison between local government and for-profit homes for registered nurses and licensed practical nurses is statistically significant at the 10% level, while the comparison between nonprofit and for-profit sectors has the sign indicated by hypothesis but is not significantly different from zero. Hypothesis 1 is therefore partially supported.

Table 11.3 Comparison of implementation of merit-based pay incentives (probit)

	Registered nurses	Licensed practical nurses	Certified nursing assistants
Nonprofit	–0.639	–0.611	–0.792
	(0.397)	(0.481)	(0.492)
Local government	–0.997*	–1.090*	–1.032
	(0.571)	(0.643)	(0.669)
Home size (total number of residents)	–0.007*	–0.005	–0.004
	(0.004)	(0.005)	(0.005)
Chain status	–0.609*	–0.857**	–0.404
	(0.317)	(0.368)	(0.379)
Hospital affiliation	0.733	0.994**	1.222***
	(0.512)	(0.474)	(0.465)
Case mix index	1.985	2.859*	3.521**
	(1.797)	(1.678)	(1.772)
Tenure	–0.021	–0.022	0.028
	(0.039)	(0.040)	(0.031)
Job complexity	0.870***	0.091	–0.434
	(0.323)	(0.317)	(0.327)
Union representation	–0.291	0.223	–0.455*
	(0.352)	(0.304)	(0.267)
Values congruence	–0.424	–0.972**	–1.555***
	(0.509)	(0.389)	(0.424)
Workload	0.066	0.172	0.023
	(0.218)	(0.215)	(0.224)
Supervisor's ability of evaluating employee's work	0.421	–0.428	–0.055
	(0.276)	(0.311)	(0.229)
Degree of market competition	–0.038	0.030	0.083
	(0.100)	(0.090)	(0.090)
Per capita income	–0.028	–0.037	–0.024
	(0.047)	(0.051)	(0.052)
N	93	93	86
Pseudo-R^2	0.190	0.190	0.230

Heteroskedasticity-robust standard errors in brackets. *Significant at 10%; **significant at 5%; ***significant at 1%. Degree of market competition and Per capita income are in thousands

Table 11.4 Comparison of fringe benefits (OLS)

	Registered nurses	Licensed practical nurses	Certified nursing assistants
Nonprofit	0.601**	0.387*	0.464**
	(0.249)	(0.230)	(0.217)
Local government	0.571**	0.432**	0.567***
	(0.241)	(0.214)	(0.195)
Home size (total number of residents)	0.002	0.002	0.003*
	(0.001)	(0.001)	(0.001)
Chain status	−0.271*	−0.319**	−0.271*
	(0.145)	(0.155)	(0.157)
Hospital affiliation	0.254**	0.293***	0.308***
	(0.120)	(0.105)	(0.111)
Case mix index	1.274	1.168	0.873
	(0.819)	(0.801)	(0.868)
Tenure	−0.020	−0.002	−0.006
	(0.017)	(0.019)	(0.012)
Job complexity	−0.038	0.092	−0.092
	(0.139)	(0.118)	(0.112)
Union representation	0.049	−0.033	−0.052
	(0.140)	(0.160)	(0.160)
Values congruence	0.024	0.014	−0.098
	(0.085)	(0.096)	(0.085)
Workload	0.132	−0.037	−0.050
	(0.134)	(0.097)	(0.121)
Degree of market competition	0.022	0.034	0.043
	(0.025)	(0.026)	(0.028)
Per capita income	0.009	0.018	0.022
	(0.017)	(0.017)	(0.018)
N	92	92	87
R^2	0.284	0.248	0.278

Heteroskedasticity-robust standard errors in brackets. *Significant at 10%; **significant at 5%; ***significant at 1%. Degree of market competition and Per capita income are in thousands

Table 11.4 presents the estimation of fringe benefit levels across sectors. The equations, estimated by OLS but producing similar results when estimated by ordered logit, are overall quite significant. We find significant evidence that nonprofit and local government nursing homes offer better fringe benefits to their employees; nurses working in a home affiliated with a hospital (which are all nonprofit in Minnesota) enjoy even better benefits. This supports Hypothesis 2.

Table 11.5 presents the results of wage estimations. These estimations yield R^2s of around 0.4, so the equations are generally well determined. Overall, we cannot detect any significant differences across sectors in the wages of any nursing group. There is weak tendency for nonprofit and local government nursing homes to pay higher wages to registered nurses, but the effects are small in magnitude and statistically insignificant. Hypothesis 3 is therefore not supported. Finally, Table 11.6

Table 11.5 Comparison of wage levels (OLS)

	Registered nurses	Licensed practical nurses	Certified nursing assistants
Nonprofit	0.012	–0.023	0.000
	(0.034)	(0.029)	(0.028)
Local government	0.029	–0.029	0.016
	(0.049)	(0.044)	(0.037)
Home size (total number of residents)	0.001*	0.000	0.000
	(0.000)	(0.000)	(0.000)
Chain status	–0.014	–0.007	0.007
	(0.031)	(0.025)	(0.026)
Hospital affiliation	0.174***	0.049*	0.068**
	(0.044)	(0.030)	(0.032)
Case mix index	0.105	0.141	0.469***
	(0.177)	(0.136)	(0.143)
Tenure	–0.003	–0.001	0.000
	(0.003)	(0.003)	(0.002)
Job complexity	–0.011	–0.018	0.005
	(0.025)	(0.022)	(0.020)
Union representation	0.027	–0.006	0.038
	(0.034)	(0.027)	(0.024)
Values congruence	0.006	0.003	0.007
	(0.016)	(0.016)	(0.014)
Workload	0.016	–0.008	–0.024
	(0.025)	(0.025)	(0.018)
Degree of market competition	–0.021***	–0.010	–0.016**
	(0.008)	(0.009)	(0.008)
Per capita income	0.008**	0.015***	0.009**
	(0.004)	(0.003)	(0.004)
N	88	89	85
R^2	0.457	0.387	0.444

Heteroskedasticity-robust standard errors in brackets. *Significant at 10%; ***significant at 5%; ***significant at 1%. Degree of market competition and Per capita income are in thousands

confirms what we found already implicitly in Table 11.5: there are no differences in wage dispersion across the three types of organization. Hypothesis 4 is thus not supported by our findings.

11.5 Discussion and Conclusion

This paper sheds light on two types of wage inequality in for-profit, nonprofit and local government organizations. We investigate wage differentials among the three types of organization, and compare within-organization wage dispersion across sectors. We obtain cleaner results associated with the type of organization than those available in the literature thanks to our focus on three job titles within a single occupation (nursing) and a narrowly-defined industry (nursing homes).

Table 11.6 Comparison of within-organization across-occupation wage dispersion (OLS)

	LPNs/CNAs	RNs/CNAs
Nonprofit	–0.041	0.018
	(0.031)	(0.069)
Local government	–0.046	0.020
	(0.049)	(0.078)
Home size (total number of residents)	0.000	0.001
	(0.000)	(0.001)
Chain status	–0.020	–0.030
	(0.029)	(0.063)
Hospital affiliation	–0.029	0.218**
	(0.047)	(0.090)
Case mix index	–0.432**	–0.745*
	(0.203)	(0.434)
Tenure (CNAs)	–0.002	0.007
	(0.004)	(0.007)
Job complexity (LPNs or RNs)	0.022	0.038
	(0.037)	(0.045)
Job complexity (CNAs)	–0.046	–0.057
	(0.030)	(0.049)
Union representation (LPNs or RNs)	–0.070	0.030
	(0.075)	(0.115)
Union representation (CNAs)	0.016	–0.043
	(0.067)	(0.079)
Workload (LPNs or RNs)	0.009	–0.029
	(0.024)	(0.036)
Workload (CNAs)	–0.036	–0.035
	(0.024)	(0.047)
Values congruence (LPNs or RNs)	0.033	0.103**
	(0.038)	(0.051)
Values congruence (CNAs)	–0.010	–0.020
	(0.029)	(0.052)
Degree of market competition	0.006	–0.004
	(0.013)	(0.019)
Per capita income	0.009	0.001
	(0.006)	(0.009)
N	85	84
R^2	0.326	0.335

Note: Estimates include an unreported constant term. OLS coefficients in plain text (marginal effects in Table 11.3); heteroskedasticity-robust standard errors in brackets. *significant at 10%; **significant at 5%; ***significant at 1%. Degree of market competition and Per capita income are in thousands

Our analysis shows that although nonprofit and local government organizations are not found paying higher-than-market hourly wages to their employees, they do provide better fringe benefits. Therefore, our prediction that nonprofit and local government organization will have better compensation is supported because efficiency wages are offered by the nonprofit and government sectors in the form of fringes. This phenomenon can be explained as the organizations' solution to ameliorate agency problems and maintain the loyalty of their employees and elicit their effort to enhance customer care. Another finding consistent with our hypotheses is that for-profit organizations are more likely to use merit-based pay than local government organizations.

Why would the efficiency wages be paid in the form of fringe benefits rather than wages? This is an important question for future research, but we believe that it may be due to the perceived ethicality of fringe benefits. Nonprofit managers report to a board of directors that is primarily concerned with resident care. This board may not like the managers to pay higher wages than the market demands because they may perceive that it takes financial resources away from other projects that could enhance resident quality of life. But unlike for-profit boards that are concerned with profitability, nonprofit boards are generally volunteers who care chiefly about the well-being of residents, and they may have other related ethical beliefs about the importance of healthcare or retirement pensions as well. These board members may be swayed by ethical arguments about the importance of health care or pension for employees, regardless of market demands. They may also be concerned about employee turnover, which can be reduced by benefit provision, or employees passing on illness to residents, which can be mitigated by the paid sick-leave.

In this paper, we subject the prediction of the wage premium in the nonprofit and government sectors by agency theory to further theoretical scrutiny: if there is indeed a wage premium in these sectors in comparison to the for-profit sector, what sources can provide the opportunity for the premium? We discuss how donations and tax advantages in nonprofits, tax dollars in local government organizations, or potentially higher efficiency relative to the private sector due to intrinsically motivated employees could be the sources of these premiums.

The second part of our analysis considered sectoral differences in wage inequality. In nonprofit and local government organizations, there may be a certain level of 'favouritism' towards certain types of employees that increases or decreases their relative wages. This could occur either by raising or lowering wages for the high end or the low end in comparison to the market level. Although neither case is evident from our data, we believe this is an important question for future studies to tackle regarding other industries or locales. Theoretically, wage inequality can be influenced by the distribution of employees' decision-making power and value congruence among employees in the organization. The first factor indicates that the degree of within-organization across-occupation wage inequality is at least partially determined by the relative bargaining power among employee groups, and therefore the wage distribution will in generally favour those employees with higher skill level and greater decision-making influence. In contrast, the second factor suggests that a stronger congruent value system among employees may encourage a climate of equality in the organization, and therefore narrower wage gaps among occupations. Differences in these two factors may determine the relative level of wage inequality within organizations, and the difference may differ across sectors.

In our data, neither the intrinsic motivation perspective's prediction of less inequality among employees in nonprofit and government sectors, nor is the agency theory prediction that higher level employees will use their influence to increase their own well-being without increasing the well-being of others, is supported. The efficiency wages in the form of fringe benefits appear to be shared equally across at least the nursing staff.

Avenues for future research include deciphering the reasons explaining higher fringe benefits among all core occupational groups in nonprofit organizations, and the relative strength of each element of agency theory and the intrinsic motivation perspective in explaining wages and wage dispersion across multiple organizational types. For example, do nonprofit and local government-owned organizations offer higher wages in order to increase the size of their applicant pool and allow them to choose higher quality workers to benefit patient care? Do nonprofit and local government-owned organizations seek to elicit additional effort from current employees due to their concern about patient care? Are more highly compensated front-line employees more pleasant to the residents because they do not feel that they are being exploited (are less likely to have their intrinsic motivation lost due to perceptions of inequality)? Or alternatively, is it because nonprofit and local government employees have more decision-making authority and have used it to increase their own well-being, as well as the well-being of lower-level staff they believe are worthy of extra compensation?

If efficiency wages are used to hire better quality workers, we should find better quality workers in the nonprofit sector. We do find that nonprofit workers have more tenure and more career experience from our data. Are these more experienced workers simply paid their worth? To address this question, we controlled for average experience and tenure in our model specification, which continues to show similar wages and extra fringes in the nonprofit and government sectors. We also conducted a robustness test using data from employees in 36 nursing homes, and after controlling for education, tenure, experience, quadratics in tenure and experience, gender, age, supervisory status, and occupation, as well as the structural firm-level variables, we also found no differences in pure wages across sectors. We leave it to future research to determine whether there are unobservable differences between nonprofit and for-profit workers.

Are nonprofit and local government workers paid more in terms of total compensation because they work harder? We cannot be sure, because we do not have an exact measure of how hard they actually work, but we do have a supervisory report of their workload that is controlled for in our equations, and we control for the severity of illness of the residents, which also affects workload. These differences in fringes persist despite these controls. Do nonprofit and local government employees provide better care? Ben-Ner and Ren (2008) found that nonprofit and local government owned organizations are more likely than their for-profit counterparts to provide the less observable aspects of care.

Do nonprofits and local government workers exploit their additional managerial discretion to better their wages? Our data show that registered nurses in nonprofit homes have more decision-making influence than their for-profit counterparts. We also observe that registered nurses have more influence over decisions than other nursing staff, but they also have higher relative levels of value congruence. Because of this value congruence, these nurses appear not to be acting as agency theory would predict, they appear not to be using their influence to raise their wages at the expense of either other employees or customer care.

It is important to note that our analysis has some limitations, most notably our small sample size and the fact that our results may not generalize to other industries or to industries where for-profit and nonprofit sectors do not compete. The benefit of this approach is to rule out the unobservable heterogeneity across multiple industries that may intervene with the interpretation of the results. However, analyses of other industries are also needed to validate our findings.

In conclusion, we believe that both the intrinsic motivation perspective and agency theory are essential to understand the dynamics of wage inequality between and within the for-profit, nonprofit and government sectors of the economy. Each theory has multiple predictions that sometimes complement each other, yet at other times conflict. The relative strength of each of these predictions will determine the wage structure in a given industry, and the relative strength of these theories may be industry-specific.

Acknowledgements We acknowledge support from Aspen Institute Grant NSRF 2005-1, "A Comparative Study of Organizational Structure, Behavior and Performance in For-Profit Firms, Government Organizations, and Nonprofit Organizations".

References

Alchian AA, Demsetz H (1972) Production, information costs and economic organization. American Economic Review 62:777–795

Arrow KJ (1963) Uncertainty and the welfare economics of medical care. American Economic Review 53:941–973

Ballou JP, Weisbrod BA (2003) Managerial rewards and the behavior of for-profit, governmental and nonprofit organizations: evidence from the hospital industry. Journal of Public Economics 87:1895–1920

Ben-Ner A (2006) For-profit, state and non-profit: how to cut the pie among the three sectors. In: Touffut J-P (ed) Advancing public goods. Edward Elgar, Cheltenham

Ben-Ner A, Ren T (2008) Does organization ownership matter? Structure and performance in for-profit, nonprofit and local government nursing homes. University of Minnesota Industrial Relations Center Working Paper 0108

Borjas GJ, Frech, III HE, Ginsburg PB (1983) Property rights and wages: the case of nursing homes. Journal of Human Resources 18:231–246

Deci, EL, Koestner R, Ryan RM (1999) A meta-analytic review of experiments examining the effects of extrinsic rewards on intrinsic motivation. Psychological Bulletin 125:627–668

DeVaro, J, Brookshire D (2007) Promotions and incentives in nonprofit and for-profit organizations. Industrial and Labor Relations Review 60:311–339

Fama EF, Jensen MC (1983) Separation of ownership and control. Journal of Law and Economics 26:301–325

Feldstein MS (1971) The rising cost of hospital care. Information Resources Press, Washington DC

Frank R (1996) What price the high moral ground? Southern Economic Journal 63:1–17

Freeman RB, Kleiner MM (2000) Who benefits most from employee involvement: firms or workers? American Economic Review 90:219–223

Frey BS (1993) Motivation as a limit to pricing. Journal of Economic Psychology 14:635–664

Frey BS (1998) Institutions and morale: the crowding-out effect. In Ben-Ner A, Putterman L (eds) Economics, values, and organization. Cambridge University Press, Cambridge UK

Gass TE (2004) Nobody's home: candid reflections of a nursing home aide. Cornell University Press, Ithaca

Glaeser EL (2003) Introduction. In: Glaeser EL (ed) The governance of not-for-profit organizations. University of Chicago Press, Chicago
Handy F, Katz E (1998) The wage differential between nonprofit institutions and corporations: getting more by paying less? Journal of Comparative Economics 26:246–261
Hansmann HB (1980) The role of nonprofit enterprise. Yale Law Journal 5:835–901
Hirth RA (1999) Consumer information and competition between nonprofit and for-profit nursing homes. Journal of Health Economics 18:219–240
Holtmann AG, Idson TL (1993) Wage determination of registered nurses in proprietary and nonprofit nursing homes. Journal of Human Resources 28:55–79
Ito T, Domian D (1987) A musical note on the efficiency wage hypothesis: programming, wages and budgets of american symphony orchestras. Economics Letters, 25:95–99
Lazear EP, Rosen S (1981) Rank order tournaments as optimal labor contracts. Journal of Political Economy 89:841–864
Leete L (2000) Wage equity and employee motivation in non-profit and for-profit organizations. Journal of Economic Behavior and Organization 43:423–466
Leete L (2001) Whither the nonprofit wage differential? Estimates from the 1990 Census, Journal of Labor Economics 19:136–170
Leete L (2006) Work in the nonprofit sector. In: Powell WW, Steinberg R (eds) The nonprofit sector: a research handbook. Yale University Press, New Haven
Mirvis PH, Hackett EJ (1983) Work and workforce characteristics in the nonprofit sector. Monthly Labour Review 106:3–12
Mocan HN, Tekin E (2003) Nonprofit sector and part-time work: an analysis of employer-employee matched data on child care workers. Review of Economics and Statistics 85:38–50
Mosca M, Musella M, Pastore F (2007) Relational goods, monitoring and non-pecuniary compensations in the nonprofit sector: the case of the Italian social services. Annals of Public and Cooperative Economics 78:57–86
Pauly MV, Redisch M (1973) The not-for-profit hospital as a physicians' cooperative. American Economic Review 63:87–99
Prendergast C (1999) The provision of incentives in firms. Journal of Economic Literature 37:7–63
Preston AE (1988) The effects of property rights on labor costs on nonprofit firms: an application to the day care industry. Journal of Industrial Economics 36:337–350
Preston AE (1989) The nonprofit worker in a for-profit world. Journal of Labor Economics 7:438–463
Preyra C, Pink G (2001) Balancing incentives in the compensation contracts of nonprofit hospital CEOs. Journal of Health Economics 20:509–525
Roomkin MJ, Weisbrod BA (1999) Managerial compensation in for-profit and nonprofit hospitals. Journal of Law, Economics, and Organization 15:750–781
Rose-Ackerman S (1996) Altruism, nonprofits, and economic theory. Journal of Economic Literature 34:701–728
Ruhm CJ, Borkoski C (2003) Compensation in the nonprofit sector. Journal of Human Resources 38:992–1021
Sesil JC (2006) Sharing decision-making and group incentives: the impact on performance. Economic and Industrial Democracy 27:587–607
Shaw JD, Gupta N, Delery JE (2002) Pay dispersion and workforce performance: moderating effects of incentives and interdependence. Strategic Management Journal 23:491–512
Steinberg R (1987) Nonprofit organizations and the market. In Powell WW (ed) The nonprofit sector: a research handbook. Yale University Press, New Haven
Steinberg R (1990) Labor economics and the nonprofit sector: a literature review. Nonprofit and Voluntary Sector Quarterly 19:151–169
Steinberg R (2008) Principal-agent theory and nonprofit accountability. In: Hopt KJ, Von Hippel T (eds) Comparative corporate governance of non-profit organizations. Cambridge University Press, Cambridge UK
Weisbrod BA (1983) Nonprofit and proprietary sector behavior: wage differentials among lawyers. Journal of Labor Economics 1:246–263

Chapter 12
Tacit Knowledge and Volunteers' Empowerment in the Fair Trade Sector

Renata Livraghi and Gabriella Pappadà

Abstract This paper presents the outcome of a fieldwork carried out in France, Italy, Malta and Spain, with the aim of providing evidence about the main features characterizing fair trade organizations and the individuals (in particular volunteers) involved in them. The case studies have been selected taking into consideration both the areas where Fair Trade has deeper roots (as in some French, Italian and Spanish regions) and is more developed, and the areas where the sector is younger, more politically oriented (like Malta and the south of Italy). It turns out that Fair Trade mainly attracts women and young people, but by different degrees, leading towards a classification of potential volunteers. However, there are some skills that emerge across all the groups, such as relational team-working skills.

12.1 Introduction

Fair trade is part of the third sector, operating in a market in order to diminish the inequalities between developed and developing countries. Consumers of developed countries decide to pay for goods at a 'fair price', that is to say, a higher price than they would pay otherwise, in order to have a say on the production methods adopted in developing countries. In the age of globalization, in which emerging countries are chosen as the centre of production of low-cost, low value-added, consumer goods, fair trade products are differentiated by their handicraft quality and by the respect for the value of fairness, and they are therefore more expensive than similar commercial products resulting from mass production.

The main targets of the fair trade relationship are the most disadvantaged producers in poor countries, whose production is based on the use of raw materials or on informally obtained professional abilities. Therefore, direct and ongoing relationships are established, bringing about satisfactory trade for both parties. On the one side, producers can lead a dignified life at both individual and collective levels. On the

R. Livraghi(✉)
Department of Education and Territorial Sciences, University of Parma,
Borgo Carissimi 10, 43100, Parma, Italy

S. Destefanis and M. Musella (eds.), *Paid and Unpaid Labour in the Social Economy*,
AIEL Series in Labour Economics DOI: 10.1007/978-3-7908-2137-6_13,

other side, consumers choose goods produced consistently with standards negotiated by international networks in the fair trade market. Consumption of these goods increases the welfare of consumers and at the same time modifies their lifestyle introducing the values of solidarity and fairness into their choices.

Moreover, the fair trade sector is an innovative segment of the labour market. Paid and, especially, unpaid workers in world shops and import organizations play a very important role in connecting consumers and (developing-countries) producers. The 2004–2007 Fair Project, *For a new recognition of skills informally and non formally developed in the fair trade sector*, co-financed by the European programme Leonardo da Vinci (http://ec.europa.eu/education/lifelong-learning-programme/doc82_en.htm) has sought to analyze the fair trade sector by focusing on the process of competence acquisition through (paid or unpaid) work in this sector. Its key question is whether workers are able to take advantage of informal learning through the work carried out in a world shop or in an import organization.

Accordingly, this paper presents the outcome of a fieldwork carried out in Italy, Spain, Malta and France on fourteen case studies with the aim of providing evidence about the main features characterizing fair trade organizations and the individuals involved in this sector in the different countries. The case studies have been selected taking into consideration both the areas where Fair Trade has deeper roots (like in some French, Italian and Spanish regions) and is more developed, entrepreneurial, and has a longer traditions, and the areas where the sector is younger, more politically oriented, and in slow growth (like Malta and Southern Italy). The project has emphasized the impact of voluntary work in the industry, interviewing volunteers that assume different managerial and practical roles. Another important criterion of case selection has been the type of structure, in order to consider both world shops (bottom-up structures) and import organizations (top-down ones).

This paper focuses on two particular issues: the competence acquired through work and the weight that informal learning has for paid workers and volunteers. We have decided to adopt a qualitative approach in order to uncover the complex process of skill acquisition. According to social constructivism (Vygotskij 1962; Cole 1978; Varisco 2002; De Koster et al. 2004), socially and economically constructed reality is an ongoing, dynamic process. Reality is reproduced by people acting on their interpretations, their ethics and values and their knowledge. When people interact, they do so with the understanding that their respective perceptions of reality are related and as they act upon this understanding their common knowledge of reality becomes reinforced. It is in this sense that reality is socially and economically constructed. We thus argue for the importance of cooperation and mutual respect in social and economic interaction as a necessary condition for learning, cognitive development and for the accumulation of social capital. More specifically, we argue that volunteers can, with help from peers who share their ethics and values, master concepts and ideas that they could not understand on their own.[1]

The remainder of the paper is organized as follows. Section 12.2 provides a descriptive overview of the fair trade sector. Section 12.3 deals with the connections

[1]This is an application of Vygotsky's (1962) "zone of proximal development". See also Cole (1978).

among Sen's capability approach, social constructivism and fair trade community. Section 12.4 reports the main results from the case studies, and Sect. 12.5 further discusses the findings for the Italian case studies. Section 12.6 concludes.

12.2 Fair Trade Market: An Overview

Fair trade avails itself of the following elements (EFTA 2001):

- Localized producers in developing countries
- Import organizations
- The world shops
- Channels of alternative distribution
- Consumers

Generally, *producers* are small, family-run, businesses that operate in isolated and difficult environments. Producers would therefore be usually constrained to sell their products to a middleman, or to compete with multinational enterprises for the commercialization of their products. Fair Trade intervenes in order to enhance the possibility set of these producers. Fair trade organizations seek to establish a trusting, cooperative relationship between producers and import organizations. Such relation involves an obligation for producers to operate and make decisions according to democratic procedures within the organizations and to actively collaborate in production decisions and processes. The fair trade organizations undertake to provide financial, technical, and educational assistance. They favour the formation of networks between producers, and the ability to offer goods at a marketable price and sufficient quantity within an agreed time period.

More precisely, producers must:

1. Aim for self-development and autonomy of local populations
2. Avoid exporting food products and scarce raw materials, as well as manufactures intensive in the above goods
3. Use local raw materials
4. Guarantee products' quality

The *import organization* links the producers of developing nations with the consumers of developed nations through the world shops. The import organizations are nonprofit organizations whose main aim is to make fair trade operational. They must:

- Provide finance to producers and favour other forms of equal credit or micro credit
- Promote reciprocal collaboration, continuous relationships, favour greater stability of the producers' market outlets, and permit an effective improvement of standards of living
- Provide support to production and exportation organizations: training, advice, market research, product development, and product and market feedback

- Assure that the principles of fair trade are known and shared by the producers and work with them in order to apply these principles
- Provide assistance to world shops, inform them about products and producers through informative reports
- Give to the other subjects of fair trade access to information regarding activities (commercial and cultural) and technical skills not available in world shops
- Allow world shops the opportunity to meet producers (and vice versa), respecting the criteria of responsible tourism

World shops are the distribution centres of produced goods in developed nations. They are nonprofit organizations, in which consumers may purchase goods and at the same time learn about the culture of the impoverished countries. They are places in which interpersonal bonds can be created. The consumer purchases goods in order to satisfy his/her needs, and at the same time becomes aware that his/her purchase will influence the economic development of a poorer country. The World Shops consumer is a member of a community who has chosen to belong to principles, which he/she intends to follow. This modifies his/her lifestyle *(functionings)* with respect to traditional consumers.

Each world shop has peculiarities, which synthesize their existing interpersonal relationships. Some are more specialized in handcrafted goods of given countries; others offer the consumer the opportunity to choose from a vast array of items. Others yet collaborate with political, cultural, social and religious institutions in their territory. World shops carry out numerous activities. They are not only businesses but also places where debates are carried out and training takes place. World shops' activity is mainly carried out by volunteers that acquire skills by interacting with the paid colleagues and the consumers.

World shops must:

- Mainly commercialize fair trade products, either imported directly from a poorer country or acquired through an import organization
- Choose a fair trade supplier organized in a nonprofit structure with democratic management
- Not entertain commercial relationships with companies that violate human rights and damage the environment
- Provide consumers with all the relevant information about the product, including a transparent price
- Support promotional campaigns, conducted at national and international levels, in order to achieve the objectives of fair trade
- Be constantly informed about the products sold, verifying that they respect the fair trade criteria
- Employ paid workers, guaranteeing an adequate wage and training
- Value and prepare volunteers and guarantee their participation in the decision-making process
- Seek to start new fair trade agreements, and to maintain a direct contact (through letter exchange, trade trips, diffusion of information to customers) with the experiences of self-development in poorer countries

The *alternative channels of distribution* of the world shops are numerous and use various methods: sales by mail, or by internet; equipment contracts with associations, communities, cafeterias, catering societies, hotels, University coffee bars, national and European parliaments; groups of families interested in responsible consumption. The growth of Fair Trade has also prompted the need to expand the distribution channels of products in traditional stores and supermarkets. The issue of selling fair trade goods in traditional stores and supermarkets is hotly debated within the fair trade community. Some members of the community are afraid of impoverishing the ethical message and depriving the consumers of the relational goods attached to the fair trade products. The alternative point of view argues that Fair Trade can be more effective by reaching a larger share of consumers.[2]

Consumers purchase the goods and interact with producers, signalling to them a given way in which they must conduct their business. They have implicitly signed, by paying the 'just price', a social contract with various agents of the fair trade network. Fair Trade could not be effective without a 'sovereign' consumer, knowing how to choose and recognize the value of the good purchased and consumed. Fair trade consumers are interested in the origin of the products and in the commercial relations that exist with the producers. "More and more consumers want to be sure that producers receive a fair deal for their products. They want to know the conditions under which the chocolate or bananas they are eating have been produced" (Fairtrade Labelling Organization 2005).

This greater attention on the part of the consumers requires a careful response from the workers and volunteers of this sector, who must know the products that are on the shelves, presenting their characteristics and relating details of their origin. The fair trade sector must respond to the needs of its customers, from a perspective that is based on the principle of solidarity with poorer countries. Fair Trade is more than a commercial activity: it recounts the history and the traditions of populations in Africa, Asia and Latin America. Workers establish a relationship of trust between the consumer and the shop, based on the training and informative significance that every act of selling assumes, which differs from that found in the commercial sector. The motto is "to dedicate time to the customers", be it when they are choosing the products, or when they come to pay for them.

The world shop is intended as a 'place of relationships' where people communicate and socialize. Sales are carried out by conveying to the customer the enthusiasm and the values of Fair Trade. Some customers have a sustained and close relationship with the world shop, while others have a more occasional relationship. To promote their projects and their activities, fair trade workers employ strategies of traditional communication (mass media and word of mouth) and of the latest generation (dedicated web-sites and links on various other sites).

Fair trade workers also set themselves the objective of making the population aware – by means of training campaigns conducted at schools, universities and fairs – about the themes of peace, earthly concerns and multiculturalism, respect for the

[2] See for instance Pricewaterhouse Coopers (2001).

traditions of the developing populations, and thoughtful and careful consumption. These relationships give evidence that Fair Trade is characterized by a 'social contract', signed by people who share its history and values.

12.3 Capabilities Approach and Social Constructivism in the Fair Trade Community

The capability approach is a broad normative framework for the evaluation and assessment of individual well-being and social arrangement, and the design of policies, and proposals for social change in society (Robeyns 2005). The approach in its present form has been pioneered by economist and philosopher Amartya Sen (1980, 1984, 1985a, b, 1987, 1990, 1992, 1993, 1995, 1999) and a growing number of other scholars (see www.capabilitiesapproach.org). It highlights the difference between means and ends, and between substantive freedoms (capabilities) and outcomes (functionings). The interest of this approach for our purposes comes from the focus it allows on the multi-faceted aspects of the well-being of paid workers and volunteers involved in the world shops and importer organizations of developed countries.

A key analytical distinction in the capability approach is between the means and the ends of well-being and development. Only the ends have intrinsic importance, whereas means are instrumental to reach the goal of increased learning, skills, well-being, justice and development. In Sen's earliest work, capability is synonymous with capability set which consists of a combination of potential functionings. The relationship between capability and functionings is influenced by three groups of conversion factors: personal conversion factors; social conversion factors; and environmental conversion factors. For example, both Sen and Nussbaum have paid much attention to the social norms and tradition that form women's preferences and that influence their aspirations and their effective choices (Sen 1990; Nussbaum 2000).

This attention means that the capabilities approach not only must advocate an evaluation of people's capability set, but also analyze the context in which economic production and social interactions take place and the circumstances in which people choose their opportunity sets. In order to do this, the analysis of the conversion factors can rely on the theory of social constructivism (Vygotskij 1962; Cole 1978; Varisco 2002; De Koster et al. 2004). Social constructivism is crucially important in outlining the conversion process in a context characterized by a group of people who have decided to devote time to an organization that pursues the values and ethics they share.

Among the various aspects of conversion, we focused mainly on the informal learning of volunteers in world shops and import organizations. Beside the three traditional groups of conversion factors we introduce another group that we call context conversion factors. The world shops have different organizational structures from import organizations and volunteers have different motivations and aspirations. The theoretical model of social constructivism, centred on the analysis of the group and the various interactions between members of the community, helps us in grasping the differences among different contexts of Fair Trade.

The context conversion factors found in the fair trade sector are:

- The intrinsic factors of the commitment and the sharing of the social network project. The *mission* of Fair Trade coincides with the values pursued by the agents operating in the sector
- The interpersonal relations set up between the various fair trade agents (consumers, producers, distributors of goods produced, and the relevant civil society)
- The organizational procedures utilized in fair trade productive units, which are very similar to situations in a *learning organization*

The Fair Project has sought to identify the competence of volunteers and employees, utilizing an appropriate methodology to bring out the qualitative aspects of the problem analyzed. Competence was understood as a set of personal traits, abilities and behaviours, which make fair trade volunteers and employees 'appropriate' and 'coherent' for their various roles and duties in the sector. This competence is 'tacit' for the time being, because it is incorporated in the person who possesses it and is not made explicit and has been learned in a 'non-traditional' manner, namely through non-formal and informal channels of learning. Certification of the competence of fair trade operators would transform tacit knowledge into explicit knowledge, thus widening their actual opportunities or *capabilities*.

The Fair Project has also brought to light that fair trade operators are prevalently volunteers, who participate in the social network to which they belong in various manners and with different expectations. In fact, volunteers are a set of heterogeneous persons, in terms of personal traits and abilities, and they have different expectations. In common, they have values such as equity and solidarity and the desire to change social structures, thanks to their actions and the interpersonal relationships they succeed in establishing (Livraghi and Pappadà 2007).

Figure 12.1 represents the process of conversion of material and immaterial resources and circumstances in outcomes (functionings). In Fair Trade, such a conversion process is influenced by the choices of individuals (who share values but may have different personal interests), their roles in the world shop or import organization, their age, their learning abilities (affected by their educational and working background) and their awareness.

Fair trade consists of organizations who act in a complex, changeable, unstable reality. They organize assets to achieve an aim. If agents have an aim in common, because they accept the 'social contract' through their actions, the decision procedure must be developed and agreed on every time. The decision procedure must involve every agent (leadership, world shop manager and volunteers). The results of empirical research show us that to explain the choice to become volunteers in the fair trade sector is very important in order to know:

- The reference frame
- Experiences, skills and knowledge accumulation process
- Agents' activity and actions

This is because social constructivism requires taking a stand on a community with constant attention to the group and interaction between partnerships. In this case, there is no dissociation between decisions taken and decision making.

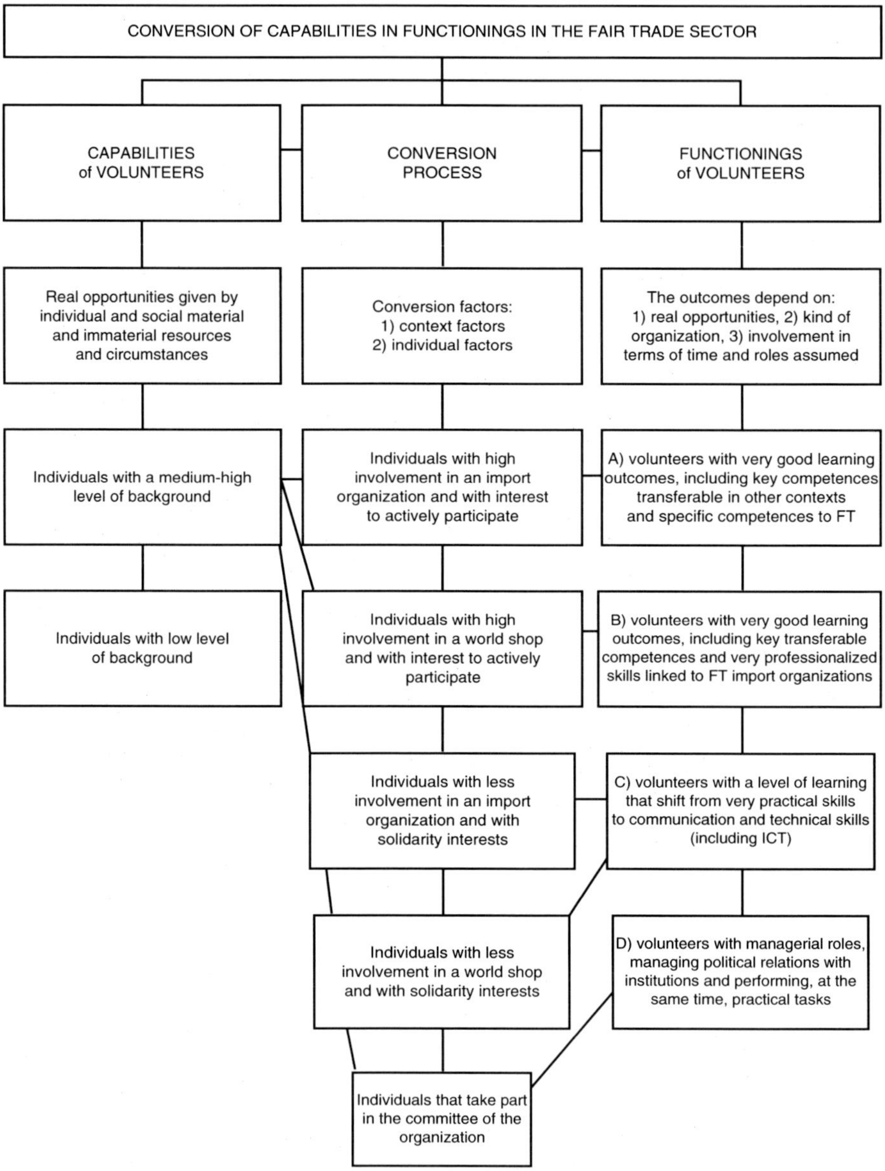

Fig. 12.1 A collective capability model

The decision procedure is individual and cooperative at the same time. It is also an opportunity to enjoy, and to appreciate involvement in the selected choice. The decision procedure has a cycle, in development, with different agents, and has several functions both symbolic and cognitive. Every decision procedure must accounted for, if we wish to understand the relationships between voluntary participation and the process to achieve well-being and competence.

12.4 Comparative Results from the Fair Project

We now present the main results from a fieldwork carried out within the Fair Project in Italy, Spain, Malta and France on fourteen case studies. This research aims to provide evidence about the main features characterizing fair trade organizations and the individuals involved in this sector in the different countries, by focusing on the process of competence acquisition through (paid or unpaid) work in this sector. Its main question is whether workers are able to take advantage of informal learning through the work carried out in a world shop or in an import structure.

According to social constructivism, when people interact, they do so with the understanding that their respective perceptions of reality are related and as they act upon this understanding their common knowledge of reality becomes reinforced. Our empirical research has studied people's arguments in depth to understand personal and community history, key topics and underlying meaning. We have chosen to make use of detailed interviews with people and we have analyzed documents following suggestions from both capability approach and social constructivism. This research strategy is in accordance with Gergen's suggestions (Gergen 1994, 1999).

We have decided to adopt a qualitative approach in order to uncover the complex process through which competence is acquired and the weight that informal learning has in it for paid workers and, especially, volunteers. The case studies have been selected taking into consideration both the areas where Fair Trade has deeper roots (like in some French, Italian and Spanish regions) and is more developed, entrepreneurial, and has a longer traditions, and the areas where the sector is younger, more politically oriented, and in slow growth (like Malta and Southern Italy). Another important criterion of case selection has been the type of structure, in order to consider both world shops (bottom-up structures) and import organizations (top-down ones). Organizational structure also depends on the history of the Fair Trade in the social context, and the years of experience of the structure. These different organizational structures are however all characterized by a mix of individuals permanently involved in Fair Trade and interested in working in such a sector and a group of marginal participants that share the values and are only interested in doing voluntary work.

In Table 12.1 we present the main characteristics of the organization under scrutiny, while a summary of the characteristics of the interviewees in each country is given in Tables 12.2–12.5.

First of all, our cross-country analysis must allow for some basic differences in the realities under scrutiny.

The French, Italian and Spanish case studies provide evidence of long lasting experience in Fair Trade. Both volunteers and customers share values and interests in such a sector for a longer period than Malta. In France, this has allowed fair trade organizations with a high level of professionalization, the establishment of fair trade organizations specialized in specific activities, such as import of environment-friendly clothes distributed in Europe, Japan and USA or the import from specific Third World areas, and sensitivity to ecological interests. In the French case studies, the board is, in general, composed of paid workers with a learning background close to Fair Trade (see Table 12.2) who provide unpaid extra work. In Italy most boards

Table 12.1 Main characteristics of the organizations in the fourteen case studies

Country	Case study(year of start up and type of organization)	Location	Organizational characteristics
France	Solidair'Ethic (1999 – world shop)	Quimper (Bretagne)	Started as a limited company and transformed in a nonprofit association in July 2007. Linked to MINGA Fair Trade network.
France	Saldac (2002 – import organization)	Montélimar (Rhône Alpes)	Started as a cooperative and transformed in limited company in 2002. It has shops in France and Switzerland and is linked to MINGA Fair Trade network.
France	Andines (1987 – import organization)	Saint Denis (Ile de France)	Constituted by two complementary structures: a cooperative that imports and distributes fair trade products and a financial company that provides the funds for the producers development. Linked to MINGA Fair Trade network.
France	Taddart (2002 – travel agency)	Paris	Fair trade travel agency creating travel packages, taking into account the local populations needs in order that the tourists' stay does not perturb the life of the community. The relationship with the customers is about helping them to evolve in their relationship with travel.
France	Les Racines Du Ciel (2005 – clothes made with environment–friendly materials in France, Italy and Tunisia)	Quimper (Bretagne)	Limited company created by two French designers to promote respect for human rights and for the environment in the fashion sector.
France	ARTASIA (2001 – import organization)	Paris	Nonprofit association with a modest turnover and a good level of organization.
Malta	KKG – Kooperativa Kummerc Gust (1996 – world shop)	Valletta	A small cooperative with a simple structure based on informal job sharing. There is a committee composed of three people and three areas of activities (shop management, administration and education area) managed by three different individuals.
Spain	Intermon-Oxfam-Vilanova (established in 1996 to organize events; first world shop in 2001)	Vilanova (Catalonia – 40 km. from Barcelona)	Shop operated by a group of seventeen women. One of these women is the shop manager. Informal but effective process to assign tasks according to volunteers' interests and skill, based on a rotational system for practical tasks. Intermon is a NGO of Spanish and Jesuit origins that joined 10 years ago the international organization Oxfam. It currently includes 30 fair trade shops in Spain
Spain	Intermon-Oxfam (1998 – world shop)	Barcelona (Catalonia)	Shop organized with one paid worker, with a social education university degree, working full time, as shop manager. There are also one part time worker and thirteen volunteers.

Spain	Ideas (import organization started informally in 1987 and established in 1997)	Cordoba (Andalusia) Some interviews gathered in Toledo and Linares	Cooperative of eighteen paid permanent workers, organized in departments with high degrees of autonomy. Role rotation, wage differences such as monthly bonus for each 3 years worked in the organization. Use of external consultancy to develop marketing and product strategies. A specific human resources department has been planned due to the growth of the organization. It is recognized as NGO
Italy	Unsolomondo (first world shop: 1998; second world shop: 2005.)	Bari (Puglia)	Cooperative with an organizational structure establishing well-defined roles, and a good spirit of cooperation.
Italy	Radici Emirandira (2004 – world shop)	Conversano (province of Bari – Puglia)	Cooperative with little formalization of roles. No volunteers, as the cooperative is in its infancy. It is linked to AGICES - General Italian Assembly of Fair Trade)
Italy	Ravinala (1987 – import organization)	Reggio Emilia (Emilia Romagna)	Cooperative with horizontal structure: everyone is his or her own manager. Strategy for recruitment of volunteers: experience required; workers are chosen from among the volunteers, whose skills are known. Good cooperation spirit involving five paid workers with permanent contracts and numerous volunteers. Linked to NGO RTM, Caritas of Reggio Emilia, Association of World shops and AGICES.
Italy	Ex-Aequo (1993 – import organization)	Bologna (Emilia Romagna)	Cooperative with horizontal structure: two heads of the cooperative and three area heads. No human resources manager, hence the roles are not very well defined, given the large size of the structure. Good cooperation spirit involving six paid workers with permanent contracts and numerous volunteers. Linked to NGO CTM.

Table 12.2 Summary of the characteristics of the interviewees in France

	Solidair'Ethic	Saldac	Andines	Taddart	Les Racines Du Ciel	Artasia
Age	54	34	53	44	39	32
Gender	Woman	Man	Man	Woman	Woman	Woman
Level of education	Secondary school	Post-university degree	Secondary school	Secondary education	University degree	University degree
Term of involvement in the structure	7 years	4 years	19 years	4 years	2 years	5 years
Values/motivations for working in the fair trade sector	To actively participate in a movement of international solidarity	His values are emphasized by the cultural familiarity with the Indian Peru community from which he has origin	Active promoter of human rights	To promote quality trips that can lead to a change of the sense of travel	To promote a change of the way of consuming, respecting human rights and environment	The result of a personal reflections, political involvement, constantly criticizing limits to the third world humanitarian help
Past working and training experience	Long lasting experience in the health sector and many years spent in West Africa. She started her Fair Trade experience selling products in the markets	Since his secondary school he started Fair Trade activities. His university degree and doctorate in economics of development are strictly linked to Fair Trade	Employed for 8 years in a metallurgy firm and trade unionist. Volunteers in a health NGO working in Columbia for 4 years	Education background in administration and economics. Past working experience as project and sales management and volunteer experience in Fair Trade in Artisans du Monde	Education background in business, 3 years of working experience in Air France and 5 years working experience in fashion business	5 years' experience in a department store as cashier. A couple of years experience in an arts events organization
Learning experience in the case studies	Informal learning favoured by the role of manager performed in the structure	Informal learning by trial and errors and by interacting with other professionals	He actively participates in the process of professionalization of Andines. The process of knowledge transfer through non formal and informal pathways is well developed	She argues that there is no, strictly speaking, method of learning. The professional constraints are the same as in another sector, but exercizing the role of manager places the professional skills that she previously acquired in another light	Informal learning favoured by the managerial role performed in the organization	Fair Trade workforce has different training needs from the for-profit sector

Table 12.3 Summary of the characteristics of the interviewees in Malta

	KKG	
	Workers	Volunteers
Age	54	Average 36 (from 19 to 67)
Gender	woman	2 men and 3 women
Level of education	3 with university degree 2 with secondary school degree 1 with compulsory school degree	
Term of involvement in the structure	From 2 to 11 years	
Values/motivations for working in the fair trade sector	Most volunteers come from the Third World Group; they are also involved as volunteers in other nonprofit organizations	
Past working and training experience	The founding members had working experience or an educational background linked to this kind of activities. Most part of them had voluntary experience in the Italian Fair Trade	
Learning experience in the case studies	Informal learning characterized by learning by interacting, and by trial and errors	

are composed of volunteers who started their working experience in Fair Trade when they were young and went on, except in some cases of drop out due to family commitments. The involvement of French managers is expected to rise in the future due to the demand of customers, the need to enhance the network with other partners and the development of some branches of the industry. On the other hand, marginal volunteers in all country case studies are tending to reduce their involvement in accordance with their family needs. In such cases the focus is different, and is not represented by Fair Trade's development, but by personal needs. In a context like Northern Italy where Fair Trade has a long-lasting history, the import cooperative has an organizational model more similar to a for-profit company than a nonprofit organization and requires workers and volunteers with fairly specific competence and knowledge. In France too, where Fair Trade maintains a clear character of humanitarian help, there is an increasing need for professionalization of the industry.

In contrast to this model, there is the Malta case study. Malta is a small country with a fair trade organization only started in 1996 thanks to the ideas of some members of the Third World Group who had work experience within Italian Fair Trade and wanted to do something more than the short spells of voluntary work they had so far experienced. They decided to transfer their experience to the Maltese third sector, creating a world shop with 10 constant members and about 100 volunteers, in part foreign people involved in Leonardo projects working in the cooperative for temporary periods, in part Maltese people employed in other contexts and devoted to Fair Trade in periods of special events, and in part Maltese people involved as

Table 12.4 Summary of the characteristics of the interviewees in Spain

	Intermon – Oxfam				
	Barcelona shop		Vilanova shop	Ideas	
	Workers	Volunteers	Volunteers (no workers)	Workers	Volunteers
Age	Average 30	Average 50	Average over 50	Average 45	Average 26
Gender	11 women and 2 men		13 women	7 women and 1 men	
Level of education	2 with university degree 6 with secondary degree 5 with primary degree		5 with secondary degree 8 with primary degree	3 with university degree 5 with secondary degree (2 are university students)	
Term of involvement in the structure	From 3 to 8 years		Average tenure: 3 years	From 2 to 10 years	From 1 to 10 years
Values/motivations for working in the fair trade sector	People with attitudes to promote justice, solidarity and peace on a global scale		The volunteer's profile is a woman over 50, active member of the city centre Catholic parish community with social sensitivity	Highly professionalized staff sharing Fair Trade values	
Past working and training experience	The staff selection is based more on attitudes and availability than on specific past working experiences of the individuals. Most employees have a long experience in working in the service sector (education, administrative tasks and commerce)		Most part of these volunteers worked when they were young and left their jobs because of family commitments.	Generally highly qualified because the number of employees is not sufficient for the level of tasks required. A large number of students carrying out practical training in Ideas and people with a university degree in business are on demand. Ideas workforce has gone through some formal training	
Learning experience in the case studies	Besides informal learning, inside the NGO there are two kinds of ongoing training for the workforce: training concerning the organization and its sales activities; and personalized training programs.		Informal learning in the workplace through learning by interacting. Practical training (management and accounting) carried out by a shop monitor on a new computer terminal.	The cooperative has a department of cooperation for development, research, social action and education that organizes courses, but they are few in comparison with the demand coming from the employees.	

Table 12.5 Summary of the characteristics of the interviewees in Italy

	Unsolomondo		Radici Emirandira	Ravinala		Ex Aequo	
	Workers	Volunteers	Workers (no volunteers)	Workers	Volunteers	Workers	Volunteers
Age	28–37 years	31 and 40 years respectively	Average 31–32 years Young cooperative consisting of young members	Average 39 Range 32–46		Average 30 R ange 23–48 (2 volunteers of 45 and 47 years)	
Gender	1 man and 2 women	1 man and 3 women	1 woman and 3 men	2 women 3 men	2 women	1 man and 3 women	3 men and 4 women (1 is also a collaborator)
Level of education	4 with university degrees 2 university students 1 with a diploma		3 with secondary degrees 1 with compulsory schooling only	2 with university degrees 4 with secondary degrees 1 with compulsory schooling only		9 with university degrees 1 about to graduate 1 with compulsory schooling only	
Term of involvement in the structure	From 2 to 14 years (those with the longest experience are the founders)		Workers from 3 to 5 years; 1 year for a female collaborator	(a) 12 years (b) 8 years months (c) 3 years (d) 18 months (e) 3	(a) 19 (founder) (b) 15	From a minimum of a few months to a maximum of 13 years for the shop's founder	
Values/motivations for working in the fair trade sector	Influence of Combonian monks. Sharing of Fair Trade ideals, interest in creating an alternative economic system, and solidarity with developing countries		Staying together, collaborating, interacting	Solidarity with developing countries, interest and sharing of Fair Trade values		Desire to redress the differences between the North and South of the world and of promotion of informed consumption. Among the volunteers there are many youths who come from the Scout movement	

(continued)

Table 12.5 (continued)

	Unsolomondo		Radici Emirandira	Ravinala		Ex Aequo	
	Workers	Volunteers	Workers (no volunteers)	Workers	Volunteers	Workers	Volunteers
Past working and training experience	Actively involved in Fair Trade for several years, as participants in various initiatives and courses, including specialized master degrees		Some experience in the for-profit sector, and training in specialized Fair Trade courses	Generally some past experience in the for-profit sector in similar jobs, and experience in Fair Trade as volunteers or attending courses regarding volunteer work in Africa		Medium to high level of study; only two persons have followed training courses. Various past work experiences, often intermittent; some involving Fair Trade or values of solidarity (e.g. assistant to the elderly and disabled) or for more technical aspects (e.g. sales assistant). Many of the current workers began as volunteers	
Learning experience in the case studies	Mainly informal training strategies based on the guidance of veteran workers. A 'come and see' strategy		Above all informal learning in the workplace	The cooperative continually organizes refresher courses		Experience at work, with guidance and collaboration, is considered important, while training courses for volunteers are considered much less effective, because of the unpredictability of the eventual roles	
Tasks carried out in the structure	Workers	Volunteers	Workers (no volunteers)	Workers	Volunteers	Workers	Volunteers
Specific/structured roles assumed	Simply structured, but with clearly defined roles: 1 manager for each shop, 1 coordinator of all activities,	No rigid division of roles. Activities are carried out flexibly according to the needs of the shop and the skills available	Flexible division of roles: all the activities can be carried out by all 3 of the members. The female collaborator is dedicated solely to the manufacture of bomboniere favours	Not subdivided into functional areas, but with some defined roles that correspond to the interviewees:	President of the cooperative. Head of training and external relations.[3]	Structured division of roles: 2 heads of shop and of the purchasing, 1 admin. head, 1 head of promotion, 1head of training	High turnover of volunteers, who carry out rather simple jobs and supporting tasks, except in the three cases involved in the administrative board

	1 training manager, and 1 manager in charge of bomboniere favours production			(a) warehouse; (b) adm.; (c) commerce; (d) adm.; (e) warehouse.			
Weekly work timetable	Average 40–45	The volunteer founder, who is also president, dedicates 15–20 h. Other, on average, 4–8 hrs according to need	2 full time (about 60 h) 1 part time flexible, 1 occasional	(a) 50 (b) 50. (c) 50 (d) 48* (e) 40/45 *50% voluntary	(a) 10 (b) 6–8 (partly paid)	From 15–25 h up to 40 h	Flexible participation (generally every other Saturday, from 3 to 10 h) except 1 permanent at 15–20 h and 2 permanent on Saturday

[3]The other volunteers (not interviewed, as they do not carry out typical activities) do various tasks (e.g. warehouse management, Internet site management).

part-time volunteers for few hours a week. Most volunteers involved in Fair Trade are also involved in other voluntary activities (see Table 12.3). This is less common in the other countries, especially if the individuals do not have much time to devote to other activities because their involvement in Fair Trade is full time or they are, at the same time, employed in other contexts. In Malta turnover is low, even if it is devoted to a wide kind of activities, typical of Fair Trade, like developing educational activities, selling fair trade products, relating with policy makers at local level, and special events involving the local community.

Among young people in Spain, France and Italy, there is a deep interest in Fair Trade, leading these people to study disciplines close to such a sector. Young volunteers are often more educated than older ones, with a view to work in the Fair Trade as paid workers and active participation in the decision-making process. Elderly people are less educated and less involved in the decision-making process, except in the case of active participation in the board. All individuals involved in Fair Trade have the opportunity to learn by doing and by interacting, although such a learning process depends both on the worker and on the environment where he/she works. The Fair project provides evidence that there are different profiles of volunteers, whose learning outcomes depend on the kind of organization

The data gathered in the four countries investigated (Italy, Spain, Malta and France) reveal common elements with respect to the organizational structure of the world shops and import organizations, and diversities in the personal characteristics of volunteers. In Italy, for example, the average age of persons is relatively lower than in the other countries. Levels of formal education are rather high. In some cases, volunteers possess post-degree specializations consistent with the professional skills required by the sector. The situation in Malta is similar to Italy, with a greater number of female volunteers.

The profile of volunteers in Spain (see Table 12.4), on the other hand, is quite different to what was shown for Italy and Malta. The body of volunteers is made up mostly of women, who are housewives or retired, of average to high age, average to medium and high levels of formal education and with extremely high value motivations. These volunteers provide a very stable contribution, whereas young people only stay for a short period. The degree of professionalization of Spanish case studies is differentiated: The Idea import organization mostly relies on paid workers and has a very small number of volunteers. The Barcelona shop has a fairly professionalized management notwithstanding the large number of volunteers, while professionalization is virtually nil in the Vilanova shop.

The Fair Project also deals with former volunteers in order to understand the reasons for quitting the sector and to analyze the professional itineraries taken by people who had had important opportunities for non-formal and informal learning in the past. The analyses brought out an extremely low rate of turnover for the Malta and France cases studies. In Italy, former volunteers made use of their learning in similar professional experiences, where the values of Fair Trade could still apply. In Spain, the sample of former volunteers was made up mostly of young students who had used the volunteer experience as general training, to facilitate entry into the labour market.

The competence acquired by volunteers can definitely be related to the context-related knowledge and to the more specifically technical-professional skills.[4] It must also be stressed that all fair trade volunteers accept participating actively in a social network, thus accepting an implicit contract binding them to a social organization involving awareness and responsibility.

Although the volunteers share belonging to a social network, on one hand, their different personal traits, abilities and expectations involve the acquisition of different tacit knowledge. The differences of professionalization among world shops and import organizations is a common outcome in each country. In Spain, the Ideas cooperative even applied to two external consultants in international business marketing coming from the University of Cordoba. However, also the Spanish world shops that recruit volunteers on the basis of their attitudes and availability, more than on specific skills, provide internal and external training plans to cover specific training needs. This is particularly developed in the Barcelona shop where the initial skill level of volunteers is low, but there are three kinds of training activities involving such volunteers. One course concerns the organization and its activities, another intervention includes personalized training programs geared to the skills that the workers lack, observed through interviews carried out by the shop manager; the final training intervention includes external initiatives not directly related to the shop.

In all case studies (see Table 12.1), an organizational structure has been revealed that is based on empowerment, assuming one's responsibilities, and strong group cohesion. The decision-making process of fair trade organizations, based on the principle that each head has the right of one vote, enhances the participation of each individual in the life of the organization. Even those who perform practical tasks have the right to participate in the decision-making process of the organization because he/she can contribute with his/her experience to the decision-making process. Such a mutual and unified decision process together with the empowerment of individuals, fosters the development of a learning organization, mainly based on informal learning. Almost all interviews provide evidence that learning was most frequently obtained by doing, by trial and error, by interacting. Moreover, most individuals state that informal learning is precious and provides outcomes which are very useful at work. It therefore appears that an the organizational structure centred on empowerment has a favourable bearing upon skill training.

The sharing of the work in a mutual and unified form - the cooperative style, according to which the decisions are taken by the group - fosters the acquisition of relationship, decision and managerial skills. The centrality of group meetings as decision-taking bodies creates an environment in which managerial and decisional abilities are shared. Relational skills emerge in two aspects: one within the cooperative, relating to the strong relationship among the shop workers, and one of a more external character, relating to the social network that is created in this sector. In particular, the workers of the largest shop examined define their relationship skills as widely transferable, as follows:

---

[4]Technical-professional skills were shown to be greater in import organizations, as compared to those in world shops.

- Teamwork
- Management of people (seeking to reconcile the different needs of everyone and to manage possible conflicts between workers and volunteers due to high workload[5]
- Problem solving
- Promotional activity

Other types of skills that unite the fair trade workers are those relating to information technology (computers, the Internet, and cash-desk instrumentation). In the case of people over 50 (such as Spanish housewives), fair trade is a fruitful tool to learn ICT besides an opportunity to feel useful for the society.

12.5 A Deeper Analysis of the Italian Case Studies

We deal with the Italian case studies in somewhat greater detail due to the larger amount of information available for them (see Table 12.5). The four Italian case studies (see also Table 12.1) include three world shops, (two in the Mezzogiorno and one in the North) and an import centre situated in the North. They are all horizontally structured cooperatives, as decisions are taken in the group according to the cooperative principle, and roles are rather well defined, often in a non-functional but spontaneous way, determined by the cohesion of the group. All case studies have some external relationships with trade associations and local institutions, with which they have formed a network, and they also involve local producers with whom they are networked (except in the case of the import centre, which provides only handmade products from a selection of developing countries, and Fair Trade package tours, because it prefers to have direct and strong relationships with customers and suppliers). The products and the services that they offer vary from organic foodstuffs to handmade goods.

From the analysis of the personal characteristics of the interviewees, we note that there is no substantial difference in age between paid workers and volunteers, and, on the whole, the target age-group ranges from 23 to 48 years. Those who are oldest work in the two oldest structures in the sector, and are often the founders of the cooperative itself. In general, those who approach the world of Fair Trade are the young, while those of a more mature age tend to have consolidated experience in the sector already. Indeed, there is a noticeable tendency for people to approach Fair Trade world at a young age, and then to remain there because they grow fond of it.

Regarding the difference of gender, there are equal numbers of men and women among the workers (8 of each sex), while the women have, without doubt, a greater presence among the volunteers (9 women vs. 4 men). Among other characteristics, it is the women who are of greater age in the group (e.g. 45, 47 and 48 years), be it as volunteers or as paid workers.

The analysis of the educational attainment reveals that on the whole it is medium to high: 15 bachelor's degrees, 11 high-school diplomas, and only 3 participants with nothing more than compulsory education. A good many of those with diplomas

[5]Differences in workload can also explain low turnover of volunteers in small shops and high turnover in large shops.

are either university students (of whom one is about to graduate) or persons who have abandoned university before completion of their courses. Education is seen as a tool for the acquisition of knowledge and learning method. Moreover, almost everybody has attended training courses that are specific to Fair Trade (almost always before becoming volunteers) and they consider these courses to have been useful.

The cooperatives that were interviewed organize training courses aimed at drawing workers towards the sector, although of the four studies examined, only the import centre regularly organizes training courses for its volunteers and workers, while the shops maintain that the best method of learning is to begin work under the guidance of a senior member. This difference is due to the fact that the import centre demands volunteers who are already in possession of a specific skill portfolio. This greater professionalization is evident also in the phase of selecting the volunteers, because the import centre is the only cooperative to apply selection rules beyond the requirement of a minimum weekly work contribution.

The work timetable is fairly constant in the cases examined. The most frequently attending volunteers work, in general, some 15–20 h per week, although there are a good many who offer about 3–4 h a week (a half-day). This lower rate of attendance is common among persons who already have another activity that occupies them full time (university, work, or looking after children), and who are not involved in the meetings of the cooperative.

In all cases, the sustaining element of voluntary activity is represented by an affinity with intrinsic Fair Trade values, to which the volunteers are often drawn by means of political ideals, the Scout Movement, or religious organizations, such as the Combonian missionaries.

12.6 Concluding Remarks

The capabilities approach is a set of theoretical assumptions, initially introduced by Sen. It lends itself to effectively explain how the capabilities of fair trade agents (workers and volunteers) can, through appropriate processes, convert into an ability to learn competences and a thus create a better quality of life. The assumptions of the capabilities approach refer to real opportunities for employees and volunteers in a given 'context' of Fair Trade: a world shop or an import organization, in a given territorial area. Social constructivism tries to explain the process of conversion of capabilities as a way of life, freely chosen as a result of self-realization and self-determination. The empirical research of this paper has tried to identify the capabilities of employees and volunteers in Fair Trade and analyze their conversion process, in a context characterized by cooperation and social interaction. These acts and activities allow them to freely pursue choices at the individual and group level because they reflect common values and shared ethics.

Social constructivism suggests paying attention to the local context, and organizational and interrelationships between different members of the group. In this way, the operational experience with other employees and volunteers of the Fair Trade is a major source of informal learning for them.

Analysis of the cases under scrutiny has allowed an empirical test of these assumptions, noting that the collective capabilities model allows a distinction between different kinds of volunteers. In Fig. 12.1 we represented the process of conversion of material and immaterial resources and circumstances in outcomes (functionings). In Fair Trade, such a conversion process is influenced by the choices of individuals (who share values but may have different personal interests), their roles in the world shop or import organization, their age, their learning abilities (affected by their educational and working background) and their awareness. Fair Trade mainly attracts women and young people, but by different degrees, leading towards the classification of four groups of potential volunteers.

Group A concerns individuals with a medium to high level of education, in certain occasions with past working experiences close to fair-trade specific skills. Its members are actively involved in a world shop in terms of time and roles assumed in the structure. This group involves many young people and women around 40 with a high-school diploma that share Fair Trade values. It is frequent in all the case studies analyzed, with particular references to Italian and Maltese ones. In the Italian case studies, many volunteers in this group are interested in transforming their voluntary commitment into a paid labour contract.

Group B is distinguished from Group A by involvement in an import organization. Its members must be considered more professional, and have the competence required to interact with producers in developing countries.

Group C is mainly characterized by people less involved in the import sector, because either they are employed in other contexts or they are involved in fair trade to support developing countries. This group is very frequent in the Spanish world shops analyzed by the project with the presence of a large number of elderly women with only compulsory education and less involvement in the organization.

Group D includes the most involved people, who play a fundamental role in the structure. The level of professionalization of the structure may affect the professional itineraries within the group, as well as the kind of commitment to the organization (volunteer or paid worker).

Finally, it turns out that workers often possess a set of highly disparate skills, whereas there are some skills that emerge across all the groups, such as relational team-working skills.

Acknowledgments The Fair project has been realized thanks to co-financing from the European Commission-Leonardo da Vinci programme Project 2004 2240/001 001 LE2-51OREF (2004 - IT/04/C/F/RF-81506).

References

Cole M (ed) (1978) Mind in society. MIT Press, Cambridge MA

De Koster K., Devisé I., Flament I., Loots G. (2004) Due applicazioni, una prospettiva, molti costrutti: implicazioni del costruzionismo sociale per la ricerca scientifica e la terapia. *Rivista di Terapia Breve Strategica e Sistemica* 1:71–77.

EFTA (2001) Fair Trade Yearbook. EFTA, Schin op Geul. http://www.european-fair-trade-association.org/efta/yb.php.

Fairtrade Labelling Organization (2005) Fair trade in europe. Facts and figures on Fair Trade in 25 members countries. Fairtrade Labelling Organization, Bonn

Gergen K (1994) Realities and relationships: soundings in social construction. Cambridge University Press, Cambridge UK

Gergen K (1999) An invitation to social constructionism. Sage, London

Livraghi R., Pappadà G. (2007) Valorisation of the tacit knowledge of Fair Trade workers and volunteers: lessons learned from the Fair Trade Project. In: Torlone F (ed), Volunteers and professionals in the Fair Trade sector. A learning pathway. European Commission-Leonardo da Vinci Project, Brussels

Nussbaum M. (2000) Women and human development: the capabilities approach. Cambridge University Press, Cambridge UK

PricewaterhouseCoopers (2001) Strong growth potential for the fair trade market. *Retail and Consumer Worlds* 39(1)

Robeyns I. (2005) The capability approach: a theoretical survey, *Journal of Human Development* 6:93–114

Sen A. (1980) Equality of what? In: McMurrin S (ed), The Tanner Lectures on Human Values. University of Utah Press, Salt Lake City

Sen A. (1984) Rights and capabilities. Resources, value and development. Harvard University Press, Cambridge MA

Sen A. (1985a) Commodities and capabilities, North Holland, Amsterdam

Sen A. (1985b) Well-being, agency and freedom. *Journal of Philosophy* 82:169–221

Sen A. (1987) The standard of living. In: Hawthorn G (ed.) The standard of living. Cambridge University Press, Cambridge UK

Sen A. (1990) Justice: means versus freedoms. *Philosophy and Public Affairs* 19:111–121.

Sen A. (1992) Inequality re-examined, Clarendon Press, Oxford

Sen A. (1993) Capability and well-being. In: Nussbaum M, Sen A (eds.) The quality of life. Clarendon Press, Oxford

Sen A. (1995) Gender inequality and theories of justice. In: Nussbaum M, Glover J (eds.) Women, culture and development: a study of human capabilities. Clarendon Press, Oxford

Sen A. (1999) Development as freedom. Knopf, New York

Varisco B.M. (2002) Costruttivismo socio-culturale. Genesi filosofiche, sviluppi psico-pedagogici, applicazioni didattiche. Carocci, Rome

Vygotskij L.S. (1962) Thought and language. MIT Press, Cambridge MA

Chapter 13
The 'Re-Emergence' of Social Enterprises in CEE and the CIS

Giulia Galera

Abstract This essay analyzes the characteristics and the role of social enterprises in CEE and CIS countries. Following a brief introduction on the relevance of institutional pluralism for economies characterized by poorly developed markets and welfare systems under construction, the importance of social enterprise for those countries is emphasized. Starting from a definition of social enterprise grounded in the European tradition, focus then shifts on the history of social entrepreneurial organizations and current social enterprise development paths in the region, with special regard to the role played by the social enterprise in fostering socio-economic development. Social enterprises are found to increase the supply of general goods and services for the community, generate new employment, contribute to a more balanced use and allocation of resources, and enhance the social capital at the local level.

13.1 Introduction

This paper aims to explore the potential role of *social enterprises*[1] as vehicles for economic and social development at both national and local levels. Reference is made in particular to post-communist and socialist countries, that is, those economies that despite the economic growth recorded, continue to include several

[1] The vast array of socio-economic institutions other than investor-owned (the market) and public agencies (the state) has been termed in various ways depending on the definition used in the specific tradition, national context, and specific features emphasized. The "nonprofit sector approach" has been developing since the second half of the 1970s to understand the US situation. It relies on strict

G. Galera
European Research Institute on Cooperative and Social Enterprises, University of Trento, Via Inama 5, 38100 Trento, Italy

S. Destefanis and M. Musella (eds.), *Paid and Unpaid Labour in the Social Economy*, AIEL Series in Labour Economics DOI: 10.1007/978-3-7908-2137-6_14,

pockets of poverty and are affected by severe problems of inequality, unemployment, and social exclusion among their populations.

Social enterprises are conceived of as private and autonomous legal entities that have an explicit social goal, and provide goods or services of general interest. They are owned and managed by groups of citizens and the material interest of both owners and investors is subject to limits. The societal and political interest in social enterprises stems from their ability to tackle crucial economic and social problems and challenges in a number of domains, including the provision of social, health, educational, and utilities (for instance, electricity, public transportation, water supply). Hence the attractiveness of this institutional arrangement for countries that are facing dramatic social and economic difficulties.

The proposed definition of social enterprise excludes third sector organizations that perform either an advocacy or a re-distributive function, regardless of their legal framework. By contrast, it embraces cooperatives with a social element to them, which form an important part of the European legacy, including eastern European countries that saw a significant development of such organizations in pre-communist times and are now witnessing a re-emergence of these institutions in a number of sectors (i.e. housing and credit, among others). Thus the key criteria for identifying social entrepreneurial organizations lie in the specific social goal to be pursued, together with the non-distribution constraint, and the assignment of ownership and control rights to stakeholders other than investors, including a plurality of stakeholders.

Following a brief introduction on the relevance of institutional pluralism for economies characterized by poorly developed markets and welfare systems under construction, the first part of the paper is devoted to analyzing social enterprises in general with special reference to conceptual aspects. Given the broad range of definitions put forward in the literature, attention is paid to a definition of social enterprise that is grounded in the European tradition, and is therefore considered more appropriate for target countries. The second part of this contribution focuses on both the history of social entrepreneurial organizations and current social enterprise development paths in the region, with special regard to the role played by the social enterprise in fostering socio-economic development. This is due to its ability to: (1) supply general goods and services

limits imposed on the appropriation of the organization's surplus in the form of monetary gain by those who run and control it (Anheier and Ben-Ner 2003). The term "voluntary sector" is mainly used in Great Britain to refer to those organizations that are located in a societal space between the State and the Market. The "social economy" approach, French in origin, was forged to bring together cooperatives, mutual societies and associations. The social economy definition stresses the specificity of the mission of these organizations, namely their aim to benefit either their members or a larger community, rather than to generate profits for investors. This paper mainly refers to third sector organizations and draws on the concept of *social enterprise* that was originally worked out by the EMES European Research Network (http://www.emes.net). See Sect. 13.2.2 for an analysis of the social enterprise concept.

for the community, (2) generate new employment, (3) contribute to a more balanced use and allocation of resources, and (4) enhance the social capital that is accumulated at the local level.

13.2 Institutional Pluralism and the Emergence of Social Enterprise as a Concept

13.2.1 Relevance of Institutional Pluralism for CEE and the CIS

Interest in institutional pluralism, which has been enhanced by the historical experience in all European countries of social entrepreneurial organizations, such as cooperative and mutual aid societies, foundations and associations, stems from the belief that it is a pre-condition for a more rapid and balanced economic development in transition economies (Borzaga and Spear 2003). In addition to investor-owned enterprises, these may include worker-owned, consumer-owned, producer-owned, and service-providing third sector organizations.

The transition from central planning to a market economy, as well as the transition from an authoritarian to a democratic regime, can be said to be primarily processes of institutional change (Raiser et al. 2001). Paradoxically, institutional issues were underplayed in the early stages of transition. The rejection of the previous system created an institutional void where all agents were expected to adapt to the spirit of neo-classical economics (Nørgaard 2000). The approach adopted to implement the transition process was in fact consistent with mainstream thinking that portrayed the market, conceived of exclusively as an ensemble of for-profit enterprises, as the sole actor capable of filling the gap left by the removal of state involvement in a short period of time (Smyth 1998). This approach was also characterized by policies supporting the development of advocacy associations and grant-making foundations funded by foreign donors. Whilst the former were challenged to contribute extensively to consolidating democracy through the development of a vibrant civil society whose deficiency was a legacy left by the previous regime (Havel 1992), the grant-making foundations were conceived of as a crucial component of the welfare systems still under construction. Thus, in the early years of transformation, the introduction of democratic rules and the freedom to associate, along with significant support from donors, had a part in revitalizing the advocacy role of newly-established third sector organizations in particular. In contrast, the potential of third sector organizations as productive entities and their ability to directly meet the social and economic needs arising in society were underestimated. As such, third sector organizations were primarily expected to act as 'safety valves' devoted to channelling dissent. They were less conceived and exploited as a 'safety net' that could take on crucial social and economic problems, including poverty and social exclusion (Bach and Stark 2002)[2].

Despite the substantial political and economic reforms undertaken since the fall of Communism in many countries of the former Soviet Union, eastern and central Europe, these countries can be said to have largely failed to guarantee both an adequate social safety-net for their citizens and satisfactory provision of goods and services for their communities. Political changes were accompanied by the liberalization of former mechanisms of social inclusion, leading to a reduction of social rights and access to social, educational, and health services. Moreover, in some countries new economic institutions were introduced at the beginning of the transformation, which were strongly criticized by some commentators as being inadequate for the state of the local economy (Leś and Jeliazkova 2007)[3]. In general terms, the last decade has shown that in the transition to democratic political systems and market-oriented economies, social welfare systems have been neglected (Schecter 2000). By and large, the transformation in most of the transition countries has resulted in a general economic decline especially in certain economic sectors and it has had a direct effect on the populations' standard of living, consumption, employment and the state of the internal market, as well as on infrastructure (e.g. electricity and roads) and social infrastructure (e.g. education and health services). In many countries, the first phase in particular revealed growing inequalities in the standard of living and a sharp rise in poverty, with a scale of deprivation that had not been widely foreseen. The security provided during the socialist period through guaranteed employment, old-age pensions, free health care and other services has given way to massive unemployment or under-employment, declining pensions and a reduction of other social services, now available only to those who can pay.

Given the failure of mainstream policies, a change in focus reinforcing the institutional perspective has come to the forefront (Murrell 2005). This implies the exploitation of a broader set of tools and goals, including the participation of citizens in various ways in making strategic decisions that affect their lives (Stiglitz 1998). This approach presupposes paying increasing attention to solutions other than public agencies and for-profit enterprises. It also coincides with both a structural evolution of third sector organizations – especially associations and foundations - towards a more entrepreneurial stance and the increasing emergence of new entrepreneurial organizations that are part of a social project.

As such, this paper is based on the assumption that, since the main goal in central, eastern, and south-eastern European countries is to achieve a more balanced economic growth, what is required is the development of an institutional framework capable of managing transactions effectively. The adoption of market-centred policies, generally

[2]Most of the laws regulating associations and foundations in the region limit the possibility of running economic activities. Hence, there is a marginal role for third sector organizations in the supply of social services.

[3]Leś and Jeliazkova quote the Polish sociologist Jadwiga Staniszki, who coined the term "structural violence" to describe this phenomenon. (Leś and Jeliazkova 2007).

relying on the creation of a market economy populated only by for-profit enterprises, has contributed to an underestimation of the role of 'alternative organizations' as vehicles for local and national development, notwithstanding the significant role historically played by these organizations in both advanced and pre-communist economies to also improve the functioning of the market.

The system of charitable service provision, which spread especially in the health and social service sector, dates back to the Middle Ages. Charities and other types of third sector organizations perform an important role until they were replaced by a system of public welfare services (Anheier 2005). Similarly, a vibrant cooperative sector developed in all European countries, including central Europe, in the middle of the nineteenth century. What is noteworthy is that charities, associations, self-help groups, and cooperatives were characterized by direct forms of participation of producers and users in service delivery and succeeded in addressing key economic and social problems of local communities (Evers and Laville 2004).

Against this background, this paper aims to shed light on the potential of social enterprises as a unique way of addressing some of the untackled socioeconomic challenges that public agencies and for-profit providers cannot cope with in an effective and efficient manner in the CEE and the CIS.

13.2.2 The Social Enterprise Concept

As illustrated in the previous section, the development of economic activities in the frame of a social project is not a new phenomenon. It can be said, however, that the use of *social entrepreneurship* and *social enterprise* as autonomous concepts is a recent accomplishment in both the United States and Europe. Nonetheless, they are both still under-researched as fields of scholarly enquiry and continue to be largely phenomenon-driven (Mair and Martì 2006). Despite their rapidly rising field of practice (Roper and Cheney 2005), social entrepreneurship and social enterprise remain ill-defined concepts that can take on a variety of meanings (Weerawardena and Mort 2006). The range of definitions of social entrepreneurship and social enterprise at the international level is such that a number of authors use social enterprise and social entrepreneurship interchangeably (Peredo and McLean 2006).

Two main approaches may be observed at the international level that are partially attributable to the specific context in which the concepts were constructed.

It was predominantly the rediscovery of nonprofit organizations (mainly associations) as social service providers and work-integration organizations coupled with the strengthening of cooperatives' concern for the community that paved the way for the conceptualization of the 'social enterprise'. The term is often used to describe a 'different way' of doing business and providing social services, which encompasses the most entrepreneurial component of the nonprofit sector and the most innovative part of the cooperative movement, while consistent with the characteristics of the activities carried out.[4] This approach has found greater resonance in Europe than in the United States.

On the other hand, a definition of social enterprise which is gaining ground especially in the United States tends to qualify social enterprises as organizations running commercial activities, though not necessarily linked to a social mission, with the goal of collecting funds for a social activity. The latter, ranging from the funding of single projects to the giving of donations, is not meant to have an entrepreneurial connotation. Given the instrumental nature of the commercial activity, whose specific aim is to support the social mission, possible tensions can arise between the two goals pursued.

Differences between the two approaches mirror a prevailing private and business focus in the United States, where private foundations provide most outside financial support for social enterprises and where the welfare state has traditionally been weak, and a government and social service focus in Europe (Kerlin 2006). In the United States, the defined concepts of social entrepreneurship, social entrepreneur and social enterprise started to be employed, often interchangeably, when nonprofits experienced cutbacks in government funding. That is to say, when nonprofit service-providing organizations started to dramatically expand commercial activity in order to fill the gap left by governmental retrenchment (Kerlin 2006) and the dissatisfaction with the pace and management of standard third sector organizations called for innovative alternatives (Barendsen and Gardner 2004). The use of these terms also reflects the need to conceptualize the increasing implementation of a variety of socially-driven economic initiatives by single entrepreneurs and entities not legally bound to the non-distribution constraint (Peredo and McLean 2006). In this respect, the existence of an entity specifically designed to pursue a social goal, or its ability to carry out economic activities in a stable and continuous way, is not considered by a large part of the literature to be a necessary condition for its classification as a social enterprise. Hence the emphasis put on the individual dimension of the social entrepreneur as an agent of change, who is capable of implementing innovative solutions and able to tackle social problems that are overlooked by other actors in a wide variety of fields of general interest. Accordingly, special attention has been addressed by some scholars to value-driven 'extraordinary individuals' that are conceived of as transformative forces (Roberts and Woods 2005).

For the purpose of this contribution, the definition of social enterprise put forward has substantial roots in European countries. Originally proposed by the EMES European Research Network, it relies on a number of social and economic criteria.[5] Briefly, the activity performed by the social enterprise must be of general interest and it has to be managed in an entrepreneurial way. In this way it becomes the commercial activity of the social enterprise but with limitations regarding those

---

[4] The evolutionary dynamics of both associations and cooperatives was emphasized for the first time by CECOP (1996).

[5] The concept of the *social enterprise* was originally worked out in Europe by a group of researchers - the EMES European Research Network. It refers to both socio-economic entities that are newly created organizations and existing third sector organizations refreshed by a new dynamics (Borzaga and Defourny 2001).

sectors eligible for social enterprise involvement. Social enterprises have to be subject to a restriction on the distribution of profits, which can be either total or limited. It is worthy of note that social and economic activities overlap, as do the goals pursued, since one becomes the condition justifying the other. An exception is provided by work-integration social enterprises whose specific goal is to integrate disadvantaged workers or people with limited possibilities of being employed by for-profit enterprises. In such social enterprises there is a clear distinction between the commercial and social activity and, consequently, a tension may become manifest between the need to accumulate income and the maximization of the number of workers to be integrated.

Drawing on the European tradition, the term social enterprise encompasses the multiplicity of entrepreneurial organizations that pursue goals other than profit in a stable and continuous way, and which developed alongside private for-profit enterprises and public organizations in market economies before the nineteenth century onwards, i.e. organizations that have an entrepreneurial connotation, even though the overall aim of their activities excludes the pursuit of profit as an ultimate goal as well as its distribution to the owners. The institutional focus adopted is clearly dissociated from the emphasis on the individual that characterizes part of the literature on social entrepreneurship. By contrast, the approach embraced emphasizes the collective nature prominent in the history of European social entrepreneurial initiatives (Borzaga and Spear 2003; Spear 2006). According to this perspective, social enterprises are conceived of as specific institutions and, more generally, as a facet of social entrepreneurship. Social enterprise is used as an umbrella term that is not defined in legal terms, and encompasses a set of initiatives and societal trends occurring through a variety of organizational forms, partnerships, and networking across organizational boundaries (Johnson 2000; Austin et al. 2006).

With regard to positioning the concept of social enterprise for post-communist countries in time and place, the adoption of a European approach is considered more appropriate in the light of the pre-communist cooperative tradition (shared by most of the countries of this geographical area), evolutionary trends and prospects for development. By referring to entrepreneurial dynamics focused on social aims, the conceptual framework proposed by EMES attempts to bridge the two existing and wide-known concepts used to define organizations other than public agencies (state) and for-profit enterprises (the market): the nonprofit sector and the social economy. More specifically, the concept of social enterprise introduced by EMES is intended to enhance third sector concepts by shedding light on entrepreneurial dynamics focused on social aims within the sector (Borzaga and Defourny 2001). Furthermore, such an approach contributes to bridging the European tradition of cooperative organizations with the new socio-economic initiatives that have recently developed in a number of European countries,[6] all of which represents a radical innovation in the traditional third sector.

[6] This is the case of *Community interest companies* in the UK and *Social enterprises* in Italy, as well as *Public benefit companies* in Czech Republic, Croatia, Slovakia, and Hungary.

13.2.3 Social Enterprise Features

Unlike social entrepreneurship, social enterprises are autonomous institutions engaged in the supply of services and goods with a merit- or general-interest nature in a stable and continuous way. The competitive advantage of social enterprises over alternative ways of organizing the production of these goods and services stems from their specific features, enabling them to provide innovative responses when public agencies fail either to supply at all or in sufficient quantity or quality, goods and services that have a merit nature, yet where for-profit enterprises eventually manage to do so, albeit charging costs that prevent people in need from accessing them.

The salient features of social enterprises are:

1. *the social goal pursued*; the goal pursued by social enterprises is explicitly nonprofit and, as such, presupposes that the end-product is characterized by merit or general interest, in consideration of the type of goods and services supplied or production/allocation process adopted. The latter can be driven by different and specific motivations, including the decision not to exploit a monopoly power or information asymmetry to the advantage of the producer, the choice not to internalize all the value produced, or the will to allocate the wealth gained in favour of those people who are unable to pay. The merit- or general-interest nature incorporated in the social enterprise is in all cases an inescapable sign of the organization's character for all stakeholders involved, namely workers, donors, users, volunteers, and the community as a whole. The activity carried out can either entail promoting the interests of specific categories of stakeholders (i.e. consumers that are unable to pay, disadvantaged workers) or of the community at large (i.e. regeneration of a depressed area).
2. *the non-distribution constraint*; the non-distribution constraint is a user-protection device (Hansmann 1988), preventing to a certain extent undesirable behaviours - including the exploitation of market power, namely the application of high prices and the adoption of low quality standards - to the disadvantage of the users (Ben-Ner and Gui 2003). The exclusion of profit maximization is a key criterion for identifying social enterprises. This implies that organizations bounded legally to the non-distribution of profits and enterprises structured to exclude profit as the main goal are considered to be social enterprises. In both cases the distribution constraint can be either total or limited;
3. *the assignment of ownership and control rights to stakeholders other than investors, coupled with an open and participatory governance model*; an additional device that strengthens the correcting power of the non-distribution constraint is the assignment of ownership and control rights to stakeholders rather than investors. Depending on the type of social enterprise under consideration, ownership and control rights can be assigned to a single category of stakeholders (users, workers, or donors) or to more than one category at a time, thereby giving ground to a multi-stakeholder ownership asset.

These characteristics play a role in shaping governance models that to different degrees enhance the participation of stakeholders and democratic management and, in so doing, contribute to the adoption of strategic decisions for the community through participatory mechanisms. Both aspects can contribute to rendering the goals pursued by the organization itself and those of the agents involved consistent to one another, thereby allowing for the improvement of the performance of the social enterprise in terms of effectiveness and efficiency (Borzaga and Tortia 2008). Depending on the degree and number of stakeholders involved, the goal pursued, and the type of services and goods supplied, social enterprises can succeed in mobilizing a plurality of resources (monetary and non-monetary, as well as economic and non-economic), in addition to those generated by the mainstream economy (commercial incomes and/or public funding). The importance of additional resources with respect to mainstream incomes depends on the degree of 'dis-advantage' taken on by the social enterprise and the level of financial cover ensured by traditional funding sources. Similarly, the degree of participation required of stakeholders for the efficient and effective management of the social enterprise depends on the type of goods and services supplied, ranging from being very important for goods and services perceived as highly meritorious by the community to being only marginally important for those goods and services that are also supplied by other actors.

To sum up, the definition of social enterprise proposed here excludes all for-profit enterprises and third sector organizations that display either an advocacy or a grant-making function, but it embraces all kinds of cooperatives, credit unions, and mutual aid societies that have important social functions. More generally, the term social enterprise is used here to identify enterprises that fulfil crucial economic and social tasks which are often disregarded by other actors or are produced in insufficient quantity or quality, and whose aim is to promote the interests of the community at large or those of specific fragile segments of society. Against this background, the activities delivered can range from the supply of social and health, work integration, environment, education, cultural and recreational services, to the provision of economic general services, including among others electricity, water supply, and transportation, as well as the production of goods below cost in order to ensure access for all those in need.

13.3 Social Enterprises in CEE and the CIS

13.3.1 A Historical Overview

Foundations, associations, and cooperatives have a long established history in pre-communist and socialist countries and they are not a 'product' of the regime transformations of 1989 (Leś and Jeliazkova 2007). Mutual support within a wide range of activities, including production, consumption, credit, and trade had developed in different spheres of public life and can be traced back to the Middle Ages. Voluntary and service organizations flourished throughout pre-World War II Europe, and have a rich and diverse history in all post-communist and socialist countries (Davis 2004).

At the end of the nineteenth century, the system of cooperative societies spawned into mass social movements, as it represented an effective mechanism apt to enhance the competitiveness of farmers, workers, and craftsmen (UNDP 2008). Cooperatives performed a significant role as economic and social institutions and were committed to dealing with the various social problems affecting the local communities, as well as specific fragile groups. The Czech Republic has had a strong voluntary and cooperative sector since the late nineteenth century, when it was still part of the Austro-Hungarian Empire. The sector thrived during the 20 years of independence between 1918 and 1938. The cooperative sector included farmers' cooperatives, consumer cooperatives, food processing cooperatives, and many others, including credit cooperatives, which were the most numerous. Credit cooperatives based on the Raiffeisen model numbered 7,500 in 1937 and were an important source of support to small farmers (UNDP 2008).

In pre-World War II Poland, foundations, associations, and cooperatives complemented the government's provision of social, educational, and health services. For instance, in 1927 there were 3,539 credit cooperatives which accounted for over one million members (Leś and Jeliazkova 2007).

In Bulgaria, after the establishment of its nation state in 1878 and until the end of World War II, the most widespread forms of cooperation were cooperatives of various kinds (mainly in the agricultural, credit, production, and consumer sector, numbering in total 4,476 in 1941), a specific form of cultural association - *chitalishte*, which supported educational and cultural activities in the local communities, an urban voluntary civil sector composed of foundations and associations, among which women's associations became rather popular. Similarly, Slovenian society has a long and extensive tradition of self-organizing associations reflecting the interests of different groups of people (UNDP 2008).

The development paths of these organizations was either stopped or transformed after World War II. Associations and foundations were dissolved in most countries of the region, whereas cooperatives were transformed into quasi-public organizations and became a pillar of the newly-established economic system. In addition, new mass organizations were created top-down with the goal of promoting the interests of the totalitarian states.

Nevertheless, considerable differences existed among the countries in the region as regards the interference of the State in the functioning of those organizations that were allowed to exist. These differences explain the various dynamics in the development and growth of third sector organizations after the collapse of communism (Mansfeldovà et al. 2004).[7]

[7] In countries which enjoyed more liberal regimes, the process of growth after the collapse of communism was slower if compared to more authoritarian regimes. For instance, in Slovenia the rise in the number of third sector organizations was the most intense in the period 1975–1985, following some democratic changes, which paved the way for the development of third sector initiatives. In contrast, in Slovakia and in the Czech Republic, third sector organizations were much more subordinated to the State. As a result, many more organizations were formed during the first years of democratic rule (Mansfeldovà et al. 2004).

It is worth noting that the rich traditions of charity, cooperative movements, and solidarity principles going back to the pre-revolutionary period, coupled with the emancipation of the newly-established civil society organizations, contributed to the renaissance of the third sector after the collapse of the communist regime (UNDP 2008). However, while the importance of advocacy organizations for the construction and strengthening of democracy was acknowledged by neo-liberal policies and western donors, the role of non investor-owned organizations, including cooperative organizations, as economic and welfare actors was quite overlooked. Indeed, an impressive boom of civil society organizations, especially associations, was recorded in all the countries of the region in the early 1990s (Mansfeldovà et al. 2004), whereas cooperative organizations saw a dramatic decrease in number (UNDP 2008).

13.3.2 State-of-the-Art Social Enterprise

Despite the dramatic development seen in third sector organizations at the beginning of transition in east, central and south-east European countries, social enterprises are by and large still a rare practice in post-communist countries (OECD 2006; UNDP 2008). Social enterprises are still underdeveloped in the face of potential demand for services and the entrepreneurial behaviour increasingly adopted by many groups of citizens.

Various factors explain the weak legal and socio-economic institutionalization of social enterprise structures. The prevalence of 'transition myths' has resulted in policies that rely heavily on the creation of a free market economy based solely on for-profit providers. This trend has been coupled with the legacies of the command economy and the absence of post-socialist welfare models. Ideological remnants of communism have led to barriers being raised against the adoption of voluntary principles and also to the political distrust for certain organizational models, such as cooperative organizations, which are still regarded as a relic of the communist era (Huncova 2003). What is worth noting is that the efforts made to build democracy by creating an independent third sector across central and eastern Europe have ignored the mass-organizations and quasi-independent associations in existence in socialist times (such as environmental organizations) that were undergoing a transformation process. This approach was insensitive to the unique social and cultural contexts of individual countries and it overlooked the various roles that third sector organizations could play (Carmin and Jehlička 2005). Most importantly, it underestimated the potential of third sector organizations as service providers and the role of cooperatives as tools of economic development in localities and sectors badly hit by the negative effects of economic transition. Nevertheless, the general distrust towards economic activities carried out by cooperatives and third sector organizations was further induced by corruptive practices involving some of these organizations in the early transition, along with the misuse of the cooperative formula for personal gain.

There are also other practical economic and social barriers that hamper social enterprise development. These include the lack of supporting environments and infrastructures, restricted access to resources, privileged positions enjoyed by some organizations, an unsuitable institutional framework and an inconsistent legal environment, all of which have given rise to the lack of formal regulations and unsuitable legal frameworks that fail to take into account the social commitment and degree of disadvantage taken on by social enterprises. In addition, the fragile political systems where social enterprises are located prevent them from building medium and longer term strategies, while the lack of skills of social entrepreneurs adds to the chronic financial instabilities of most social enterprises. Overall, the roles played by non investor-owned organizations and public agencies in the social systems and economies of post-communist countries are still widely untapped and overlooked. Social enterprises are still considered as 'filling the gaps' agents rather than long-term welfare and economic actors (Leś and Jeliazkova 2007).

Notwithstanding the above-mentioned constraints that hinder the development of social enterprises, these organizations are becoming more widespread in a number of fields of activity. More specifically, social enterprises are increasingly turning into innovative agents in the local economies, owing to their capacity to introduce new institutional models apt to solve socio-economic problems and meet basic needs. The potential economic and social contribution of social enterprises is important since they are increasingly engaged in the production of innovative services, especially general-interest services, and they contribute to generating new employment.

Three main trends may be pinpointed. First, the institutionalization of social enterprises in some new member countries where new legal frameworks designed for social enterprises have been introduced. This is the case of Poland and Hungary, where laws on social cooperatives aimed at integrating disadvantaged people into work have been enacted (Kuti 1990). Service-providing organizations named Public Benefit Companies have been introduced in the Czech Republic, Croatia, Slovakia and Hungary, which are committed to supplying services that are of public benefit. Similarly, an income-generating third sector organization has been introduced in Slovenia: the Private Not-For-Profit Institute, which operates in the field of education, science, culture, sports, health, social affairs and whose main source of income comes from commercial activity within the market (OECD 2006; UNDP 2008). Nonetheless, several shortcomings of these laws still prevent the new legal frameworks being fully exploited.

Second, the strong presence of enterprises integrating disadvantaged people. Despite a general mistrust of economic activities carried out by third sector organizations, social enterprises appear to be more accepted when integrating disadvantaged workers into work. The Polish, Hungarian and Croatian examples are in this respect a case in point. A possible interpretation of this more favourable attitude is the long-standing tradition of cooperatives for the disabled that were set up under communism and continue to perform in all post-communist and socialist countries.

Third, the creation of subsidiary commercial enterprises, set up and owned by associations and foundations, and whose aim is to earn income to support the social activities of their founding entities. The economic activities carried out are normally not consistent with the social goal pursued by the founding associations and foundations. This trend involves countries where the economic activities conducted by third sector organizations is limited by legal inconsistencies (Bulgaria and Croatia) and countries where social enterprises are strictly outlawed (Macedonia and Belarus). It should be noted that the trend towards the division of these two economic and social spheres gives rise to an increase in added costs.

A pre-condition for sustaining social enterprise development is the political recognition of social enterprises as fully-fledged socio-economic actors of the market economy. Hence the need to raise the interest of all stakeholders involved with social enterprises, including policy makers at the national and local level, social entrepreneurs, the third sector community, trade unions, and the donor community, as well as the need to strengthen their awareness of the potential of social enterprises.

13.4 Social Enterprise, Economic and Social Development

Given the conception of development as a social process where such factors as the economic, social, historical and cultural are constantly at play, social enterprises emerge as institutions apt to contribute effectively to the social and economic development of a given territory, while also contributing to economic growth at national level.

The historical analysis of social entrepreneurial organizations provides evidence of the crucial role played by these institutional arrangements in supporting development and especially in promoting the interests of the weakest stakeholders of society that would otherwise have been excluded from mainstream economic life. The positive impact of social enterprises on social and economic development can be seen from various perspectives: they supply general services and goods, contribute to a more balanced use and allocation of resources, generate new employment, and play a role in enhancing the social capital that is accumulated at the local level.

First, social enterprises complement the supply of general services that public agencies and for-profit enterprises fail to deliver for a number of reasons, including budget constraints, the inability to recognize new needs arising in society, and market failures (i.e. induced by information asymmetries or positive externalities). All these aspects are of crucial importance in target countries, which in a number of cases still lack basic public services and facilities. Several countries of the region, especially former Soviet Union republics, are characterized by settlements which have no electricity, lack safe drinking water, and are cut off from gas supplies. Furthermore, gaps in service delivery also affect other public and merit goods, such as social, educational and health services. Interesting experiences from target countries show that these services can be provided efficiently through the self-organization and self-reliance of the citizens concerned. Social enterprises show a high innovation potential, since they have the capacity to react to external challenges and meet new needs arising at the local level. As locally-embedded institutions, they adapt to the evolution of the local context and, as such, can be considered problem-solving devices apt to tackle crucial social and economic problems and adhere to the specific social and economic context dealt with (Borzaga and Tortia 2008). Interesting examples of community organizations that manage to resolve severe difficulties, such as the provision of reliable drinking water supplies and adequate water for irrigation in rather complex situations, can be found for instance in Crimea in the settlements of Bakhchisaray, Tenistoye and Sevastyanovka, which have also become important references for other villages (Christen 2004).

Second, social enterprises contribute to a more balanced use and allocation of locally-available resources, to the advantage of the community, as they have a direct influence on the management of economic and social development at the local level. Thanks to the participation of local stakeholders, they succeed in promoting inclusive governance models that empower the local community in strategic decision-making (Sugden and Wilson 2005). Through the decentralization of power stakeholders can fulfil the needs of various social groups, by virtue of their ability to grasp them at the local level and of their greater flexibility (Elstub 2006). Community involvement through social mobilization also contributes to positive changes in attitude, since communities become aware that they can take stock of their own situation and contribute towards finding solutions to their own problems via the setting-up of a participatory institutional arrangement (Christen 2004). The latter ensures that the social goals pursued will reflect the general interest of the community rather than particularistic interests. Indeed, thanks to the relations established with other sectors, including public agencies and for-profit enterprises, social enterprises can contribute to transforming the social and economic system where they operate, to the advantage of the community as a whole.

Third, social enterprises play a crucial role in generating new jobs. In general, they develop new activities and contribute to creating new employment in the sectors where they operate, i.e. the social and community service sectors, which show high employment potential. Moreover, in a number of cases they enable the unemployed, for instance mothers seeking flexible jobs (part-time jobs, for example) to become employed, and they contribute to creating innovative models of industrial relations (Borzaga and Depedri 2005; Borzaga and Tortia 2007). More specifically, the aim of some social enterprises is to integrate into work disadvantaged workers with little possibility of finding a job in traditional enterprises and to train these workers (Nyssens 2006). The capacity of social enterprises to generate employment in target countries is particularly relevant/important, considering the high unemployment rates that affect certain segments of the population that are especially at risk of exclusion from the traditional labour market (i.e. women with children/mothers, unskilled young people with low qualifications, minority groups, disadvantaged people, immigrants, homeless people, and former prisoners).

Fourth, social enterprises help foster social cohesion and enhance social capital within society and the economy because they supply goods and services that are endowed with a high social potential, which strengthens relations of trust among the agents involved. Furthermore, the inclusive and participatory approach favoured by some social enterprises leads to citizens' active participation in the social and economic issues affecting the local community. This contributes to enhancing the sense of social responsibility towards the community to which they belong and the accumulation of social capital embedded in a community. Social enterprises engaged in the production of general services indirectly contribute to tackling a major problem found in post-communist and post-socialist countries, i.e. the low level of citizen trust in political institutions and participation in democratic processes. This is a crucial problem affecting especially former Soviet Union republics whose stock of social capital is particularly low (Raiser et al. 2001).

13.5 Concluding Remarks

Social enterprises are engaged in very different activities related to co-ordination difficulties faced by the 'market' and the 'state', such as the national and local government inability to deal with certain welfare issues and challenges driven by global and regional economic trends.

Significant differences can be found in countries and localities with regard to the diffusion of social enterprises when compared to alternative institutional settings, i.e. public and for-profit arrangements (Ben-Ner 2006). Various forces at play contribute to defining to different degrees both the importance of social enterprises compared to other institutions, and the specific features taken on, including political and cultural considerations. Indeed, the advantages and disadvantages associated to each institutional arrangement are not immutable. Policies can be developed to improve weaknesses and enhance strengths of the various organizational forms found in the real world. More specifically, policies can foster a more efficient distribution of economic activity across sectors by exploiting the strengths of each sector (Ben-Ner 2006) or, alternatively, they can jeopardize the development of certain organizational forms. In particular, social enterprises are extremely sensitive to changes in public policy, especially regarding their eligibility for public subsidies (Bacchiega and Borzaga 2003). A country's legal system can play either an enabling or a restrictive role in the development of social enterprises. In turn, legal solutions are greatly influenced by cultural considerations, which may be more or less keen to acknowledge the role of certain organizational typologies, i.e. third sector organizations as service providers.

While underestimating the role of non investor-owned enterprises in the pursuit of important social goals in the new market economies, traditionally-inspired mainstream policies have failed to support a balanced economic growth and to govern economic activities and localities in the interests of the community at large. Given the crucial economic and social issues affecting transition economies, including gaps in social service delivery, poverty, and high rates of unemployment, what emerges is the importance of governance in the development of localities and, as a result, of social enterprises as economic actors devoted to pursuing general-interest goals that have been ignored or underestimated by both public and for-profit enterprises.

To conclude, effective strategies and policies apt to sustain the development of social enterprises should be developed by the actors concerned, in addition to national governments, western donors, international agencies and international non-governmental organizations. These strategies and policies imply the introduction of adequate public schemes that acknowledge the responsibilities taken on by social enterprises and suitable legal frameworks consistent with the specificities of the national context (legal tradition, socio-economic conditions, etc.) by adopting a participatory approach (involving every important stakeholder). Indeed, only a conducive environment will enable the strengths of social enterprises to be utilized as poverty reduction agents that provide access to basic public services (social, educational, health, etc.) for local communities, including people who are unable to pay. In this way social enterprises can complement the roles already played by other socio-economic actors (including, among others, public agencies, traditional cooperatives, and advocacy organizations) in addressing crucial problems of target countries. Specifically, they can contribute to supporting the economic and social development of many depressed regions of post-communist and socialist countries, create new employment as a result of the new services supplied, and favour the integration into work of disadvantaged people (minority groups, single women, people with disabilities, etc).

Acknowledgment I thank Carlo Borzaga for his comments. However, the responsibility of any errors remains only mine.

References

Anheier HK (2005) Non-profit organizations. Theory, management, policy. Routledge, London

Anheier HK, Ben-Ner A (2003) The Study of the nonprofit enterprise. Theories and approaches. Kluwer, New York

Austin JE, Stevenson H, Wei-Skillern J (2006) Social Entrepreneurship and commercial entrepreneurship: same, different, or both. Entrepreneurship Theory and Practice 30:1–22

Bacchiega A, Borzaga C (2003) The Economics of the third sector: toward a more comprehensive approach. In: Anheier HK, Ben-Ner A (eds) The study of the nonprofit enterprise. Theories and approaches. Kluwer, New York

Bach J, Stark D (2002) Innovative ambiguities: NGOs' use of interactive technology in Eastern Europe. Studies in International and Comparative Development 37:3–23

Barendsen L, Gardner H (2004) Is the social entrepreneur a new type of leader? Leader to Leader 34:43–50

Ben-Ner A (2006) For-profit, state and non-profit: how to cut the pie among the three sectors. In: Touffut J-P (ed) Advancing Public Goods. Edward Elgar, Cheltenham UK

Ben-Ner A, Gui B (2003) The theory of nonprofit organizations revisited. In: Anheier, HK, Ben-Ner A (eds), The study of the nonprofit enterprise. Theories and approaches. Kluwer, New York

Borzaga C, Defourny J (eds) (2001) The Emergence of social enterprises. Routledge, London

Borzaga C, Depedri S (2005) Interpersonal relations and job satisfaction: some empirical results in social and community care services. In: Gui B, Sugden R (eds) Economics and social interaction: accounting for interpersonal relations. Cambridge University Press, Cambridge UK

Borzaga C, Spear R (eds) (2003) Trends and challenges for co-operatives and social enterprises in developed and transition countries. Edizioni31, Trento

Borzaga C, Tortia E (2007) Social economy organizations in the theory of the firm. In: Clarence E, Noya A (eds) The social economy. Building inclusive communities. OECD, Paris
Borzaga C, Tortia E (2008) Social enterprises and local development: an evolutionary approach. Mimeo, University of Trento Department of Economics
Carmin JA, Jehli ka P (2005) By the masses or for the masses? The transformation of voluntary action in the Czech union for nature protection. Voluntas 16:397–416
CECOP (1996) Social enterprises: an opportunity for Europe. First European Conference on Social Co-operation. Research on social co-operation in Europe, Brussels.
Christen J (2004) Peace and stability through sustainable and economic development. Swiss Agency for Development and Co-operation, St Gallen
Davis RJ (2004) The rebirth of the non-profit sector in post-communist Eastern Europe. Civil Society International, Seattle. http://www.civilsoc.org/resource/eenoprft.htm
Elstub S (2006) Towards an inclusive social policy for the UK: the need for democratic deliberation in voluntary and community associations. Voluntas 17:17–39
Evers A, Laville JL (2004) The third sector in Europe. Edward Elgar, Cheltenham
Hansmann H (1988) Ownership of the firm. Journal of Law, Economics and Organisation 4:267–304
Havel V (1992) Politics and the world itself. Kettering Review (Summer):8
Huncova M (2003) The Czech co-operative. Reality and its social aspects. In: Borzaga C, Spear R (eds) Trends and challenges for co-operatives and social enterprises in developed and transition countries. Edizioni31, Trento
Kerlin J (2006) Social enterprise in the United States and Europe: understanding and learning from the differences. Voluntas 17:246–262
Kuti E (1990) The possible role of the non-profit sector in Hungary. Voluntas 1:26–41
Johnson S (2000) Literature review on social entrepreneurship. Canadian Centre for Social Entrepreneurship, Edmonton
Leś E, Jeliazkova M (2007) The social economy in Central, East and South East Europe. In: Clarence E, Noya A (eds) The social economy. Building inclusive communities. OECD, Paris
Mair J, Martì I (2006) Social entrepreneurship research: a source of explanation, prediction and delight. Journal of World Business 41:36–44
Mansfeldovà, Nalàcz S, Priller E, Zimmer (2004) A civil society in transition: civic engagement and nonprofit organizations in Central and Eastern Europe after 1989. In: Zimmer A, Priller E (eds) Future of civil society. VS Verlag Für Sozialwissenschaften, Wiesbaden
Murrell P (2005) Institutions and firms in transition economies. In: Ménard C, Shirley MM (eds) Handbook of new institutional economics. Springer, Heidelberg
Nørgaard O (2000) Economic institutions and democratic reform. Edward Elgar, Cheltenham UK
Nyssens M (2006) Social enterprise. Routledge, London
OECD (2006) Seminar on emerging models of social entrepreneurship: possible paths for social enterprise development in Central, East and South East Europe. OECD, Paris. http://www.oecd.org/document/11/0,3343,en_2649_34459_36925515_1_1_1_1,00.html
Peredo AM, McLean M (2006) Social entrepreneurship: a critical review of the concept. Journal of World Business 41:56–65
Raiser M, Haerpfer C, Nowotny T, Wallace C (2001) Social capital in transition: a first look at the evidence. EBRD Working Paper 61
Roberts D, Woods C (2005) Changing the world on a shoestring: the concept of social entrepreneurship. Business Review 7:45–50
Roper J, Cheney G (2005) The meanings of social entrepreneurship today. Corporate Governance 5:95–104
Schecter K (2000) The social sector: a failure of transition. In: Karatnycky A, Motyl A, Piano A (eds) Nations in transit 1999–2000. Civil society, democracy and markets in East Central Europe and the newly independent states. Freedom House, Washington DC
Smyth R (1998) New institutional economics in the post-socialist transformation debate. Journal of Economic Surveys 12:361–398

Spear R (2006) Social entrepreneurship: a different model? International Journal of Social Economics 33:399–410

Stiglitz JE (1998) More instruments and broader goals: moving towards the post-Washington consensus. Wider Annual Lectures, Helsinki

Sugden R, Wilson J (2005) Economic globalisation: dialectics, conceptualisation and choice. Contributions to political economy. Oxford University Press, Oxford

UNDP (2008) Social Enterprises: A new model for poverty reduction and employment generation. UNDP Regional Bureau for Europe and the CIS, Bratislava. http://europeandcis.undp.org/home/show/02F5569C-F203-1EE9-BD529F7FE21C9320

Weerawardena J, Mort GS (2006) Investigating social entrepreneurship: a multidimensional model, Journal of World Business 41:21–35